The Measurement and Evaluation of Library Services

by
F. W. LANCASTER

with the assistance of
M. J. Joncich

INFORMATION RESOURCES PRESS

Published May 1977. Fourth Impression March 1979.
Printed in the United States of America.

Available from
Information Resources Press
2100 M Street, N.W.
Washington, D.C. 20037

Library of Congress Catalog Card Number 77-72081

ISBN 0-87815-017-X

This book is dedicated to my son Aaron, and also to Knut Thalberg and his colleagues at the Library of the Norwegian Institute of Technology, University of Trondheim, who (although they may not have realized it) in 1973 gave me the whole idea of undertaking a work of this kind.

Contents

Foreword

Evaluation is one of the important steps in the administrative process. In brief, it consists of the comparison of performance with the objectives of the agency, in order to determine (a) whether there has been any change in performance for a given time period, (b) if so, whether the change is in the desired direction, and (c), if so, to what extent. The theory of evaluation is quite simple; you need to have specific and clear objectives, and you need to have measurement tools which are easy to apply and are adequate for the purpose.

In practice, the process of evaluating library services is usually difficult and often completely lacking, precisely because the requirements in the theory are almost never met. Most libraries, as well as many other institutions, have no clearly defined, up-to-date, and well-thought-out objectives to govern their policies and determine their practices. Sometimes libraries espouse traditional clichés, such as to serve the curricular needs of the students and the research interests of the faculty, or to meet the educational, informational, and recreational interests of the general public. All too often, libraries continue doing whatever it is they have traditionally done without taking a long hard look to determine whether a particular activity should be discontinued or whether new activities should be added.

When concrete and meaningful objectives are adopted and implemented, evaluation of the resulting services and products becomes critical. In such a situation, evaluation closes the loop and provides feedback on whether or how well the system is working. If the results indicate that the objectives are not being met, one desirable step is to reexamine the objectives to see if they are realistic in terms of the library's resources and total situation. Any casual attempt at evaluation should quickly reveal the inadequacies of traditional, superficial, and essentially meaningless objectives. Objectives, to be useful, require evaluation, and the evaluative process needs objectives as its criteria.

The second major element needed for the evaluative process consists of measures of performance which, ideally, are easy to apply, relevant, and reliable. Traditionally, libraries have measured that which was easiest to measure (e.g., book accessions, circulation, etc.), but, unfortunately, these usually are input or process variables rather than output variables. In other words, libraries do not exist merely to acquire books or to maximize the work load at the circulation desk; presumably, libraries are in some way concerned more with certain uses of books and with certain desired outcomes of the reading process.

Difficult though it may be to devise valid measures of library service, it is heartening to observe the great activity and progress in this regard during the last decade or two. One of the virtues of this book is that it brings together all the worthwhile advances in this field of endeavor, explains them in the clear and simple language that is Professor Lancaster's usual style, and examines them critically. He would be the first to say that the results most to be desired from wide use of this volume are continued improvement of these measures and the development of new and better ones.

As more and better measures of performance are devised and used, the difference between an effective and ineffective library will become more obvious and more easily documented. This is desirable for the sound development and future influence of the profession. In other words, measurement is necessary and useful, not only for the library administrator, but also (and in some ways even more so) for governing bodies, library staff members, patrons, accrediting agencies, and others. Heightened awareness of the adequacies and inadequacies of the present performance of libraries will inevitably hasten reevaluation of the scope and mission of libraries, and will enable earlier decisions to be reached concerning proposed or possible services. In short, improved measurement of library service will surely increase the tempo of change in the profession on a sound basis.

This book has been written in that spirit. Technically, it is comprehensive and analytical. Substantively, it deals both with traditional library services and with modern services of computerized information storage and retrieval. With his work experience and research background, Professor Lancaster is one of the best-qualified and competent people to write this book. I predict that it will be of great help and stimulation to many people and that it will quickly become a standard reference in the profession.

HERBERT GOLDHOR, *Director*
Graduate School of Library Science
University of Illinois

Preface

In the past 10 years, librarians, in common with other professionals, have become increasingly interested in techniques that might be used to evaluate the services they provide. One reason for this concern is, of course, financial: growing competition for funds, inflationary pressures, and the need to justify the importance of library services to those responsible for funding them. It seems important, then, that graduate programs in librarianship should include courses relating to the measurement and evaluation of library services, the major objectives being to survey work already done in this area, and, perhaps more importantly, to encourage students to adopt an "evaluative attitude" toward library activities. Such a course has been offered since 1970 at the Graduate School of Library Science, University of Illinois.

The present volume was developed primarily as a textbook for this course and, perhaps, for similar courses in other schools. It should be regarded largely as a survey and synthesis of, as well as a guide to, published literature in the field. It should not, however, be regarded as a substitute for reading the various studies directly. A serious effort has been made to include all important or interesting approaches to evaluation and to put these into meaningful and, where appropriate, critical perspective. The book concentrates primarily on techniques that can be used to evaluate the public service of a library, preferably by means of reasonably objective procedures, although some consideration also is given to the evaluation of technical services. The emphasis is on evaluation methodology; however, in reviewing studies which have been conducted, major findings are frequently presented to show the types of results that have been achieved by various procedures. As pointed out in the first chapter, the book is concerned only with how well the library satisfies the immediate tangible needs of its users. It deliberately excludes any consideration of the evaluation of libraries in terms of their broader, intangible, and largely unmeasurable "benefits" to society.

I would like to express my appreciation to Walter Allen, Michael Buckland, Charles Bunge, George Bonn, and Don Swanson for reading and commenting on various chapters, and to Herbert Goldhor for reviewing the entire volume.

I also would like to thank two of my graduate assistants, Elana Hanson and Gini Gale, for their assistance at various stages of the manuscript. Both made significant and useful contributions. Jane Gothard helped immeasurably with her efficient typing. My greatest debt, however, is to Mary Jane Joncich, who helped me both as a graduate assistant and as a critic, and who was largely responsible for writing Chapters 10 and 11.

Acknowledgements

Figure 7 and Tables 2–7 were reproduced by permission of the American Library Association. Tables 8–10 and 12 were reproduced by permission of ASLIB. Tables 11, 13 and 14 were reproduced by permission of Pergamon Press. Figure 8 was reproduced by permission of Yale University. Tables 15–17 were reproduced by permission of the Graduate Library School, University of Chicago. Figure 9 was reproduced by permission of the Library Association. Table 20 was reproduced by permission of the New Zealand Library Association. Tables 21–24 were reproduced by permission of the American Library Association. Figure 10 was reproduced by permission of ASLIB. Table 25 was reproduced by permission of the Enoch Pratt Free Library. Tables 26–30 were reproduced by permission of the Medical Library Association. Tables 31–37 were reproduced by permission of Scarecrow Press. Figures 11–22 were reproduced by permission of Hughes Dynamics, Inc. Figures 23 and 24, Table 38, and the Appendix to Chapter 3 were reproduced by permission of the General Electric Co. Tables 42–44 were reproduced by permission of the American Library Association. Table 45 was reproduced by permission of the State University of New York. Table 46 was reproduced by permission of the author. Table 47 was reproduced by permission of the University of Chicago Press. Figure 26 was reproduced by permission of the American Society for Information Science. Figures 27 and 28 were reproduced by permission of *Libri*. Table 48 was reproduced by permission of the American Library Association. Table 49 and Figure 29 were reproduced by permission of the American Society for Information Science. Figures 30 and 31 and Table 50 were reproduced by permission of MIT Press. Table 51 was reproduced by permission of the University of Lancaster. Figure 32 was reproduced by permission of the Medical Library Association. Figures 33 and 34 were reproduced by permission of the Library Association. Tables 53–59 were reproduced by permission of ASLIB. Figures 35–37 and Table 60 were reproduced by permission of the Graduate Library School, University of Chicago. Figure 38 was reproduced by permission of the University of Lancaster Library. Tables 61–63 and Figures 39–48 were reproduced by permission of the Medical Library Association. Figures 49 and 50 and Table 64 were reproduced by permission of the Indiana State Library. Table

65 was reproduced by permission of the author. Tables 66–68 were reproduced by permission of the Library Association. Tables 71–73 were reproduced by permission of the Graduate School of Library Science, University of Illinois. Figure 51 was reproduced by permission of MIT Press. Table 80 was reproduced by permission of the American Library Association. Table 81 was reproduced by permission of Crosby Lockwood. Tables 82–84 and Figures 54–56 were reproduced by permission of ASLIB. Tables 85 and 86 were reproduced by permission of *Nature*. Figures 57 and 58 and Table 87 were reproduced by permission of ASLIB. Figures 60–62 were reproduced by permission of Spartan Books. Figure 64 was reproduced by permission of the H. W. Wilson Co. Table 88 was reproduced by permission of the University of Lancaster. Tables 89–91 were reproduced by permission of MIT Press.

1

The Evaluation of Library Services: An Introduction

Levels of Evaluation

It is feasible to evaluate any type of service at three possible levels: effectiveness, cost-effectiveness, and cost-benefit.

Effectiveness must be measured in terms of how well a service satisfies the demands placed upon it by its users. Such an evaluation can be subjective (e.g., conducted by gathering opinions via questionnaires or interviews), objective (e.g., the measurement of success in quantitative terms), or a combination of the two.

An evaluation of a system's *cost-effectiveness* is concerned with its internal operating efficiency. Such a study measures how efficiently (in terms of costs) the system is satisfying its objectives; that is, meeting the needs of its users.

A *cost-benefit* evaluation is usually the most difficult to conduct. It is concerned with whether the value (worth) of the service is more or less than the cost of providing it. In other words, a *cost-benefit* study attempts to determine whether the expense of providing a service is justified by the benefits derived from it.

The expression *cost-performance-benefit* refers to the interrelationships among costs, performance (level of effectiveness), and benefits. These interrelationships, as pointed out by Lancaster,[11] cannot be completely separated. In practice, it is difficult to differentiate between cost-effectiveness and cost-benefit studies: a particular change in a system may increase its effectiveness, its cost-effectiveness, and its benefits. This book deals primarily with the effectiveness of library services, although cost-effectiveness also will be considered from time to time. The ultimate benefits of library service (i.e., the value to users of having these services available) will not be discussed in any detail.

Another distinction worth making, first explicated by King and Bryant,[9] is the difference between *macroevaluation* and *microevaluation*. The effectiveness of a system or service may be evaluated by either method. Macroevaluation measures *how well* a system operates, and the results usually can be expressed in quantitative terms (e.g., percentage of success in satisfying requests for interlibrary loans). It reveals that a particular system operates at a particular level, but does not, in itself, indicate why the system operates at this level or what might be done to improve performance in the future. Microevaluation, on the other hand, investigates *how* a system operates and *why* it operates at a particular level. Because it deals with factors affecting the performance of the system, microevaluation is necessary if the results of the investigation will, in some way, be used to improve performance.

Library Functions and Objectives

The functions of all libraries are essentially the same: to acquire bibliographic materials related to the interests of a particular user population, actual or potential; to organize and display these materials in various ways; and to make them available to users.* In a wider context, libraries are part of the entire process of transferring information via the published record. This information transfer process is illustrated in Figure 1, which is adapted from King and Bryant.[9] The diagram represents the composition, publication, and distribution of a document; its acquisition by libraries (and others); its organization and control (i.e., the library processes designed to make the document accessible to users, including cataloging, classification, indexing, abstracting, shelf arrangement, and related activities); its physical presentation to the user; and its assimila-

---

*Throughout the book, I use the expressions "bibliographic materials," "bibliographic resources," and "documents" interchangeably, to refer, in general, to books, journals, pamphlets, reports, films, manuscripts, records, prints, drawings, and other message-carrying units. The word "user" simply refers to a member of the specific population that a particular library or other information center is designed to serve, and should be considered to embrace potential users as well as actual users. In library literature, the words "reader" or "patron" are sometimes substituted for "user."

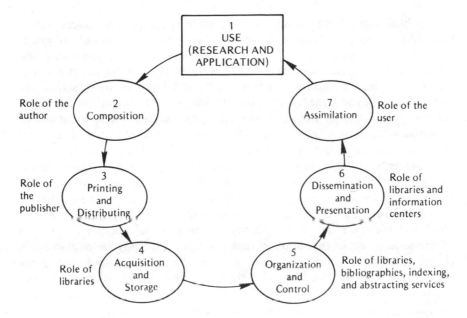

FIGURE 1   The transfer of information by published documents.

tion by the user. This transfer process may be considered as a cycle. Assimilation, the stage at which the user is "informed" by a publication (i.e., his state of knowledge on a subject is changed), may lead to some application of this newly acquired knowledge (e.g., in research); and this may, in turn, result in the composition of a new document.

While librarians should be interested in all the activities illustrated in this diagram, libraries are directly concerned only with the fourth, fifth, and sixth steps shown (except insofar as libraries themselves may be responsible for composition and publication). The assimilation of a document by a user, once it has been supplied, is generally outside the library's sphere of influence; that is, libraries exist to bring documents and users together. The responsibility of a library is to ensure that the user gains access to publications that are pertinent to his interests and comprehensible to him (i.e., written in a language he can read and at a level he can understand). Thereafter, the librarian has no direct control or influence over the user, and usually does not know whether the latter makes use of or is "informed" by the items supplied; it is for this reason that the ultimate "benefits" of library service are difficult to measure.

Others have claimed, however, that the ultimate product of the library is not the circulation of books. Armstrong,[1] for example, claims that, in the case of a farmer who borrows books on how to construct a house, the house built is the real product. This approach is completely unacceptable. The library has served its function adequately if it has a supply of good, readable, up-to-date books on how to construct a house and can make these available at the time the user needs them. Whether or not the reader does construct the house is governed by a myriad of factors that are completely beyond the control of the library. Moreover, of all these factors, the availability of suitable reading materials is likely to be one of comparatively minor importance. Assume, for example, that user A and user B come to a library seeking books on house construction. Both borrow materials that they consider suitable for their present purposes. A subsequently builds a house, B does not. It is doubtful that anyone could say that the library succeeded in the first case and failed in the second. It could, however, be legitimately claimed a failure if user B was unable to find suitable materials in the library at the time he needed them. The attitude adopted in this book is that a library can only be evaluated in terms of whether or not it is able to provide the materials sought by users at the time they are needed. What the user subsequently does with these materials is completely outside the librarian's control (and, some users might say, none of the librarian's business).

Over the years various individuals and groups have published statements of "objectives" for various types of libraries. These published objectives vary widely in scope. Some are specific and practical, while others, especially those relating to public libraries, are somewhat nebulous and even platitudinous. Many of these have been summarized by Hamburg et al.[8] Consider, for example, the following:

To aid in the creative use of leisure time for promotion of personal development and social well-being.

To assist people to become better members of their families and communities by promoting rational, democratic attitudes and values.

To assist people to discharge political and social obligations, thereby establishing an enlightened citizenship.

To develop creative and spiritual capacities.

To sustain the increasingly complex operations of government.

To assist people in their daily occupations, thereby sustaining economic growth.

Social, spiritual, and economic "objectives" of this type sound impressive, but they have very little real meaning and utility except, perhaps, to persuade librarians of their value to society or, perhaps, to convince society of the value of libraries. Such objectives may be related to the ultimate benefits of library services. They certainly do not relate directly to the immediate function of the library, are not easily (if at all) measurable, and are too vague and impractical to be used as criteria by which one can readily evaluate a library or its services.

As Drucker[5] has pointed out, a "public service institution" may have long-term objectives that are relatively intangible, but this is no excuse for its inefficient management or lack of self-evaluation. Drucker goes on to indicate that such institutions also have various shorter term goals which are both tangible and measurable.

"Saving souls," as the definition of the objectives of a church is, indeed, "intangible." At least the bookkeeping is not of this world. But church attendance is measurable. And so is "getting the young people back into the church."

"The development of the whole personality" as the objective of the school is, indeed, "intangible." But "teaching a child to read by the time he has finished third grade" is by no means intangible; it can be measured easily and with considerable precision.

"Abolishing racial discrimination" is equally unamenable to clear operational definition, let alone measurement. But to increase the number of black apprentices in the building trades is a quantifiable goal, the attainment of which can be measured.

Achievement is never possible except against specific, limited, clearly defined targets, in business as well as in a service institution. Only if targets are defined can resources be allocated to their attainment, priorities and deadlines be set, and somebody be held accountable for results. But the starting point for effective work is a definition of the purpose and mission of the institution—which is almost always "intangible," but nevertheless need not be vacuous.

Fortunately, all libraries have one overriding objective that is practical, that, to a certain extent, is measurable, and that may be used as a basis for evaluation. As illustrated in Figure 2, the library exists as an interface between the universe of bibliographic resources (using "bibliographic" in the widest sense) and a particular user population (restricted geographically or by institutional affiliation). The overall objective of the library is to make this universe (or at least that portion having the most immediate relevance and interest) maximally accessible to its users. The Hamburg[7,8] studies stated this objective differently: to maximize the exposure* of library users to the universe of bibliographic materials. These two objectives (accessibility/exposure) are really opposite sides of the same coin. Maximization of accessibility suggests a somewhat passive information service—one in which the library makes materials available, but waits for users to request them. Maximization of exposure, on the other hand, carries a more active connotation—such as bringing materials to the attention of potential users through some form of dynamic service (e.g., a current awareness service of the Selective Dissemination of Information [SDI] type). Generally, public and academic libraries are

---

*As mentioned later in this chapter, the exposure may be direct or indirect. An example of indirect exposure would be the provision of an answer, over the telephone, to a factual question posed by a library user.

OBJECTIVES

{
To Maximize Accessibility
of Materials to Users

To Maximize Exposure
of Users to Materials
}   (EFFECTIVENESS)

To Maximize
Accessibility/Exposure   (COST-EFFECTIVENESS)
per $1 of Expenditure

FIGURE 2   The interface function of libraries.

relatively passive (i.e., they provide services "on demand" only), whereas many industrial libraries and other specialized information centers are more dynamic (e.g., they provide services—not directly solicited—designed to keep users current with literature in their areas of specialization).

The major criterion by which one can evaluate the *effectiveness* of a library is the degree to which it maximizes either accessibility, exposure, or both; the major criterion by which one can evaluate the *cost-effectiveness* of a library is the degree to which it maximizes accessibility/exposure per dollar expended.

The accessibility/exposure objectives of the library were perhaps enunciated most clearly in the studies by Hamburg. These broad objectives, however, have been presented in various ways by many other writers. Ranganathan[14] discussed them in considerable detail in 1931, when he presented his five "laws" of library science:

1. Books are for use.
2. Every reader his book.
3. Every book its reader.
4. Save the time of the reader.
5. The library is a growing organism.

The first law implies the entire concept of the library as an interface between users and bibliographic resources; the second implies the notion of accessibility (in the sense that the library provides required services on demand); and the third implies exposure (in the sense that the library, as a more active information service, makes bibliographic resources known to potential users). In his fourth law, Ranganathan recognized a secondary, but still important, objective relating to the internal efficiency of the library; namely, to make bibliographic resources accessible in ways most convenient to the user. Rzasa and Baker[15] restated this in terms of the primary goals of a library:

1. To maximize user need satisfaction.
2. To minimize time loss to the user.

They also recognized a secondary goal; namely, to increase the number of actual library users. These goals all involve the maximization of exposure and the minimization of cost to the user.

During the last 15 years, a considerable amount of work has been done on the evaluation of information retrieval systems—particularly automated systems; and a group of "user requirements" for such systems has been identified. These requirements, which may be considered as criteria for evaluating retrieval systems, have been presented in various forms by Bourne et al.,[2] Cleverdon et al.,[3] and Lancaster.[10] Summarized, they are:

1. *Coverage* of the collection. The scope of the collection in terms of the extent to which it is complete in various subject areas.

2. *Recall.* The ability to retrieve literature relevant to a particular subject when a request for such literature is made to the system.

3. *Precision.* The ability not to retrieve irrelevant literature in response to a request to the system. Jointly, *recall* and *precision* measure filtering capacity: the ability to let through what the user wants and not let through what he does not want.

4. The amount of *effort* the user must spend in exploiting the system. If the effort required is excessive, the system will not be used. Some people may even prefer to do without needed information, if the task of locating such information is particularly burdensome to them. This point was well explicated by Calvin Mooers[13] in 1960 as "Mooers' Law":

An information retrieval system will tend *not* to be used whenever it is more painful and troublesome for a customer to have information than for him not to have it!

5. The *response time* of the system. How long the user has to wait to obtain needed literature or references to such literature.

6. The *form of output* provided by the system.

It is readily apparent that coverage and recall relate directly to the accessibility/exposure objectives of information services, and that the other four criteria relate directly to the additional objective of providing this accessibility/exposure as efficiently as possible—"save the time of the reader," as Ranganathan puts it.

These six criteria are applicable to the evaluation of library service in general. They provide a more precise restatement of the overall accessibility/exposure objectives of libraries and are clearly within the spirit of Ranganathan's five laws. Unfortunately, many of these requirements are in conflict. There tends, for example, to be an inverse relationship between recall and precision. What one does to improve one aspect may well cause a decrease in the other.

Criteria for evaluating library services also have been discussed by various other investigators, including Evans and Borko[6] and Wellisch et al.[16] Evans and Borko, after an extensive review of the literature, identified six possible performance criteria: accessibility, cost, user satisfaction, response time, cost-benefit ratio, and use. Obviously, these criteria are not restricted to the evaluation of library effectiveness, but also include cost-effectiveness and cost-benefit considerations. This list is somewhat unsatisfactory, because it represents a number of different levels of performance evaluation. *Response time* and *accessibility* are really factors affecting *user satisfaction,* while *user satisfaction* is presumably the major factor determining extent of *use.* Likewise, the *cost-benefit ratio* presumably indicates some relationship between *cost* of library services and *user satisfaction* with these services.

In summary, a library exists as an interface between a particular user population and the universe of bibliographic resources. The objective of the library is to maximize the accessibility of these resources to the user or to maximize the exposure of the users to the resources. In addition, the library should be organized to minimize the amount of effort required to obtain access to needed bibliographic materials, and to supply such materials as soon as possible when the need for them arises. The effectiveness of any library can be evaluated in terms of how well it satisfies these objectives. Cost-effectiveness can be evaluated in terms of how efficiently it makes use of available funds in the satisfaction of these objectives, the goal being, as Hamburg has put it, to maximize accessibility/exposure per capita (i.e., per user served), per dollar expended. A better goal, from the viewpoint of cost-effectiveness, would be to maximize the satisfaction of demands per dollar expended.

Library Organization

To satisfy its overall objectives, a library generally is organized into technical services and public services. The former, "behind the scenes" services, interface directly with the universe of bibliographic resources and provide a bridge between these resources and the user, while the latter interface directly with the user community (see Figure 3) and provide a bridge between the user and the resources. The library staff is involved in both types of activity; "management" directs and coordinates both. The library may cooperate with other institutions in both public and technical services, and today may apply automated procedures to many of them, particularly in the larger libraries.

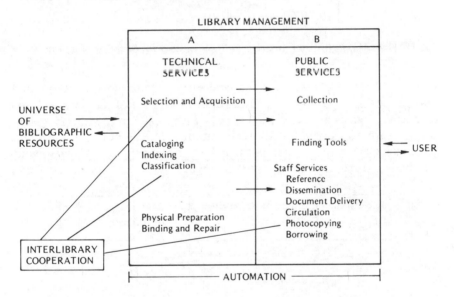

FIGURE 3   Organization of a library to serve the interface function.

As illustrated in Figure 1, and again in Figure 4, libraries are involved primarily in three major activities: (a) acquiring materials and storing them, (b) identifying and locating them, and (c) presenting these materials to library users in a variety of forms. The library staff also is involved in all three of these activities, and library costs are distributed over all of them. The activities are manifested to the library user in the form of the stock (collection), the tools available to exploit this stock (including shelf arrangement, catalogs, and indexes), and the services provided to the

PRINCIPAL FUNCTIONAL COMPONENT   PUBLIC MANIFESTATION

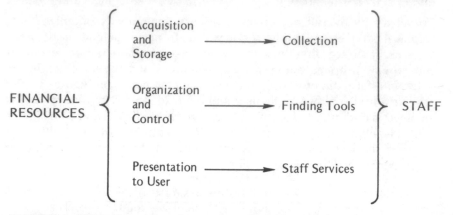

FIGURE 4   Major library functions and manifestations of these functions.

user. All three facets (stock, tools, and services) are closely interrelated, and all must be considered in any overall evaluation of the library. While technical services are concerned mostly with inputs to the library, public services are concerned mostly with outputs. This is not to suggest that technical services are less important than public services. Clearly, without input, there can be no output. Figure 5 depicts the three major

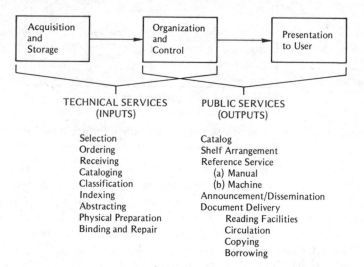

FIGURE 5   Major library functions and the most important services, public and technical, associated with them.

library activities and the most important services—technical and public—associated with them.

Measurement of Exposure

The most complete discussion of procedures for measuring exposure is given by Hamburg et al.[7,8] Exposure of library users to library materials may be direct or indirect. Direct exposure implies the exploitation of library materials by library users, and can be measured quantitatively by the number of items borrowed or consulted in the library, the number of photocopies made, and so on. Indirect exposure implies the exploitation of the library's collection by library staff on behalf of the library's users. It can be measured by the number of telephone inquiries handled or the number of individuals attending a library function (e.g., a book discussion or a storytelling session for children). Exposure is always measured quantitatively.

Hamburg and his colleagues recognize three possible measures of exposure, of increasing sophistication; namely, exposure counts, item-use days, and exposure time.

In the exposure count, each single use of the library's resources counts as a single exposure, either direct or indirect. Although this method provides an easy way to measure exposure, it has a number of disadvantages.

1. Dissimilar events (e.g., the borrowing of a book, the consultation of an index, the answering of a telephone inquiry) may be lumped together into one overall count. Of course, it is possible to divide these various events into separate counts, but this may complicate subsequent manipulation and analysis of the data collected.

2. Volume of use is measured, but amount of use is not. For example, five separate uses of *The Official Airline Guide*, each involving one minute, would count as five separate exposures. On the other hand, a book borrowed and used continuously for five days would count as a single exposure.

3. It is possible to increase exposure counts by artificial means. For example, a reduced loan period would presumably result in more individual loans per year. The exposure count would thus increase, while the actual level of service offered might not.

Item-use days measures exposure by number of days of use. For example, an item used within the library for part of one day counts as one item-use day, while a book borrowed for five days may be counted as five item-use days. This measure, which appears to have been first suggested by Meier,[12] is a more precise indication of use than the exposure count, but it too has disadvantages:

1. A book borrowed for five days is not necessarily used for five days or, indeed, used at all. This can only be determined by interviewing users, or a sample of users, at the time they return materials to the library—a difficult and time-consuming process. Also, the accuracy of the measures thus made is entirely dependent upon the accuracy of the users in remembering how much use they made of a particular publication. This problem may be avoided by sampling, to determine the average number of use days per circulation, and using this estimate as the basis for all item-use calculations of material used away from the library.

2. Events that should be considered approximately equal in value may be weighted differently. For example, a document used for one hour on each of five days counts as five item-use days, while the same document used for five hours in one day counts as only one item-use day.

Exposure time measures the actual hours of use. This is a more exact measure of the amount of use, and can only be determined by sampling: the observation of users—selected at random—in the library, and questioning users—again at random—when they return borrowed materials (a difficult and costly process). The object of the sampling is to determine the average amount of time associated with each type of exposure.

All of these exposure measures are quantitative rather than qualitative. A unit of use does not indicate the quality of the use. The loan of a novel for recreational reading, for example, may count the same as the scholarly use of a rare manuscript in the library. It is, however, theoretically possible to incorporate some qualitative elements into exposure measures by weighting the various exposures according to type of user, type of use, or both. It is unlikely, however, that much consensus would be reached (among librarians or others) as to what weights should be assigned to these different use categories.

Ultimately, all activities in which the library engages are designed to increase accessibility/exposure. As pointed out by Hamburg, one should be able to assess the effect of changes in stock, tools, and services in terms of exposure. For example:

The more branch locations provided, the greater the exposure.
The more hours the library is open, the greater the exposure.
The more titles provided, the greater the exposure.
The more copies provided, the greater the exposure.

The more physically accessible the collection, the greater the exposure.
The more liberal the usage period (up to a point), the greater the exposure.
The more explicit the shelf arrangement, the greater the exposure.
The more assistance given to users, the greater the exposure.
The more accessible the catalog, the greater the exposure.
The more indexes provided, the greater the exposure.
The more widely publicized the services, the greater the exposure.

While all library activities are designed to increase exposure, not all are intended to increase immediate exposure. Some activities, including purchase of new materials and publicizing of services, represent investment in future exposure.

De Prospo et al.[4] developed a completely different method of measuring exposure; namely, effective user hours—the number of hours of actual use recorded during a sampling period, divided by the number of hours in that period. Take, for example, a sampling period of 50 consecutive hours during which a library is open: 620 hours of actual use are accumulated (the sum of all hours spent in the library by all users during the sample period). The "effective user hours" are, therefore, 620/50, or approximately 12.4 hours of user time for each hour that the library is open.

Microevaluation of Library Service

Exposure is a measure of the amount or volume of use. It is an appropriate measure of a library's effectiveness (presumably, the more effective the library, the more it will be used). Amount of use per dollar expended is an appropriate measure of cost-effectiveness.

But volume of use is a relatively gross, quantitative measure, suitable only for macroevaluation. Microevaluation of library services involves the identification of factors affecting the amount of use and degree of user satisfaction (Figure 6). In general, microevaluation of any service should take into account factors of quality, time, and costs (including costs represented by human effort). A sample of some quality, time, and cost criteria by which the various technical and public services of a library may be evaluated is shown in Table 1.

The public services of a library must be measured ultimately in terms of degree of user satisfaction. The extent to which the library is used (i.e., the amount of exposure actually provided) presumably reflects the degree of user satisfaction, which may be measured by subjective procedures

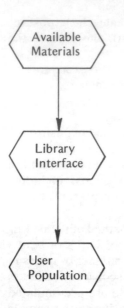

FIRST LEVEL
(Macroevaluation)

Measurement of amount of exposure. May simply be in quantitative terms with no explanation of why this amount of exposure is achieved, with no attempt to identify failures in service, and with no identification of ways in which exposure might be increased.

SECOND LEVEL
(Microevaluation)

Diagnostic. Goes beyond simple quantitative measurement and attempts to determine why a particular level of exposure is achieved (i.e., the factors affecting library performance) and what might be done to increase exposure in the future.

FIGURE 6   Relationship between macroevaluation and microevaluation.

such as questionnaires or interviews. This has a certain amount of value, but is somewhat limited in its utility for microevaluation. Users are not always able to recognize "failures." For example, a user who cannot locate a particular item in the catalog may be unaware of entries filed under headings he did not think of consulting. Or, a user seeking a particular item on the shelves may not know that he is looking in the wrong place. To be able to identify various types of failures in library services—and particularly to identify their causes—more objective, quantitative measures of performance are needed, such as percentage of user success in finding items on the shelves, or of staff success in answering telephone inquiries.

It is true, of course, that some aspects of library service are more easily evaluated than others. Generally, the more "concrete" the user requirement, the easier it is to measure user satisfaction in absolute terms. For example, if a user comes to a library seeking a particular book for which no substitute is acceptable, he either finds this book and is presumably completely satisfied, or he does not, in which case he is dissatisfied. The degree to which a "known-item" requirement is met is relatively easy to measure; and it is relatively easy to identify the factors determining

TABLE 1 Examples of Possible Performance Criteria Applied to Various Services of a Library

	Technical Services	Public Services

Quality	1. Selection and acquisition
	    Size, appropriateness, and balance of
	    collection
	2. Cataloging and indexing
	    Accuracy, consistency, and completeness
		1. Range of services offered
		2. Helpfulness of shelf order and guidance
		3. Catalog
		    Completeness, accuracy, and ease of use
		4. Reference and retrieval
		    Completeness, accuracy, and percentage success
		5. Document delivery
		    Percentage success

Time	1. Delays in acquisition 2. Delays in cataloging and other processing 3. Productivity of staff	1. Hours of service 2. Response time 3. Loan periods

Cost	1. Unit cost to purchase
	2. Unit cost to process
	    Accession
	    Classify
	    Catalog
		1. Effort to use
		    Location of library
		    Physical accessibility of collection
		    Assistance from staff
		2. Charges levied

whether or not particular books are available when needed. A less concrete case is that of the user who comes to the library seeking bibliographic material about a particular subject. It is not too difficult to determine whether or not he finds *some* material on this subject. It is, however, much more difficult to determine whether he finds "the best" material, or whether he finds *all* relevant material (assuming that he wants a comprehensive search). Whereas a "known item" search can be scored as 0 or 1, depending on its outcome, a subject search is not as readily amenable to such an absolute scoring system. Moreover, a user may come to a library, particularly a public library, with no specific requirement in mind beyond finding an "entertaining" book. The degree to which this user is satisfied is more difficult to evaluate and is certainly not susceptible to any absolute numerical score. It can easily be determined whether this user borrows one or more books, but it quite difficult to discover if he is actually entertained by them. If he is not entertained, the reason may be completely beyond the control of the library. Although the entertainment value of libraries may be hard to quantify, it should not necessarily be regarded as unimportant.

The satisfaction of this "browsing" type of requirement, although less easy to measure and certainly to express in quantitative terms, is not completely unmeasurable; but it may be necessary to express the results as completely subjective statements of user satisfaction. Moreover, factors influencing the satisfaction of various types of users certainly can be identified to ensure that library shelves contain a wide selection of materials of various types and levels likely to satisfy at least the majority of all browsers.

The technical services of a library, unlike the public services, cannot be evaluated directly in terms of user satisfaction. Technical processes must be evaluated from two viewpoints: (a) internal efficiency and (b) external, long-term effects (i.e., effects on public service and, ultimately, user satisfaction). Internal evaluation is concerned largely with time and cost factors; for example, how much it costs to acquire a book and to catalog it accurately, and how long it takes to process a new book (i.e., the time lag between receipt in the library and appearance on the shelves). From such calculations, various comparisons can be made, for example, with published standards, with other organizations, and with performance in other periods of time. Some qualitative internal evaluation of technical processes also may be possible. For instance, consistency and quality checks can be made on cataloging activities, as is often done in both descriptive and subject cataloging.

The external evaluation of technical processes involves longer term considerations: the effect of the technical processes upon the public services of the library. Selection and acquisition, for example, obviously determine adequacy of the collection and thus greatly influence use, whereas the quality of indexing and cataloging obviously influence use of the catalogs and other tools, as well as the degree of success achieved in locating needed documents.

Conclusion

Before any eligible individual can make use of the services of a particular library, he must be made aware of its existence and of the resources it provides. One important factor affecting the extent of library use is physical accessibility. Libraries must be conveniently located—within a building, on campus, or in the community. The typical person visits a library because he has some need for its services, which may fall into one of four major categories:

 1. The need to obtain one or more bibliographic items whose existence is already known.
 2. The need to obtain one or more items dealing with a particular subject.
 3. The need to obtain the answer to a specific factual question.
 4. The need to find a book solely for entertainment.

The extent to which these needs are promptly satisfied is directly dependent upon the size and quality of the library's collections, the adequacy of collection organization, the usefulness of the tools—especially catalogs and indexes—providing access to the collections, and the ability and willingness of the staff to exploit these resources. Whether or not a user is satisfied with the service of the library depends largely upon how long it takes—and how much effort he needs to expend—to obtain a particular known item, one or more items dealing with a particular subject, or the correct answer to a specific reference question. Evaluation of library service should be regarded as a management tool, applied to determine how effectively and how efficiently the library is serving the needs of its users, to identify limitations and failures of service, and to suggest ways in which the service might be improved. Moreover, it is reasonable to assume that improvements in immediate service will also lead to improvements in the ability of the library to reach its longer term, largely unmeasurable goals.

The following chapters discuss the evaluation of specific facets of library service and their effects on accessibility, exposure, factors affecting use of the library, and degree of success in satisfying requirements of users.

REFERENCES

1. Armstrong, C.M. "Measurement and Evaluation of the Public Library." *In: Research Methods in Librarianship: Measurement and Evaluation.* Edited by H. Goldhor. Urbana, Ill., Graduate School of Library Science, University of Illinois, 1968, pp. 15–24.
2. Bourne, C. P. et al. *Requirements, Criteria, and Measures of Performance of Information Storage and Retrieval Systems.* Menlo Park, Calif., Stanford Research Institute, December 1961. AD 270942.
3. Cleverdon, C. W. et al. *Factors Determining the Performance of Indexing Systems.* Vol. 1, *Design.* Cranfield, England, Cranfield Institute of Technology, 1966.
4. DeProspo, E. R. et al. *Performance Measures for Public Libraries.* Chicago, Public Library Association, 1973.
5. Drucker, P. F. "Managing the Public Service Institution." *The Public Interest, 33:*43–60, Fall 1973.
6. Evans, G. E. and Borko, H. *Effectiveness Criteria for Medical Libraries. Final Report.* Los Angeles, Institute of Library Research, University of California, 1970. ED 057813.
7. Hamburg, M. et al. "Library Objectives and Performance Measures and Their Use in Decision Making." *Library Quarterly, 42:*107–128, 1972.
8. Hamburg, M. et al. *Library Planning and Decision-Making Systems.* Cambridge, Mass., MIT Press, 1974.
9. King, D. W. and Bryant, E. C. *The Evaluation of Information Services and Products.* Washington, D.C., Information Resources Press, 1971.
10. Lancaster, F. W. *Information Retrieval Systems: Characteristics, Testing and Evaluation.* New York, Wiley, 1968.
11. Lancaster, F. W. "The Cost-Effectiveness Analysis of Information Retrieval and Dissemination Systems." *Journal of the American Society for Information Science, 22:*12–27, 1971.
12. Meier, R. L. "Efficiency Criteria for the Operation of Large Libraries." *Library Quarterly, 31:*215–234, 1961.
13. Mooers, C. N. "Mooers' Law or, Why Some Retrieval Systems Are Used and Others Are Not." *American Documentation, 11:*204, 1960.
14. Ranganathan, S. R. *The Five Laws of Library Science.* 2nd ed. Bombay, Asia Publishing House, 1957.
15. Rzasa, P. V. and Baker, N. R. *Measures of Effectiveness for a University Library.* Atlanta, School of Industrial and Systems Engineering, Georgia Institute of Technology, 1971. ED 054833. Also appeared in *Journal of the American Society for Information Science, 23:*248–253, 1972.
16. Wellisch, J. B. et al. *The Public Library and Federal Policy.* Westport, Conn., Greenwood Press, 1974.

2

Studies of
Catalog Use

A catalog is the single, most important key to a library's collections. Its major function is to show whether the library owns a particular bibliographic item whose author and/or title are known (known items) and, if so, where it is located. The catalog also reveals the library's holdings in specific subject areas and indicates where they are located, reveals the library's series holdings, and provides bibliographic information.

Library catalogs, in some form, have existed for centuries, but only in comparatively recent times have serious attempts been made to evaluate their effectiveness as finding tools. There are two main reasons why catalog use studies have gained increasing attention in recent years. First, librarians are becoming more concerned with the evaluation of library services and operations. They want to know how well the catalog performs, what its deficiencies are, and how its level of effectiveness can be increased. Second, it is likely that many of the present card and printed catalogs will someday be replaced by machine-readable catalogs capable of being searched through on-line terminals. To design effective on-line catalogs, more information is needed on how existing catalogs are being used, how successfully they are being used, and their major problems and limitations.

While it is relatively easy to measure the volume of catalog use within a library, it is far more difficult to measure the effectiveness of catalog use (i.e., to determine whether the user is able to find entries for items or subjects he is seeking, and how long it takes to locate relevant entries). Microevaluation of a catalog requires differentiation between successes and failures, identification of specific instances of failure, and determination of precise causes of failure. This is not an easy task, and it is certainly not readily susceptible to unobtrusive observation.

Questionnaires administered to library users, eliciting opinions on catalogs, are of limited value, because they are heavily dependent upon what respondents remember about past experiences; and human memory is notoriously unreliable. Moreover, a study of this kind can gauge only general reactions. It does not deal with specific instances of use and, thus, cannot quantify successes and failures, or precisely identify instances of failure, to allow the recognition of their underlying causes.

A diagnostic study of catalog use must measure the individual user's degree of success in locating an item or in finding material on a specific subject when he consults the catalog. Clearly, a study of each catalog use can be made only in the very smallest of libraries, and only within a very restricted time period. A true picture of the volume and effectiveness of catalog use can, however, be obtained on the basis of a well-constructed sample of individual uses over a reasonable length of time. The sample must be drawn to represent all types of users and all types of uses in proportion to their occurrence in the total pattern of catalog use within a specified period. An example of such a sample is provided by Lipetz[20] in his study of the catalog at the Yale University Library.

But sampling is only the beginning of the problem. Having identified a sample of specific catalog uses, the next step is to determine what the user is seeking and how successful he is in his search. One approach would be to have users complete a brief questionnaire at the conclusion of each catalog search. While this technique is inexpensive in staff time, it does present several problems. Many people dislike questionnaires and will either refuse to complete them or will do so in such a hurried and careless fashion that the results are of little value. Many users are in a hurry to select some books and to leave the library, which could have an adverse effect on any questionnaire study. It also may be difficult to obtain from a questionnaire the detailed level of information needed for the identification and analysis of failures. Or, particularly in the case of subject searches, the user may not recall exactly what he was looking for when his search began (i.e., the original conception of his information need may have changed somewhat during the course of the search).

Because of the difficulties inherent in using questionnaires, the most valuable studies of catalog use have been conducted through interviews with users at the time they search the catalog. Although an interview study requires a much greater expenditure of staff time, at least in the data-gathering phase, the resulting data are likely to be more precise and more reliable. The technique is not, of course, perfect. To obtain the data needed for analysis, the interviewer may have to approach the user when he begins to search the catalog, to determine what he is seeking and must again interview the user when the search is completed, to determine his degree of success. To record a precise sequence of entries consulted during the search, the interviewer must remain in close proximity to the user throughout the entire process. The problem is not one of user cooperation, but of over-cooperation—it has been found in several studies of this kind that users are quite willing, and sometimes even eager, to participate. A subject who knows he is being observed may not, however, behave the same as he would when unobserved; there is, for example, a strong tendency to be more careful or to expend greater effort than under normal conditions. This "Hawthorne effect" can be avoided if the interview is conducted only at the conclusion of the search, but at this point it may be difficult to collect accurately all the data needed for subsequent analysis. With on-line catalogs, it may be possible to monitor catalog use "transparently." Studying the use of card catalogs and book catalogs, however, is largely restricted to questionnaires and interviews, particularly the latter. Following are some major studies of catalog use, including their principal findings.

ALA Catalog Use Study

The first large-scale study of catalog use was conducted by the Resources and Technical Services Division of the American Library Association and published in 1958.[2] This study, conducted over a 12-week period, was based on 5,494 completed interviews of catalog users in 39 libraries: 2 large research libraries, 15 college and university libraries, 3 metropolitan-central public libraries, 2 small-city public libraries, 6 special-subject libraries, 5 public branch libraries, and 6 high school libraries. Two characteristics of the sample should be especially noted. First, each library was asked to interview 15 users during each week of its participation in the study; thus, the samples from the smaller (and presumably less-used) libraries would provide better representations of total catalog use than those from the larger libraries. Second, because of the large number of academic libraries included, the total population represented in the sample contained a high proportion of students. Library staff were deliberately included in the sample, but only 203 interviews of this type took place.

The objectives of the investigation were to identify actual user demands on the catalog and to measure the extent to which these demands were satisfied. The 137 interviewers collected such data as the user's objective in searching the catalog, the knowledge he brought to it, the way he used it, and his successes and failures. The user was approached as he neared the catalog. Having obtained his agreement to participate, the interviewer accompanied the user to the catalog and recorded data on a standard preestablished questionnaire (reproduced as Figure 7).

This large sample revealed that, in public libraries, subject searches were conducted more often than known-item searches, but the reverse was generally true in academic and special libraries. The overall distribution for the entire sample was quite even: 48% were known-item searches and 52% were subject searches. Rarely did a user change from one type of search to another at a single session. In the academic libraries, the distribution between the two types of searches varied with the "seniority" of the user: undergraduate students conducted more subject searches, graduate students more known-item searches, while the majority of faculty searches were of the known-item type.

Table 2 shows the percentage of successes and failures for the known-item searches. Overall, there was a 66% success rate. A search was

TABLE 2   Known-Item Searches: Patron Successes and Failures[2]

Library Category	Type of Entry Found			Successful Searches		Failures		Total Searches
	Main (Item 3)	Title (Item 4)	Subject (Item 5)	No.	%	No.	%	
College and University, Type A	175	26	31	232	60	152	40	384
College and University, Type B	208	30	13	251	68	116	32	367
College and University, Type C	208	17	10	235	78	67	22	302
College and University, Type D	80	29	7	116	80	29	20	145
Large Research	75	11	16	102	59	70	41	172
Special-Purpose	159	16	13	188	51	178	49	366
High School	110	104	66	280	80	69	20	349
Metropolitan—Central	98	17	14	129	63	76	37	205
Small City	63	26	12	101	69	46	31	147
Metropolitan—Branches	105	28	17	150	60	100	40	250
Not Coded	2	1		3				3
TOTAL	1,283 (72%)	305 (17%)	199 (11%)	1,787	66	903	34	2,690

INTERVIEW REPORT.   Agency: _____ 1. ____

Date _____ Interview began _____M   Ended _____ M

Day _____ Patron's occupation _____ 2. ____

(Be as specific as possible, e.g., Undergrad.; Grade-school teacher, Plumber)

SEEKING A KNOWN ITEM (Please record patron's data on verso)

3. Found author or title-main-entry card for desired item	3.	☐
4. Found title card for desired item	4.	☐
5. Found item by looking for author or title-main-entry under a SUBJECT	5.	☐
6. Did not find item	6.	☐
7. Patron's information about author or title was incorrect or incomplete	7.	☐
8. "Author" was not main entry but added entry (like translator)	8.	☐
9. No entry for "author", altho there *was* a main entry card	9.	☐
10. No title card, altho there *was* an author card (permanent or temporary)	10.	☐
11. Filing arrangements under this author, or before and after him, were unclear to patron .	11.	☐
12. Item was not in this catalog	12.	☐
13. Other reason _____	13.	☐
14. Source of patron's information: _____	14.	____

LOOKING UP A SUBJECT

15. Wanted material on (HIS WORDS) _____	15.	____
16. That "subject"-field was already familiar to the patron	16.	☐
Found catalog cards on that "subject" by locating		
17. This subject heading or SEE reference: _____	17.	☐
18. Title(s) with the meaning he wanted, altho his "subject" was not a Library subject . .	18.	☐
19. Partial or inverted title(s) with the meaning wanted (again, not a Library subject) . . .	19.	☐
20. Relevant title(s) under an AUTHOR known to write on patron's "subject"	20.	☐
21. Additional subject headings pertinent to search	21.	☐
22. Did not find any catalog cards on his "subject"	22.	☐
23. Patron's "subject" was not a subject heading and there was no SEE reference to the subject heading that was used	23.	☐
24. There was a SEE or SEE ALSO, but it was not understood or not found	24.	☐
25. Following up SEE's or SEE ALSO's became burdensome or threatened to; was abandoned	25.	☐
26. Time was lost at heading _____ which proved little or no help	26.	☐
27. There were no cards on the subject in this catalog	27.	☐
28. Other reason _____	28.	☐
29. Took down call numbers for all entries under subject(s) used	29.	☐
Took down call numbers for only *some* (or *none*); selection was based in good part on:		
30. Alphabetical position of entries	30.	☐
31. Desire for works in English	31.	☐
32. Desire for works in other language(s)	32.	☐
33. Connotation of wording of title(s), subtitle(s)	33.	☐
34. Date of publication	34.	☐
35. Prominence of particular classifications (i.e., Where are most books on the subject?) . .	35.	☐
36. Author's reputation	36.	☐
37. "Illus." statement	37.	☐
38. Bibliography note	38.	☐
39. Tracing	39.	☐
40. (Other) _____	40.	☐

41. Patron had used this catalog before	41.	☐
42. Sought help at some point(s) from staff member	42.	☐
43. Differences among author, title and subject cards were not clear to patron	43.	☐
44. Lack of guide-card(s) contributed to confusion, loss of time, or failure	44.	☐
45. Interviewer believes catalog entries were sufficient to meet patron's need	45.	☐

INTERVIEWER'S (and Patron's) COMMENT: OVER

FIGURE 7 Questionnaire used in ALA study.[2]

characterized as successful if the user was able to locate an entry for the item sought when he first approached the catalog. The failures, occurring in 34% of all uses of this type, were of two distinct types: (a) failure to find an entry for an item *not held* by the library (a collection failure rather than a catalog failure)* and (b) failure to find an entry for an item held by the library and actually represented somewhere in the catalog.

These two types of failure are depicted in Table 3, wherein the "Failures" column displays the total number of failures, and the "Failures, Adjusted" column, the catalog failures only (i.e., instances of user failure to find an entry for an item that actually appeared in the catalog). Catalog failures numbered 450, or approximately 20% of the 2,237 searches in the sample. These data might be summarized as follows: the users had a 66% overall chance of finding the bibliographic item they sought when they first approached the catalog; the item they sought was actually held by the library in 2,237 of the 2,690 cases, a coverage of approximately 83%. In one case out of every five, however, the user was unable to locate an entry that was actually present in the catalog, and this 20% failure rate may be a low estimate. A user was recorded as not having found an existing entry only when the librarian-interviewer was able to find one for the item the user had sought unsuccessfully. But the searches of the librarians, themselves, certainly were not perfect, and it is likely that they too were unable to find entries for some items that were included in the catalog. The figure of 453 items "Not in Catalog" may thus be high, and the figure of 450 items not discovered in the catalog may be correspondingly low. This possibility is supported by the fact that, of the 203 sample searches conducted by staff members of participating libraries, 16% produced failures to locate entries for items that were actually in the catalog. Thus, on the average, the librarian user fared little better than the nonlibrarian user.

The main entry (author or title) was used in 72% of the successful searches, a title-added entry in 17%, and a subject entry in 11%. The results of the study suggest that users had little difficulty with cataloging rules pertaining to main entry form. Of the 2,690 searches for known items, only 62 (2.3%) failed or were delayed because the user tried a different form of main entry from that actually in the catalog; and in half of these cases, some form of reference or added entry provided an easy link to the main entry. It was noted that added entries for joint authors, as well as descriptive bibliographic data provided on the catalog cards, were little-used.

* As Krikelas[14] has pointed out, a catalog search that correctly indicates that the library does not hold an item sought must be regarded as successful in terms of the role of the catalog, even though the user may not be "satisfied" with this result.

TABLE 3   Incidence of Failure in Known-Item Searches[2]

Library Category	Known-Item Searches	Failures No.	Failures %	Not in Catalog	Total, Adjusted	Failures, Adjusted No.	Failures, Adjusted %
College and University, Type A	384	152	40	54	330	98	30
College and University, Type B	367	116	32	53	314	63	20
College and University, Type C	302	67	22	46	256	21	8
College and University, Type D	145	29	20	25	120	4	3
Large Research	172	70	41	20	152	50	33
High School	349	69	20	49	300	20	6.7
Special-Purpose	366	178	49	83	283	95	34
Metropolitan—Central	205	76	37	36	169	40	24
Small City	147	46	31	34	113	12	11
Metropolitan—Branches	250	100	40	53	197	47	24
Not Coded	3				3		
TOTAL	2,690	903	34	453	2,237	450	20

The user's author or title information was incorrect or incomplete in 13% of all known-item searches. This type of inaccuracy occurred less frequently in small libraries and was most prevalent in large academic libraries, where it affected 22% of the searches. Accuracy of information brought to the catalog was the single most important factor determining the success or failure of a search, although there were some indications that degree of success also varied directly with the user's experience with the catalog and inversely with its size.

Table 4 presents data on the incidence of failures and successes in 2,792 subject searches. The user was successful in 80% of the searches; that is, he was able to find one or more entries on the subject he was seeking when he approached the catalog. No attempt was made to determine whether the user found all relevant entries or whether the items he did find were the "best" (i.e., most directly related to the subject sought).

Table 5 depicts the two types of subject search failures. Of the 551 searches that uncovered nothing on the topic sought (20% of the total subject searches), 195 were unsuccessful because the catalog actually contained nothing on the subject matter sought, while 356 were unsuccessful because the user was unable to find entries that did exist. If the first group were omitted from the sample, it is clear that, in 356 of the

TABLE 4   Subject Searches: Patron Successes and Failures[2]

Library Category	Types of Entry Found				Successful Searches		Failures		Total Searches
	Subject (Item 17)	Full Title (Item 18)	Partial Title (Item 19)	Author (Item 20)	Number	%	Number	%	
College and University, Type A	210	26	6	23	265	77	80	23	345
College and University, Type B	242	13	3	8	266	84	51	16	317
College and University, Type C	224	10	1	12	247	86	40	14	287
College and University, Type D	164	20	1	6	191	92	16	8	207
Large Research	124	7	1	13	145	86	23	14	168
Special-Purpose	179	10	5	17	207	75	68	25	275
High School	268	18	5	2	293	83	60	17	353
Metropolitan—Central	185	18	6	9	218	80	56	20	274
Small City	153	7	2	3	165	90	19	10	184
Metropolitan—Branches	228	9	1	5	243	64	138	36	381
Not Coded		1			1				1
TOTAL	1,977 (89%)	139 (6%)	27 (1%)	98 (4%)	2,241	80	551	20	2,792

TABLE 5   Incidence of Failure in Subject Searches[2]

Library Category	Subject Searches	Failures		Not in Catalog	Total, Adjusted	Failures, Adjusted	
		No.	%			No.	%
College and University, Type A	345	80	23	24	321	56	17
College and University, Type B	317	51	16	18	299	33	11
College and University, Type C	287	40	14	13	274	27	10
College and University, Type D	207	16	8	9	198	7	4
Large Research	168	23	14	3	165	20	12
High School	353	60	17	26	327	34	10
Special-Purpose	275	68	25	18	257	50	19
Metropolitan—Central	274	56	20	19	255	37	15
Small City	184	19	10	10	174	9	5
Metropolitan—Branches	381	138	36	55	326	83	25
Not Coded	1				1		
TOTAL	2,792	551	20	195	2,597	356	13

2,597 searches (13%), the user was unable to find an entry for a subject represented in the catalog. For the reasons previously discussed, this figure of 13% failure may be somewhat low. As with the known-item searches, Table 5 indicates some degree of correlation between rate of failure and size of catalog, although the metropolitan branch libraries had a very high rate of failure and did not conform to the general pattern. The investigators hypothesize that, in addition to the size (complexity) of a catalog, another factor affecting the success of a subject search may be the amount of time the user is able to spend on a search. They suggest that metropolitan branch users, as a whole, because they might be less pressed for time, are less intensive in their efforts at the catalog. The users of academic catalogs, on the other hand, may be more pressed for time, resulting in greater concentration and level of effort at the catalog.

An alternative, and perhaps more plausible, explanation is that success in catalog searching is directly related to user motivation, and that the academic users were more highly motivated than the branch library users.

The study found that the typical user consults only a single subject heading (which perhaps casts some doubt on the value of *see also* references). On the average, only one of five users consulted a second heading. Searching other headings occurred most in the large research libraries and least in the metropolitan branches and high schools, which again reflects a relationship between intensity of effort and motivation. Tracings were rarely used as an additional source of subject headings.

The major reason for subject-search failures was lack of an appropriate subject heading or cross-reference, but detailed analyses were not conducted to determine why these were not present in the catalogs under study. Data from five college libraries indicate that failures were more prevalent in specific searches than in broad ones. It was found that, frequently, subject headings were not sufficiently specific and that (following common subject cataloging practice) references rarely were made from the specific heading that the user sought to an appropriate, more general, heading.* It also was discovered, however, that some users expect the catalog to function as a type of encyclopedia, using it to seek information on a topic too restricted in scope to have a book devoted to it.

Analyses of failures indicate that the performance of the subject catalog could be improved considerably with more *see* references—from synonyms and nearly synonymous expressions, from popular names to the more scientific or technical names used in the catalog, from inverted to noninverted forms of entry (or vice versa), and from specific to appropriate, more generic, terms. But the catalog itself was not responsible for all subject failures. Other reasons can be attributed to lack of perseverance or, in some cases, lack of intelligence on the part of the searcher.

A breakdown of failures by subject area is given in Table 6, which also shows two types of failure: (a) subject not represented in the catalog, and (b) subject represented, but not found by the searcher. It is clear that searches were most successful in the fields having precise vocabularies (e.g., technology, biography). Subject areas with less precise and more abstract language (e.g., education, literature) had a far higher rate of failure. This general finding has been apparent several times since 1958 in evaluations of information retrieval systems: such systems tend to perform at a higher level overall in subjects (e.g., chemistry) with relatively "hard" languages than they do in subjects (e.g., sociology or the behavioral sciences) with "soft" languages.

Evidence (see Table 7) from the study also suggested that the failure rate in a strict dictionary catalog (authors, subjects, and titles interfiled) was greater than the failure rate in a divided catalog (authors and titles separated from subjects).

A final area of interest in the ALA study was the investigation of criteria by which users selected individual entries under particular subject head-

---

*This failure also is common in computer-based and other types of information retrieval systems, in which context it has been referred to by Lancaster[18] as "lack of an adequate entry vocabulary."

TABLE 6 Incidence of Subject Search Failures by Principal Subject Fields[2]

Subject	Searches	Failures		Not in Catalog	Total, Adjusted	Failures, Adjusted	
		No.	%			No.	%
Education	114	37	32	5	109	32	30
Literature	228	51	22	12	216	39	18
Biography	316	56	18	30	286	26	9
Science	191	33	17	14	177	19	11
Technology	377	63	17	42	335	21	6
Economics	194	32	16	11	183	21	11
History/ Description	227	34	15	13	214	21	10
All Classes	2,792	551	19.7	195	2,597	356	14.5

ings. The title of a book was, as might be expected, the most-used indicator of its contents, and the majority of items were selected on this basis. The investigators pointed out that titles are not always descriptive, and that the user frequently had trouble selecting the books most likely to be relevant to his precise interests, especially when he was consulting many entries under a relatively broad heading. They also suggested that selection of the most useful items would be much easier if more specific subject headings were available and used. Date of publication was used more frequently as a criterion for selection than name of author, which suggests that arranging entries under a subject heading in reverse chronological order might be more useful than arranging them alphabetically by author.*

TABLE 7 Incidence of Failures by Structure of Catalog (College and University Libraries, Types A, B, C, and Special-Purpose Libraries)[2]

	Known-Item Searches	Percent Failure		Subject Searches	Percent Failure	
		Unadj.	Adj.		Unadj.	Adj.
Dictionary	905	39	28	712	23	18
Divided (A–T;S)	419	32	15	423	14	9

*Other studies, however, described later in this chapter, have discovered that some users with incomplete author/title information actually approach a known-item search by subject heading. It is much easier to find "Browne's Textbook on Economics" under the heading ECONOMICS if the author sequence is maintained.

The ALA study was very important, and it gathered many interesting and valuable data. It strongly suggested that certain established cataloging practices (e.g., failure to refer from the specific to the general in subject catalogs) were adversely affecting the performance of the catalog, while other features (e.g., the elaborate network of *see also* references) were comparatively little-used. This study was the first large-scale, systematic attempt to identify the major factors that determine whether a catalog search will be successful or unsuccessful. But a multilibrary study of this type must deal mostly in generalities. The major limitations or defects of a single catalog must be identified by a similar investigation restricted to that catalog and to its particular users; however, since most library catalogs, as well as user needs, are similar in many aspects, all libraries can derive some benefit from the findings of a general multilibrary study of this type.

Studies at the University of Michigan

A major catalog-use study conducted at the University of Michigan was described in 1970 by Tagliacozzo et al.[41] and by Tagliacozzo and Kochen.[42] This large survey of searching-behavior patterns was conducted via 2,681 interviews with a randomly selected sample of catalog users at three University of Michigan libraries and, for purposes of comparison, at the Ann Arbor Public Library. The interviews, conducted between February 1968 and April 1969, were distributed as follows: 887 searches in the general university catalog, 659 in the undergraduate catalog, 618 in the catalog of the medical library, and 517 in the public library catalog. The interviews were open-ended, orally administered, and supported by observation of user behavior at the catalog. Users were interviewed before and during their searches. Most of the university catalog users were students—approximately one-half graduate and one-half undergraduate. Of the 2,681 searches in the sample, 1,745 were for known items, 786 for particular subjects, and 150 for other purposes.

Known-item searches clearly outnumbered subject searches at all three university libraries. In the public library, the known-item searches also outnumbered subject searches, but by a close margin (49.5% known-item, 41.6% subject, and 8.9% "other"). The proportion of subject searches declined markedly with the increased "seniority" of the searcher. Subject searches by underclassmen comprised 42.4% of all catalog searches in this group, the corresponding figures being 31.7% by upperclassmen, 19.8% by graduate students, and 12.6% by faculty.

Table 8 presents data on the success and failure rates of known-item searches in all four catalogs. The failure data reflect both collection

TABLE 8　Results of Catalog Searches, Michigan Study[41]

Libraries	Known-Item Searches	Successes		Failures	
		Number	%	Number	%
University of Michigan					
General Library	636	515	81.0	121	19.0
Undergraduate Library	448	298	66.5	150	33.5
Medical Library	405	287	70.9	118	29.1
Ann Arbor Public Library	256	155	60.5	101	39.5
TOTAL	1,745	1,255	71.9	490	28.1

failures (inability to find an item because it was not in the catalog) and searching failures (inability to find an entry that was included in the catalog).

Table 9 shows the relationship between total failures and searching failures. For example, out of a total of 150 failures (33.5% of all searches) in the undergraduate catalog, only 27 (8.3%) were failures to find existing entries.

The proportion of collection failures tends to decrease as the size of the library increases, while the proportion of searching failures tends to increase. This can be seen by comparing the data from searches in the general library (approximately 4 million catalog entries) with searches in the undergraduate library (approximately 268,000 entries). A large proportion of total failures in the former were caused by inability to find an entry that was present, while in the latter, there were very few failures of this type, and most were of the "not-in-collection" variety. This relationship, however, is not valid when one compares failures in the undergraduate library with failures in the medical library. Even though these catalogs are approximately the same size, failures to find existing entries

TABLE 9　Collection Failure Versus User (Searching) Failure, Michigan Study[41]

Libraries	Total Failures		User (Searching) Failures	
	Number	%	Number	%
General Library	121	19.0	82	13.7
Undergraduate Library	150	33.5	27	8.3
Medical Library	118	29.1	76	20.9
Public Library	101	39.5	12	7.2

were much more prevalent in the medical library. The Michigan investigators suggested several possible reasons for this, the most plausible being that the undergraduate catalog contained far more title-added entries than did the medical library catalog. Their suggestion that the high failure rate in searching the medical library catalog might be partly due to its being divided (whereas the undergraduate catalog is a straight dictionary arrangement) appears less likely in view of the findings of the ALA study.

As in the ALA study, the Michigan investigators determined the completeness and accuracy of title and author information brought by users to their catalog searches. Table 10 presents data for title information. The categories A–G represent a scale of accuracy and completeness: A, the title is complete and accurate in every respect; B, the first two words are correct, but the remainder of the title is incomplete, incorrect, or both; while G (the worst possible case), the user knew nothing about the title. It can be seen that the majority of users (70%) had complete and accurate title information, but 8.1% had no title information at all.

The accuracy level of title information was much higher than that of author information. If only the personal (as opposed to corporate) authors are considered, only 41.9% (573/1,367) of the users had perfect information. As Tagliacozzo et al.[41] point out, "the chance that a user would approach the catalog with perfect or nearly perfect information is much higher in the case of titles than in the case of authors (70.0% versus 41.9%)." This is partly explained by the fact that "the meaning of a title usually acts as a built-in corrective mechanism which tends to eliminate minor errors of the orthographic or grammatical type."

Titles brought to the catalog in written form were more likely to be accurate than those that were memorized by users—81.9% as opposed to 71.6% accuracy. The difference between written and memorized author

TABLE 10   Degree of Correctness and Completeness of Users' Titles, Michigan Study[41]

Libraries	Title Categories							
	A	B	C	D	E	F	G	Total
General Library	405	22	20	17	39	11	55	569
Undergraduate Library	309	23	8	10	27	12	29	418
Medical Library	219	24	14	16	37	26	33	369
Public Library	178	10	9	1	15	7	12	232
TOTAL	1,111	79	51	44	118	56	129	1,588
%	70.0	5.0	3.2	2.8	7.4	3.5	8.1	

information was very slight and not statistically significant, although written citations contained a higher proportion of accurate, but not perfect, information. It should be noted, however, that written citations were in a variety of forms, including printed bibliographies, typed reading lists, and handwritten notes. Handwritten notes, possibly compiled from imperfectly memorized information, would obviously be as inaccurate as an original citation committed to a user's memory. No attempt was made to distinguish between types of written information.

Table 11 reveals the comparative effect of inaccurate or incomplete author and title information in known-item searching. These data indicate that users were able to compensate reasonably well for defective titles— even grossly defective ones. They also were able to compensate reasonably well for inaccurate or incomplete author information, except in the grossly defective category, where 28.3% of all searches failed.

Almost two-thirds of the users observed in the conduct of known-item searches chose the author as first access point, while less than one-third chose the title. A very small number of users looked first under the subject heading. First, second, and third search attempts are summarized in Table 12, which includes data for searches in which the user had no search option (e.g., he had author information, but no title information, or vice versa). When users did have a choice between author and title, 85.2% began with authors. As Tagliacozzo and Kochen[42] indicate, "there seems to be a marked preference, therefore, for the author over title as first access point." Despite this preference, however, users' title information tends to be more accurate than their author information. A distinction was made in this study between "access" and "recognition" (or verification) in catalog searching. When a user searches for a particular item by the

TABLE 11   Failure of Search in Relation to Degree of Correctness and Completeness of Author or Title Information, Michigan Study[42]

Author	Number of Searches	Failure of Search	Title	Number of Searches	Failure of Search
Group I (high precision)	459	4.1%	Group I (high precision)	670	5.8%
Group II (moderate precision)	292	6.8%	Group II (moderate precision)	63	14.3%
Group III (low precision)	67	14.9%	Group III (low precision)	93	10.7%
Group IV (grossly defective)	46	28.3%	Group IV (grossly defective)	38	10.5%
TOTAL	864			864	

TABLE 12   Sequence of Choice of Access Points, Michigan Study[41]

Access Point	1st Attempt (N=1,718)	2nd Attempt (N=295)	3rd Attempt (N=62)
Author (and Editor)	65.5%	34.5%	19.3%
Title	28.9%	37.3%	17.7%
Subject Heading	5.6%	28.1%	62.9%

author, the author's name is used as the point of access, while the title plays a subordinate role—that of allowing recognition of the item sought. The reverse situation is true in a title search: the title is used as the point of access and the name of the author for recognition. Citation information must be reasonably accurate to allow access to the catalog, but less accuracy is needed for the purpose of recognition or verification. Because most users approach the catalog by author rather than title, it is unfortunate that author information tends to be less accurate than title information. Overall catalog searching would clearly improve if users came to the catalog with better author information or, alternatively, if they searched more often under the title and used the less-accurate author data for recognition only.

The Michigan study also considered the perseverance of the searcher at the catalog. A "persevering" searcher is one who continues to look for a particular item after initial failure to locate it. It is interesting to note that more than half of the searchers whose first attempt met with failure did not continue the search.

Subject searching also was investigated in the Michigan study, but not in as much detail as known-item searching. Table 13 is a result of this phase of the investigation, and it presents the correlation between users' terms for material on the subject sought and headings that appeared in the catalog. On the average, in all four libraries, approximately 75% of the

TABLE 13   The Matching of Query Terms to Catalog Entries, Michigan Study[42]

Type of Match	General Library N=293	Undergraduate Library N=259	Medical Library N=298	Public Library N=273
Exact Match	66.6%	55.6%	57.7%	50.0%
Partial Match	16.0%	18.2%	15.4%	21.9%
TOTAL	82.6%	73.8%	73.1%	71.9%

"trials"* were successful in the sense that user terms matched the catalog entries exactly or partially. A "partial match" was one in which user terms and catalog entries, while not identical, were sufficiently close to permit the searcher to locate the necessary headings.

A successful match does not necessarily mean a successful subject search. It is possible that a searcher's heading will match a catalog entry, but that he will not find any items under this entry that he considers "relevant" to his information needs (e.g., the searcher might not have chosen an appropriate heading in the first place). Table 14 compares two kinds of subject-search failures. The first column represents failures in which the user was unable to match his search term with the catalog

TABLE 14 Zero-Match Searches and Unsuccessful Searches, Michigan Study[42]

Libraries	Zero-Match Searches	Unsuccessful Searches
University of Michigan		
General Library	4.2%	15.7%
Undergraduate Library	8.7%	19.1%
Medical Library	10.7%	14.8%
Ann Arbor Public Library	14.4%	14.4%

heading, while the second column shows the total percentage of unsuccessful subject searches. For example, in 19.1% of all subject searches in the undergraduate library, the user failed to select any book as a result of his catalog search. In 8.7% of the searches, this failure was due to the user's inability to match his search terms with headings in the catalog. In 10.4% of the searches (19.1% minus 8.7%), his search terms matched the catalog headings partially or exactly, but the entries did not meet his information needs. In the public library, the number of unsuccessful searches equaled those in which the user was unable to match his terms with catalog headings. In other words, when users succeeded in matching their terms with subject headings, they always found a book to satisfy their needs, at least in part. Tagliacozzo and Kochen[42] discuss the factors affecting the effectiveness of subject searches as follows:

*A "trial" is a single user attempt to match one of his own subject terms with a catalog entry. Some subject searches may have involved several trials, although the great majority of searches involved only a single trial. The data in Table 13 relate to "trials" rather than searches; for example, 71.9% of the "trials" in the public library produced an exact or partial match.

Success or failure of the search results from the interplay of two basically distinct sets of variables. The first set, which is related to the matching of the user's query term to a catalog entry, may include such things as the skill and resourcefulness of the user, his persistence, his familiarity with catalog rules; it may also include the availability of subject headings relevant to the topic of his query and the availability of cross-references connecting related subject headings in the area of the search. The second set of variables has to do with the user's acceptance of the retrieved material and therefore concerns the user's expectations and attitudes, his satisfaction with the retrieved information, his knowledge of the topic and his ability to discriminate between what is relevant and what is not.

The study also found that the majority of searchers (approximately 60%) relied entirely upon terms they themselves had generated and did not allow the catalog to lead them to additional subject terms (by means of the alphabetical proximity of related headings or its cross-reference structure). In observing this, the authors[42] suggest that:

... some users fail to try catalog-generated terms because they lack confidence in the catalog's associational structure or do not understand its use, or perhaps because the catalog is inadequate in the area of their search.

Another study at the University of Michigan was reported by Palmer[31] in 1972. This study was conducted in the general library, to determine who used the catalog, for what purpose, in what way, with what degree of success, and whether most user requirements could be met satisfactorily with some form of computer-based catalog that would provide abbreviated bibliographic data for each book. Questionnaires were distributed to more than 4,400 catalog users—graduate students comprising the largest group—over an eight-week period in 1967. The 5,067 completed "survey units" represented a 10% sample of all catalog uses during that period. Approximately 70% of all searches were of the known-item variety, and 84% were reported as successful (note how close this figure is to the known-item success rate—81%—in the other Michigan study). Palmer also determined that a computer-based catalog which included an abbreviated citation of only five elements—author, title, call number, subject headings, and date of publication—would satisfy approximately 84% of the user requirements in this study. He estimated that this satisfaction rate could be raised to 90% if a sixth item, contents note, were added.

Yale University Library

A major study of the Yale University library catalog was conducted during the period 1967–1969 and has been reported by Lipetz.[19,20] The public card catalog at Yale, arranged in a single alphabet, consists of approximately 8 million cards in 7,000 drawers and provides access to approximately 5 million volumes. The study was conducted to determine volume of catalog use, characteristics of users, types of searches conducted, and degree of success attained. Its major purpose was to provide data to aid in the eventual computerization of the catalog and to improve the existing catalog during the interim.

The investigation was conducted through interviews with a carefully constructed, random sample of catalog users. Each day some 1,000 searches were conducted in this catalog. After the volume and distribution of use were carefully observed over an initial 10-week period, a schedule for interviewing was established to yield approximately a 1% sample of all catalog uses during a one-year period.

As users began their search in the catalog, the interviewer endeavored to determine the objective of each search. Information was gathered on the type of search to be conducted, motivation for the search, "clues" that the user either had in mind or had written on paper (these were photocopied), intended search approach, and various personal details about the user (including frequency of library use and length of time at Yale). An interview guide—in the form of a multiple-part questionnaire—was followed uniformly by all interviewers. Refusal to cooperate was very rare (less than 1% of all users approached), and most were delighted to participate. Approximately 2,100 interviews were completed during the study year.

After the initial interview, the user was observed from a distance. Some data, including time spent on the search, were gathered by this method. After the user's search was completed, he was reinterviewed to ascertain the number of terms he had looked under and how successful the search had been. In particular, the interviewer noted the call numbers of items the user had selected as likely to be relevant to his needs. (Later, catalog cards for these items, as well as the items themselves, were examined to determine how well the catalog matched or might have matched the user's original clues.) If, during the second interview, the user was uncertain about the success of his search and intended to continue elsewhere (e.g., the stacks), he was given a simple follow-up form on which to report the results. Note that the technique used in the Yale study, with interviews only before and after catalog use, differs from the technique used in the ALA and Michigan studies, where interviewers accompanied catalog users through their searches.

In the Yale study, 73% of the users interviewed were looking for a known item, and 16% were conducting subject searches. The remaining 11% were conducting other types of searches (e.g., using the catalog as a source of bibliographic data or to determine which books the library held by a particular author). Lipetz[19] found that a significant portion of the known-item searches were actually subject searches "in disguise." The searcher already happened to know of one book on the subject, so he looked for it, although there may have been others of equal value. Perhaps, Lipetz suggests, this indicates the inadequacy of our present catalogs for subject searching. Actually, only 56% were known-item searches; 33% were subject searches (16% directly by subject and 17% indirectly by the known-item approach). Unlike the other studies described, the Yale investigation did not identify any significant relationships between type of search and academic status of the user.

Of the known-item searches, 84% were successful, a rate identical to that determined by Palmer[31] at Michigan. Approximately 10% failed because the item sought was not represented in the catalog at the time of the search (collection failure), and approximately 5% because the user was unable to find an entry for an item that actually existed in the catalog (searching failure). When a follow-up study was conducted some months later, approximately one-fifth of the items not represented in the catalog at the time of the original search had been added. Presumably, then, these particular failures can be categorized as "due to delays in processing."

In 62% of the cases, the user approached a known-item search by author, and in 28.5% by title. Subject headings were used in 4.5% of the searches. As in the earlier investigations reported, the Yale study also found that title information, as opposed to author information, was more likely to be complete and accurate, although the difference between the two was not as great as reported in the other studies. Catalog users usually were able to identify desired documents in their searches despite incomplete or inaccurate data brought to the catalog.

The success rate for subject searches reportedly was approximately the same as for known-item searches, but no detailed analysis has been reported on the reasons for failures in the former; however, a study was made of the factors that determine which items a user selects under a particular subject heading. As in the ALA study, the publication date was found to be important, and it was suggested that entries arranged chronologically under a subject heading would be more useful than entries arranged on the basis of main entry.* The typical user tried many clues other than date to decide whether or not a particular item was likely to be useful. These included annotation, author, title, subtitle, and language. Subject searches frequently identified more potentially useful documents than the user could profitably examine.

*See footnote on page 29.

Lipetz[20] also reports that "no evidence of frustration or diminishing catalog use was found among catalog users in their first year of experience with the Yale libraries. Success rates appear to be about the same for all types of users."

An important element in the Yale study was the measurement of volume and distribution of catalog use. Traffic at the catalog can be plotted by time of day, day of week, and period of academic year. Figure 8 is a sample plot showing distribution of catalog use by time of day. These kinds of data have immediate value in planning schedules of reference assistance in the catalog area. They have long-term value in indicating the peak, simultaneous-access capacity that would be needed in an on-line catalog.

The ratio of catalog use to volume of book circulation remained almost constant from week to week. Lipetz points out that measurements of catalog use can be used to predict rates of borrowing, or vice versa. At Yale, graduate students were the major users of the catalog, with undergraduates a close second. Faculty use was comparatively light.

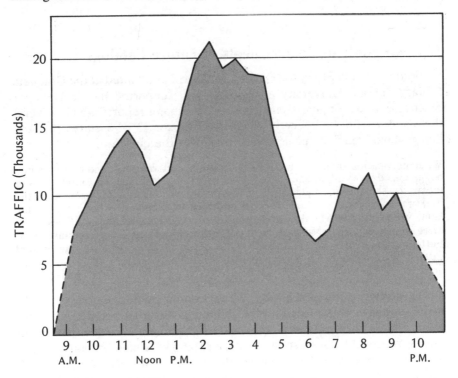

FIGURE 8 Yearly total of catalog traffic by half hour of the day, Yale study.[20]

An earlier study of catalog use, conducted at the Yale Medical Library, is reported by Brooks and Kilgour.[5] Observers recorded the amount of catalog activity during a single week in a period of expected heavy use (October–November 1963). To determine type of use, researchers, during the same week, conducted standardized interviews for six hours each day (30 hours altogether), staggered over the period when the library was open. Use by library staff was almost equal in volume to use by the public. The author approach, found to be clearly predominant, was used in 227 (90.8%) of the 250 searches conducted by the staff and in 136 (54.2%) of the 251 searches conducted by the public. Other approaches used were by title-added entry (11.2% of the public searches and 16.4% of the staff searches) and by title main entry for periodicals (20.3% of the public searches and 2.4% of the staff searches). Overall, a subject approach was made in only 12.8% of the searches (17.9% in the case of public searches), and the investigators pointed out that a significant number of these were conducted either to locate a known item or to find a classification number to gain access to the shelves.

Chicago Study of Requirements of Future Catalogs

A "Requirements Study for Future Catalogs," conducted at the Graduate Library School, University of Chicago, and supported by the National Science Foundation, has been described in a major report[43] and in several theses. A useful summary is given by Swanson,[40] who states that the major objective of the project was to answer the question:

What information should be recorded in future library catalogs, and how should it be organized, presented, and searched in order to be best adapted to the needs of those who seek library materials? . . . We do not assume that it is necessarily the user of present catalogs alone whose needs must be ascertained, for it may be the latent needs of those who do *not* use present catalogs because such catalogs fail to meet their needs that should be most cogent in influencing design requirements. Furthermore, it may be assumed that the needs of those who *do* use present catalogs are conditioned by their expectations of what catalogs can do, and so the need for new capabilities might not be perceived even by the user himself.

The study was devoted largely to known-item catalog searches, and the major emphasis was placed on the characteristics that people remember about a book they once saw, especially those characteristics they might use for retrieval from existing or future catalogs. A memorability experiment was conducted by exposing 104 subjects, mostly students, to a collection of 180 psychology books, and having each participant choose 5 books of interest, examine them closely, and write a brief comment on some aspect of each book that particularly interested him. Several weeks later, the subjects were tested to determine which of some 38 different characteristics they remembered about the books they had previously examined. In this test, they were given their own comments on the books, but no other means of identification.

It is remarkable that, of 440 usable responses, only 10 provided a complete and correct bibliographic citation. In 110 cases (25%), sufficient author/title information was provided to allow the items to be located in the catalog of the Harper Library, University of Chicago; 312 responses (71%) provided enough information on author, title, or subject to allow the book to be located, but, in many cases, only after a lengthy catalog search. Recall of author data is shown in Table 15, recall of title data in Table 16, and recall of subject data in Table 17. As Table 15 indicates, only 16% (approximately) of the responses allowed any form of author approach to be made in the catalog, and a high proportion of these involved last name only, requiring examination of many catalog entries. Title information (Table 16) was more accurate: 22.8% of the titles supplied were complete and correct.

These data were analyzed in considerable detail by Hinkley,[11] who found that approximately one-fourth of the inexact titles supplied could be found by searching in a conventional card catalog (because the first word or two, or at least the first five letters, were correct). A conventional card catalog, with title-added entry for every item, would allow a successful search for more than 30% of all titles (exact plus inexact match). Hinkley claims that an index that permutes the words in titles, making each significant word an access point, would allow retrieval of most of the remaining titles if allowance were made for partial matches, plurals, and variant word forms, and if subtitles were included. He concludes that such an index would allow title matching for 80% of the responses. As one

TABLE 15   Recall of Author's Name, Chicago Study[43]

Type of Response	Number	%
Correct first and last name	37	8.5
Correct last name, first initial	2	.5
Correct last name only	31	7.0
Incorrect name	22	5.0
(Misspelled or partial name only, 10 cases; wrong author named, 12 cases)		
No response	348	79.0
TOTAL	440	100.0

TABLE 16   Recall of Title, Chicago Study[43]

Type of Response	Number	Percentage
Correct	100	22.8
Incorrect		
Synonym error	84	19.2
Permutation	30	6.8
Incomplete	55	12.5
Unrecognizable	95	21.5
Total incorrect	264	60.0
Null	76	17.2
TOTAL	440	100.0

might expect, an inverse relationship appears to exist between length of title and accuracy of recall—shorter titles are recalled more accurately than longer ones.

Two types of subject data were gathered from respondents: (a) subject headings under which it was estimated a book would appear in the library catalog, and (b) unstructured written descriptions of a book's contents. Both types were recorded on questionnaires during the test session and are summarized in Table 17. Subject headings were supplied in 192 cases, of which 18.2% exactly matched headings used in the catalog of the Harper Library. An additional 52.6% of the headings would have led, via cross-references, to the correct subject entry. A total of 70.8% of the responses, then, would have allowed location of the sought entries in the catalog. The success rate for the unstructured subject descriptions was somewhat higher: 29.8% contained words or phrases that exactly matched subject headings used in the catalog, and an additional 45.8% contained words or phrases that would ultimately have led to correct subject headings, bringing the total potential match to 75.6%.

An analysis also was conducted to determine the degree of correlation between words in the titles of the experimental collection in psychology and in Library of Congress subject headings. Ninety-four percent of all "substantive" words in the former completely or partially matched the latter: in 37% of the cases, the subject headings had actually been assigned to the book by the University of Chicago or the Library of Congress; in the remaining 57%, the headings had not been assigned. It was concluded from this analysis that catalog searching on the basis of words contained in book titles could, in principle, be quite successful. This facet of the investigation has been described by Vaughan.[44]

Participants in the study were 78% successful in matching their written comments on a book with a complete bibliographic citation contained within a list of approximately 600 citations. There was 96% success in identifying the selected books when the subjects were again exposed to

TABLE 17   Congruence of Subject Responses to Actual Subject Headings, Chicago Study[43]

| Type of Response | Accuracy of Response | | | Base N |
	Directly Congruent	Ultimately Congruent	Total	
Unstructured subject description	29.8%	45.8%	75.6%	440
Estimated subject heading	18.2%	52.6%	70.8%	192

the same experimental collection, shelved in the same way. These experiments revealed no significant variations in behavior between subjects with and without experience in the field of psychology.

The Chicago study was concerned not only with the memorability of book characteristics, but also with the relationship between memorability and potential use in retrieval. The investigators pointed out that some characteristics, while remembered rather accurately, have little real value in searching. For example, more than 90% of the interviewees were able to remember that the book examined was complete in a single volume, and 65.4% were able to recall correctly whether or not a book was translated from another language. Neither of these characteristics is of great use in retrieval, because neither is particularly discriminating. A very high percentage of books in any collection is likely to consist of single volumes, and a very high percentage is likely not be be translated. Therefore, these characteristics narrow the scope of a search very little. Besides memorability as such, there are various factors that significantly affect the value of a book's attributes for purposes of searching in a catalog, including *permanence* (its physical condition is not permanent; neither is its color, which may change through rebinding), *unambiguity* (color, for example, is an ambiguous characteristic, because different people will give different names to the same shade), and *specificity*—or discriminating capacity (the size of a book is one attribute that is not very discriminating because, unless it happens to be an unusual size, it will be common to a very large porportion of items in the collection).

Swanson[40] summarizes the findings pertaining to the relationship between memorability and utility of the standard book characteristics as follows:

For each of the 440 responses, the information recalled about author, title, and subject was searched in the card catalog, and the length of search, in terms of the number of cards examined before finding the right one, was recorded and analyzed. Out of the 440 responses, sixty-eight (15 percent of the total) author searches were successful, with an average search length* of twenty-seven cards. Seventy-six (17 percent of the total) title searches were successful, with an average search length of 1.7 cards. Two hundred thirty-four (53 percent of the total) subject searches were successful, with an average search length of 156 cards. The total number of successful searches (by one or more methods) was 312, or 71 percent of the total.

Further evidence on the value of using titles in catalog searching was provided by a supplementary study reported by Grathwol,[10] who took a sample of 400 citations to published monographs on psychology in English from class reading lists, abstracts, and publications cited in the *Annual Review of Psychology* and checked each one in the catalog at Chicago. Approximately 82% (327) were found to match; of those not matching, approximately 71% were verified as correct citations, thus representing items presumably not in the collection at the time of the search. A major goal of this study was to determine search length for the citations that could be matched. Search length for personal authors varied considerably with the amount of information given in the citation. Had all personal names in the citation sample been given in exactly the same form (surname and forenames) used in the catalog, the average search length would have been 7.8 cards; however, in 168 citations supplying initials only (while the catalog filed under complete forenames), the number of cards the searcher would have had to examine could have been as high as 26 per search.† When the citation provided the surname without forenames or initials (15 cases), the search length could have been as long as 139 cards per search.

Grathwol's comparison of author searches with title searches also is enlightening. Of 319 titles identified in citations, 231 matched catalog entries exactly, 24 differed slightly, and 64 could not be located. Most titles constituted a file of one; that is, only one entry in the catalog matched the title exactly. The average search length for titles was 1.32 cards. Thus, where title entries exist, this approach is more efficient for locating a record than searching by author, which, under the best conditions, could involve an average search of 7.8 cards, and many more in the worst cases.

---

*"Average search length," a measure of the effort required to locate a particular entry, is expressed by the number of cards the searcher needs to examine in the catalog in order to locate the sought entry.

†For example, an author is cited as R.A. Brown. If the catalog includes full forenames, the searcher may have to look at every entry from Brown, Ralph to Brown, Ryland—say, 75 entries—because the name identified by the initials R.A. could appear either at the end of this sequence or at the beginning.

The Chicago findings on the comparative success of title versus author searching parallel the findings of the other studies mentioned earlier in this chapter.

The relationship between memorability and retrieval potential for 24 nonstandard book characteristics was examined by Cooper.[6] The most useful nonstandard characteristics for catalog search were, in descending order, date, type of work (handbook, textbook), number of pages, binding, color, level of treatment, and height. While none of these clues alone would be particularly useful for retrieval of entries from a catalog (because none is sufficiently discriminating), two or more together, in some form of mechanized search, might be quite effective in restricting the search to a small set of possibly matching entries. The greatest value of such characteristics would be to help narrow a search when information on author and title is inexact or incomplete.

In attempting to summarize the significance of the Chicago investigations, Swanson[40] highlights four results that, in his opinion, have special significance:

1. The relatively small proportion, 26%, of the searches in a conventional catalog in which the search length is less than 10 cards.

2. The relatively large proportion, 80%, of remembered titles that match actual titles completely or partially.

3. The rather large extent to which successful subject headings match terms occurring in book titles.

4. The reduction in search length that might be achieved were it possible to exploit the nonstandard clues in some way.

He concludes that future catalogs:

. . . should incorporate principles of redundancy and multiple-access routes to a much greater extent than they do presently . . . Unquestionably, title entries are of especial importance. Access should be provided not only by the title taken as a whole but by each word of the title taken separately as an alphabetic entry and with suitable provision for entry by means of singular/plural and other types of word-form variation, as well as synonyms. Whether such multiple-access points to titles are provided by means of an extra title-entry card for each word of the title or whether a separate printed index is created for the catalog is more a matter of design efficiency than it is a basic requirement. It would seem fairly clear that the separate printed index makes more sense than allowing the catalog to burgeon by multiplication of added entries. This is especially so if mechanized procedures are used to assist in the production of such title indexes.

In the on-line catalog, of course, it is relatively easy to provide access by any word in a title.

In considering the use of "nonstandard data," Swanson advocates catalogs that provide access by logical combinations of various attributes. No single attribute alone would narrow a search appreciably, but two or more together could have a very significant discriminating effect. He proposes that fragmentary author/title information should first be exploited, thereby narrowing the search to perhaps a few hundred entries. Nonstandard data could then be used to narrow the search even further. This type of searching, not possible in a card catalog, is quite feasible in an automated catalog and would be especially amenable to searching an on-line system.

Of course, the use of several "nonstandard" elements in catalog searching presupposes that the searcher is looking for an item he has previously seen or used or which has been vaguely described to him by someone else (color or size, for example), rather than an item he has discovered in a bibliography or reading list. The overall value of such nonstandard elements is at least partly dependent on the proportion of all catalog uses that involve searching for an item previously seen. It is unlikely that many data exist on this, and catalog searches of this type may be relatively small. Blackburn,[4] for example, in interviews with 100 catalog users at the University of Chicago, found that 71% had not previously seen the item they were seeking. These figures are biased, however, because, presumably, a person who has only "nonstandard clues" to an item will not be trying to find it in a conventional catalog. It is also interesting to note that, in this study, the users who had previously seen the item they sought had, as a group, less bibliographic and less accurate data than those who had not seen the sought item before, suggesting that searchers who have used an item earlier may rely more heavily on memory than on a printed citation.

Survey of Catalog Use in the United Kingdom

In 1971, a study of catalog use in 39 libraries was undertaken by staff and students from a number of British library schools. Conducted under the aegis of the Cataloging and Indexing Group of the Library Association, this study has been summarized by Maltby[25] and by Maltby and Sweeney.[27] Unfortunately, the published accounts give very little detail of methodology, especially of the sampling methods used. The study was conducted through interviews, and a structured questionnaire was followed by all interviewers. The questionnaire, which is reproduced as Figure 9, was administered to a sample of visitors to the cooperating libraries at specified times, and not only to those who were observed using the catalog. It was, therefore, unlike the studies mentioned previ-

LIBRARY ASSOCIATION – CATALOGUING & INDEXING GROUP
CATALOGUE USE STUDY

Library School Coding for this Library

We are undertaking a nationally organised study, on behalf of the Library Association Cataloguing & Indexing Group, of the use made of library catalogues.

It is hoped that the results will help librarians to make catalogues more effective and we would like your assistance with regard to the compilation of this questionnaire.

First a general question   Please tick boxes

Q.1. Do you normally visit this library

Monthly or less (e.g., twice per year)?	1
Weekly, fortnightly or at three week intervals?	2
More than once a week?	3
Can't say	4

Q.2. Have you ever been shown how to use THIS LIBRARY'S catalogue?

YES	5	Go to Q4
NO	6	Go to Q3

Q.3. Have you ever had, or seen, an explanation of how to use ANY library catalogue?

YES	7	Go to Q4
NO	8	Go to Q6

Q.4. Was this explanation by:

(Interviewers to tick more than one category if necessary)

a) A librarian?	9
b) A teacher?	10
c) A printed guide?	11
d) A film or filmstrip?	12
e) Slides or closed circuit TV?	13

f) Someone else or by other means, please specify

FIGURE 9   Questionnaire used in U.K. Catalog Use Study.[25]

ously, in that it included nonusers as well as users of the catalog. The inclusion of nonusers in a survey of this kind is certainly desirable. The survey, however, was designed only to ask people about their use of the catalog *in general,* and was not geared to specific examples of catalog use. Such data usually are far less reliable than data obtained by observing

Please tick boxes

Q.5.   Did you find the instruction sufficient for you to be able to use the catalogue?

YES | 14
NO | 15

Q.6.   Do you use THIS LIBRARY'S catalogue?

YES | 16 | Go to Q8
NO | 17 | Go to Q7

Q.7.   Is this because of any of the reasons shown on this card? (SHOW APPROPRIATE CARD)

a)   It doesn't give the information wanted. | 18
b)   I can manage without it. | 19
c)   I prefer to ask the staff. | 20
d)   Crowding makes it difficult to use. | 21
e)   I find it difficult to understand. | 22
f)   Some other reason. Please describe.

In the case of interviewees who have answered Q.7, the interviewer can now go straight to the classificatory data at end of questionnaire.

Q.8.   Do you normally use the catalogue

Monthly or less (e.g., twice per year)? | 23
Weekly, fortnightly or at three week intervals? | 24
More than once a week? | 25
Can't say | 26

Q.9.   When you use the catalogue do you (Interviewers to tick more than one category, if necessary)

THINK OF — a)   the AUTHOR'S NAME — and look under that? | 27
— b)   the TITLE of the work — | 28
— c)   what the book is about — | 29
THE SUBJECT

Q.10.   Do you use the catalogue to discover where you should look on the shelves for a book?

YES | 30
NO | 31

FIGURE 9   (Continued)

what people do on a particular occasion. A study of this kind can deal only in generalities and cannot identify specific instances of catalog failure. It is, then, suitable for macroevaluation, but not for microevaluation. Nevertheless, it produced some interesting results, which are not incompatible with those derived from the other investigations.

A total of 3,252 completed questionnaires was obtained, falling some-

Please tick boxes

Q.11. Do you use the catalogue to find additional information about the book such as:
(INTERVIEWER TO SHOW APPROPRIATE CARD.
IF ANSWERS TO ALL SECTIONS OF THIS SECTION
ARE 'NO', LEAVE BOXES BLANK)

a) publisher	32
b) date of publication	33
c) price	34
d) edition	35
e) whether it is illustrated	36
f) number of pages or volumes	37
g) anything else. Please specify.	

Interviewer to supply a prompt. See 'Notes for Interviewers'.

Q.12. Are you aware of any other sources from which details of books can be obtained?

YES	38
NO	39

Q.13. NOTE: Either all of A or all of B is to be answered here, depending upon the type of library catalogue in use. If only an author catalogue is provided, ignore 13A and merely answer appropriate column in 13B.

A. Classified Catalogue

Do you find the catalogue(s) are	Author/Title/Name Section		Subject (Classified)		Subject (A–Z Index)	
Easy to use and understand		40		43		46
Difficult to use and understand		41		44		47
Can't say		42		45		48

B. Dictionary Catalogue

Do you find the catalogue(s) are	Author/Title/Name		Subject entries and references (incl. alphabetico-classed)	
Easy to use and understand		49		52
Difficult to use and understand		50		53
Can't say		51		54

Q.14. Is there anything else you would like the catalogue to include and do you have any ideas for its improvement?

_____

_____

_____

FIGURE 9 (Continued)

what short of the original goal of 100 usable questionnaires from each library. The sample of libraries included 1 national and 18 public libraries; the remainder were in universities, colleges, or other academic institutions. Well over half the respondents (more than 1,800) were full-time students.

CLASSIFICATORY DATA

In conclusion, I would like to obtain a few details about yourself.

A. Sex

Male	55
Female	56

B. Age Group

Under 18	57
18–21	58
22–40	59
41–60	60
Over 60	61

C. Educational background

When did you finish your full-time education?

At age	14–15	62
	16–18	63
	19–21	64
	22–25	65
	Over 25	66

THANK YOU VERY MUCH FOR YOUR HELP

Interviewer's comments (if any)

_____

_____

_____

_____

Interviewer's name   Date   Time at end of interview

_____   _____   _____

FIGURE 9   (Continued)

Data on users versus nonusers are summarized in Table 18. Proportionally, far more visitors to academic libraries than to public libraries use the catalog. Most of the nonusers (approximately 67%) believed they could manage without a catalog; others (approximately 22%) preferred to seek help from the library staff; a few (approximately 5%) indicated difficulty in using a catalog.

Data on types of approaches made by catalog users are summarized in Table 19. Note that these data were derived by asking library visitors which approach they used, rather than by observation of the approach actually made on a particular occasion, and that the use categories were not mutually exclusive (i.e., several interviewees made use of two or more approaches). The national library in the sample—the National Library of Wales—has only an author catalog.

TABLE 18   Library Users Who Make Some Use of the Catalog[25]

	All Libraries	Public Libraries	Academic Libraries	National Libraries
Catalog users	1,914 (59%)	546 (32%)	1,275 (73%)	93 (93%)
Catalog nonusers	1,338 (41%)	853 (68%)	479 (27%)	6 (6%)

One of the aspects given most attention in the U.K. study was the relationship between catalog use and degree of instruction that people have had in using the catalog. The investigators concluded that those who had received instruction were more likely to be catalog users and, thus, were more likely to be frequent users. No statistical techniques were used to test the strength of these associations. Krikelas,[15] in his critical review of the study, pointed out that the relationships indicated by the data are, in fact, quite weak.

Another valuable aspect of this study dealt with user needs and preferences for the various descriptive details included on catalog cards. The majority of users considered certain imprint details—date of publication, publisher, and edition—most important, but rarely mentioned place of publication. Information about illustrations was requested by only 68 of the 1,914 catalog users, and pagination by 61. On the other hand, publication price, an item rarely included in library catalogs, was requested by 119 respondents. Maltby and Duxbury,[26] in a supplementary study, reported that many readers would like more use of contents notes or annotations. This leads to the reasonable claim that "this kind of information is of greater potential utility than much of the data which it is customary to provide in the body of the catalogue entry."[27]

Interestingly enough, these findings were quite similar to those in a study conducted by Akers[1] almost 40 years earlier. Akers found that publication date was judged of value by 91.5% of a sample of liberal arts students and contents note by 83.3%. Palmer[31] has summarized the findings of several studies as they relate to the elements on a catalog card actually used by library patrons. He points out that only author, title,

TABLE 19   Types of Approaches Made to the Catalog by Library Users[25]

	All Libraries (N=1,914)	Public Libraries (N=546)	Academic Libraries (N=1,275)	National Libraries (N=93)
Author approach	1,554 (81%)	422 (77%)	1,039 (81%)	93 (100%)
Title approach	468 (24%)	133 (24%)	335 (26%)	—
Subject approach	781 (41%)	264 (48%)	517 (41%)	—

subject headings, call number, and publication date are "heavily used." "Moderate use" is made of place of publication, publisher, edition, and contents notes. The remaining items (e.g., pagination, size, series notes, illustrations) are used very little (each item was used by less than 10% of the patrons included in the various studies).

The questionnaire developed for the British study also was used, substantially unchanged, in a survey of catalog use in New Zealand. Results from six public libraries, two academic libraries (one a teachers' college), and two "technical institutes" were reported by MacLean.[22] The survey was undertaken by students of the New Zealand Library School, at libraries in or near Wellington. The students filled out the questionnaires while interviewing library users. Samples were quite small.

The proportion of library users claiming they used the catalog breaks down as follows: 95% in the two academic libraries, 66% in the large public libraries, 43% in the small public libraries, and 45% in the technical institutes. The distribution of type of use is shown in Table 20. Except in the technical institutes, author approach predominated over title approach. In interpreting the results of the use of various bibliographic items on the catalog card, MacLean concluded that, other than title and author, the only items of real importance to the typical library user were publisher, date of publication, and edition. Just as in the British study, most nonusers of the catalog indicated that they could "manage without it."

TABLE 20   Types of Approaches Made in the New Zealand Study[22]

	Large Public Libraries	Small Public Libraries	Academic Libraries	Technical Institutes
Author approach	58%	70%	72%	46%
Title approach	34%	32%	24%	49%
Subject approach	54%	37%	41%	55%

Other Catalog Use Studies

Over the years, many other studies of catalog use have been conducted. Montague[28] has summarized those studies conducted during the period 1949–1965, and Irwin[12] and Frarey[7] have discussed some of the earlier investigations. Other useful summaries have been made by Palmer,[31] Krikelas,[14] and Stevens.[39]

In addition to the ALA study, Montague analyzed 15 others, mostly conducted in a single library, and many of them recorded as master's degree theses. Ten of the studies deal with academic libraries: most involved collecting data from users as they were conducting searches in a card catalog during specific test periods or after a catalog search had been completed; some used questionnaires or interviews; and others used a combination of approaches. In a few investigations, catalog use was ascertained by an analysis of requests made for material from closed stacks, where each call slip was assumed to represent a successfully completed search in the catalog. Sample sizes varied widely, from as few as 40 to more than 2,000. Montague, as did Lipetz[20] later, criticized investigators for neglecting to use scientific approaches to sampling, with the result that truly representative samples of users and uses were lacking in many cases. She presents a useful summary of the 16 projects in terms of (a) who uses the catalog, (b) how the catalog is used, (c) difficulties encountered, and (d) factors influencing success or failure of a search. Some of Montague's major findings have been summarized by Swanson[40] as follows:

Of some 8000 searches analyzed in the sixteen studies reviewed, 60 percent were for known items, 38 percent for subject search. (Most but not all of the studies made no third distinction). Seventy-five percent of the known-item searches used author entries to complete the search, 20 percent used title entries, and 10 percent subject entries. Sixty-two percent of the sources of bibliographic information for the known-item searches fell into three categories: oral citation (29 percent), course reading list (18 percent), footnote or chapter bibliography (15 percent).

This is a somewhat gross overview, the figures being largely dominated by the few studies with large samples (e.g., that from ALA). Nevertheless, it presents a reasonable picture of use in the majority of studies. A few sets of results were, for various reasons, atypical of the general pattern (e.g., all studies measuring catalog use by high school students found a preponderance of subject searches) or represented extremes in mode of catalog use. For instance, Rothrock[36] reported that, in a sample of 199 searches, 81.4% were of the known-item variety. This investigation, however, was concerned solely with locating material relating to French, Spanish, and Italian literature, an area in which subject headings are unlikely to be of prime importance. Montague's sample included a number of other specialized investigations, such as that of Wolfert,[45] on use of a card catalog of music scores at the University of Chicago.

Montague also found that students predominated among catalog users, not only in academic and high school libraries, but also in the large research and public libraries. Faculty use of catalogs, where this was measured, was always very small and almost exclusively devoted to searches for known items.

Few studies attempted to measure the proportion of failures in catalog searching. When failures were identified, little systematic analysis was provided on how and why they occurred. Failures and other problems in searching were most frequently revealed by asking users—during interviews or through questionnaires—about the difficulties they encountered, or by questions asked of reference assistants stationed in the catalog area. An example of this latter approach is the study by Lyon,[21] who stationed herself at the public catalog of the main library at the University of Chicago. During the study period, she was asked 111 questions relating to catalog use. She identified 52 as user failures to find desired entries; of these, 13 were searches for items not included in the catalog, 11 were examples of failure to find an existing entry because of an incorrect or incomplete citation, and 28 were failures to find an existing entry through lack of familiarity with the filing rules or, in some cases, actual filing errors.

A somewhat different approach, a study of searching effectiveness by simulation, was used by Malcolm[23] at the University of Pittsburgh. One hundred graduate and undergraduate students were tested on their subject-searching abilities by asking them which subject headings they would consult to find 10 different items that were briefly described in a questionnaire. In 62.6% of the cases, the search could have been successful, but in only 16.8% of the cases would it have been successful on the first attempt. In 20.9% of the cases, the search would have been successful only if the user had pursued the leads given by catalog cross-references. In 38.4% of the "simulated searches," the heading suggested was completely wrong and could not have led to the correct entry.

An unusually high occurrence of searching problems was reported by Riddle[35] in interviews with 1,265 catalog users at the Texas State College for Women. Problems occurred in 1,676 (74%) of the 2,244 separate searches studied, but only 3.68% were unsuccessful because the items sought were not in the catalog. The major problem (43%) was that users came to the catalog with incomplete or incorrect author or title information, or both. An additional 32% of the users failed to understand catalog entries.

A good example of catalog use analysis by a study of call slips was conducted by Spalding[38] at the Library of Congress. He evaluated 2,214 call slips presented at the circulation desk in the general reading room. Users had marked these slips with the specific entry used to locate a desired item. The entries were compared with the total number of entries contained in the catalog for the item, the general object being to determine which types of entries were used most and which were used least, to arrive at some form of utility index for each type of entry. Main entries and subject entries were used about equally, whereas, in a parallel study, advanced research workers using special facilities of the library used the main entry approximately two-thirds of the time. Of the call slips from the general reading room, approximately 9% were made from title-added entries, but only 2.3% from personal, corporate, or series-added entries, suggesting that the latter have only marginal utility to users of the general reading room.

The analysis of Frarey[7] briefly covers 27 studies of catalog use conducted during the period 1930–1952. Most of these studies were performed through interviews or questionnaires administered to catalog users, but some were performed by other techniques: the analysis of reference questions to determine the proportion which could best be answered by the use of standard reference works and which by use of subject catalogs; the study of records indicating books selected for borrowing after use of the subject catalog; the evaluation of call slips submitted by users; and even the "measurement" of extent and type of catalog use through observation of the soiled condition of catalog cards. Most of the studies reviewed were quantitative, dealing with who used the catalog, how much, and for what purpose. Some studies, however, attempted to determine how successful the user was in searching the catalog for information on a particular subject. Success was measured by the proportion of searches in which a user was able to find an appropriate subject heading. Another consideration was whether or not the user found the required entry at the first attempt. Success rates varied widely, but several fell in the 40%–50% range for finding relevant material under the first heading examined.

One example of an investigation in which success rates were measured is an analysis by Quigley[34] of subject requests received from branch libraries by the interbranch loan office of the New York Public Library. Subject requests were recorded in the patron's words by a library assistant at the branch and submitted to this office. During a one-month test period, a total of 261 requests was recorded and analyzed to determine which could be satisfied through the subject catalog (and how directly) and which could not. In approximately one-half of the cases, some of the request words exactly matched a subject heading under which relevant literature could be found. The remaining 50% were grouped into three categories: (a) words in the request did not match subject headings exactly, but were so close that "any intelligent reader" might be expected to locate the relevant heading without cross-references or the help of a librarian; (b) instances in which words did not match, but where a cross-reference would lead the user to the correct heading; (c) problem requests that were difficult or impossible to handle because of inadequacies in the subject headings or cross-reference structure, because of lack of clear understanding of what the user really wanted, or simply because material on the requested subject was not available. This type of analysis has some value in exposing the limitations of the catalog: the need for changes in headings to reflect new terminology, the need for more analytical entries, and the need for additional cross-references.

Perrine,[32,33] in 1967 and 1968, reported on two studies of catalog use undertaken by the Catalog Use Committee, Reference Services Division, American Library Association. Twelve university libraries participated in one study and 11 public libraries in the other. Reference staff in the cooperating libraries, during a three-month test period, used a special form to record catalog problems brought to their attention by library users or encountered directly by members of the library staff. A total of 284 forms were submitted by the university libraries, and 363 by the public libraries. The major problems were attributed to filing arrangements, lack of sought headings or cross-references, and lack of sufficient title-added entries.

A more recent study of catalog use in a particular library was conducted in England at the University of Newcastle upon Tyne. This survey, reported by Morris,[29] involved the use of an "instant diary" technique during two days in November 1969 and one day in November 1970. During these days, each user entering the library was handed a survey card and was asked to complete it while in the library and to return it to the library staff on departure. The card recorded details about the user and his use of library resources on that particular visit. If the catalogs were used, various questions were asked about the type of use; the degree of success in finding sought items on the shelves also was recorded. An analysis was subsequently conducted to determine why failures had occurred. It is remarkable that, in 1969, 26% of all respondents (2,384 cards) used the catalog, and that an identical percentage was achieved in the 1970 survey. In fact, the results for both survey periods are closely similar in most respects.

In 1969, users searched the catalog for 1,455 items and found 1,026 (a success rate of 71%). In 1970, the comparable ratio was 581/791, or 74% success. Of 896 items sought on the shelves in 1969, 408 (46%) were found. The comparable ratio for 1970 was 271/512, a success rate of 53%.

The author catalog was used more frequently than the subject catalog by all user categories, but members of the academic staff were more likely to use the catalog to determine if the library held a particular item than to actually locate the item on the shelves. The reverse was true in the case of students.

Seymour and Schofield[37] mention a library-use survey of 21 British universities, which showed that, on the average, only 39% of undergraduate users consulted the catalog in known-item searches, many preferring to go directly to the shelves. They pointed out that this figure is close to that obtained in another survey, at Southampton University, in which the catalog was consulted first in only 37% of known-item searches.

These authors also report on a catalog-use study conducted at four academic libraries (London University Institute of Education, Cambridge University Library, Leicester University Library, Bradford University Social Sciences Library) in England. The study, designed by the Library Management Research Unit of Cambridge University, was conducted in two parts. The first involved the use of "catalog query slips," which were available in the catalog area and were to be completed by catalog users when they were unable to find a known item in the catalog. These slips were collected daily, counted, and checked against the catalog to determine if the item had been overlooked. If not found in the catalog, the item was verified in bibliographies to establish positive identification. A second search was conducted if the actual bibliographic citation was found to be substantially different from that brought to the catalog by the user. An item verified to exist, but not in the catalog, was checked against records of books on order and books "in process."

The second part of the survey involved interviews with catalog users. These were conducted for two 30-minute periods each day during peak catalog use. The main purpose of the interviews was to obtain a reasonable estimate of the proportion of catalog users who completed query slips. They also were used to determine whether or not users completing query slips were representative of all types of catalog users, to obtain a better idea of the proportion of catalog failures, and to discover what users who failed at the catalog intended to do, if anything, as a next step.

Table 21 shows the major results of the interviews for each of the four libraries in the study. Between one-fourth and one-third of all users

TABLE 21   Results of Interviews with Catalog Users at Four University Libraries[37]

Profile of Responses	Cambridge	Leicester	Institute of Education	Bradford
Readers interviewed	446	262	369	193
Readers not fully satisfied	110	90	105	69
Reader failure rate	25%	34%	28%	36%
Readers filling in query slips	31	14	7	7
Reader cooperation rate	28%	16%	7%	10%
Individual items looked for	1,370	713	827	413
Individual items not found	193	204	179	106
Item failure rate	14%	27%	20%	26%
Query slips reported filled in	39	15	10	7
Item cooperation rate	20%	7%	5%	7%
Estimated full item failure	2,035	2,200	960	557

interviewed reported at least partial failure (i.e., failure to find all items sought). Rate of cooperation in completing query slips was quite low: 7% of all readers interviewed reported catalog failures at one library; 10%, 16%, and 28%, respectively, at the others. At Cambridge, for example, 110 (25%) of the 446 catalog users interviewed reported at least partial failure; of these, only 31 had completed query slips, a cooperation rate of 28%. "Item failure rate" refers to the number of sought items that were not found by catalog users. Of the 446 readers at Cambridge, 193 reported item failures, an overall item failure rate of 14%.

Based on the survey data collected at Cambridge, it was estimated that approximately 2,035 "catalog failures" occurred during a five-week period. In this case, catalog failure means failure to find a known item in the catalog, either because the library did not hold the item or because the searcher was unable to find an entry (i.e., both collection and catalog-searching failures were included).

In all four libraries, the rate of failure was lower for undergraduate students than for graduate students or for academic staff. Table 22 shows the intended action of users who were not successful in a catalog search. Variations in local conditions are quite apparent in these data. Note, for example, that 39% of the Institute of Education group intended to try another library. This may be explained by the close proximity of the main library of London University.

The major causes of failure at Cambridge and Leicester are summarized in Table 23. Approximately one-half were collection failures, but a

TABLE 22   Action Planned by Library Users After Encountering Failure at the Catalog[37]

| Action Planned After Failure | Proportions of readers intending different types of action in | | | |
	Cambridge	Leicester	Institute of Education	Bradford
Total no. of readers failing	110	90	105	69
Recheck reference	5%	—	—	7%
Look on shelf	2%	17%	10%	9%
Ask library staff	11%	18%	35%	13%
Ask supervisor/colleague	12%	4%	5%	2%
Look in bibliography	6%	2%	5%	1%
Attempt to purchase	6%	3%	10%	—
Try another library	18%	14%	39%	25%
Try interlibrary loan	2%	12%	3%	9%
Recommend to library	2%	—	1%	3%
Try to find substitute	4%	1%	4%	7%
Other	4%	2%	17%	4%
Forget it	28%	29%	11%	19%

TABLE 23   Major Causes of Searching Failures at Two University Libraries[37]

	Cambridge Number	%	Leicester Number	%
In catalog but not found by user	106	26	25	16
In library but not yet cataloged	64	16	22	15
On order	8	2	6	4
Identified as not in collection	198	49	82	53
Unidentified citations	31	8	19	12
TOTAL	407	101	154	100

substantial number of true catalog searching failures also were encountered. Note that a significant number of failures probably could have been avoided by reduction of delays in cataloging materials by the library.

As in previous studies, this study revealed that many users came to the catalog with incomplete or incorrect author/title information. Some, however, failed to find a correctly filed entry even when their information was complete and correct. See Table 24 for a full categorization of catalog searching failures at Cambridge and Leicester.

This study is an example of a true microevaluation of catalog use. Its major purpose was diagnostic. From such a study, which is relatively easy for a librarian to administer, one can identify weaknesses in the collection, the extent of problems caused by processing delays, and difficulties in the actual catalog search that might be reduced by changes in cataloging rules, by improved guiding in the catalog, or by training of library users.

Further evidence on the comparative accuracy of title versus author data brought to the catalog is provided in a study conducted at the Atomic Weapons Research Establishment, Aldermaston, England, reported by Ayres et al.,[3] who analyzed a group of 450 known-item requests, the results of which are summarized in Figure 10. The study revealed that 90.4% of titles were correct, and an additional 2.9%, although incorrect, were traceable in the catalog. Authors were correct in 74.7% of the cases and traceable in an additional 14%. Untraceable authors (11.3%) exceeded untraceable titles (6.7%). The authors suggest that the mnemonic value of titles has been underestimated in the past. They also point out that many of the titles judged not traceable in this study could, in fact, have been traced in an on-line catalog or a computer-based title catalog with rotated entries. This conclusion was essentially the same as a major conclusion of the Chicago studies.

Another study, reported by Blackburn,[4] investigated the data brought to the catalog by users and the accuracy of these data. The study was conducted at the Harper Library of the University of Chicago, and involved relatively small samples of each type of data. When the searcher

TABLE 24   Categorization of Catalog-Searching Failures at Two University Libraries[37]

CAMBRIDGE

Source of Reference

Reader Problem in Finding Book in Catalogue	Lecturer/ Supervisor	Reading List	Book/Per Article	Separate Bibliography	Colleague/ Friend	Reviews	Publicity/ Bookshops	Other	(2 sources given)	(3 sources given)	TOTAL	PERCENT
Author's surname	17	4	2	2	1		1	4	(1)		30	28
Author's forename(s)	4	1	1								6	6
Title	8	1	2		1			1			13	12
Corporate body	1					1					2	2
Form heading	3	1	2	1		1		3	(1)		10	9
Edition	1		1								2	2
Insufficient information	4	2			1			1	(2)		6	6
Other	9	4	7	2	2	1	4	2	(3)	(1)	26	25
No apparent problem	10	4	4	1	1	3	2	3	(3)		25	24
TOTAL	57	17	19	6	6	6	7	14	(10)	(1)	120*	
PERCENT	54	16	18	6	6	6	7	13				

*This total is more than the 106 items found in the catalogue because several query slips showed evidence of more than one point of confusion or misinformation on the part of the reader. Percentages given, however, are based on the actual total of items (106) rather than on the augmented total (120).

LEICESTER

Source of Reference

Reader Problem in Finding Book in Catalogue	Lecturer	Tutor/ Supervisor	Reading List	Book/Per Article	Separate Bibliography	Colleague/ Friend	Reviews	Publicity/ Bookshops	Other	(2 sources given)	(3 sources given)	TOTAL	PERCENT
Author's surname	2	1	3	1								7	28
Author's forename(s)			1									1	4
Title			2									2	8
Corporate body			1									1	4
Form heading									1			1	4
Edition					1							1	4
Other	2	1	1							(2)		2	8
No apparent problem	2	2	3	3	1					(1)		10	40
TOTAL	6	4	11	5	1				1	(3)		25	
PERCENT	24	16	44	20	4				4				

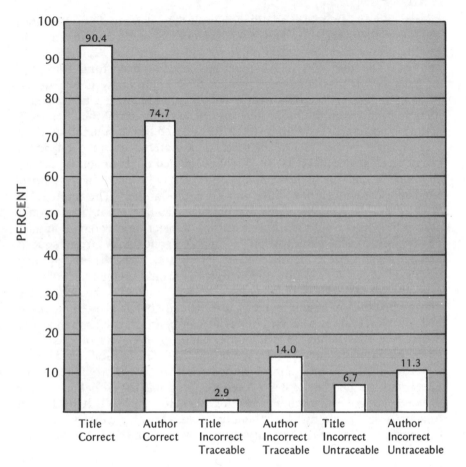

FIGURE 10   Accuracy of citation data brought to catalog in a group of 450 searches, expressed in percentages.[3]

had an author's surname, it usually was correct (63 of 65 cases). The author's initial was correct in 15 of 16 cases, but author's first name was correct in only 31 of 37 cases. The title of a book was correct in 48 of 55 cases, but the title of a journal was correct in 21 of 22 cases (95% of the time). Blackburn also discovered that users were 76% successful in finding a catalog card for a known item sought and, as expected, the successful users, as a group, brought more accurate data to the search than those who were unsuccessful.

It is a well-known phenomenon that the observed behavior of people does not always coincide exactly with what they claim to do or what they claim to be their preferences. This is evident in a study conducted at the International Labor Organization (ILO) and reported by Kenney.[13] The purpose of the study was to investigate the "needs of users for the design of a catalogue." It was conducted in two steps: by an analysis of requests made at various ILO centers over a 10-week period, with a tabulation of "angles from which the requesters described the material they needed"; and by questionnaires, administered to users of ILO documentation services, designed especially to determine their preferences and habits in the use of catalogs and indexes. In the 70 completed questionnaires, catalog approaches, ranked in descending order of importance, were subject heading, personal author, title, and corporate author. The approaches actually made in requests, however, produced a different ranking (again in descending order): title, corporate author, subject, and personal author. The two sets of data are not strictly comparable: one derives from requests for documents made to members of the library staff, while the other derives from user statements of how they search, or would prefer to search, the catalog. This type of discrepancy, nevertheless, indicates the danger that may be involved in assuming that a user actually behaves as he *claims* to behave. Observation of actual behavior can be more useful than asking people how they behave. On the other hand, the behavior of a user at a given time is conditioned by his experience of existing capabilities. How he now uses a catalog, for example, may not be the way he would use it if it were modified, perhaps to make it more appropriate to his real needs. For example, users of a particular catalog may not approach it by title as frequently as they do by author simply because they have discovered that title entries are provided for only a small proportion of total items.

Union Catalogs

A special type of catalog study is the evaluation of a union catalog, exemplified by Neely's[30] investigation of the North Carolina Union Catalog. It was analyzed in terms of effectiveness, coverage, and arrears in the filing and processing of cards. Effectiveness was judged by the degree of success achieved in using the catalog to locate specific items desired by users. Statistics collected during a single month—April 1964—indicated that 361 of the 573 titles sought were located in the union catalog, a success rate of 63%. Coverage was judged primarily by the number of North Carolina libraries contributing cards (this number was substantially less than the number represented in the catalog), by the number of cards contributed by libraries in the state in comparison with the total number of volumes added to collections by these libraries, and by the number of different locations provided for each entry in the catalog. Filing arrears of approximately 420,000 cards were reported in June 1968. Neely was able to make some recommendations for improvement of the catalog. It was reported later that filing arrears had been eliminated, the rate of card contributions had increased, and the volume of catalog use also had increased.

Other studies have been made of several union catalogs in terms of their size and other characteristics and the extent to which they reflect holdings of libraries in a region, although most are not true evaluations because they do not measure the degree of success achieved in satisfying demands placed upon them. One example is the study of the Nashville Union Catalog, reported by Gleaves and Martin.[8] The characteristics of this catalog (e.g., size, growth rate, types of entries, distribution of entries by date and subject, distribution of numbers of libraries holding each title) were determined by random sampling. The catalog's physical condition also was examined. Attitudes of librarians in the region toward the union catalog were determined by questionnaires and interviews, and these techniques also were used to discover how consistently and completely the cooperating libraries contributed new cards and issued withdrawal slips for discarded items.

Summary

This chapter has provided an overview of studies that measured or evaluated the use of the card catalog in libraries. Major emphasis has been placed on the scope of these studies and the procedures used. The importance of such investigations has been well summarized by Gorman,[9] who claims that "the most vital aspect of cataloguing theory and practice which remains unexamined is the use made of the catalogue. Until the aim of catalogue construction has been clearly stated on the basis of objective and accurate surveys of catalogue use, all cataloguing theory will remain unscientific and open to doubt." Since Gorman wrote this, in 1968, a number of valuable studies have been completed, but the subject is certainly far from being exhausted.

The catalog is the major key to a library's collections, and accessibility/ exposure should be improved if more people use it and use it effectively (i.e., to find the known items they are seeking, or items on a subject of current interest, as quickly and accurately as possible). As these various studies have shown, whether or not a particular catalog search is successful depends on many factors:

1. The accuracy of the information brought to the catalog by the user, and the form in which it is brought.

2. The type of approach (author or title) made to a known item by the searcher.

3. The amount of user experience and training.

4. The average number of entry points per item provided in the catalog.

5. The extent to which title entries are included.

6. The number of cross-references provided.

7. The size and complexity of the catalog.

8. The quality of the labeling and guiding given in the catalog.

9. The perseverance, diligence, and intelligence of the searcher.

The various catalog studies reviewed have provided some interesting and useful data on who uses the catalog in different types of libraries, for what purpose, how much, and (to a lesser extent) with what degree of success. Most studies used interviews or questionnaires, although a few other techniques also were tried. Some of the investigations produced estimates of failure rates in catalog searching—both failures to find entries for items actually present (searching failures) and failures to find entries for items not present (collection failures). Many cases of failure to find entries known to exist in the catalog were documented, and limited analyses to determine causes of these failures were undertaken. Several studies revealed generally that title information brought to the catalog by users is more accurate than author information; searching under titles, where title entries are provided, is more successful than searching under author; and title searches can be conducted more quickly. The searcher generally is able to compensate more easily for incomplete or partially inaccurate title data than for incomplete author data. Despite the greater overall accuracy of title data, however, and greater probability of success in title searching, users were more likely to approach a known-item search by author than by title.

Analyses of searching by subject suggested that insufficient entry points were provided in many catalogs and that subject headings lacked sufficient specificity for some purposes. Success rate in subject searches is likely to be much higher if more *see* references are provided, particularly references from specific terms not used as headings in the catalog to the appropriate, more generic, terms that are used. The *see* references of the catalog are equivalent to the *entry vocabulary* of other types of information retrieval systems; and it has been shown in several evaluations that adequacy of the entry vocabulary is a very important factor influencing the performance of such systems.[17,18] The need for more *see* references was reinforced by the fact that many catalog users lacked perseverance, giving up on a search if they were unable to locate sought items under the first entry point they tried. It also was evident that *see also* references were used comparatively little in subject searching. Because of the fragmentary author/title information that many users brought to the catalog, there appears to be a need for greater redundancy in future catalogs. The Chicago study suggested the desirability of a permuted title approach and the use of supplementary "nonstandard" search keys. The need for more annotations or scope notes on catalog cards also was indicated.

Although a number of valuable and careful catalog use studies have been conducted, as pointed out by Maltby,[24] more measurement and evaluation is needed in this area. As long as card catalogs are retained, there appears to be no feasible way of observing catalog use unobtrusively—at least in any detail—therefore, interviewing catalog users is likely to be the preferred technique for some time to come. Computerized, on-line catalogs offer great new opportunities for observing how a catalog is used, for what purpose, and with what degree of success. This will be discussed further in Chapter 9.

Thus far, there has been more measurement of catalog use than true evaluation. Further studies are necessary to determine success rates in catalog searching and, more importantly, to identify in greater detail the major factors determining the success or failure of such searches. Several of the aforementioned studies have attempted to measure success rates, but have not analyzed in sufficient numbers, or sufficient detail, the precise reasons why various searches failed. More diagnostic analyses, of the type applied in the evaluation of mechanized information retrieval systems,[16] are needed to identify more clearly the factors that most importantly affect the performance of library catalogs and to determine what might be done to increase their effectiveness and efficiency in the future. The Chicago study is the only one that addressed itself directly to potential improvements in future catalogs; it also is the only study that systematically measured the time and effort involved in catalog searching.

More work has been done on known-item searches than on subject searches. This is reasonable, because the prime purpose of the catalog is to indicate whether or not a library possesses a particular item and because, in many libraries, known-item searches outnumber subject searches. Nevertheless, the evaluation of subject searching in library catalogs has been somewhat neglected, and those studies that have addressed this point have been rather superficial. The success of a subject search generally has been measured by whether the heading chosen by the user was actually present in the catalog or, at best, whether the user selected one or more items as a result of his catalog search. Very little work has been done to distinguish types of subject searches (e.g., the search for one "good" book on a particular topic as opposed to a comprehensive search in which the user tries to locate everything that the library possesses on a subject); to determine whether or not a user is able to find an item that completely satisfies his present information need; to determine (in the case of a more comprehensive search requirement) how much of the relevant literature the user can find in the catalog and whether he finds the items that are in some sense most relevant to his interests; to determine, in detail, reasons why users fail to locate entries for books that are relevant to their interests; and to measure the amount of time expended in conducting subject searches. All of these matters require investigation.

Finally, the studies discussed in this chapter concentrate primarily on catalog users. But many people use libraries without ever consulting the catalog and, in some cases, are not even aware of its existence. Characteristics of nonusers of the catalog—and how these characteristics differ from those of users—and reasons why they do not use it are matters that require much more study.

A useful and concise summary of the major findings of several important catalog use studies appears as an appendix to this chapter.

REFERENCES

1. Akers, S. G. "To What Extent Do the Students of the Liberal Arts Colleges Use Bibliographic Items Given on the Catalogue Card?" *Library Quarterly*, *1*:394–408, 1931.
2. American Library Association. *Catalog Use Study*. Edited by V. Mostecky. Chicago, 1958.
3. Ayres, F. H. et al. "Author Versus Title: A Comparative Survey of the Information Which the User Brings to the Library Catalogue." *Journal of Documentation*, *24*:266–272, 1968.
4. Blackburn, M. "The Information Known by Users of the Catalog Who Are Looking for a Particular Work." Master's Dissertation. Graduate Library School, University of Chicago, 1968.
5. Brooks, B. and Kilgour, F.G. "Catalog Subject Searches in the Yale Medical Library." *College and Research Libraries*, *25*:483–487, 1964.
6. Cooper, W. S. "The Potential Usefulness of Catalog Access Points Other than Author, Title, and Subject." *Journal of the American Society for Information Science*, *21*:112–127, 1970.
7. Frarey, C. J. "Studies of Use of the Subject Catalog: Summary and Evaluation." *In: Subject Analysis of Library Materials*. Edited by M. F. Tauber. New York, School of Library Service, Columbia University, 1953, pp. 147–166.
8. Gleaves, E. S. and Martin, I. M. *An Investigation of More Effective Means of Organization and Utilization of the Nashville Union Catalog*. Nashville, Tenn., George Peabody College for Teachers, 1970. ED 051825.
9. Gorman, M. *A Study of the Rules for Entry and Heading in the Anglo-American Cataloging Rules, 1967*. London, Library Association, 1968.

10. Grathwol, M. "Bibliographic Elements in Citations and Catalog Entries: A Comparison." Master's Dissertation. Graduate Library School, University of Chicago, 1971.
11. Hinkley, W. A. "On Searching Catalogs and Indexes with Inexact Title Information." Master's Dissertation. Graduate Library School, University of Chicago, 1968.
12. Irwin, R. "The Use of the Card Catalog in the Public Library." Master's Dissertation. Graduate Library School, University of Chicago, 1949.
13. Kenney, L. "The Implications of the Needs of Users for the Design of a Catalogue: A Survey at the International Labor Office." *Journal of Documentation*, 22:195–202, 1966.
14. Krikelas, J. "Catalog Use Studies and Their Implications." *In: Advances in Librarianship, Vol. 3*. Edited by M.J. Voigt. New York, Seminar Press, 1972, pp. 195–220.
15. Krikelas, J. "Review of the U.K. Catalogue Use Survey." *Newsletter on Library Research*, 9:7–10, 1974.
16. Lancaster, F. W. *Evaluation of the MEDLARS Demand Search Service*. Bethesda, Md., National Library of Medicine, 1968.
17. Lancaster, F. W. *Information Retrieval Systems. Characteristics, Testing, and Evaluation*. New York, Wiley, 1968.
18. Lancaster, F. W. *Vocabulary Control for Information Retrieval*. Washington, D.C., Information Resources Press, 1972.
19. Lipetz, Ben-Ami. "Catalog Use in a Large Research Library." *Library Quarterly*, 42:129–139, 1972.
20. Lipetz, Ben-Ami. *User Requirements in Identifying Desired Works in a Large Library*. New Haven, Conn., Yale University Library, 1970.
21. Lyon, S. A. "Assistance for Users of the Catalog in a University Library." Master's Dissertation. Graduate Library School, University of Chicago, 1963.
22. MacLean, H. "Using the Library Catalog." *New Zealand Libraries*, 35:165–172, 1972.
23. Malcolm, R. S. "The Student's Approach to the Card Catalog." Master's Dissertation. Carnegie Library School, Carnegie Institute of Technology, 1950.
24. Maltby, A. "Measuring Catalogue Utility." *Journal of Librarianship*, 3:180–189, 1971.
25. Maltby, A. *U.K. Catalogue Use Survey: A Report*. London, Library Association, 1973.
26. Maltby, A. and Duxbury, A. "Description and Annotation in Catalogues: An Attempt to Discover Readers' Attitudes and Requirements." *New Library World*, 73:260–262, 273, April 1972.
27. Maltby, A. and Sweeney, R. "The U.K. Catalogue Use Survey." *Journal of Librarianship*, 4:188–204, 1972.
28. Montague, E. A. "Card Catalog Use Studies 1949–1965." Master's Dissertation. Graduate Library School, University of Chicago, 1967.
29. Morris, W. E. M. *Catalogue Computerisation Project: Final Report to OSTI, 1967–1971. Part 2. Catalogue Use Survey*. Newcastle upon Tyne, England, University of Newcastle upon Tyne, 1971.
30. Neely, E. T. *The North Carolina Union Catalog: An Examination and Evaluation*. Occasional Paper No. 99. Urbana, Ill., Graduate School of Library Science, University of Illinois, 1971.
31. Palmer, R. P. *Computerizing the Card Catalog in the University Library: A Survey of User Requirements*. Littleton, Colo., Libraries Unlimited, Inc., 1972.
32. Perrine, R. H. "Catalog Use Difficulties." *RQ*, 7:169–174, 1968.
33. Perrine, R. H. "Catalog Use Study." *RQ*, 6:115–119, 1967.
34. Quigley, H. "An Investigation of the Possible Relationship of Interbranch Loan to Cataloging." *Library Quarterly*, 14:333–338, 1944.

35. Riddle, M. S. "The Use of the Card Catalog in the Library of a Typical Women's College." Master's Thesis. Department of Library Science, Texas State College for Women, 1952.
36. Rothrock, I. S. "Use Made of the Card Catalog of the University of Texas Library in Locating Material in the Fields of French, Spanish, and Italian Literature." Master's Dissertation. School of Library Science, University of Texas, 1954.
37. Seymour, C. A. and Schofield, J. L. "Measuring Reader Failure at the Catalogue." *Library Resources and Technical Services, 17*:6–24, 1973.
38. Spalding, C. S. "The Use of Catalog Entries at the Library of Congress." *Journal of Cataloguing and Classification, Fall:* 95–100, 1950.
39. Stevens, R. E. *A Summary of the Literature on the Use Made by the Research Worker of the University Library Catalog.* Occasional Paper No. 13. Urbana, Ill., University of Illinois Library School, 1950.
40. Swanson, D. R. "Requirements Study for Future Catalogs." *Library Quarterly, 42*:302–315, 1972.
41. Tagliacozzo, R. et al. "Access and Recognition: From Users' Data to Catalogue Entries." *Journal of Documentation, 26*:230–249, 1970.
42. Tagliacozzo, R. and Kochen, M. "Information-Seeking Behavior of Catalog Users." *Information Storage and Retrieval, 6*:363–381, 1970.
43. University of Chicago, Graduate Library School. *Requirements Study for Future Catalogs. Progress Report No. 2.* Chicago, 1968.
44. Vaughan, D. "Titles as Sources of Subject Headings." *In: Requirements Study for Future Catalogs. Final Report. Appendix 1.* Chicago, Graduate Library School, University of Chicago, 1972, pp. 1–10.
45. Wolfert, R. J. "Use of the Card Catalog of Music Scores in a University Library." Master's Dissertation. Graduate Library School, University of Chicago, 1959.

APPENDIX TO CHAPTER 2
SOME IMPORTANT FINDINGS IN CATALOG USE STUDIES*

The following list is broken down into five categories of findings. They are:

1. Findings about the behavior of catalog users, the knowledge they bring to it, and why many people do not use the catalog.
2. Findings about known-item searches.
3. Findings about subject searches.
4. Findings about the physical structure of the catalog
5. Some miscellaneous facts.

The following abbreviations after each item listed indicate from which study or studies this information was obtained.

ALA=American Library Association study
UC=University of Chicago study
UM=University of Michigan study
UK=United Kingdom study
YU=Yale University study

Findings About Catalog Users

1. Most people avoid the catalog when they can. Many, particularly in public libraries, never use it at all. (UK)
2. Most people have little knowledge of the structure of the catalog. (ALA, UK)
3. Few people ever remember complete bibliographic data. Quite often the bibliographic information they do have is incorrect. (ALA, UC)
4. People with written bibliographic information are only a little more likely to have it accurate than those who come to the library with memorized information. (UM)
5. Most people remember titles better than authors. (UM, UC)
6. People often remember key words in titles even when they do not remember exact titles. (UC)

---

* This summary was prepared by Alan Meyer, a student in the Graduate School of Library Science, University of Illinois, during 1973–1974. It is reproduced with his permission.

7. People generally use authors for entry to the catalog before they use titles. This is true in all libraries, not just academic ones. It is especially surprising considering that it usually takes longer to find a book by author than by title. (UC)

8. Most searches in the catalog are for known items. (UM)

9. Many known-item searches are, in fact, subject searches in which the user is using the known item only as an entry to a subject area. (YU)

10. Most people do not persevere very long in catalog searches. More than 50% will look up only one entry and then stop, regardless of whether or not they have found what they are looking for. Most subject searches are attempted under a single subject heading. (UM)

11. People generally ignore collation and physical description notes. (UK)

Findings About Known-Item Searches

1. Searching under author requires an average of five times as many card examinations as searching under title. With inaccurate bibliographic information, which is very common, that ratio increases considerably. (ALA, UM, UC)

2. Permuted title indexes greatly raise the success rate of searching for incomplete and half-remembered titles. (UM, UC)

3. Present catalogs are fairly adequate if the user is willing to work hard at searching. Improvements should aim at decreasing the amount of user effort (both in time spent searching and in time spent verifying bibliographic information) needed to search the catalog. (UM, UC)

4. Searching for known items under subject headings is very inefficient. Many cards may need to be looked at; however, this method generally provides results if all others have failed. (UM)

5. Multiple access and redundancy greatly increase the chances of success when searching under incomplete or inaccurate bibliographic information. (UC)

6. Nonstandard bibliographic clues (e.g., imprint, color, size, etc.) are individually of very little use for finding half-remembered items; however, taken together they can be of great significance in narrowing a search. (UC)

7. The most useful nonstandard clues are date of publication, type of book (e.g., handbook, textbook, novel, etc.), number of pages, binding, color of cover, level of treatment, and height. (UM)

8. How much bibliographic or subject information the user has affects, to a considerable degree, the success of his search. (UM)

9. Search strategy and perseverance greatly affect success. (UM)
10. Joint authors are rarely used for entry to the catalog. (ALA)

Findings About Subject Searches

1. The richer the reference structure of a catalog, the better it is for subject searches. *See* references are particularly important. (ALA)
2. About one-half of all users think up a subject heading or entry word that gets them an entry or *see* reference in the catalog on the first try. (ALA, UC)
3. Subject searches often fail because of failure to search on the right word or heading. (UM)
4. Subject headings are not specific enough to meet the needs of most users. (ALA)
5. Subject searches very often fail because the user cannot tell from the cards he finds whether or not the books they represent are relevant to his needs. (UM)
6. Contents notes and succinct annotations are more useful than descriptive notes and collation. (UK)
7. Subject searchers select individual items on the basis of date of publication more frequently than by name of author. (ALA)

Findings About the Physical Structure of Catalogs

1. Larger catalogs have a higher incidence of search failure than smaller ones. Small catalogs are easier to search. (ALA, UM, UC)
2. A computer-based cataloging system would be the best way to permit searching the catalog with nonstandard clues. (UC)
3. Since permuted title indexes and other search aids would greatly clutter a card catalog, one way to increase the number of entries while decreasing clutter would be to establish a single main entry card catalog with auxiliary title, subject, permuted title, etc., indexes in book form. (UC)
4. Card catalogs can be manually searched more quickly than book catalogs. (UC)

Miscellaneous Findings

1. Present catalogs are basically successful. Present policies should be continued with change introduced slowly and cautiously. (ALA, YU)

2. The main reason for overall search failure is that the item desired is not in the collection. (YU)

3. Many librarians do not have a good understanding of the catalog, as evidenced by their own success in searching. (ALA)

4. The lack of call numbers for fictional works confuses many patrons. Some fiction identifier is desirable for the catalog cards. (ALA)

3

Evaluation of Reference Service

The "measurement" of reference service has been discussed in the professional literature for many years, but only recently has anyone attempted to evaluate reference work objectively. Most of the studies surveyed in Rothstein's[35] excellent review (1964)* are either purely quantitative or largely subjective, with little attempt made to distinguish successes from failures. Of course, the measurement of success in reference work is not an easy task, as will be discussed later.

A useful statement of the scope of reference service, which distinguishes between *direct* and *indirect* service, was prepared by the Committee on Reference Standards and Statistics of the American Library Association's Reference Services Division and reported in 1961 by Shores.[37] Direct service involves personal assistance to users by library staff, and includes answering questions of a factual type, conducting literature searches, and instructing and guiding patrons in their use of library resources. Indirect service, on the other hand, is concerned with the preparation of tools (e.g., catalogs and bibliographies) to improve access to the collections. These tools may, of course, be used in direct service at some future date. Members of the reference staff also may be

*A useful review of the literature for the period 1964–1973 has recently been made by Weech.[47]

engaged in activities which support the reference function, such as selecting and ordering materials, building files, training and supervising personnel, and handling interlibrary loans. In some libraries, they may be involved in other related activities, such as abstracting and the preparation of translations.

Most direct service in public and academic libraries is of a "reference assistance" type, which involves answering questions of a factual nature—by telephone, in person, or, less commonly, by mail—and helping users find needed bibliographic materials. Much of this work is of a "quick reference" nature, although this term is used rather loosely. A question may be answered in seconds from a standard reference tool or may require an hour or more of searching, possibly beyond the bibliographic resources of the library. Rothstein[35] claims that approximately 90 to 95 percent of the questions handled by libraries may be of the "ready reference" type, capable of being answered in 10 minutes or less. Public and academic libraries have varying policies in relation to the amount of time they are willing and able to spend on a particular question. In cases where no formal policy exists, the time spent will depend on the inclinations and priorities of individual staff members. Rarely will they undertake comprehensive literature searches for an individual. Industrial and certain other special libraries, however, do get involved in this type of service. In fact, a literature search in an industrial library may involve many hours, or even days, of research. But "reference assistance" service constitutes the bulk of direct service to the public in most libraries, and it is this aspect upon which this chapter will focus.

Presumably, the quality of any reference activity depends largely upon (a) the quality of the collection of reference materials (or perhaps of the library's total resources) and (b) the ability of the staff to exploit this collection effectively. Also, the quality of the service must be judged in terms of how completely, accurately, and efficiently all user demands are satisfied. To get a reasonably good picture of how well a reference department performs in answering user questions, the following data are needed:

1. The total number of questions received (during a specified period).

2. The proportion of these questions the staff makes some attempt to answer.

3. The proportion of the "attempted" questions for which the staff provides an answer.*

---

*For a more complete picture, the number of questions that are referred elsewhere (e.g., to other libraries or information centers, or to other types of agencies) would perhaps need to be known. A question correctly referred to another, more appropriate, source may be counted as a success for the referring library.

4. The proportion of the "answered" questions that are answered completely and correctly.

5. The average time it takes to answer a user's question.

These data, at least, are needed for the macroevaluation of reference service. Microevaluation would require, in addition, an analysis to determine why certain questions are attempted and others are not, why answers are found for some questions and not for others, and why some questions are answered more quickly than others. Some libraries gather a few of these data, but it is unlikely that any one library has attempted to gather all of the data that are needed to conduct a complete evaluation of the performance of a reference division in answering even a small sample of questions submitted by users.

It is common for libraries to maintain statistics on the volume of reference questions they handle, although methods of counting them may be somewhat haphazard, and the total count, as Rothstein[35] points out, may be incomplete by as much as 40 percent.* Gross counts of this kind have value in indicating a library's volume of business, and information on the pattern of query distribution throughout the day and the week is useful in developing efficient staff schedules, but in themselves they provide no basis for evaluating the quality of reference service. Somewhat more illuminating are counts that categorize reference questions—by subject, time needed to answer them, materials or sources used, types of users, or types of questions. Rothstein[35] identifies four types of questions: *directional* (those referring a user to a particular book or location), *ready reference* (those having simple factual answers), *search* (those involving more time and, usually, more sources), and *readers' advisory* (those providing assistance in the choice of a book). This kind of categorization has some value—it is certainly desirable to know who the users are and what types of questions they are asking—but it is not a form of evaluation.

Hieber[21] has proposed a different method of categorization, based upon the type of response given to the inquirer. She recognizes five major types, the last two of which are similar:

1. *Exact reproduction.* The information need is satisfied by seeing a particular piece of text or illustration (e.g., the inquirer needs to see a picture of Durham Cathedral or a copy of a particular statute).

2. *Fill-in-the-blank.* This is the common "factual" type of inquiry. The user is satisfied by a particular name, term, or figure, or by a list or table of names, terms, or figures (e.g., a table of statistics or numerical data).

3. *Descriptive.* The information need is satisfied by some text describ-

---

*Rothstein cites Christ[9] for this figure.

ing an object, person, place, or activity (ranging from a dictionary definition to a lengthy and complete description of a particular manufacturing operation). Generally, any of several possible descriptive statements may satisfy this category of inquiry, whereas only one specific item can satisfy the *exact reproduction* category.

4. *Information-about*. A requester looking for documents on a specific subject area is given one or several documents to satisfy his need.

5. *List of references*. The information need is satisfied by furnishing the requester with a list of references to documents.

Hieber derived her method of categorization by analyzing a sample of 272 questions received at the reference desk of Lehigh University Library. In terms of the aforementioned five categories, she found the 272 inquiries were distributed as follows: 12.1%, 47.8%, 19.5%, 15.5%, and 5.1%, respectively.

More recently, Jones,[25] analyzing questions received at Northwestern University, arrived at the following categories: *orientation* (those requiring orientation of users to the library or to the location or use of materials), *directory* (those requiring specific data to be supplied), *topical* (those requiring descriptive material on a particular subject), *citation*, and *holdings*.

Kronick[27] analyzed information requests received at the Cleveland Medical Library over a two-year period and divided them into four groups: direct (factual), indirect (subject-related), biographical and directory, and citation-verification. More than half the requests were of the second type, requiring literature on a particular subject—the majority requiring only a limited number of documents (five articles or less) of recent origin (last five years). Requests for citation verification represented 25% of the total; direct (factual) inquiries, 12%; and biographical and directory inquiries, 9%.

It is not, of course, necessary to analyze all questions handled by a reference department during the course of a year or to maintain daily statistics. A very accurate picture can be achieved by appropriate sampling procedures. Halperin[18] has described, in simple form, methods that can be used to determine the number of days on which questions should be counted (and, possibly, analyzed) in order to achieve a given level of precision and confidence in the results. A more elaborate approach to work sampling in libraries, as applied to interlibrary loan and photocopying activities, has been described by Spencer,[39] whose sampling technique is based on the use of random alarm devices: Members of the library staff record the activities in which they are engaged when an alarm device is sounded. These devices are set for random times during the day.

The sum of the staff observations, recorded at random times during the working day, provides a good composite picture of a department's activities.

Rothstein[35] mentions several other approaches that have been made to the measurement or analysis of reference work. Users have been categorized (e.g., by occupation or academic rank), public awareness of reference services has been measured, and degree of user satisfaction has been determined by interviews or questionnaires.

Existing evidence suggests that many people are unaware of the reference function of libraries or, at least, of their capabilities in this area. For example, Campbell and Metzner,[6] in their national survey of public libraries, found that only a small minority of the people questioned had considered consulting a library for information. Harlan,[19] in a study of a public library in Michigan, discovered that approximately half the users did not know they could request information from the library by telephone. Studies of the information-seeking behavior of various professional groups (scientists, engineers, behavioral scientists) also have consistently revealed that "consulting a librarian" ranked low on the list of actions taken when information was needed. It appears probable, then, that only a very small percentage of the population makes any use of the library reference services available to them. Those that do use reference services are generally in the lower age group.

White,[49] describing a survey of reference services in 108 metropolitan Atlanta libraries, pointed out that 81% of the users were age 25 or younger, while only 8% were age 40 or over.

Despite the fact that library reference services may be comparatively little-used, and even little-known, when library users were asked their opinions of reference services, the results, in Rothstein's words, "could hardly be bettered by paying for testimonials." He cites a number of studies, of both public and academic libraries, in which the great majority of users felt the services were satisfactory and were judged good or excellent by many; other studies have shown that users feel their questions are answered satisfactorily in most cases.

Referring to the survey conducted in the Atlanta area, White[49] says:

The very favorable responses of the reference users to the existing services was surprising and a little disturbing to the interviewers. If so many patrons are satisfied with services, a danger exists that they do not recognize the limitations or that the problems which they bring are relatively simple and easily resolved.

Swope and Katzer[41] have reported a small-scale study conducted at Syracuse University on the tendency of library users to ask reference staff for assistance. A random sample of 119 people present in various sections of the library were interviewed. Of those, 49 (41%) were seeking information (i.e., had legitimate reference questions), but little more than one-third (17, or 35%) indicated they would ask a librarian for assistance. Reasons given for not seeking such assistance included a desire not to bother the librarian, feeling that the question was too simple, and dissatisfaction with previous service. Many users indicated, however, that they would seek help from another student.

A reference collection itself can be evaluated in various ways, although few such studies are reported in the literature, and the method used almost exclusively is that of checking the collection against standard bibliographies and lists. Little has been done to evaluate the performance of reference personnel, but much has been written on the qualifications and attributes desired of such staff and on the staff levels needed to operate a satisfactory reference service in different size libraries. Some investigators have measured the staff time consumed in answering reference questions and have derived figures for the direct labor costs involved in answering a typical question.

Standards for Reference Service

One possible way of assessing the reference service of a particular library is by comparison with various published standards. A good example is *Standards for Reference Services in Public Libraries*,[40] prepared by the Library Association of Great Britain and published in 1970. These standards provide recommendations on the range of services offered; size and composition of the reference collection; organization of the reference service; accommodations and facilities; and size, qualifications, experience, and salaries of staff. They recommend, for example, that one seat be provided for each 500 members of the population served, that each seat be allocated 25 square feet of floor space, that open-shelf reference stock be not less than 200 volumes per 1,000 population served, and that the ratio of staff to population be at least 1:20,000, with a lower ratio in libraries serving urban populations of 300,000 or more.

Standards for reference service do not appear to go beyond such broad quantitative statements. Indeed, it seems doubtful that they could. The Standards Committee of the Reference and Adult Services Division of the American Library Association has been able to produce only "developmental guidelines." The committee has stated that, because of the diversity existing in modern information services, "standards of quantity, quality, extent, level, or correctness are virtually impossible."[1]

Effectiveness of Reference Service

Standards provide useful guidelines on minimum requirements for collections, facilities, and staff. The counting of reference facility users and the analysis of requests are valuable criteria for determining how much the reference services are used, by whom, and for what purposes. Interviews and questionnaires can indicate "user satisfaction" in broad, subjective terms. Factors likely to affect the ultimate success or failure of a reference service, including the size and composition of the collection and the size and composition of the reference staff, also can be examined. None of these by itself provides a true or complete evaluation of reference service.

Real evaluation, as implied earlier, entails the identification of success ses and failures and the analysis of reasons for failures. This type of evaluation rarely has been applied to reference service.

The closest approach to real evaluation by most libraries (and even this is not done by all of them) is to maintain a record of the proportion of questions that the reference staff are able to answer and, ergo, the proportion they are unable to answer. Where such figures have been quoted by libraries, the percentage of success claimed is almost always extremely high, rarely below 90%. Unfortunately, these figures do not necessarily portray a true picture of the effectiveness of reference service.

First, it is not always clear whether the figures quoted represent a percentage of success for questions *received* during a particular period or whether they represent a percentage of success for all questions *attempted* by the reference staff (i.e., after certain questions have been rejected for one reason or another). Some questions may be rejected for legitimate reasons (e.g., they are out of scope for the library or they are of a type that the library will not answer as a matter of policy), but others may be rejected because the reference librarian knows he will be unable to find the answer or is only likely to find an answer after an arduous, time-consuming search. A thorough evaluation should record all requests as they are made. Questions that are rejected should be tallied, and reasons for rejection categorized. An analysis of the reasons for rejections could reveal the kinds of legitimate questions the library is poorly equipped to handle, perhaps because of weaknesses in the collection or of inadequate tools for exploiting the collection. Or it could reveal lack of experience or training among staff members (e.g., questions are rejected that actually could be answered, if not from the library's own resources then from some readily accessible outside source).

Second, the figures quoted by libraries for percentage of success reflect only those questions for which some answer was found and given to the user. The answer given is assumed to be correct, but there is reason to believe that not all answers provided by libraries, even to factual questions, are completely correct. Nevertheless, there is certainly some merit in maintaining, or at least collecting for a particular period of time, statistics on the number of questions answered. Libraries that do maintain such statistics are one step closer to an evaluation of their reference service.

An example of this type of data gathering is Goldhor's[17] analysis of reference service at the Evansville (Indiana) Public Library. A single reference assistant recorded data on inquiries received during a three-month period, November 12, 1957 to February 14, 1958. Altogether, the library received 2,645 questions, and answered approximately 96% of them. In addition, 100 of these inquiries, occurring on 31 different days, were studied in greater detail. This group did not comprise a systematically derived sample; it was merely a set of questions for which the reference assistant had time to record more complete data. Of the 100 questions, 63 were received by telephone and 37 were from users visiting the library. For each question, the reference assistant recorded the number, type, and location of the sources used, as well as various characteristics of the inquirers, and the length of time required to produce an answer. Averaging nine minutes per question, direct labor costs were calculated at approximately 30 cents per question, based on the rate of pay received by the assistant who participated in the study. Goldhor states that, of the 100 questions under review, "97 percent were answered successfully and the other three were answered partially."

A somewhat similar study, but covering a number of libraries, was reported earlier by Cole.[10,11] It was based largely on questions received by 13 libraries, mostly in the Chicago area, during April 1941, but questions received at the St. Louis Public Library on a single day in January of that year also were included. The sample of institutions consisted of public libraries of various sizes, junior and liberal arts colleges, university departmental libraries, and special libraries. It was intended that all questions received by these libraries during the designated test period were to be included in the analysis, but some undoubtedly escaped the net as a result of work pressures. A total of 1,026 questions was collected. A member of the staff at the cooperating library recorded an exact statement of each question, the occupation of the inquirer, the specific reference sources used in finding the answer, and whether or not the question was answered "satisfactorily." The questions later were categorized by type, subject, sources used, and type of inquirer. Success rate was judged high:

About 4 percent of the public library questions, 9 percent of the college and university questions, and 12 percent of the special library questions were unanswered or only partially answered.[11]

Thoreen[43] reports on two surveys of reference requests handled by the Bay Area Reference Center (BARC), one conducted during a one-month period in 1972 and the other during a one-week period in 1973. Of 263 requests handled during the earlier period, 58% were answered "totally satisfactorily"; 20%, "partially satisfactorily"; 8%, with "negative success"; and 12% were "unanswered." The "negative success" category were those requests judged "impossible" for one reason or another. Success was judged by librarians in member libraries served by BARC.

In a survey of an industrial library—the Thornton Research Centre of Shell Research Ltd.—Mote and Angel[31] reported a failure rate of only 9% in responding to technical inquiries. This figure was derived from an analysis of several hundred inquiries collected over a 10-year period. A major purpose of this analysis was to determine the distribution (number and type) of sources used in answering the inquiries (including date of publication and distinction between published and unpublished sources) and the occupation and status of the inquirers. Sabel et al.[36] quote a failure rate of only 6% in a similar analysis of several hundred inquiries collected at the Atomic Energy Research Establishment in Harwell, England; and Cole[12] gives the same figure in his analysis of reference question records at the British Petroleum Company.

Attempts have been made at various times to collect information on questions that libraries in general have been unable to answer. The British publication, *Unanswered Questions* (London, Department of Scientific and Industrial Research), published for a number of years in the 1950s, was virtually a clearinghouse for questions of this type. Jahoda and Culnan[23] conducted a survey of unanswered questions at 26 science and technology libraries in the United States. During the one-month period of the study, they collected 47 such questions and attempted to determine why answers could not be found.

In 1968, the Enoch Pratt Free Library in Baltimore, Maryland[3] conducted perhaps one of the most complete evaluations of telephone reference service within a single library. It included staff evaluations, telephone interviews with selected users (of a random sample of 37 people contacted, 4 judged the service inadequate, 24 judged it adequate, and 9 considered it exceptionally good), and "staff monitoring of incoming calls." Table 25 summarizes the types of questions that could not be answered satisfactorily during one year of operation. As the footnote to the table indicates, only 0.2% of all questions received fell into this category.

Palmour and Gray[33] present the results of a cost analysis associated

TABLE 25   Telephone Reference Service Evaluation, Enoch Pratt Free
Library, November 1968[3]

Statement of Questions which T.R.S. and the Central Library Subject Departments Were
Unable to Answer or Fill to the Caller's Satisfaction

The Pratt Library has nothing on the subject	82
The Pratt Library does not own the material in the form requested (recording, foreign language edition, etc.)	36
The Pratt Library does not have the subject material in the required depth or in the specific detail desired (surgical techniques, schematic drawings, etc.)	62
Unsuccessful historical event or historical significance search (last date that milk was delivered by horse and wagon in Baltimore)	20
Unsuccessful first use, beginning of, or origin of type search (origin of the tomato, book about the origin of the bayberry candle, when were indelible pencils first used)	7
Unsuccessful searches for titles, authors, or biographical information	136
Unsuccessful searches for addresses (firms, organizations, societies, institutions, manufacturers, dealers, fraternities, foundations, etc.)	81
Unsuccessful legal information search	8
Patron called back to halt action	5
Unsuccessful quotation search (nothing we have ever done will ever be good enough again)	20
Other [including library does not answer such questions] (who is the greatest living philanthropist in Baltimore?)	27
Total:	484

NOTE: There were 160,298 telephone questions answered by T.R.S. staff. Another 20,900 telephone questions were referred to Central Library subject departments, making a total of 181,198
questions handled. Only 484 fall into the above categories; these represent only 0.2% of all
telephone questions.

with answering reference questions at seven major libraries in Illinois.
Daily logs were used to record time spent in answering queries. Costs
were derived by relating time spent to average salary rates for reference
staff at the seven libraries. The costs, thus, are direct salary costs only
and do not reflect the total costs involved in operating the reference
services. (A more realistic method would be to divide the total number of
questions handled during one year into the total cost of operating the
reference service. Based on sampling, the amount of time spent on each

type of reference activity could be estimated, and the total cost allocated over the various activities; a realistic unit cost could be derived for each telephone inquiry, each case of personal assistance to users, and so on.) Palmour and Gray cite the unit cost for inquiries of varying levels of complexity: "bibliographic citation," "simple fact," "multiple fact," and "complex fact." Averaged over all seven libraries, they were $0.49, $0.32, $1.04, and $2.77, respectively. A wide range of cost figures for each type of inquiry is provided for the seven libraries in the group.

A useful study of time considerations in reference work was conducted by Jestes and Laird[24] at the University of California, Davis campus. The object was to determine what proportion of the total time spent by a librarian at the reference desk was directly spent with library users or in answering their questions. It was discovered that librarians were actually spending less than one-quarter of their time performing these duties and that only one-half of this time (i.e., one-eighth of the total time) involved activities for which professional training was needed. The authors suggest that efficiency might be considerably improved through a careful reallocation of responsibilities among professional librarians and "technical assistants."

Obtrusive Testing of Effectiveness

In the aforementioned studies, an inquiry was judged successfully handled if the reference staff was able to provide some information to the inquirer. The accuracy of the information supplied was not considered in any of these studies, and the time taken to supply the information was disregarded in some of them. Childers[8] points out another problem:

. . . the fact that the recorders of the unanswered questions are usually the very people responsible for answering them casts doubt on the objectivity of that measure.

It is exceedingly difficult, if not impossible, to assess the accuracy of information supplied by a reference department under normal operating conditions, because it requires the cooperation of a very large number of users, who have to be identified either just before or immediately after use of the reference services. While it might be feasible to identify users making a personal visit to the library, it would be quite impossible to identify those making telephone inquiries. The sample, therefore, would not be fully representative of all types of users and of all types of questions. Once users willing to cooperate in the investigation were identified, it would be necessary to record the questions asked by each and the answers they received. Then each answer would have to be checked with extreme care to identify which questions were answered correctly and which were not. The complete operation would be difficult to implement, and the size of the sample would have to be very large before any reasonable level of confidence could be obtained. It is small wonder that this type of evaluation has not been attempted.

If a study cannot be conducted under realistic conditions, one alternative would be an evaluation of reference staff performance by means of a controlled set of questions, for each of which an unequivocal answer is known to the investigator. A number of studies of this type have been undertaken, the first, perhaps, being that conducted by the Committee on Public Library Service of the State of New York,[13] as reported in 1958. "A list of 10 reference questions, ranging from the common to the unusual, designed to test the extent of the library's general collection of subject materials more than its reference facilities" was applied under test conditions to 33 public libraries having varying levels of expenditure. This was clearly a reference test, but the report of the committee did not provide details of the exact methodology used in applying the test questions, except that questions answered by a library from its own resources were distinguished from those answered through outside resources. Moreover, the results presented are somewhat confusing.

An evaluation of the New York State public library system,[15] conducted during the period 1963–1966, included a test of reference performance in public libraries of varying sizes. The investigators concluded that public libraries serving even small populations were able to provide a considerable level of user satisfaction, and that performance on the test was not always directly related to library size and resources available.

A careful and detailed test of the ability of reference staff to answer a prescribed set of test questions was conducted by Bunge,[5] in 1967. The investigation was conducted in medium-sized public libraries in the Midwest, the major objective being to determine if there was a relationship between the degree of success in answering inquiries and the level of professional education of reference personnel. The subjects consisted of nine pairs of reference assistants in seven libraries. Each pair was "matched" so they would be "as similar as possible with regard to such variables as amount of undergraduate education and years of reference experience, while differing in amount of formal library training."The study used a group of factual questions selected from a large sample collected from medium-sized public libraries in various parts of the country. The final set of questions represented a range of difficulty, a range of question type, and a range of subject area. A total of 27 questions was administered, but many of the resulting data were based only on the 17 questions that all participants had attempted.

After each test question, the investigator "followed the participant about as he attempted to find the answer." The amount of time necessary to find the answer was recorded by stopwatch, and "each observable step was noted on the observation schedule and each relevant verbal comment was recorded." A single search was allowed a maximum of 15 minutes "unless it appeared that the next step would produce the answer."

The form in which Bunge presents the results of his study is number of questions attempted, number of correct and incorrect responses, amount of time necessary for each, and number of sources used. Success rate for the 17 questions varied from 17/17 (2 of the 18 staff members answered all questions correctly—one in 55.2 minutes and the other in 80.2 minutes) to 11/17 (91.2 minutes). The longest time recorded was 114.5 minutes for 14/17 correct answers. Bunge found:

> . . . some apparent relationship between having a professional library degree and answering the test questions accurately, but it was not statistically significant. Those participants with library training did handle the questions more quickly. Combining accuracy and speed, it was found that efficiency in reference performance was significantly related to having had formal library education, as predicted by the study hypothesis.

Two controlled tests for assessing the performance of reference library staff were developed by the Institute for the Advancement of Medical Communication (IAMC), working under contract with the National Library of Medicine. These tests have been described briefly by Pizer and Cain[34] and, in more detail, by Orr and Olson.[32] The first was designed to test the ability of reference staff in verifying incomplete or inaccurate bibliographic citations; it was referred to as a "citation-cleaning performance test." The reference assistant being tested was given a set of 50 citations, each incomplete or inaccurate in some way, and was required to "verify" (i.e., correct or complete) as many of these citations as possible in a four-hour test period. The full instructions for the test are presented in Table 26, an illustrative sample of the citations in Table 27, and the scoring procedure used in Table 28.

The main purpose of this test was to determine the ability of the reference assistant to exploit the resources available in his library. A list of secondary sources (indexes, bibliographies) that could be used to verify each faulty citation was prepared by the project staff and was checked against the holdings of the library participating in the investigation. For each library, the investigators were able to determine what the maximum score of the reference staff could be; that is, if in a particular library it was theoretically possible to verify 42 of the 50 citations (no tools exist to permit verification of the other 8), the reference assistant was judged by how many of the 42 citations he or she was able to complete correctly during the four-hour test period.

TABLE 26   Instructions for Staff-Mediated Citation-Cleaning Perform-ance Test[32]

1. The aim is to clean and complete as many of the sample citations as possible in a *4-hour* period. *They do not have to be done in any fixed order,* and it is expected that the "easy" ones will be selected to be done first.

2. All citations should be verified by the staff member who *customarily* handles such work in your library. Whatever is the *customary* practice with regard to consulting other members of the staff may be followed, but the work *cannot be divided up* among several individuals. Likewise, *usual* practices in asking help from other libraries may be followed *as long as no mention is made that this is a test situation.*

3. Citations may be verified either with original documents or with one of the *standard* bibliographic tools. If the tool used happens to give an incorrect citation, it will not be counted as an error.

4. The correct citation should be written below each of the items together with a note specifying the verifying source, giving the page if a bibliographic tool is used. Also note the *time* that the verification was completed.

5. The test will be scored on the basis of the number of *complete* and *correct* citations verified within the 4-hour period. If all elements required for a complete citation cannot be verified (e.g., the title of a chapter in a contributor-type book), partial credit will be given.

6. For the purposes of this test, a complete citation includes *all* details that any journal might require for a bibliographic entry. Such details include the following, *in addition* to the minimum bibliographic information necessary to identify the document uniquely:

   A.   Last names and initials of *all* the authors. (If the citation is to a specific section of a contributor-type book, the authors of the section *as well as* the editors of the book should be included.)

   B.   *Inclusive* pages for journal articles and for cited sections of contributor-type books.

   C.   Titles of journal articles or sections in contributor-type books. (These may be given in either the original language of publication or in English translation.)

   D.   Titles of serials may be given in full or as abbreviated in any of the *standard* bibliographic tools used for verifying the citation.

NOTE TO TEST ADMINISTRATOR: The test questions on the attached sheets should be cut apart, and each of the citations should be mounted at the top of a blank sheet of regular size paper. The individual taking the test will then be able to sort the citations as desired and will have adequate space for answers.

This test, although limited to a very narrow facet of reference service, is a useful one. It can be used as one measure of the quality of the reference collection itself, especially in terms of the library's basic bibliographic tools. More importantly, perhaps, it can be used to determine how far the actual performance of a reference staff falls below the maximum score it could possibly achieve if the available bibliographic resources were fully exploited. Of course, the reference assistant tested is not prevented from using outside sources (e.g., calling another library) when appropriate and necessary (see Table 26). It is, therefore, theoretically possible for a reference assistant to verify more citations than the collection of his own library would permit.

The second test developed by IAMC was a "question-answering performance test," designed to determine the ability of reference staff in answering questions of a factual nature, and was very similar to the type devised by Bunge. A particular reference assistant was asked to answer as many of the questions as possible in a four-hour test period. The instructions for the test are presented in Table 29, and a sample of questions in Table 30. The test questions were arrived at by asking a group of medical librarians and medical practitioners to review a sample of articles on medicine and to formulate from each "one or more questions of simple fact that the author would probably have had to look up, or ask someone about, during the course of the work reported, or

TABLE 27   Illustrative Sample of 10 Test Items for Citation-Verification Test[32]

1. About humoral cholinesterases. Histochemistry of Cholinesterase, Symposium, Basel, 1960. Bibl. anat. 2, 228–235 (1961).

2. Proc. Conf. of Profess. Sci. Soc. Chicago, 1963

3. Dordick, H.S., et al. IRE Tr. 4th Internatl. Conf. on Medical Electronics, July 1961

6. Behnke, A.R. & W.A. Taylor. 1959. Some aspects of recent findings pertaining to the body composition of athletes, obese individuals & patients. U.S. Naval Radiological Defense Lab. Rept. TR-339. San Francisco, Calif.

8. Broca, A. & Sulzer, D., 1902. La sensation lumineuse en fonction du temps. J. Physiol. et Path. Gen. 4, 632.

10. Conway, W.J. Microdiffusion Analysis & Volumetric Error, London, Crosby Lockwood, 1947.

12. Erickson, E.H. (1959). Identity and the Life Cycle. New York: International Universities Press.

13. Estes, W.K. & Skinner, B.F. Some quantitative properties of anxiety. J. Exp. Psychol. 29:390, 1941.

15. Friedman, M.H. J. Am. Vet. Med. Assoc. 130, 159–62 (1957)

16. Goldiamond, I. & Hawkins, W.F. Vexierversuch: The log relationship between word-frequency and recognition obtained in the absence of stimulus words. J. exp. Psychol. 1958, 56, 457–463.

TABLE 28   Scoring Procedure for Citation-Verification Tests[32]

In scoring the results of the staff-mediated test, not only the *number* of citations verified in the 4-hour period, but also the *accuracy* of verification (judged by comparison with the criterion set) have to be considered. Errors and omission of details that would prevent or slow location of the cited document, or replicating the document once it is found, should carry a greater penalty than errors and omissions that do not have such practical consequences. Since a user should be able to trust the accuracy of a citation that has been verified by a librarian, it seemed that the more serious errors should carry a greater penalty than no verification at all. Based on this philosophy, and a maximum score of 100% if all 50 citations in a test sample are fully and correctly verified, the following tentative scoring procedure was adopted for the pilot trials:

For each citation matching the criterion set	+2.0%
For citations with a *wrong* article title, journal or book title, volume, year, or initial pages; or with journal or book title, year, or initial page missing	−1.0%
For citations with errors in last page, or edition (for books); or with the name of first author missing	+0.5%
For citations with last page or article title missing	+1.0%
For citations with miscellaneous small errors or omissions (e.g., incomplete journal title, author initials incorrect, author names misspelled, series note missing, editor not given, conference sponsor not given, all authors not given, etc.)	+1.5%

Weighting for scoring can, of course, be varied to reflect whatever value system one desires. The above method was adopted for the pilot trials on a tentative basis and, for any definitive tests, should probably be validated by group consensus.

when writing the document."[34] The test, however, was made more difficult because the investigators eliminated from the sample "all questions that could be answered authoritatively by referring to a single secondary source, such as a handbook, directory, or standard text . . ."[34]

Pizer and Cain[34] have this to say about the two tests developed by IAMC:

Trials of the citation-verification and question-answering tests were carried out in academic, industrial, and hospital libraries to assess their practicality and reliability. Unlike the methods described thus far, these tests were never intended for use in a national survey, rather they were designed primarily for library self-assessment. A library's administrator can employ these tests to assess his collection of bibliographic and reference tools and the skill of his staff in using these tools. They can also be useful for "in house" training programs. Although the present test materials are appropriate only for libraries serving biomedical scientists, materials suitable for testing other libraries can be prepared by anyone willing to make the effort.

Goldhor[16] also used an obtrusive test, consisting of 10 questions, to assess the quality of reference service at 12 public libraries in the Minneapolis-St. Paul metropolitan area. The questions were submitted in writing, and no time limit was imposed. Library staff were scored according to the following scale: 2 for a correct answer; 1 for a partially correct answer or if the correct source was known, but was not in the collection; 0 for no answer or for an incorrect answer. Out of a possible score of 20, the performance ranged from a low of 6/20 to a high of 17/20. The overall average was only 50% (10/20). Three of the questions were correctly answered by all 12 libraries, and one was not answered successfully by any library. The aforementioned tests do have certain value in examining the ability of a reference librarian to operate under a controlled set of conditions, because the same set of test questions can be applied to the reference staff in a number of different libraries under similar conditions, and the performance of one group can be compared

TABLE 29 Instructions for Staff-Mediated Question-Answering Performance Test[32]

---

1. The aim is to provide answers to as many of the sample questions as possible in a *4-hour* period. *The questions do not have to be answered in any fixed order, and it is expected that the "easy" ones will be selected for answering first.*

2. All questions should be answered by the staff member who *customarily* provides such service in your library. Whatever is the *customary* practice with regard to consulting other members of the staff may be followed, but the work *cannot be divided up* among several individuals. Likewise *usual* practices in asking help from other libraries may be followed *as long as no mention is made that this is a test situation.*

3. The "quality" of answers will be judged by the *authority* and *currency* of the source. The questions were selected as ones having answers that might be found in a *single reference-type* source.

4. The answer should be written on the sheet that gives the question, together with a note specifying the *source* and giving specified page location. Also note the *time* that the answer was found.

5. All the questions have short answers, i.e., less than 200-300 words. Many can be answered by a few words or numbers. Where a paragraph or two are required (e.g., a description of a method, or specifications for a piece of equipment), rather than copying an answer in longhand, the source should be specified, and a photocopy of the appropriate section should be made and appended to the question sheet *after* the 4 hours are up.

NOTE TO TEST ADMINISTRATOR: The test questions on the attached sheets should be cut apart, and each of the 50 questions should be mounted at the top of a blank sheet of regular size paper. The individual taking the test will then be able to sort the questions as desired and will have adequate space for answers.

TABLE 30   Illustrative Sample of 10 Test Items for Question-Answering Test[32]

1-01 What is the present address and title of Ewing, W.H.?
(He is probably a bacteriologist and has published in U.S.)

1-13 What is the incidence of Down's syndrome (mongolism) in the U.S.?

1-14 What is the dosage of chlorthiazide diuretics in adult hypertensives?

1-18 What is the Ceriotti indole method for determining DNA (deoxyribonucleic acid)?

1-26 What is the average weight of the normal human heart (adult males)?

1-35 What is the Archibald method for determining the molecular weight of proteins?

1-38 What are the specifications of the Ostwald Viscosimeter, Model G-25?

1-43 What is the dosage of desoxycorticosterone acetate for replacement therapy after adrenalectomy in man?

1-50 What is a Svedberg unit? (ultracentrifugation)

2-50 What is the structural formula of the alkaloid, ajmaline?

---

with that of another. Moreover, tests of the "citation-verification" type can be used to assess the adequacy of a library's collection of certain types of bibliographic tools. This type of test, however, also has certain basic limitations, the most obvious being that the subject of the evaluation is completely aware of the test situation. When he knows he is being observed and evaluated, he may not behave as he would under "normal" working conditions; an inevitable "Hawthorne effect" is created. As a result of being in the spotlight, a reference assistant may operate more carefully or more diligently than he would otherwise, and his performance under test conditions may be somewhat better than under "normal" circumstances. Or the situation may be completely reversed. Knowing he is being observed and tested, the librarian may become tense and nervous. Working under "stopwatch" conditions also places undue pressure on the subject, and his efficiency may deteriorate, or he may make more errors than usual. On the other hand, he knows the test questions are likely to have "findable" answers, which is not always true in actual conditions.

Ideally, it would be preferable to administer a controlled test, with the subject unaware that he is being studied. Such a test is likely to be more satisfactory in many ways than an obtrusive test because it could measure the performance of the reference librarian under actual working conditions rather than under the artificial conditions of an obtrusive study. Although a controlled, unobtrusive study of reference service is not particularly easy, some successful attempts have been made recently.

Unobtrusive Observation of Reference Performance

The most important work on unobtrusive evaluation to date is represented by two studies conducted in New Jersey. The investigators, Crowley and Childers,[14] reported the results of their separate surveys in a single publication.

The Crowley study[14] was designed to test the hypothesis that:

Libraries with high expenditures and high per capita support will answer a larger proportion of information questions than will libraries with low expenditures and low per capita support.

The study was conducted among medium-sized libraries open a minimum of 60 hours per week (to allow questions to be posed during different periods of library activity: weekday, weeknight, Saturday). Out of 40 candidate libraries in New Jersey, 6 high-expenditure and 6 low-expenditure libraries were selected for evaluation.

The questions asked in the test were "made up" by the investigator. In this sense, they were "artificial," but they also were "realistic," in that they were of a type that a public library reference department could reasonably be expected to answer. Clearly, the questions must be real enough to be accepted by the library being tested. Crowley pretested a number of questions before choosing a final set, selecting those that were neither too difficult nor too easy. A question was rejected after the pretest if it had been answered correctly by more than 75% of the libraries tested or if more than 75% had failed to answer it correctly. The justification for this was to identify questions that would be the best discriminators of performance among libraries. Another requirement was that the test question be of a factual nature and have a reasonably unequivocal answer.

Eight questions were actually used in Crowley's study, but one of these was administered three times to determine consistency in library responses. Each library, therefore, was asked 10 questions, a total of 120 for the 12 libraries tested. The unobtrusive character of the evaluation was achieved by posing questions anonymously (i.e., the library staff members had no idea that they were "test" questions and did not represent an actual information need of a library user). All but one of the questions were posed by telephone. Approximately one-half were asked by Crowley himself; the remainder, by eight "proxies." Eight of the 10 test questions were asked consistently by the same person in each of the 12 libraries. Different questions were asked during the various time periods when the libraries were open (to cover both "slack" and "busy" periods), but each question was asked during the same time period in each library. In most cases, a particular question was asked on the same day in each library. In other cases, the same question was asked a few days apart in each library.

"No library received more than one inquiry a day, and in most cases several days or weeks separated the inquiries."[14]

Table 31 shows the 10 questions used, the correct response for each, and the actual answers received from the six high-expenditure and six low-expenditure libraries. The first four questions dealt with current events relating to national political figures. The first was asked eight weeks after Thurgood Marshall had been sworn in as Associate Justice. Questions 2, 3, and 4 were essentially the same inquiry in slightly different forms. The first version was asked nine weeks after Secretary Connor had resigned and Trowbridge had been appointed Acting Secretary. The second version (question 3), used four weeks later, was asked of all 40 libraries in the New Jersey "medium size public library" category to compare the success rate of the sample group with that of all 40 libraries.

TABLE 31   Questions Used by Crowley,[14] with Library Responses

QUESTION 1

"Who on the Supreme Court was appointed
by President Johnson?"

Asked November 28, 1967
Answer—Abe Fortas and Thurgood Marshall

Library	Response	Library	Response
H_1	Fortas	L_1	Fortas
H_2	Fortas	L_2	Fortas & Marshall
H_3	Fortas	L_3	Fortas & Marshall
H_4	Fortas	L_4	Fortas
H_5	Fortas & Marshall	L_5	Fortas
H_6	Fortas & Marshall	L_6	Fortas

QUESTION 2

"What is the name of the Secretary of Commerce?"

Asked March 21, 1967
Answer—Alexander Trowbridge, Acting Secretary

Library	Response	Library	Response
H_1	Trowbridge	L_1	Trowbridge
H_2	Trowbridge	L_2	"There is no secretary now."
H_3	Trowbridge	L_3	Connor
H_4	Connor	L_4	Connor
H_5	Connor	L_5	Connor
H_6	Connor	L_6	Trowbridge

TABLE 31 (Continued)

QUESTION 3

"Who is in charge of the Department of Commerce?"

Asked April 21 and 24, 1967
Answer—Alexander Trowbridge, Acting Secretary

Library	Response	Library	Response
A*H	Trowbridge	U	Connor
B*H	Trowbridge	V	Connor
C*	Connor	W	Trowbridge
D*	Connor	X	Trowbridge
E	Trowbridge	Y	Not called
F H	Trowbridge	Z	Connor
G*H	Connor	AA	Connor
H	Connor	BB L	Connor
I*H	Connor	CC	Connor
J	Connor	DD L	Trowbridge
K*H	Connor	EE	Not called
L	Trowbridge	FF	Not called
M L	Connor	GG	Connor
N	Trowbridge	HH	Connor
O	Not called	II L	"Vacant"
P	Connor	JJ	Trowbridge
Q*	Connor	KK	"Vacant"
R	Connor	LL	Not called
S*	Trowbridge	MM L	Connor
T	Trowbridge	NN L	Connor

* - Area Library
H - "High" Sample Library
L - "Low" Sample Library

Summary

	All Libraries		Sample Libraries		Area Libraries	
Connor	21	53%	7	58%	6	67%
Trowbridge	12	32%	4	33%	3	33%
Vacant	2	5%	1	9%		
Not called	5	10%				
	40	100%	12	100%	9	100%

TABLE 31   (Continued)

QUESTION 4

"Would you give me the name of the Secretary of Commerce?"

Asked October 19, 1967
Answer—Alexander Trowbridge

Library	Response	Library	Response
H_1	Trowbridge	L_1	Trowbridge
H_2	Trowbridge	L_2	Connor
H_3	Trowbridge	L_3	Connor
H_4	Connor	L_4	Trowbridge
H_5	Trowbridge	L_5	Trowbridge
H_6	Trowbridge	L_6	Trowbridge

QUESTION 5

"Could you tell me when the New Jersey
primary election will be?"

Asked April 29, 1967
Answer—September 12, this year

Library	Response	Library	Response
H_1	June 6	L_1	Sept. 12
H_2	Sept. 12	L_2	Sept. 12
H_3	Sept. 12	L_3	First Tuesday
H_4	September		after first
H_5	Second Tuesday		Monday in Sept.
	after first	L_4	Sept. 12
	Monday in Sept.	L_5	Sept. 12
H_6	Sept. 13	L_6	Third Tuesday
			in April

QUESTION 6

"Who said 'The medium is the message'?"

Asked May 9, 1967
Answer—Marshall McLuhan

Library	Response	Library	Response
H_1	Don't know	L_1	Don't know
H_2	Marshall McLuhan	L_2	Marshall McLuhan
H_3	Marshall McLuhan	L_3	Don't know
H_4	Marshall McLuhan	L_4	Don't know
H_5	Marshall McLuhan	L_5	Don't know
H_6	Don't know	L_6	Marshall McLuhan

TABLE 31 (Continued)

QUESTION 7

"How did Senator Case (R., New Jersey) vote on the
1957 Civil Rights Bill?"

Asked April 12, 1967
Answer—He voted YES

Library	Response	Library	Response
H_1	He voted NO but he was *for* the bill	L_1	We can't find it
H_2	He voted YES	L_2	He voted YES
H_3	Sorry, we can't help you	L_3	He voted YES
H_4	He voted YES	L_4	We can't find it
H_5	He voted YES	L_5	We can't find it
H_6	We can't find a record of his vote	L_6	He voted YES

QUESTION 8

"Could you find a recent salary estimate for a
high school teacher in California?

Asked April 20–26, 1967
Answer—U.S. *Statistical Abstract* gives
$8,600, other estimates accepted

Library	Response	Library	Response
H_1	Only more detailed data available	L_1	We can't locate it
H_2	Only more detailed data available	L_2	Only more general data available
H_3	$8,600	L_3	$7,900[3]
H_4	$8,600[1]	L_4	$8,600
H_5	$8,600	L_5	$8,600
H_6	$8,150[2]	L_6	$8,400[4]

1—Obtained by referral from State Library.
2—From *Publishers' Digest of Educational Statistics*.
3—From 1964 *Statistical Abstract*.
4—From 1966-67 *Statesman's Yearbook*.

TABLE 31   (Continued)

QUESTION 9

"What was 'The Specialist' about?"

Asked April and May, 1967
Answer—Constructing outhouses

Library	Response	Library	Response
H₁	Substan-tially correct	L₁	Substan-tially correct
H₂	Can't find it	L₂	Substan-tially correct
H₃	Substan-tially correct	L₃	Substan-tially correct
H₄	Can't find it	L₄	Substan-tially correct
H₅	Substan-tially correct	L₅	Can't find it
H₆	Can't find it	L₆	Can't find it

QUESTION 10

"What is the address of the *William Feather Magazine?*"

Asked April, 1967
Answer—9900 Clinton Road, Cleveland, Ohio

Library	Response	Library	Response
H₁	9900 Clinton Road Cleveland, Ohio	L₁	We can't find it
H₂	9900 Clinton Road Cleveland, Ohio	L₂	We can't find it
H₃	9900 Clinton Road Cleveland, Ohio	L₃	We can't find it
H₄	9900 Clinton Road Cleveland, Ohio	L₄	We can't find it
H₅	We can't find it	L₅	We can't find it
H₆	9900 Clinton Road Cleveland, Ohio	L₆	9900 Clinton Road Cleveland, Ohio

As Table 31 indicates, the difference in performance was slight. Success in identifying Trowbridge was 32% in all libraries and 33% among the sample libraries. The third version (question 4 in Table 31) was asked six months later, after Trowbridge had been sworn in.

Question 5 was another current events question, but this time in the area of state politics. It was asked eight days after the enactment of a bill to change election day from June 6 to September 12. Question 6 was intended to test the general knowledge of the reference library staff, because McLuhan's famous aphorism was then too recent to have appeared in any standard sources of quotations. The 10th question was the only one asked during personal visits to the 12 libraries.

Table 32 summarizes the results for all 10 questions and all 12 libraries. It can be seen that, overall, the high-expenditure libraries scored higher (36/60 correct) than did the low-expenditure libraries (29/60 correct), but this difference in performance is not statistically significant (i.e., the hypothesis could not be supported on the basis of a chi square test). The overall score for the entire group of libraries, 65/120 or 54.2%, is not especially impressive.

The repeated questions (2, 3, and 4) yielded especially interesting results. One would expect that, as more time elapsed between the appointment of Trowbridge and asking of the question, the degree of

TABLE 32   Summary of Results from Crowley Study[14]

	Q_1	Q_2	Q_3	Q_4	Q_5	Q_6	Q_7	Q_8	Q_9	Q_{10}
H_1	−	+	+	+	−	0	−	0	+	+
H_2	−	+	+	+	+	+	+	0	0	+
H_3	−	+	−	+	+	+	0	+	+	+
H_4	−	−	−	−	+	+	+	+	0	+
H_5	+	−	+	+	+	+	+	+	+	0
H_6	+	−	−	+	−	0	0	+	0	+

Proportion of correct
answers for High libraries $P_1 = \dfrac{36}{60}$

	Q_1	Q_2	Q_3	Q_4	Q_5	Q_6	Q_7	Q_8	Q_9	Q_{10}
L_1	−	+	−	+	+	0	0	0	+	0
L_2	+	+	+	−	+	+	+	0	+	0
L_3	+	−	−	−	−	0	+	+	+	0
L_4	−	−	+	+	+	0	0	+	+	0
L_5	−	−	−	+	+	0	0	+	0	0
L_6	−	+	−	+	−	+	+	+	0	+

Proportion of correct $P_2 = \dfrac{29}{60}$
answers for Low libraries

+   = correct answer
−   = incorrect answer
0   = unable to provide information requested

success in responding correctly would increase substantially. The first time the question was asked, exactly one-half the libraries (6/12) answered it correctly, but one month later, the proportion of correct responses actually dropped to 5/12. Even after Trowbridge had been officially sworn in, the proportion of correct answers was only 9/12. More significant perhaps is the consistency of responses. From Table 32 it can be seen that only two libraries consistently answered all three versions of this question correctly. Eight libraries were inconsistent, sometimes correct and sometimes incorrect. The other two libraries, one in the high- and one in the low-expenditure groups, were consistently wrong.

Crowley's study was valuable for two reasons: (a) he produced for the first time a reasonable, unobtrusive approach to testing the quality of reference work, and (b) he cast serious doubts on the quality of reference work conducted in certain public libraries. Moreover, he clearly demonstrated that it is not enough to judge reference work by the number of questions that are answered; the proportion of questions answered correctly must be determined.*

It also should be recognized, however, that the questions used by Crowley were, in one respect, difficult to answer correctly, because they contained an unusually high proportion of highly current information not available in standard bibliographic tools. The librarian would have to be generally knowledgeable in current events in order to recognize that the answers could not be located in standard reference tools, but would have to be sought in newspapers or other current news sources. In other words, the questions used by Crowley were probably more difficult to answer correctly than a group of 10 questions that might have been drawn at random from all inquiries submitted to a library by telephone over a particular period. This, of course, does not excuse the poor performance of some of the libraries involved in the study. Crowley's study does, in fact, indicate that the reference departments of public libraries may not be thoroughly reliable sources of up-to-the-minute information. The evidence suggests that many public libraries may rely almost entirely on published tools, with little attempt made to update these with more current information sources; that these libraries may be disseminating

---

*It is not clear whether Crowley was the first investigator to use the unobtrusive technique. A survey of Pennsylvania libraries reported by Martin[29] in 1967 refers to the use of a "reference performance test based on actual patron inquiries." No details are given, however, on the questions used in this test or how they were administered. It also is interesting to note that Crowley was one of the research associates participating in the Pennsylvania study. It is quite clear, however, that Crowley was the first to describe the unobtrusive technique in detail. Although Crowley was not the first person to cast doubts on the quality of reference service provided by public libraries, he was the first investigator to produce real evidence on this point.

outdated and inaccurate information without knowing it; that some reference assistants may lack adequate knowledge of current events; and that the user has little assurance of obtaining the same answer to a question he poses several times, the answer he receives being at least partly dependent upon which staff member he happens to reach when he contacts the library.

As reported by Martin,[28] Crowley also applied his techniques for unobtrusive evaluation of reference service to the Chicago Public Library Survey. Test questions were posed anonymously at the main library and at branch libraries. The results of this evaluation were summarized as follows:

Actual service has been evaluated by test questions, and by asking patrons their opinion. Many questions have been answered quickly and correctly, a few with imagination, but too often the service is perfunctory, and unnecessarily limited to answers found in published reference books. Thus on questions which require some "current awareness" on the part of the staff member, the responses suggest that this awareness is lacking. To a question requiring current knowledge about the U.N. members, ten agencies gave a total of five different answers, none correct. Another question went unanswered by nine agencies before a sub-branch provided the correct answer. One question asked on successive days in a Main Library Subject Department drew two different answers, one correct and one incorrect. The level of some service at the Main Library is not noticeably higher than at some branch libraries, despite the greater collections and staff qualifications.

Evidently more and better training is needed in modern reference techniques and attitudes; trained personnel must be recruited to allow flexibility in staff assignments, time for training, and completion of other duties. Perhaps most important is the principle of periodic or continuous evaluation with corrective feedback to the appropriate supervisors. Personal service can make or break the library over a period of time; there must be a mechanism for judging the quality of that service, at least for such factors as courtesy, self-confidence, and basic reference knowledge.

The Childers[8,14] study was very similar to that of Crowley. It was conducted at 25 public libraries in New Jersey, representing varying levels of expenditure, although 80% of these had smaller budgets than those in Crowley's sample. Using simple factual questions with relatively unequivocal answers, administered unobtrusively by telephone, Childers attempted to discover whether or not any relationship appeared to exist between library expenditures and percentage of correct answers supplied. The performance of the libraries also was correlated with various types of descriptive statistics available from them (e.g., size of collection and number of professional employees).

Childers included a wider range of questions than did Crowley. A total of 26 questions, shown in Table 33, was administered to the libraries in the

TABLE 33   Test Questions Used in Childers Study[14]

1. What is the gap specification for the 1963 Chevy Corvair? (2)
2. What is the two-letter Post Office abbreviation for Alaska? (6)
3. Who is the poet laureate of the United States? (5)
4. Could you identify this piece of poetry for me: "O pardon me, thou bleeding piece of earth. . ."? (4)
5. What was the federal budget expenditure in 1936? (3)
6. What is the long word that means stamp collector? (1)
7. How do you pronounce Gibran's first name? (8)
8. What are the names of the books that make up Henry Miller's *Rosy Crucifixion?* (7)
9. How many families are there in [this] county? (9)
10. Is Jack Ruby dead? If he is, when did he die? (8)
11. Where is the nearest commercial airport to Rio Grande, Ohio? (9)
12. Who painted the "Yellow Christ"? (5)
13. What was the Pulitzer Prize novel of 1930? (7)
14. What does the O.J. in O.J. Simpson stand for? (5)
15. How much does an assay ton weigh? (2)
16. What is the translation of this phrase from a Christmas card from Hawaii "Hauoli makahiki hou"? (1)
17. Would you tell me where to look for man-made satellites tonight—with a telescope? (9)
18. What was the slogan of Henry Krajewski, the pig farmer from New Jersey, who ran in three presidential elections? (8)
19. What does the phrase "gnomes of Zurich" refer to? (1)
20. Who is the author of the poem that goes something like: "Thou mayst in me behold that time of year/When yellow leaves or none or few do hang/Upon those boughs. . ."? (4)
21. What is the book that the Peter Sellers movie "The Battle of the Sexes" was taken from? (7)
22. What is the salary of the President of the United States? (2)
23. When was the fraternity Alpha Tau Omega founded? (3)
24. What is the address of the J. B. Van Sciver Co., a manufacturer of furniture? (6)
25. Do I need a passport to visit the Bahamas? (9)
26. What were the exact words of John F. Kennedy when he was asked how he became a war hero? (4)

Categories of Questions

Type of question	Number in the test
1. Meaning type	3
2. Numerical or statistical type	3
3. Historical type	2
4. Exact wording type	3
5. Proper names	3
6. Addresses of individuals or societies	2
7. Books and publishing	3
8. Biography	3
9. Geographical facts	4
	26

sample. All questions for each library were posed by telephone in exactly the same way. Twenty-five "inquirers," comprised of housewives and graduate students—mostly library school students—were used in the project. The investigator (Childers) himself posed two questions; all the other inquirers, one each. A specific question was posed by each inquirer to all libraries in the sample, usually within a three- or four-day period. For each question, the libraries were called in a random sequence at various times, distributed randomly over the hours during which the libraries were open. An example of instructions to inquirers is shown in Table 34.

Unlike Crowley, who judged a response to be either correct or incorrect, Childers developed a scale of "correctness," as follows:

1. Wholly correct.
2. The correct answer is included in the response, but some incorrect information also is included.
3. The correct answer is given, but is "obscured" in some way by the respondent (e.g., he indicates uncertainty as to whether or not the answer given is correct).
4. Part of the correct answer is given.
5. The answer is wholly incorrect, or no answer is found.
6. No attempt is made to answer the question.

Problems involved in conducting a telephone survey of this kind have been discussed in the volume by Crowley and Childers[14] and in an article by Childers.[8] They found it most important to ensure that the libraries being evaluated accepted the questions submitted to them as "real" ones from "legitimate" users, and that they remained unaware of their participation in any kind of evaluation. Because many public libraries, as a matter of policy, reject questions falling into certain categories (e.g., quiz questions, or questions that are an integral part of a homework assignment), the investigator supplied the inquirers with credible reasons for asking particular questions (e.g., "My father needs this information in order to fix his car."), which could then be given to the reference assistant if the legitimacy of a request was questioned.

The cause of another problem was that the libraries being studied were dispersed over a wide geographic area in New Jersey, resulting in many long-distance telephone calls. Such calls must not be evident to the library being called, because some libraries, as a matter of policy, will answer questions only from residents of their own community. Others, while not refusing to answer outsiders, might well be suspicious of any question that is made via a long-distance call, particularly if the inquirer is from a

TABLE 34   Example of Instructions to Inquirers as Used by Childers[14]

The Question:

For a week now I've been trying to remember the author of a poem. It goes something like:

"Thou mayst in me behold that time of year
when yellow leaves or none or few do hang
Upon those boughs. . . ."

(That's all I remember. No, I don't even remember the title. We had to learn it in high school.)

[NOTE: "something like." Make sure that is part of your introduction.]

Beginning at 7 p.m. o'clock Tuesday, April the 15th, apply the above questions to these libraries, in order. Make at least one call during every whole half-hour you are free (study time is considered "free" time).

You will find that some of the libraries, as you come on them in order, are not open when it is their turn to be called. Put that sheet on the bottom of the pile and do the next library. When you come to the unopen library again, and if that library again isn't open, repeat the procedure. This process will quickly narrow your uncalled libraries to a few that are seldom open. Arrange to call these libraries during their next open period.

Record everything: As well as filling in the blanks, in the Comments section include all other information that reflects favorably *or* unfavorably on the library, the respondent, the resources, etc. (A mention of a reference book used, other libraries called, persons consulted, etc.)

The Question. Put the question in your own words, but be consistent in the information you give, in your tone, and your rationale (the information in parentheses). Sometimes, NOTES and IF ASKED information are supplied. Heed these. They are usually critical to what we're looking for. Don't give information in square brackets to the library.

The rationale (in parentheses) should be volunteered if the respondent allows you to get it in. Make it natural. Its purpose is to identify your request as a serious one. (Not homework or a quiz contest or something.)

Pursue the question only to the extent that you repeat what you are asking for, or your rationale. It will be very tempting, but *don't help.* Don't be reluctant to be silent on the wire for several seconds—give them a chance to make a statement. (Bell Telephone says folks can't keep silent more than 6 seconds.)

When a library offers to call you back, tell them any way you want that it's easier for *you* to return the call (so they won't know it's long-distance). Ask them when you should call back: if you can't call at that time, negotiate for a time suitable to both of you.

Generally, all your calls will be completed within two days; one day may be sufficient. But some libraries that are open short hours may necessitate extending your calling into a second, even a third or fourth day. There is even the possibility that you will be asked to call back a week later. This is perfectly acceptable.

Of major importance to the success of the study:

1. Consistent application of the question.
2. Unbiased time-sampling,
3. Objective recording of the responses,
4. Unobtrusiveness.

If there are problems, questions, confusing instructions, call me at home or leave a message with the Library School office.

Thank you.

community having an adequate public library of its own. The problem of the long-distance call usually does not arise if the reference assistant contacted is able to find the needed information immediately (although "static" may give the caller away). It does arise, however, if the reference assistant wishes to call the questioner back at a later time. In such cases, Childers' inquirers offered to call the library back. This was not wholly successful, however, because some libraries became suspicious and began refusing to answer questions from users who would not leave their telephone numbers.

A further problem relates to overload. Childers discovered that, in very small public libraries, even the few questions used in his investigation were enough to create an unusually heavy load and to arouse suspicions. A final problem, although Childers did not find it very important, can be caused by communications between staff members of the various libraries being studied. Suspicions can be aroused if a reference assistant from one of these libraries happens to mention to someone from another library one of the "test" questions he has received recently; or if library A contacts library B for assistance in answering an unusual question that library B has answered earlier in the day or perhaps a few days before. In all of these situations, the objective is not so much one of hiding the specific fact that an evaluation is taking place, as it is of preventing the various libraries from feeling that some type of "unusual" situation is occurring.

The major problems discovered by Childers during his study were overloaded conditions in the smaller libraries and suspicions caused by long-distance telephone calls. He decided against further calls to any library once a "reactive" situation occurred (e.g., refusal to seek an answer when the questioner would not leave his telephone number).

The gross results of the Childers study are presented in Table 35. Note that, because of the "reactive" situation, three of the libraries were asked fewer than 26 questions. Others made no attempt to answer several of the questions. If the number of correct answers provided is divided by the number of questions asked (346/632), the average of success is 54.75% (Scale *a*), a figure that agrees almost exactly with Crowley's. If, on the other hand, success is expressed by the number of correct answers over the total number of questions attempted (346/542), the average is 63.84% (Scale *d*). The same data, arranged question-by-question in Table 36, show that a few questions were answered correctly by most libraries, but not a single one was correctly answered by all. Some questions were answered poorly by almost all libraries. The performance range varied from 23.8% to 80.8% on the *a* scale (percentage of questions asked that were answered correctly) and from 41.7% to 84.6% on the *d* scale (percentage of questions "attempted" that were answered correctly).

The type of question asked was found to influence the success rate. For

TABLE 35   Correct Answers, by Library—Childers Study[14]

Library	Number of responses (Scale *a*)	Correct answers	Number of "attempts" (Scale *d*)
A	26	17	26
B	26	6	10
C	26	14	23
D	26	14	23
E	26	21	26
F	26	14	24
G	20	11	19
H	26	14	24
I	26	14	24
J	26	13	23
K	26	13	23
L	26	14	24
M	26	12	22
N	26	14	23
O	26	18	24
P	26	15	23
Q	26	6	8
R	26	12	19
S	26	8	17
T	26	18	25
U	26	18	26
V	25	20	25
W	15	11	13
X	26	10	24
Y	26	19	26
Total	632	346	542

54.75%   63.84%

example, questions relating to proper names (category 5 in Table 33) produced a relatively high rate of success, while questions concerning geographic facts (category 9) produced a relatively low success rate.

Generally, Childers discovered that libraries having greater resources tend to produce more correct answers to telephone requests than those with lesser resources, although certain "resource measures" did not correlate significantly with performance in this reference task. Virtually no association was found between per capita expenditures and degree of success, but a significant correlation was found between an absolute figure of total expenditures and degree of success in answering questions:

TABLE 36   Correct Answers, by Question—Childers Study[14]

Question	Number of responses (Scale *a*)	Correct answers	Number of "attempts" (Scale *d*)
1	25	9	18
2	25	12	23
3	25	17	23
4	25	19	23
5	25	15	23
6	25	22	25
7	25	11	23
8	25	13	24
9	25	5	20
10	25	21	23
11	25	4	16
12	25	21	24
13	25	20	23
14	25	17	23
15	25	23	24
16	24	6	13
17	24	7	17
18	24	12	20
19	24	8	21
20	24	14	21
21	23	5	17
22	23	12	22
23	23	16	19
24	23	12	18
25	23	16	21
26	22	9	18
Total	632	346	542

54.75%   63.84%

The data indicated that there is a significant variation in the correctness of response [see Table 37] . . . when the libraries are stratified according to Total Expenditures. That is, the libraries in the lowest of the four categories of Total Expenditures respond accurately to significantly fewer questions than do the libraries in the highest category. However, the differences, while statistically significant, are not great.

The results from Childers' study support Beasley's[2] claim that the quality of reference service is dependent both on the strength of the library staff (number of professional employees) and the size of the collection. In fact, the Childers data show a stronger correlation between

TABLE 37   Percentage of Correct Responses (Scale *a*), Stratified by Library Expenditures[14]

	Correct Responses		
Total $	n	Mean	Standard deviation
		%	%
10,000–24,999	4	47.5	20.6
25,000–49,999	10	44.0	10.8
50,000–99,999	7	62.9	12.5
100,000 +	4	70.0	8.2

number of professional employees and reference success than between collection size and reference success.

Since the original study reported by Crowley and Childers, a great deal of interest has been generated in the technique of unobtrusive measurement of reference service. For example, in June 1972, a two-day workshop on the subject (conducted by Childers) was sponsored by the Division of Library Development of Maryland's Department of Education. It was attended by 30 representatives of public libraries throughout the state. Participants at the workshop tested the unobtrusive technique by telephoning several public libraries in Maryland, Virginia, and the District of Columbia. The impressions of one participant were summarized as follows:

When the unobtrusive technique was first explained to us, the initial reaction was one of fear and uneasiness. Many seemed to feel that to test any reference librarian without his knowledge was unfair to him, a bit unethical, and perhaps might even be looked upon as a threat to his job security. Most seemed to feel that they would not like to have themselves tested in such a manner. Many of these attitudes completely reversed themselves, however, by the time the two-day workshop ended. Everyone, it seemed, came to realize the usefulness of such a technique and felt it was needed. Many were eager and excited about the whole idea. Some wanted to try the method out on their own library systems.

Why this change in attitude?—because of what each of us discovered when we saw telephone reference service from a user's point of view. The biggest single impression that we got from our two days of telephone testing was the great divergence in the quality of service one might receive—not only within the same library system but sometimes within the same library![30]

In March 1973, the Suburban Library System (SLS), located in the metropolitan Chicago area, went one stage further, by proposing to set up a mechanism for the continuous monitoring of services in member libraries:

The Suburban Library System in a small attempt to assist librarians in evaluating certain services proposes that "snoop groups" be formed. These groups will be composed of resident volunteers from the library's community who will anonymously at unpredetermined times make reference and title requests at the local library. The questions and requests, devised by SLS, will be of varying difficulty. Questions will include those which can be answered with local resources as well as those which require referral to SLS Reference Service. The volunteers will report to SLS when each request was made, their evaluation of how the request was handled by the library, and when the answer or material was supplied.

SLS will submit to each participating library a confidential report of the results of the survey as submitted by the volunteers. SLS will also compile the results of all the libraries—retaining anonymity—to be published as a summary in the SLS NEWS.

Each member library board will determine its willingness to participate in the accountability survey—only those voluntarily agreeing to the test will be tested. The tests will be made if a sufficient number of member libraries indicate participation to assure anonymity.[38]

A later announcement from SLS indicated that the term "snoop group" (an unfortunate designation if ever there was one) was being dropped, and reemphasized that only libraries indicating willingness would be studied.

An unobtrusive technique also was used in a survey of reference service in academic and public libraries in Ohio.[45] Telephone calls were made to a group of public and academic libraries between 8:00 a.m. and 2:00 p.m. on a Saturday, and two questions were asked: "Can you give me the address of the National Council for the Social Studies?" and "How many people committed suicide in the United States in 1968?" Each question was asked of all libraries by the same person. The first was answered successfully by 13/14 of the public libraries attempting it, while 8 others were unable to give any answer. Overall success, thus, was 13/22. The overall success for the second question was 12/19 (only 15 of the 19 libraries called could provide an answer and, of these, 3 were incorrect, a success rate of 12/15). The performance of the academic libraries was better—5/5 for the first question and 3/3 for the second.

King and Berry[26] describe a pilot study of the telephone information service at the University of Minnesota libraries. Volunteers called in questions to several divisions of the library in order to determine (a) factual accuracy of responses, (b) amount of "negotiation" between librarian and questioner, and (c) "attitude" of the librarian. Results indicated that the negotiation process was inadequate in many instances and that sources of factual answers rarely were cited by the librarian. The Reference Division answered 60% of the questions correctly, 25% incorrectly, and was unable to find an answer for the other 15%. Accuracy of responses in other divisions varied from a low of 40% correct to a high of

90%. The attitude of the librarian was judged "pleasant" in 95% of the calls.

Before leaving this subject, it may be worthwhile to compare the unobtrusive evaluation technique used by Crowley and Childers with the obtrusive method used by Bunge. These techniques have one thing in common: Both make use of questions that are "artificial," in the sense that they do not represent "actual" information needs of "real" library users. Nevertheless, the questions used were certainly realistic and of the type that might reasonably be asked of the reference staff of a library. In both types of studies, too, the questions were of a factual nature and had reasonably unequivocal answers. The major difference between the two techniques is that in one case the staff member knew he was being observed and evaluated and in the other case he did not.

Some of the dangers and disadvantages of the obtrusive mode of study have already been discussed. The unobtrusive method has the great advantage of observing a staff member under operating conditions that are assumed to be "normal"; however, it also has some disadvantages. In the unobtrusive studies conducted in New Jersey, the library was viewed essentially as a "black box"—a question is inserted and an answer comes out (sometimes): the answer being correct, partially correct, or incorrect. This type of study can measure degree of success in answering questions and response time, can identify types of questions that appear to present difficulties, and can observe the attitudes of the reference staff. It also enables the investigator to conjecture why certain questions are answered incorrectly (e.g., outdated information is given because the reference staff relies solely on published reference books and makes no attempt to update these tools by means of newspaper clippings or other current events files). What it cannot do (by telephone) is allow the inquirer to see how the reference assistant performs the task of answering a question (as Bunge did in his study, by actual observation of library staff).

It is convenient to use the telephone for an unobtrusive study, but perhaps is not essential. If sufficient volunteers can be induced to participate, no doubt an extensive unobtrusive study could be conducted through personal visits to a single library, or to a whole group of libraries, over an extended period of time. The major requirement is that the questions used be of the type that the library staff would be inclined to answer rather than to hand the questioner a book and telling him to look for the answer. Through personal visits, it might be possible to combine the advantages of unobtrusive observation (and, at the same time, avoid some of its problems) with the advantage of being able to observe the reference librarian in action (as in an obtrusive situation). In fact, House[22] has mentioned a study in which the same question was asked during personal visits to 19 libraries.

Another difference worth mentioning is that the obtrusive study is certainly ethical, since the subject knows he is being observed and evaluated, while the unobtrusive evaluation may be regarded as unethical: a form of "spying" or "eavesdropping." Such a technique may be justified if it is applied with the ultimate objective of raising the level of performance. It also is interesting to note that the studies which have been conducted have produced similar results, regardless of the method used.

Bunge, Crowley, and Childers have demonstrated the feasibility of evaluating the quality of reference work, at least the question-answering aspect. All three studies were conducted as doctoral research projects in schools of library science, involved several libraries, and were concerned with identifying factors that might affect the quality of library reference service in general. The greatest value of these types of analyses, however, lies in their diagnostic possibilities. Evaluation procedures need to be applied intensively to individual libraries, or to the libraries in a particular system, to identify weaknesses and sources of failure and to lead to corrective actions designed to improve future performance. Such corrective actions could take the form of improving procedures for selection and training of staff, improving the reference collections in specific areas, developing new tools to exploit the collections, or changing practices in the reference division (e.g., establishing new files, routine clipping of newspapers, assigning responsibility for keeping various reference tools current). A well-designed evaluation program, which may employ several techniques, should be capable of identifying types of failures prevalent in a particular library. Such failures may be traced to specific subject areas, types of questions, or staff members. The true value of such studies will be realized only when librarians apply them routinely as a means of improving the performance of their own institutions.

Observation and Analysis of Reference Procedures

Closely related to the evaluation of reference performance is the observation and analysis of how the reference librarian functions. This can be accomplished by observing the reference librarian in action, obtrusively, unobtrusively, or by retrospective analysis of records accumulated during reference activities. Excellent examples of studies of reference activities through analysis of records of previous inquiries are provided by Mote and Angel,[31] Cole,[12] and Sabel et al.,[36] representing industrial or scientific research libraries in the United Kingdom.

Cole analyzed the records of 410 technical inquiries made to the Technical Information and Library Service of the British Petroleum Co. Ltd. Because of the detailed records maintained by this organization,

Cole was able to categorize the requests by type, by source from which the answer was supplied (e.g., 58% of all answers were supplied from journals, 14% from pamphlets), and by type of answer supplied (e.g., 69% of all inquiries required location of a few articles on a particular subject, 18% sought a single fact or figure, and only 1% required an extensive literature survey over a wide subject field). From data on the sources of journal articles (or references to them) supplied to users, Cole was able to produce a ranked list of journals by amount of use and to show the distribution of all journal references supplied, both by journal title and by age (date of publication).

The Mote and Angel study, conducted at the Thornton Research Centre of Shell Research Limited, involved an analysis of technical inquiries collected over a 10-year period. For all inquiries requiring more than 30 minutes to answer, data were maintained on cards to record: terminology of the inquiry, name and location of inquirer, date received, sources consulted, answers produced, date inquiry was closed, and time expended. These cards were then classified by subject and filed in the form of an index of inquiries handled. Analysis of the records in this file permitted the categorization of inquiries by sources used, age of sources, number of documents supplied, status of inquirer, and complexity (measured in terms of number of facets involved in an inquiry).

Sabel, Terry, and Moss studied the Library of the Atomic Energy Research Establishment in Harwell, England, where details of technical inquiries handled were recorded on edge-notched cards to permit subsequent analysis. Inquiries were then categorized by type and (Civil Service) grade of inquirer, subject, sources used, and time required to produce an answer. One product of this analysis was a list of sources, ranked in order of usefulness.

Herner and Herner[20] conducted an extensive analysis of approximately 5,000 inquiries in the field of atomic energy handled by 14 organizations in the United States. The objective of this analysis was to define user requirements for atomic energy information. All inquiries were categorized by type (e.g., 25% of all the technical inquiries requested a description of a process or method of procedure; another 25% required physical, chemical, and engineering properties of substances) and by complexity of conceptual structure. A major purpose of this study was to determine requirements for a classification or indexing scheme for organizing scientific information to allow manual or machine retrieval.

Another analysis of the conceptual structure of questions was conducted by Whaley[48] at the Linde Company. Some 260 questions, searched by a punched card retrieval system, were examined and divided into 11 categories representing logical expressions of varying levels of complexity. The logical complexity of reference questions collected at three libraries—one public and two academic—also has been analyzed by Vavrek.[46]

Many studies over the years have recorded all of the reference questions received by a particular library or group of libraries, during a certain time period, and have categorized them in various ways. These studies are too numerous to summarize or enumerate here. Rothstein's review mentions many of them. Occasionally, this type of study will go beyond the mere categorization of questions and will attempt to identify "problem" questions and to determine the major causes of these problems. One example is Breed's[4] study of 6,000 questions received over a 17-week period in a large academic library. He undertook a fairly detailed analysis of the relatively small number of "difficult" questions in this group and categorized them by type, subject matter, forms of bibliographic material involved, and primary causes of difficulty. He also attempted to identify the extent of knowledge required by members of the reference staff to answer these questions satisfactorily.

A detailed analysis of search procedures used by reference librarians, conducted by Carlson[7] for Hughes Dynamics, Inc. in 1964, had four main objectives:

1. To illustrate that human search behavior can be precisely described. The accuracy of this description can be verified by simulating the librarian's behavior on a general purpose digital computer. The results of this simulation can then be compared with the actual human search behavior.
2. To improve the present search procedures used by humans by highlighting the human's inconsistencies and ambiguities. The major decision points are where the human inconsistencies become most apparent.
3. To develop new training procedures for librarians.
4. To make it possible to develop computer routines that could assist the human in making complex searches of a file.

Carlson's study involved the search procedures used by three members of the reference staff at a university medical library. Four techniques were tested to record these procedures:

1. A portable tape recorder recorded all spoken words.
2. A stenographer recorded everything spoken.
3. The tape recorder and the stenographer were both used, and the data they collected were supplemented by notes taken by an observer.
4. Two observers were used to record everything they saw or heard.

The fourth procedure provided the most details, and was used in all final analyses. The following example of the details recorded during a search on the "function of glial cells" is given by Carlson:

> He skimmed over other books and came back and looked at the title of Ferrier again, and said, "When I browse I am continually amazed at the number of old dated books we have!" Mr. E. now went to the general physiology section, QS, of the stacks. He skimmed briefly in the section and paused on Cunningham's *Textbook of Anatomy*, 5th edition. There was a blue, a red, and a green copy. He took the blue one. Mr. E. checked the index for neuroglia and found a bold heading, *neuroglia*, turned to page 848 and said, "This was clear and concise. It doesn't give anything about glia cells within the neuroglia. Ah, here it is, glia cells are responsible for forming all types of tumors. This really doesn't tell us anything we didn't already know. It does say it better, so I'll take this along. I think we have spent too much time up here; a waste of time" . . .

From this type of detailed observation, Carlson depicted the behavior of reference librarians on flow charts. These charts are reproduced as Figures 11 thru 22. Figure 11 charts the overall reference technique; the remaining figures present details of each process outlined on the first chart.

Carlson concluded that human search behavior was, in general, quite regular: "Most of the flow charts can apply to different searches by the same librarian and also to searches made by different librarians." He also reported, however, that many techniques used by humans are inconsistent, but could be improved by an awareness of such inconsistencies and by retraining in better search techniques. Carlson pointed out that the reference librarian "has no consistent way of improving the quality of his search," because there is rarely any feedback from the user, and that he is almost always unaware of the amount of potentially relevant information he may have missed.

A related study was conducted by Torr, Fried, and Prevel[44] in 1966. Working under contract with the National Science Foundation, the investigators were concerned with developing procedures to study how people search in printed indexes and to evaluate the results of such searches. Four possible methods for collecting data on actual use of indexes were tested: written protocol, oral protocol, guided protocol, and observer photographic protocol. In the first of these, the searcher is "asked to write an introspective report of his thoughts as he searches for information. He is asked to state what he is doing and why he is doing it." From these written records, the investigators hoped to "reconstruct the variety of paths followed by an index user in his search for information." This method produced disappointing results, because the "process of introspection" does not come easily to most people. Moreover, the laborious and time-consuming task of recording one's behavior may interfere with the conduct of an efficient search.

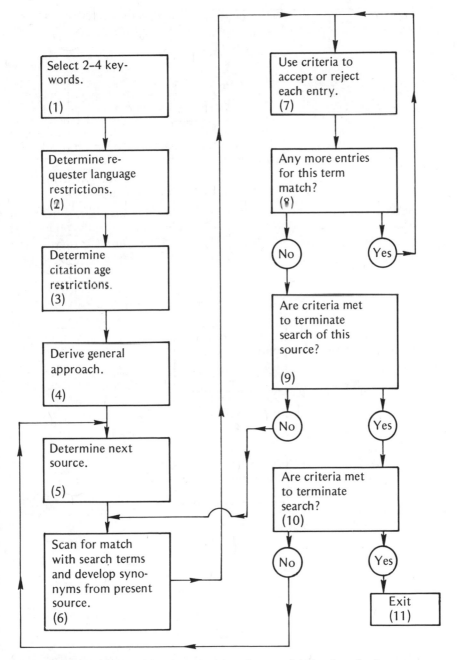

FIGURE 11   General flow chart showing the search behavior of reference librarians.[7]

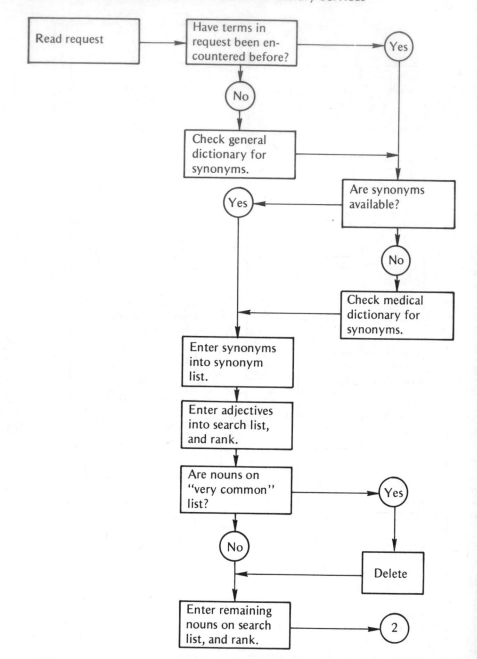

FIGURE 12 Flow chart showing the search behavior of reference librarians:
(1) Select 2–4 keywords.[7]

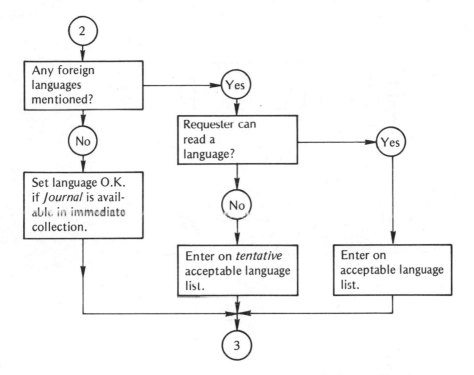

FIGURE 13   Flow chart showing the search behavior of reference librarians:
(2) Determine requester language restrictions.[7]

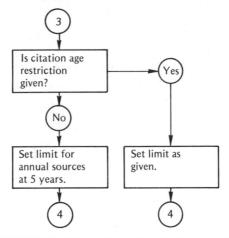

FIGURE 14   Flow chart showing the search
behavior of reference librarians: (3) Determine
citation age restrictions.[7]

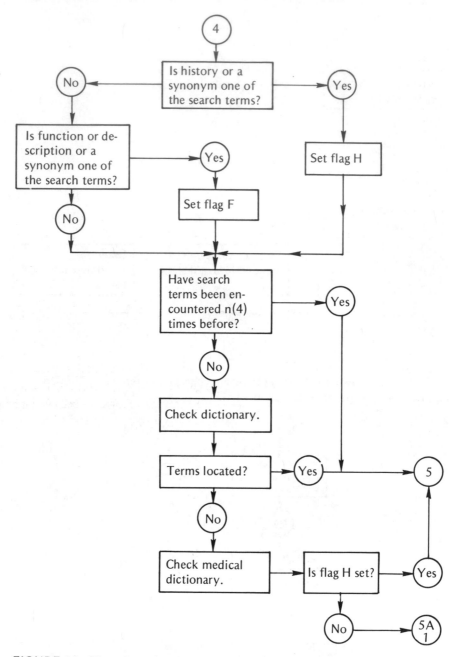

FIGURE 15   Flow chart showing the search behavior of reference librarians: (4) Derive general approach.[7]

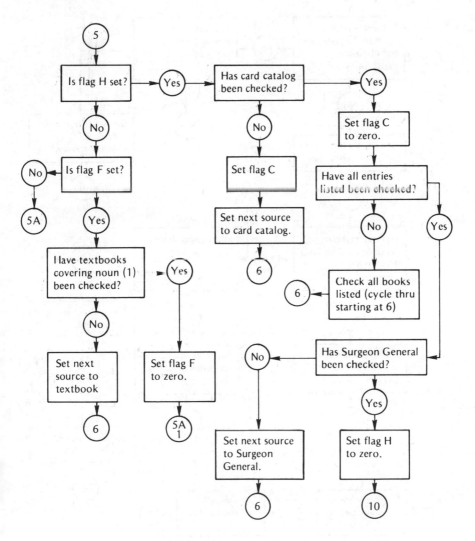

FIGURE 16   Flow chart showing the search behavior of reference librarians:
(5) Determine next source.[7]

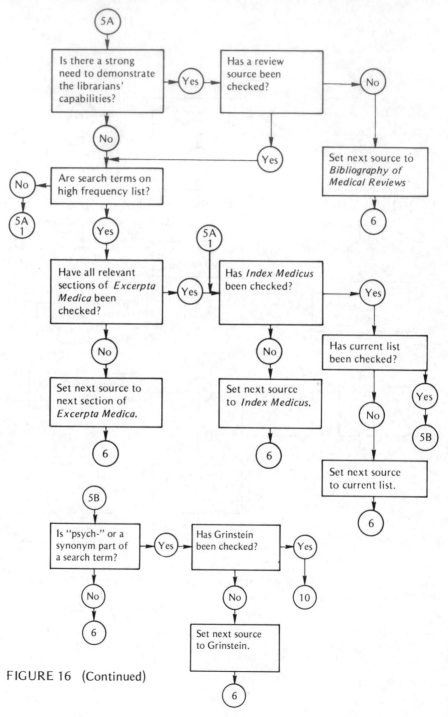

FIGURE 16   (Continued)

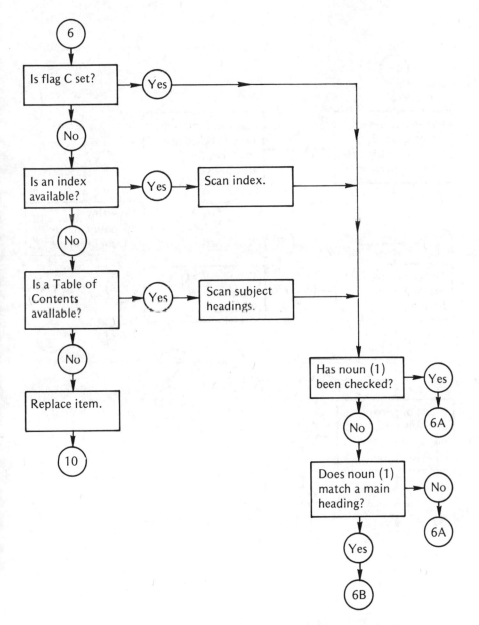

FIGURE 17   Flow chart showing the search behavior of reference librarians:
(6) Scan for match with search terms and develop synonyms from present
source.[7]

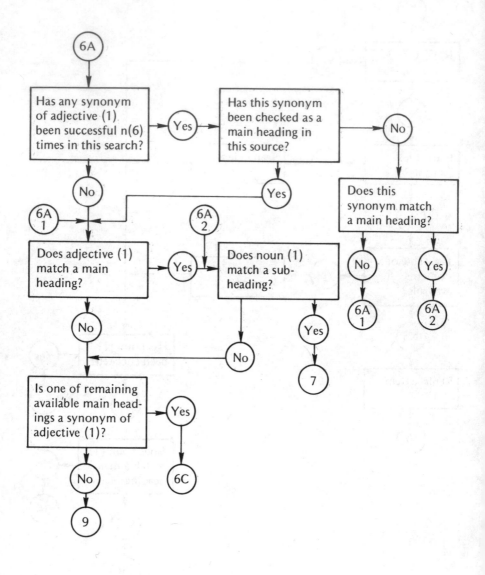

FIGURE 17 (Continued)

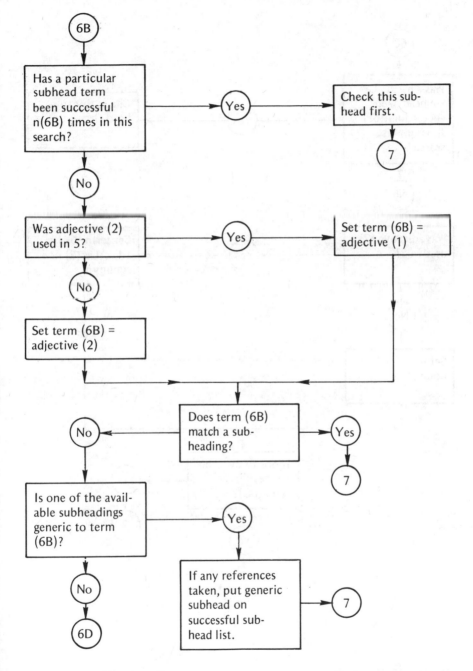

FIGURE 17   (Continued)

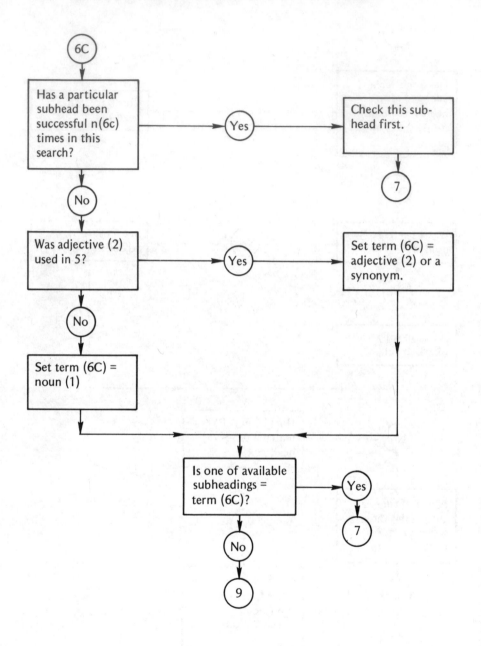

FIGURE 17   (Continued)

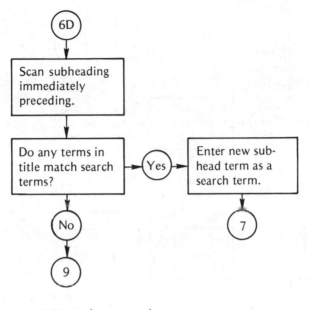

FIGURE 17   (Continued)

In the oral protocol method, the searcher wears a small microphone, into which he makes oral commentaries on his searching behavior, which are recorded on tape by means of an FM transmitter in the searcher's pocket, and an FM receiver. This technique was found feasible "to record the thought processes of a cooperative searcher as he moved freely about within a library environment, passing from indexes to periodical shelves and to other reference material."

The guided protocol method involves the use of an observer, who accompanies and questions the searcher throughout the search process, or, in a sense, conducts a running interview with the searcher. The investigators did not consider this technique to be very practical, because it required a considerable amount of cooperation from the searcher and tended to interrupt the normal thought processes used during a search.

The observer photographic method, the most elaborate of the four, requires a combination of human and photographic observations, as well as tape-recorded interviews after a search is completed. The Torr, Fried, and Prevel study was directed specifically at the use of various printed indexes, wherein the searcher uses the indexes at a viewing table. A camera at this viewing table records, at one-second intervals, how the searcher uses the index. The portion of the table the searcher uses for

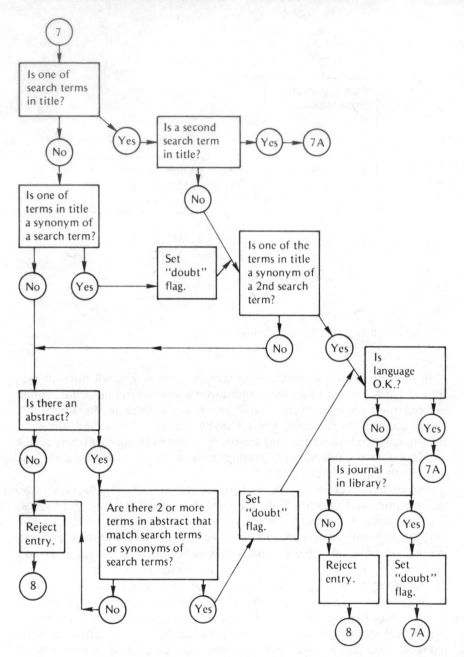

FIGURE 18   Flow chart showing the search behavior of reference librarians:
(7) Use criteria to accept or reject each entry.[7]

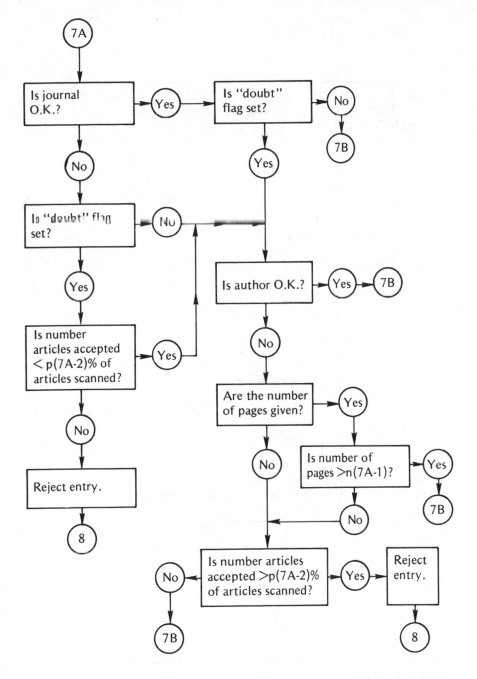

FIGURE 18   (Continued)

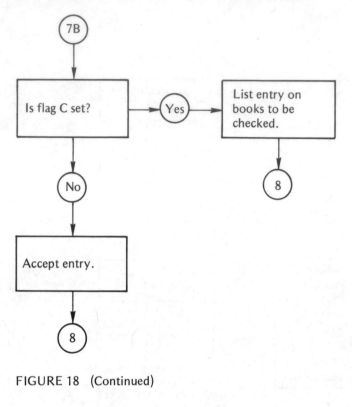

FIGURE 18   (Continued)

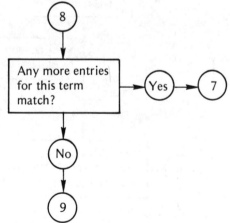

FIGURE 19   Flow chart showing the search behavior of reference
librarians: (8) Any more entries for this term match?[7]

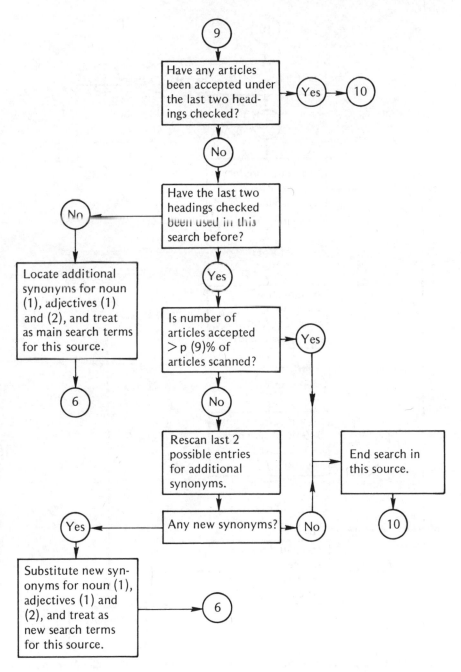

FIGURE 20 Flow chart showing the search behavior of reference librarians: (9) Are criteria met to terminate search of this source?[7]

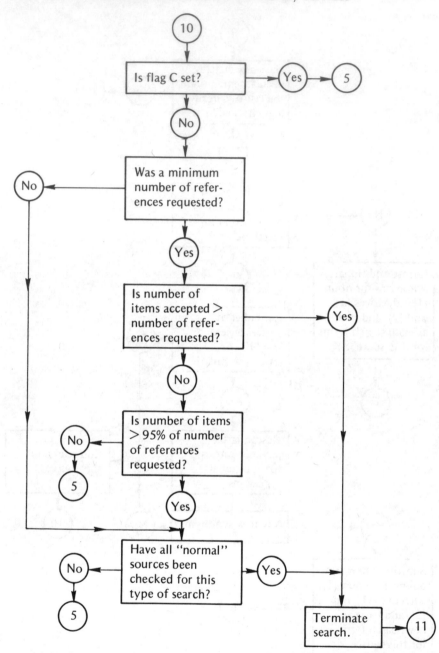

FIGURE 21   Flow chart showing the search behavior of reference librarians: (10) Are criteria met to terminate search?[7]

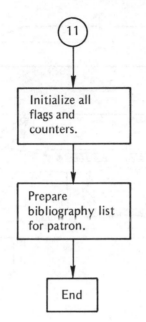

FIGURE 22   Flow chart showing the search behavior
of reference librarians: (11) Exit.[7]

making notes also is within the camera's field of vision (see Figure 23).

The entire procedure works as follows. The searcher, who has previously agreed to cooperate, conducts his search in the normal manner, except that, when he needs to consult a printed index, he does it at the viewing table. Meanwhile, an observer records the major activities of the searcher (e.g., his use of the card catalog, reference to journals) and the time required for each of these activities. When the searcher goes to the viewing table, the observer starts the camera and continues his written observations. This procedure is continued until the search is completed. After the film is processed, a recorded interview takes place with the searcher, during which the searcher and observer reconstruct details of the search from the film record and the observer's notes. The searcher is asked to explain why he went to a specific index at a particular time, why he consulted a specific heading, what he found there, and so on. This process was designed to provide a detailed record of a complete search while interfering with the searcher's thought processes as little as possible.

In addition to using the viewing table for observing actual searches of printed indexes, it also can be used for observing subjects using an index

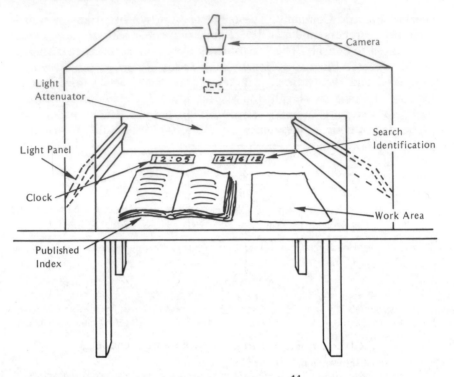

FIGURE 23   Sketch of portable photographic unit.[44]

under experimental conditions. The intention here is to make a detailed analysis of a search for information on a specific subject in a printed index. The search is conducted under controlled conditions, wherein the investigators record data on the number of relevant citations found, the number of irrelevant citations scanned, the time required for the search, and the search methods employed. The photographic method enables them to observe exactly which headings are consulted, which citations under each heading are selected, how many citations are scanned, and how long the searcher spends consulting each portion of the index. To assist in this observation, the searcher traces with his finger the headings he is consulting and the citations he is selecting.

As indicated previously, Torr, Fried, and Prevel attempted to devise procedures that could be used to observe and evaluate the use of printed indexes. The procedures developed were tested for feasibility on a limited scale, but were not implemented in any large-scale program. The feasibility studies were conducted mainly with professional staff members of the

General Electric Company. The subjects were not librarians or trained literature searchers, and many were quite unfamiliar with the indexes they were asked to consult. The experiments were conducted at two libraries of the General Electric Company, the Index Room of the Library of Congress, and the National Library of Medicine. The subjects at the Library of Congress were given a topic and were required to search a particular index, recording (on paper) their thoughts and actions as they proceeded. A typical "introspection" of this type is illustrated in Table 38.

TABLE 38   A Representative Protocol of an Introspection Made during a Search at The Library of Congress Index Room[44]

Statement: Provide a bibliography on spacecraft stabilization and attitude control using the *Air University Periodical Index.*

a.   Looked for AUPI—key words: spacecraft, satellite, control, stabilization.
b.   Looked up spacecraft—referred to space vehicles, space stations. Looked for subheading in space vehicle—found guidance control titles that do not seem relevant.
c.   Went to inertial guidance—looked for satellite—found satellite artificial—looked for guidance and control. Found one relevant article.
d.   Looked under control—nothing; looked under guidance—nothing; looked under stabilization—nothing.
e.   Skimmed for suggestions—noted heading on space projects—referred to 20 articles—none relevant.
f.   Tried gravity gradient control—nothing.

The oral protocol (dictation) method was tested at the Whitney Library of the General Electric Company. Two of the investigators, acting as subjects, used the microphone and pocket FM transmitter to record the exact details of their searches. An example of a recorded search narrative appears on page 137.

Another investigation that recorded the actual steps undertaken in a search for information, "Studies in the Man-System Interface in Libraries," was conducted at the Center for the Information Sciences, Lehigh University. One aspect of this project, as reported by Taylor,[42] involved the recording and flowcharting of information-seeking strategies used by a number of undergraduate students taking courses in information science. The aforementioned thesis by Bunge[5] also includes a useful description and flowchart of question-answering procedures.

Any complete study of reference work in a particular library should include some observation of how the reference staff operates, as well as some analysis designed to categorize inquiries by subject, type, date span, sources consulted, and other useful characteristics. Records of inquiries sufficiently detailed to allow this type of analysis are maintained routinely in some libraries. In others, however, they are not sufficiently detailed (if they exist at all), and the investigator must request that more extensive records be maintained for a designated period of time for analysis purposes. Any obtrusive evaluation of reference work can include some detailed observation of the reference staff at work (as Bunge did in his study, for example), but it is difficult to make detailed observations unobtrusively. Much can be learned, however, about the performance of a reference department through some form of unobtrusive observation of the staff in action, coupled with a more detailed analysis of records of reference inquiries conducted in the past.

Evaluation of Literature Searching Activities

Earlier in this chapter, a number of activities performed by reference librarians were mentioned. In terms of direct service to the public, a reference librarian is most concerned with answering questions, assisting patrons in their use of library resources, and conducting literature searches to locate bibliographic materials or to produce a bibliography on a particular subject. As previously mentioned, the staff of a public or an academic library normally will not undertake an extensive literature search for an individual, although such a search might be undertaken to compile a bibliography, perhaps annotated, that could be duplicated or printed for wider distribution. Librarians in these institutions will, however, undertake less extensive searches to find one or more papers, reports, or books on a topic of interest to a user.

Some libraries, on the other hand, particularly industrial libraries, will undertake comprehensive literature searches for individual requesters. The results of such searches may be a set of documents delivered to the user or, more commonly, a list of citations or abstracts for his perusal. Unlike the question-answering situation, results of this type of reference activity cannot be judged dichotomously as correct or incorrect. They must be evaluated by other means. An important criterion is *relevance* to the needs of the user. If a particular search leads to the delivery of 10 journal articles to a requester, he will judge it in terms of how many of the items are directly relevant (or pertinent) to the information need that prompted his request. This can be referred to as the *precision* of the search. For the user who needs only a few papers or reports dealing with a particular topic, the *precision* of the search is perhaps the most important criterion of success, although other criteria will include *response time* (how long he had to wait to get results) and the *amount of effort* he himself had to expend in order to obtain the search results.

But for the requester who is looking for comprehensive results (i.e., trying to collect all the literature on a particular subject), another criterion will be paramount; namely, the *completeness* of the search within a particular collection or data base. This is frequently expressed in terms of *recall* or, more specifically, a *recall ratio*. Suppose that a scientist visits his company library and requests that a search be conducted in *Chemical Abstracts* to locate all relevant papers on a particular substance. Suppose also that, within the last 10 years, 80 papers on this topic were included in *Chemical Abstracts,* but the librarian is able to find only 63 of them. The recall ratio of this particular search is 63/80, or approximately 80%. For the serious research worker who would like to locate all publications on this chemical, this search is far from perfect. It failed to uncover 17 papers, or 20% of the relevant items, and these may include some of the key contributions on the subject.

Unfortunately, the requester usually has no way of knowing how complete a particular search has been. He may have suspicions that it was incomplete, because it did not uncover one or two papers he was previously aware of, but he will have no idea of how incomplete it was. The completeness of a literature search in a particular tool or a particular collection can be estimated only by means of a deliberate test and an analysis of the results. This is an activity that librarians have rarely been willing to undertake. Moreover, for the individual who requires a comprehensive search on a subject, another important consideration is the *coverage* of the collection or data base in which the search is conducted. Even if the reference librarian had been able to find all 80 relevant papers in the hypothetical search in *Chemical Abstracts,* the question arises as to how complete the source is in its coverage of the literature on the subject for which the search was conducted.

Thus, the results of a literature search may be evaluated by various criteria—coverage, recall, precision, response time, and effort. These performance criteria, first mentioned in Chapter 1, have rarely been applied to the evaluation of literature searches conducted in conventional printed tools. More often they have been applied to the evaluation of searches conducted in so-called *information retrieval systems,* especially systems of a mechanized or semimechanized nature. The evaluation of this type of system, and the relevance of these techniques to the more conventional literature searching in printed tools, will be discussed in Chapter 4.

REFERENCES

1. "A Commitment to Information Services: Developmental Guidelines." *RQ*, *14*:24–26, 1974.
2. Beasley, K. E. *A Statistical Reporting System for Local Public Libraries*. University Park, Pennsylvania State University, 1964.
3. Bell, M. V. Personal Communication. March 23, 1973.
4. Breed, P. F. "An Analysis of Reference Procedures in a Large University Library." Masters Dissertation. Chicago, Graduate Library School, University of Chicago, 1955.
5. Bunge, C. A. "Professional Education and Reference Efficiency." Doctoral Thesis. Urbana, Ill., Graduate School of Library Science, University of Illinois, 1967.
6. Campbell, A. and Metzner, C. *Public Use of the Library and of Other Sources of Information*. Revised Edition. Ann Arbor, University of Michigan, Institute for Social Research, 1952.
7. Carlson, G. *Search Strategy by Reference Librarians. Part 3 of Final Report on the Organization of Large Files*. Sherman Oaks, Calif., Advanced Information Systems Division, Hughes Dynamics Inc., 1964. PB 166 192.
8. Childers, T. "Managing the Quality of Reference/Information Service." *Library Quarterly*, *42*:212–217, 1972.
9. Christ, R. W. "Recording Reference Service." *College and Research Libraries*, *8*:23–27, 1947.
10. Cole, D. E. "An Analysis of Adult Reference Work in Libraries." Master's Dissertation. Chicago, Graduate Library School, University of Chicago, 1943.
11. Cole, D. E. "Some Characteristics of Reference Work." *College and Research Libraries*, *7*:45–51, 1946.
12. Cole, P. F. "The Analysis of Reference Question Records as a Guide to the Information Requirements of Scientists." *Journal of Documentation*, *18*:197–207, 1962.
13. Committee on Public Library Service. *Report of the Commissioner of Education's Committee on Public Library Service, 1957*. Albany, State Education Department, University of the State of New York, 1958.
14. Crowley, T. and Childers, T. *Information Service in Public Libraries: Two Studies*. Metuchen, N.J., Scarecrow Press, 1971.
15. *Emerging Library Systems: The 1963–66 Evaluation of the New York State Public Library Systems*. Albany, University of the State of New York, 1967.
16. Goldhor, H. *A Plan for the Development of Public Library Service in the Minneapolis-Saint Paul Metropolitan Area*. Minneapolis, Metropolitan Library Service Agency, 1967.
17. Goldhor, H. "Reference Service Analysis." *Illinois Libraries*, *42*:319–322, 1960.
18. Halperin, M. "Reference Question Sampling." *RQ*, *14*:20–23, 1974.
19. Harlan, H. "Satisfying the Needs of the Community's Library Users." *In: The Library as a Community Information Center*. Champaign, Illini Union Bookstore, 1959, pp. 18–27. Urbana, Graduate School of Library Science, University of Illinois, Allerton Institute No. 4.
20. Herner, S. and Herner, M. "Determining Requirements for Atomic Energy Information from Reference Questions." *Proceedings of the International Conference on Scientific Information*. Washington, D.C., National Academy of Sciences-National Research Council, 1959, pp. 181–187.
21. Hieber, C. E. *An Analysis of Questions and Answers in Libraries*. Bethlehem, Pa., Center for the Information Sciences, Lehigh University, 1966.
22. House, D. E. "Reference Efficiency or Reference Deficiency." *Library Association Record*, *76*:222–223, 1974.

23. Jahoda, G. and Culnan, M. "Unanswered Science and Technology Reference Questions." *American Documentation, 19*:95–100, 1968.

24. Jestes, E. C. and Laird, W. D. "A Time Study of General Reference Work in a University Library." *Research in Librarianship, 2*:9–16, 1968.

25. Jones, W. O. "How Many Reference Librarians Are Enough?" *RQ, 14*:16–19, 1974.

26. King, G. B. and Berry, R. *Evaluation of the University of Minnesota Libraries Reference Department Telephone Information Service, Pilot Study.* Minneapolis, Library School, University of Minnesota, 1973, 58 pp. ED 077 517.

27. Kronick, D. A. "Varieties of Information Requests in a Medical Library." *Bulletin of the Medical Library Association, 52*:652–669, 1964.

28. Martin, L. A. *Library Response to Urban Change: A Study of the Chicago Public Library.* Chicago, American Library Association, 1969, pp. 27–28, 269.

29. Martin, L. A. *Progress and Problems of Pennsylvania Libraries: A Re-Survey.* Pennsylvania State Library Monograph No. 6. Harrisburg, Pennsylvania State Library, 1967.

30. "Measuring the Quality of Public Library Service—Workshop Report." *Branching Out (Newsletter of the Baltimore County Public Library), 10*:1, 2, 5, 1972.

31. Mote, L. J. B. and Angel, N. L. "Survey of Technical Inquiry Records at Thornton Research Centre." *Journal of Documentation, 18*:6–19, 1962.

32. Orr, R. H. and Olson, E. E. *Quantitative Measures as Management Tools.* Materials prepared for use in a continuing education course, CE7, of the Medical Library Association. Chicago, Medical Library Association, 1968.

33. Palmour, V. E. and Gray, L. M. *Costs and Effectiveness of Interlibrary Loan and Reference Activities of Resource Libraries in Illinois.* Springfield, Illinois State Library, 1972, pp. 24–29.

34. Pizer, I. H. and Cain, A. M. "Objective Tests of Library Performance." *Special Libraries, 59*:704–711, 1968.

35. Rothstein, S. "The Measurement and Evaluation of Reference Service." *Library Trends, 12*:456–472, 1964.

36. Sabel, C. S. et al. "Edge-Punched Card Examination of Retrieval Patterns in Information Offices, and Related Investigations." *Journal of Documentation, 18*:111–132, 1962.

37. Shores L. "The Measure of Reference." *Southeastern Librarian, 11*:297–302, 1961.

38. "Something New—Snoop Groups." *Suburban Library News, 7*:1, 1973.

39. Spencer, C. C. "Random Time Sampling with Self-Observation for Library Cost Studies: Unit Costs of Interlibrary Loans and Photocopies at a Regional Medical Library." *Journal of the American Society for Information Science, 22*:153–160, 1971.

40. "Standards for Reference Services in Public Libraries." *Library Association Record, 72*:53–57, 1970.

41. Swope, M. J. and Katzer, J. "The Silent Majority: Why Don't They Ask Questions?" *RQ, 12*:161–166, 1972.

42. Taylor, R. S. *Question-Negotiation and Information-Seeking in Libraries.* Bethlehem, Pa., Center for the Information Sciences, Lehigh University, 1967.

43. Thoreen, B. "Evaluating Reference Service." *Synergy, 42*:14–20, 1973.

44. Torr, D. V. et al. *Program Studies on the Use of Published Indexes.* Bethesda, Md., General Electric Co., 1966. 2 Vols.

45. "Unobtrusive Testing Used in Ohio Survey." *News from State Library of Ohio*:88–89, 1974.

46. Vavrek, B. F. "Communications and the Reference Interface." Doctoral Dissertation. Pittsburgh, Graduate School of Library and Information Science, University of Pittsburgh, 1971.

47. Weech, T. L. "Evaluation of Adult Reference Service." *Library Trends, 22*:315–335, 1974.

48. Whaley, F. R. "Retrieval Questions from the Use of Linde's Indexing and Retrieval System." *Proceedings of the International Conference on Scientific Information.* Washington, D.C., National Academy of Sciences-National Research Council, 1959, pp. 763–769.
49. White, R. W. "Measuring the Immeasurable: Reference Standards." *RQ, 11*:308–310, 1972.

APPENDIX TO CHAPTER 3
NARRATIVE ACCOUNT OF A LITERATURE SEARCH*

QUESTION: Information on Land's color theory as a two-color technique
for presenting color on displays

"I have in mind a display on a television screen. I am not too clear as to
where to start. I'll try to look for an index that will deal primarily with
Vision and Psychology. This library is rather incomplete in these two
areas. So, I'll just have to guess where to look.

"I'll start with the *Applied Science and Technology Index,* and look up
Land, 1964. Then I will look up Color. The headings are not very
extensive here; so I'll check all of the major headings for Color.

"Just quickly scanning, I see under the heading Color Sense an article
by Land in the *American Scientist,* page 247. I am going to list this one
and keep on looking.

"They are not too descriptive as to how they pertain to Land's work. I
will go on to the next heading which is Color Matching. No relevant titles
here. The next one is Color Plastics. Nothing here.

"There is an extensive *See also* section. I have found one good
reference and that only because of the author's name. I will now return
the *Applied Science and Technology Index* to the shelf. I will now pick up
the 1961, 1962, and 1963 copies of *Applied Science and Technology,* also
the most current issues that they have for 1965 of this index.

"In this index, they tend to come out quarterly, and No. 3 is a
cumulative for January, February, and March. This is March 1965 that I
am looking at.

"I will scan Color Architecture, Color Planning, and Color Matching
headings. Nothing here. Now here is one: Color Sense. There is an article
entitled, 'Color Vision' and it's in the *Scientific American.* There is also
another article, 'Three Color Pigment Vision' but that one doesn't seem
relevant. This article on Three Color Pigment Vision seems to be a
commentary on Land's work.

"Now I'll go into the second quarter of 1965 and see what I can find. I'll
check again under Color. Here is Color Matching, Color Measurement,
Color Names, and Color Photography. Now, I'll go into the September
1965. Color Codes, Color Matching, Color Measurement, Color Photography. The October 1965 is only for one month. This index comes out
every month and then every three months. There is a cumulative index of

*Reproduced from Torr et al.[44]

the preceding three months. Then, also at the end of the year, there is an annual cumulation.

"Well, since there is nothing here in 1965, I'll go back to 1962 of the *Applied Science and Technology Index*. I'll look under Color here at a heading called Dichroism. So let me check the titles to see if it pertains to my particular area. No, it doesn't. So I am going to drop this particular heading and return to the heading of Color.

"Color Coding, Color Filters, Color Matching, Color Measurements, Color Photography, Color Sense.

"Color Sense seems to be the most appropriate one.I would imagine that it would have most of the psychology articles under the heading of Color Sense.

"Well, 1962 does not have any relevant titles, so I will go back to 1961. Check Color Sense this time. There is no heading in the 1961 Color Sense.

"So I'll just start again under the heading of Color. Now, here they have a *See also*, and maybe I'll look under Color Measurement heading. Well, no titles here are relevant. Color Photography; now, here is one: 'Land's System of Two-Color Projection' by Wilson. This is in a *British Institute of Engineering Journal*. Here is another one: 'Range of Colors Cited by a Two-Color Reproduction System'; this is in a *British Institute of Radio Engineers (sic)*.

"Well, I guess that the heading Color Photography is better than I thought.

"Now, I am going to the 1963 *Science and Technology Index (sic)*. This time I will look both under Color Photography and Color Sense. I'll now go to the heading of Color Photography. Check each of the titles. None of the titles seem to have any relevance to Land's work. Before I go out into the stacks, I'll take another look around the Index Room to see if any of the indexes by title will be relevant to my question area. In order to provide some other relevant journals. The Index Room is heavily steeped in the chemical area.

"Here is one. I'll try *Dissertation Abstracts*. I'll look under the heading of Color. Here is a heading that looks pertinent: Color Psychology, and also Color Sense. There are titles underneath each of these headings. I'll see which of them pertains to Land's work; since my interest is only in the very current work, I'll turn to the 1964 index of the *Dissertation Abstracts* and I'll also get the first 6 months of the 1965s. Look under Color Psychology and Color Sense. Looking under these particular titles, nothing seems to be relevant at all. So I'll drop this abstract and see if I can find anything else in this room.

"Well, I can't find anything else in the Abstract Room, so I'll go into the stacks. Look for 4 relevant articles that I have located. First, I'll look for the *British Institute of Radio Engineers Journal*. The journals are alphabetically listed on the shelf. Here it is. Since I am here in the stacks, will also get the issues of *Scientific American* that I need and I'll take them all back into the Index Room to find the particular articles.

"I am now looking through the *British Institute of Radio Engineers (sic)*, June 1961. Here is one that I wanted on color. It seems to be a *Proceedings* that were held in England. I'll look at the remaining part of that issue and see if there is anything else that might be relevant. Here is an article about colors that are excited by a two-color reproduction system.

"Now I will find the other articles. I will now look in the *Scientific American*, December 1964. This article seems pertinent to Color. Now I am looking up in the *American Scientist*, June 1964. Here it is, and it looks like a good short description of Land's Theory.

"Now as a means of finding out about current work in this area, I'll list some of the authors from the list of references of the two articles I had found that were relevant. Here is one that includes a cycle numerical of 1959, for the National Academy of Science. Looks like an appropriate title. Here is one on Color and Perception in the *Contemporary Physics*. Here is one in the *Psych. Bulletin* by Wald. Judd also wrote an article in the *Journal of Optical Society of America*.

"Now, let's see, Land also makes some references to his own work. These go back into the 30s and the early 40s so I won't get to them since they only probably contain the historical background for his work.

"Now, I'll go the *British Institute of Radio Engineers Journal*. Here is the article by Wilson, and I'll look at the list of references. They refer to Land's article in the *International Academy of Science (sic)*. So this is one article I really must get.

"Now here is an article that Land also referred to in *Nature*, and they also list Wald's article, which I must also get. Now, I feel that I have a group of references that will be particularly valuable. One is Wald's article in *Psych. Bulletin* which several authors refer to.

"A *Science American (sic)* article by Land which two authors refer to, and the issue of the *Journal of Photographic Society*. Now, I am going back into the stacks again to get the specific issues that I had found in a list of references of the original four articles I have found from referring to the indexes.

"I am going to look up the articles that I found in the stacks, the journals of which I found in the stacks. The first is the *Optical Society of America (sic)*, 1960, Judd's articles, an appraisal of Land's work. This is an excellent article. Now one in *Contemporary Physics*. Here is one 'Color Image Synthesis'; this one is in *Nature*, 1959. Now, looking at the *Scientific American;* this is the first article that started it all. This one, I think, is appropriate for my requirement and I'll read it until I have enough information for my question."

4

Evaluation of Literature Searching and Information Retrieval

This chapter will discuss, in relatively general terms, criteria by which any type of literature-searching activity, manual or mechanized, can be evaluated. It also will briefly touch upon evaluation methodology. "Literature searching" here means any activity in which a search of the literature is conducted to find bibliographic material on a particular subject. The search may be performed in a "conventional" manner, using card catalogs, printed indexes, and other manual tools; or it may be conducted less conventionally, using a subject index in a form that is not completely manual. The most sophisticated and "least manual" of such approaches would involve an index stored in machine-readable form, searched via a computer; that is, a computer-based information retrieval system. The end product of a completely manual literature search is likely to be a group of actual documents delivered to the requester, although it may be simply a typed list of references to, or abstracts of, documents. The end product of a machine literature search is likely to be a printed list of citations or abstracts that satisfy some logical search requirement—such list generated on a computer high-speed printer or some other piece of equipment peripheral to a computer installation.

Performance Criteria

The major criteria by which any type of information service will be evaluated by its users are presented in Table 39, a somewhat expanded version of the list presented in Chapter 1. Note that information services, like most other services, generally will be evaluated in terms of time, cost, and quality factors. "Cost" does not necessarily mean monetary cost; although, if the information service does charge its users directly, the actual cost of the service will be an important characteristic by which the service will be judged. In cases where no direct charge is made for service, other types of "cost" factors still are important. One of these is the amount of *effort* a user must expend (a) in using the system (and in learning how to use it), (b) in interpreting the form of output provided by the system (some forms will require more effort than others, especially in trying to identify the documents that are actually relevant in lists of document representations delivered by the system), and (c) in obtaining the actual documents referred to by the system.

TABLE 39 Criteria by Which Users Evaluate Information Services

---

Cost

    Direct charges
    Effort involved in use
      Ease of interrogating system
      Form of output provided
      Backup document delivery capability

Response Time

Quality Considerations

    Coverage (completeness)
    Recall
    Precision
    Novelty
    Accuracy of data—completeness and accuracy of response

Cost-Effectiveness (i.e., the relationship between cost and quality)

    Cost per relevant document or reference supplied
    Cost per new relevant document or reference supplied
      (i.e., novelty-cost ratio)

Cost-Benefit Considerations

While it is relatively easy to observe the cost and time factors of an information service, it is difficult to measure its quality and, consequently, the relationship between cost and quality (i.e., the cost-effectiveness of the service). Several measures of quality are shown in Table 39. Completeness and accuracy of response, as indicated in Chapter 3, are the major criteria by which the effectiveness of reference service can be evaluated when a single factual answer is sought. But in the evaluation of literature searching, when there is no single correct answer, other measures of quality must be sought. Recall and precision are two such measures.

Whether a literature search is manual or mechanized, and whether the end results are actual documents or some form of document surrogate, its performance can be evaluated against the same principal criteria. The results of any literature search can be depicted in a 2 × 2 table, as illustrated in Table 40.

To clarify this table, consider a user coming to a library or other information center to find bibliographic materials on a particular subject, general or specific. A finite number of items are "relevant" to his information need; that is, were this library user to look at every item in the collection, he would consider relatively few (in relation to the total collection) relevant and the others (the great majority of the collection)

TABLE 40   Results of a Literature Search

	Relevant	Not Relevant	Total
Retrieved	a HITS	b NOISE	a + b Total Retrieved
Not Retrieved	c MISSES	d Correctly Rejected	c + d Total Not Retrieved
Total	a + c Total Relevant	b + d Total Not Relevant	a + b + c + d Total Collection

not relevant to his information need. "Relevance" is a personal quality; that is, each user will have a different interpretation of what is and what is not "relevant" to his information need. In this discussion, the assumption will be that the user is the sole judge of relevance. (It should be recognized, however, that many factors influence relevance decisions, and that the subject of relevance has generated a great deal of argument and literature reflecting this argument.) The user would like to find the relevant items in the collection (or at least some of them) with a minimum of effort on his part and usually with the least possible delay. These user requirements exist regardless of the "data base" or collection being searched—the book collection of a library, one or more printed indexes (e.g., *Chemical Abstracts* or *Resources in Education*), or a machine-based retrieval system (e g , the MEDLARS service of the National Library of Medicine). For the purposes of evaluation, the situation is complicated by a number of factors, the most important of which are:

1. That users have different "recall" requirements.
2. That, in some cases, the information seeker will conduct his own search (e.g., in the library catalog or in one or more printed indexes) and, in other cases, the search will be conducted for him by a librarian or other information specialist.

The "recall ratio" of a search, as discussed in Chapter 3, is the proportion of all relevant items in a particular collection or data base that the search is able to retrieve. Referring again to Table 40, the recall ratio is expressed by the fraction $a/(a + c)$. If a library holds 15 books on a particular subject, and the user finds 12 of these, but misses the other 3, the recall ratio of his search is 12/15, or 80%.

Change the situation somewhat and hypothesize that a user is conducting a search in the printed index *Resources in Education* for reports discussing a specific aspect of the teaching of reading. If the user were omniscient, he would know that this index cites 18 reports that he would consider directly relevant to his information need. But he is not omniscient. So he must conduct his search for these items by looking under the subject terms (descriptors) that appear to be most appropriate. He locates 13 of the 18 reports, but he misses the other 5; the recall ratio achieved is 13/18, or approximately 72%. The recall ratio would be equally valid if, instead of conducting his own search, he had delegated the search responsibility to a librarian or other information specialist. Suppose, instead, he requests a computer-based search of the machine-readable *Resources in Education* data base. A search strategy prepared by an information specialist is used to conduct the search, and the results—a machine listing of citations that match this strategy—are delivered to the user. If this machine search retrieved 13 of the 18 relevant citations, the recall ratio again is 72%.

As previously mentioned, the user, when evaluating any type of retrieval "system," whether it be a library catalog, a printed index, or a computer-based service, will be concerned with its ability to retrieve relevant items (recall), with the amount of effort he must expend, and with elapsed time. Every user will require some recall (except in comparatively rare situations, when the search is conducted to confirm that nothing exists), otherwise, presumably, he would not have approached the system. But recall requirements will vary among users. The person searching *Resources in Education* may have a high recall requirement; he would like to find all the relevant references contained in this data base, and might be dissatisfied if he knew he had missed 30% of the relevant reports. The recall ratio, expressed in absolute terms, is a very meaningful measure of the success of his search. But the typical user approaching a library for books on a particular subject might not require a comprehensive search. It is more likely that he will want to find *some* relevant books, but not all of them. Absolute recall is meaningless in this case. The user may find 3 books (out of a total of 18 in the collection) that are relevant to and that completely satisfy his need. He will not be too concerned that he has overlooked the other 15 relevant books, unless the items he has missed are in some sense "better" than those he found (i.e., more directly relevant or up-to-date).

Even when a person requires a comprehensive search, recall is not the only criterion by which the results should be evaluated. Time and effort also are important considerations because, presumably, if the user is prepared to work assiduously and long enough, eventually he will find all relevant items in the "system" and will achieve 100% recall. The efficiency of a search, regardless of the system used, must, therefore, be judged by the amount of effort expended and how long it takes to achieve a particular level of recall, whether it be three books or all of the relevant references in a particular index or machine-readable data base.

It is in the measurement of time and effort that the delegated search (in which the information seeker does not conduct his own search) differs most from the nondelegated search. In the latter situation, user effort may be equated directly with elapsed time; that is, how long it takes the user to identify a number of seemingly relevant items in the library catalog and then to find the actual items on the shelves, or how long it takes him to search the printed *Resources in Education* before he finally identifies 15 relevant reports. One method of measuring the efficiency of a nondelegated search (whether conducted in the catalog and collections of a library, a printed index, or an on-line information retrieval system) would be to divide the total searching time by the total number of relevant items discovered, thus producing a *unit cost* (in time) per relevant item found. For example, if it takes the library user 15 minutes to find three relevant books, the unit cost (in time) would be five minutes per item.

Suppose, on the other hand, that a delegated search is being evaluated. Here the search is conducted on behalf of the user by a librarian or other information specialist, and the results will be delivered to the user at a later time. In this case, a user cost (in time) cannot be derived directly. Instead, the success of the delegated search is measured in terms of the recall ratio, the response time (time elapsing between submission of the search request and receipt of the results), and the relevance of the results.

Relevance of search results requires further explanation. When a delegated search is conducted, the user may look upon the system as a "black box" into which he places his request and out of which, eventually, he receives a group of documents or, at least, references to them. The amount of direct user effort is relatively minor; it consists of negotiating his requirement with the system (e.g., discussing his information need with a librarian). The user will judge the results of the search primarily by their relevance to his requirement and secondarily by how long it took to get the results. In the delegated search situation, it is customary and meaningful to express the relevance of results in terms of the proportion of items (whether actual documents or references to them) retrieved and delivered that the requester judges relevant. This proportion frequently is referred to as a *precision ratio*. In Table 40, the precision ratio is expressed as a/(a + b). To illustrate, suppose a scientist asks his company librarian to undertake a comprehensive literature search in *Chemical Abstracts* (*CA*) on a specific topic. The results of this search are presented to him a few days later, either as a typed list of references or photocopies of abstracts appearing in *CA*—a total of 65 references. After examining the retrieved references, he judges 41 to be relevant to his information need and the remaining 24 not relevant, a precision ratio of 41/65, or approximately 63%. The precision ratio, then, is a valid measure of the performance of any type of delegated search in which the information seeker submits a request to some "system" and awaits the results, whether the search is manual or fully mechanized.

Note that the precision ratio actually is an indirect measure of user time and effort; that is, the higher the precision ratio (proportion of relevant items among the total retrieved), the less effort the user will need to expend in separating relevant items from those that are not relevant. In a search of very low precision ratio, in which, say, only 10 items among 80 retrieved are relevant, considerable user time and effort might be required to identify the relevant items in a printed or typed list, especially if this list contains only bibliographic citations, and the user must retrieve copies of many of the documents before he can decide which are and which are not relevant.

The precision ratio is not especially meaningful when applied to the nondelegated search. Here, the user conducts his own search and makes relevance decisions continually as he proceeds; that is, when he consults a subject heading in a catalog or printed index, he rejects irrelevant citations and records only those that are relevant. A precision ratio could be derived from this type of search by counting the total number of citations the user consulted in the catalog or index and the number he judged relevant, the precision ratio being: number of relevant citations found/total number of citations consulted. This is a rather artificial measurement, however, because user effort in the nondelegated search situation can be measured more directly by the time required to conduct the search and, from this, determining the unit cost (in time) per relevant item found. Presumably, the higher the precision of a nondelegated search (proportion of relevant items examined to the total items examined), the less time it will take, all other things being equal.

Four performance criteria by which any type of literature search may be evaluated from the viewpoint of user satisfaction have been discussed thus far: recall, precision, response time, and user effort. The salient points of these performance measures are:

Recall. Important to all users of information services who are seeking bibliographic materials on a particular subject. In some cases, only a minimum level of recall is required (e.g., one book or "about three books" on a particular subject), and this is likely to be the typical situation for a user consulting the library catalog. In other cases, maximum recall is sought (e.g., the user who wants a comprehensive search conducted in *Chemical Abstracts*).

Precision. A meaningful measure of the performance of a delegated search conducted in any form of system, manual or mechanized. It is an indirect measure of user time and effort—not particularly appropriate in the evaluation of nondelegated searches.

User effort. In a nondelegated search, effort is measured by the amount of time the user spends conducting the search. In a delegated search, it is measured by the amount of time the user spends negotiating his inquiry with the system and by the amount of time he will need, when the search results are delivered to him, to separate the relevant items from those that are not relevant (which is directly influenced by the precision ratio).

Response time. In a delegated search, this represents the elapsed time between submission of a request by the user and his receipt of the search results. In a nondelegated situation, it represents the time involved in the actual conduct of the search; in this case, it also is a measure of user effort.

Chapter 1 discusses two other performance criteria which have been applied in the evaluation of information retrieval systems; namely, *coverage* and *form of output*. Coverage actually is an extension of recall; it is expressed in terms of how much literature coverage is provided on a specific subject by a particular collection. Suppose, for example, that a scientist wishes to find all possible references to the use of lasers in eye surgery. An obvious source would be the printed *Index Medicus* or, even better, the computer-based MEDLINE service operated by the National Library of Medicine. Suppose also that the search in both sources retrieves everything of relevance (i.e., achieves 100% recall)—a rather unlikely situation. Even if the search *is* complete, so far as the data base is concerned, the user who needs a really comprehensive search also will want to know the exact coverage of this data base (i.e., what proportion of all the literature on eye surgery using lasers is contained in the data base). Searching a particular data base may result in 100% recall, but may be low in overall coverage of the literature. Absolute coverage of the collection is only of direct concern to the person who needs a comprehensive search. It is probable that the user whose need is satisfied by finding, on the library shelves, one or two books on a subject of interest is quite unconcerned as to how complete the library's collection may be in this subject area. At a later time, however, he may require a comprehensive search on this or some other topic, and the coverage of the collection consulted would then be important to him. Coverage, like recall and precision, can be expressed as a percentage. If, for example, the results of a search conducted in *Chemical Abstracts* were being evaluated, it could be estimated (although not easily) that the recall ratio is 75%; it also could be estimated (even less easily) that the coverage in *Chemical Abstracts* of the subject area of the search is 40%. With an estimated coverage of 40% and recall of 75%, the overall estimate of the comprehensiveness of the search is 30%.

Form of output is the form in which the results of a search are presented to a user, which could be the actual documents, or microfiche copies, abstracts, full bibliographic citations, titles, or other forms of these items. This is not a performance measure that is quantifiable, but it is certainly a factor affecting user satisfaction. The form in which bibliographic information is presented is especially important to the user in judging the relevance of particular items to his information need. If he is looking through a listing (e.g., printed bibliography or machine printout) containing abstracts, it should be easier for him to decide which items are relevant than if the citations only are given. Generally, the more complete the information supplied, the easier it will be to judge the relevance of the item and, in the case of a delegated search, the lower the precision ratio that the user will tolerate.

Another performance measure that may have some value is the *novelty ratio* (the proportion of relevant items retrieved in a search that are new to the requester, that is, brought to his attention for the first time by the search). The novelty ratio is particularly appropriate in the evaluation of literature searches conducted for current-awareness purposes, for example, some form of Selective Dissemination of Information (SDI).

Considerable effort has been expended in the last 15 years on the evaluation of information retrieval systems, with special emphasis on mechanized systems. This work has been covered by Lancaster,[14,16] in both complete and summary form, and will not be repeated here, except in very general terms. A comprehensive evaluation of a literature searching service, in this case MEDLARS, can be found in another report by Lancaster.[15] Evaluations of information retrieval systems usually have been based on the performance criteria discussed earlier in this chapter, although some investigators have used variations of the recall ratio/precision ratio combination (i.e., different methods of expressing the results shown in the 2 × 2 table illustrated in Table 40).

The aforementioned performance measures are potentially relevant in the following library applications:

1. The evaluation of literature searches conducted by members of the library staff using conventional printed bibliographic tools.
2. The evaluation of literature searches conducted by members of the library staff using on-line computer-based systems.
3. The evaluation of subject searches conducted in the card catalog by staff or users of the library.
4. The evaluation of a service offered by some outside information center.
5. The evaluation of a printed bibliographic tool.

Before examining each of these possibilities further, it might be well to reemphasize that diagnosis should be the major objective of any type of evaluation program; that is, through microevaluation the user should seek to discover how a particular service is operating and to identify the major factors contributing to failures in the system. Once failures have been identified, the library can make decisions as to how some of them might be avoided in the future. The remainder of this chapter will focus on the diagnostic evaluation of literature-searching activities.

Evaluation of Literature Searches

As previously mentioned, while industrial and certain other special libraries are willing to undertake comprehensive literature searches for their users, which result in the production of bibliographies, such searches are far less common in public and academic libraries. This situation may be changing, in academic libraries at least, through the increasing availability of on-line bibliographic systems, such as the MEDLINE service operated by the National Library of Medicine, and the services now offered commercially by Lockheed, the System Development Corporation, Bibliographic Retrieval Services, and other retailers of information. Many libraries have on-line terminals connected, via telephone lines, to one of these service centers, through which they routinely undertake fairly complex and comprehensive bibliographic searches of the recent literature on behalf of their patrons. Some libraries also offer a computer-based current-awareness service, Selective Dissemination of Information (SDI), tailored to the needs of individual users. While medical libraries have been at the forefront of these developments, other types of libraries have followed suit as additional on-line bibliographic systems have become more widely available.

Whether using conventional printed indexes or an on-line terminal, a literature search, conducted for a library user by a librarian, can be evaluated against the criteria discussed heretofore. *Precision* can be determined by submitting search results to the requester and having him decide which of the retrieved items are and which are not relevant to his information need. It would be preferable to design some type of form to record the relevance decisions. Why the user judges certain items to be relevant and others not relevant also is important.

Response time (how long the user must wait to obtain the results of the search) is easily recorded. The major problem in evaluating any type of literature search is the estimation of *recall*, but, as previously explained, this is of real importance only when the user requires a comprehensive search.

Although it is unlikely that the absolute recall ratio can be determined for an actual search in any data base (the situation is even more complicated when trying to determine recall for a search in multiple data bases), there are a number of ways in which recall can be estimated. Various possible techniques have been discussed by Lancaster.[14,16]

Perhaps the most viable technique in the typical library situation is to compare the actual search against one or more searches conducted solely for the purpose of evaluation. Suppose that a particular literature search conducted for a library user is to be evaluated. When the search has been completed, and the results are presented to the requester, he is asked to cooperate in the evaluation of the search. First, he is asked to examine the citations delivered and to assess their relevance. This provides a precision ratio for the search. Next, the written statement of the user's information need (it is always desirable to have this in the user's own words) is given to one or two additional members of the library staff, and they are asked to conduct a literature search on the same subject. The results of these "parallel" searches are pooled and compared with the results of the original search; any new citations (i.e., those not listed in the original results) are identified and submitted to the requester for assessment of relevance. Using this technique, an estimated recall ratio for the original search can be developed, as follows:

$$\text{Recall ratio of search A} = \frac{\text{Number of relevant items found by searcher A}}{\text{Total number of unique relevant items found by A, B, and C combined}}$$

Note that the results of the second and third searches are not being evaluated, but are merely being used as a means for estimating the performance of the first search.

To clarify the purpose of this type of evaluation even further, suppose that A—a member of the staff of an industrial library—has conducted a search, for a scientist who needs a comprehensive bibliography on some specific topic, and has found 42 citations that he deems to be relevant. The list of citations is submitted to the requester, who judges 25 to be relevant. The precision ratio of the search, which took three hours of staff time over a two-day period, is 25/42, or almost 60%. Two other staff members, B and C, conduct separate searches on the same topic. Together they find 18 items that they deem to be relevant which were not found by A. These 18 items are submitted to the requester, who judges 12 to be relevant. The recall estimate for the original search conducted by A would then be 25/(25 + 12), or approximately 67%. This is really an *upper bound* estimate of the recall of A's search. The assumption is that the sum of all the relevant references found by A, B, and C, using the full resources of the library, is the total of relevant references that can be located in this particular collection of bibliographic resources. This assumption may not be completely valid; that is, there may be some additional relevant items that were not found by any of the three searchers. For evaluation purposes, it is not always essential, however, to determine absolute recall. In fact, it is extremely difficult to do so and, when possible, requires a considerable expenditure of effort. The comparative recall estimate, derived as described above, will be adequate for most purposes.

The fact that the precision estimate for this search is 60%, and the recall estimate 67%, is less important than the fact that some searching "failures" have been identified. In particular, searcher A was unable to locate 12 relevant citations. These must be regarded as definite failures, because the library user required a comprehensive search. The 17 citations that the user considered not relevant also may be regarded as failures, although the precision failures are less important than the recall failures.

The important diagnostic purpose of the evaluation is served by making an analysis to determine why the failures occurred. If reasons for failures can be identified, perhaps some corrective action can be taken to avoid similar failures in the future. Presumably, the precision failures in this case are largely due to the searcher's misinterpretation of what the user really wanted; possibly because of inadequate interaction with the user at the time he made his request or because the librarian did not completely understand the subject matter. Inadequate interaction or lack of complete understanding of the subject matter also might have contributed to some or all of the recall failures. It is more likely, however, that the failures were caused by an imperfect search strategy on the part of the librarian, who may not have checked all of the appropriate bibliographic tools or may have overlooked some relevant subject headings in one or more of the indexes consulted. If, using the results of all three searches (A, B, and C), A's search can be reconstructed, noting apparent failures to use a particular index or to check all appropriate headings, it may be possible to determine how to reduce such failures in the future. If this type of analysis is undertaken for a significant number of searches, involving several members of the library staff, a fairly clear picture can be formed of how the library is performing its literature-searching function and what might be done to improve future performance. Corrective action might involve the development of better procedures for interacting with the requester to determine precisely what is wanted, the reallocation of searches to staff members in subject areas each is most qualified to handle, or the additional training of certain staff members. Training might involve instruction on the capabilities of useful, but neglected, tools (e.g., *Science Citation Index*), instruction in techniques for developing a systematic searching strategy, instruction on searching particular subject areas, or instruction in techniques of using a particular source (e.g., *Biological Abstracts*).

It is important to recognize, however, that some possible causes of searching failures are beyond the control of the library. Such failures, which may be termed *data base failures*, are due to indexing or vocabulary inadequacies in published bibliographic tools (e.g., it may be found that some recall failures in a particular search occurred because an index used by the searcher was inadequately cross-referenced). Although the library has no direct control of such areas, it still may be useful to identify this source of failure and to be aware of such weaknesses and limitations in the available tools.

The scope of this type of evaluation might be expanded to consider certain coverage factors. For example, a search could be extended into the resources of another, larger library, thus enabling the librarian to identify useful bibliographic tools that are missing from his own collection. Another aspect of coverage would be the proportion of articles judged relevant (in a group of literature searches) that the library can supply from its own resources. If this proportion is small, it may indicate inadequacies in the library's holdings of the primary literature on a particular subject.

The same procedures that are used in the evaluation of a literature search conducted by a librarian in the printed bibliographic tools held by a library also would be applicable to the evaluation of a search conducted in an on-line retrieval system. In fact, the latter situation is somewhat simpler, because only a single data base is involved. The same would be true for the evaluation of a search conducted in a single printed tool (e.g., *Engineering Index*).

Evaluation of Printed Bibliographic Tools

There are times when a librarian may wish to evaluate a particular printed indexing or abstracting publication (e.g., when a new and expensive tool appears and the librarian must decide if it is sufficiently useful to merit a subscription). The aforementioned criteria and techniques would be applicable, with some modification, for this type of investigation. Actually, comparatively little work has been done on the systematic evaluation of published indexes, although Lancaster[17] and Torr et al.[21] have discussed possible procedures, and Farradane and Yates-Mercer[10] have applied systematic evaluation methods, on a limited scale, to the *Metals Abstracts Index*.

From the librarian's viewpoint, perhaps the most important criterion in the evaluation of a published index is its *coverage*. A second important factor, however, relates to the ease with which a searcher can use the index to locate relevant references on a topic (i.e., its recall capabilities): an index could be comprehensive in its coverage of a subject, but almost impossible to use in the retrieval of citations on this subject, because of inadequate indexing.

It is possible to evaluate a printed index, in terms of coverage and ease of use, by means of a controlled test. One way of achieving this is through the use of specialized bibliographies in subject areas within its stated scope. Review articles are good sources of such bibliographies. Suppose one wants to determine how comprehensive *Index Medicus* is in its coverage of a particular area of medicine, say, nutrition disorders. This can be accomplished easily by locating one or more review articles covering specific aspects of this subject in the *Bibliography of Medical Reviews*. The more review articles located, and the more complete they are, the better they will fulfill this purpose. Suppose three recent review articles covering various aspects of nutrition disorders are found and that, collectively, they cite 120 unique papers in various sources. These citations are then used to assess the extent to which *Index Medicus* (*IM*) covers the literature of this subject field; that is, each citation is checked against the author index of *IM* to determine which items are and which are not included until, eventually, the proportion of the 120 citations covered by this index is known.

To undertake a comprehensive evaluation of the coverage of a particular index, it will be necessary to obtain several well-chosen review articles representing various facets of the subject matter under consideration. For example, a comprehensive study might be made of the coverage of the *Current Index to Journals in Education* (*CIJE*) through the use of, say, 12 review articles, each in some specific area of education. The same technique can be used to compare the coverage of two or more indexes. One or more specialized bibliographies could be used to compare, for example, the coverage of *CIJE* with the coverage of *Education Index*. Some interesting and valuable studies of the coverage of indexing and abstracting publications, notably by Martyn and Slater,[19] Davison and Matthews,[7] and Bourne,[2,3] have already been conducted, using a technique similar to, or identical with, the aforementioned method. Interestingly enough, the coverage of some of the major published tools has been found far from complete.

Specialized bibliographies also can be used to study the efficiency of printed tools in literature-searching activities (i.e., their ability to allow retrieval of relevant citations and the factors of time and effort involved in conducting a search). First, take a bibliography already used in studying the coverage of the printed index. We already know whether or not each item in this bibliography is included in the index (this was established by checking the author section of the index). Now study the scope of the bibliography (those attached to review articles are likely to be carefully defined) and write a full statement of the scope in the form of a request for a literature search. Next, ask a member of the library staff to conduct a search on this subject in the appropriate index, in accordance with the request statement. The staff member should be given a special form on which to record, in sequence, the subject headings consulted, a brief identification of each citation selected as relevant under these headings, and the time taken to conduct the search. A data-collection form of this type, as used by Torr et al.[21] in the study of *Index Medicus,* is shown in Figure 24.

Since this case concerns the evaluation of a printed index rather than the ability of one particular searcher, it is highly desirable that the entire process be repeated with several searchers. The results can then be averaged so that the variable of the individual searcher is reduced.

Index:

SUBJECT:

J. P.

Index Medicus   YEAR: ___1963___

Heading	Author (Last Name)	Article Title (first 3 words)
Start Time 9:30		
Eye	Beaver Crompton Goldsmith	The quantitative evaluation Avoidance of the Fine structure of
Eye Injuries	Gordon Howsam	The management of Injuries of the
Eye Manifestations	Fujii Hertzberg	Eye symptoms in Ocular signs
Eye Neoplasms	—	—
Facial Injuries	Gaisford	Airway maintenance of
End Time 10:10		

FIGURE 24   Sample form used in the evaluation of a printed index.[21]

As a result of these procedures, various measures of the performance of the index may be derived:

1. An estimate of recall, based on the proportion of known relevant items retrieved by these searches. Suppose, for example, that 37 relevant items are known to be contained in the index (these 37 were items included in the original bibliography and confirmed to be in the printed tool through checking of the author index). The results of, say, three separate searchers are averaged, indicating that they were able to locate 31/37 of these citations, a recall ratio of approximately 84%.

2. An average precision ratio for the searches. To obtain a precision ratio, it is necessary to know the total of relevant citations found by a particular searcher. Because it is likely that the searcher will have found relevant citations over and above those appearing in the original bibliography, each citation selected by the searcher (and recorded on his data form) will have to be assessed for relevance. This is not as easy as it sounds, because it requires some knowledge of the subject matter, and it may require an examination of the actual articles cited or, at least, abstracts of them. The assessments should be made by someone other than the original searchers. This relevance "judge" may be someone on the library staff with technical expertise, or it may be an independent subject specialist. Perhaps the best way of performing this operation would be to give the judge a copy of the original bibliography and ask him to base his relevance decisions on the same criteria, as far as possible (i.e., to select, as relevant, items that seem to be completely appropriate to the subject matter as "defined" by the scope of the original bibliography). When the relevance assessments are made, the precision ratio may be derived in one of two ways: (a) by dividing the total number of relevant citations found in a search by the total number of citations *selected* by the searcher and recorded on his data form, or (b) by dividing the total number of relevant citations found in a search by the total number of citations *consulted* by the searcher. This will require a count of the total number of citations appearing under all the headings consulted in the index. These two alternative procedures will provide precision ratios that essentially measure different things. The second is actually a measure of the specificity of the subject terms used in the index. To take a very simplistic example, the search may have been conducted on the subject of heart transplantation, but the most appropriate term in the index is TRANSPLANTATION. The searcher must look through all of the citations in order to identify those that appear to deal with heart transplants. In a large index, this may be a time-consuming operation, and most of the citations consulted may not be relevant to heart transplants (i.e., precision will be

low).* In the first procedure, the precision ratio is influenced both by the specificity of the vocabulary and by the ability of the searcher to recognize relevant citations. The second method, then, is a better reflection of the properties of the index itself, reducing the variable of the individual searcher.

3. As mentioned earlier in this chapter, the precision ratio is a measure of user effort. A better and more direct measure of effort in this case is searching time. If the total time taken in a search is divided by the total number of relevant citations found in that search, it will result in a unit cost (in time) per relevant citation found.

By the methods discussed above, using a number of bibliographies and several searching staff, it should be possible to conduct a comprehensive evaluation of any printed index—both its coverage and its efficiency as a searching tool (measured in terms of the recall it provides and the accompanying precision or unit cost per relevant citation retrieved).

These procedures can be used to compare the value of several indexes covering essentially the same subject area. By means of a diagnostic analysis, it also would be possible to identify causes of searching failures. Perhaps most important is identifying the reasons why all known relevant citations were not retrieved in a particular search (i.e., recall failures). Although some of these failures may be due to poor searching strategies, others may be caused by imperfect or inadequate indexing in the tool studied, or perhaps by the wide scattering of related material without adequate cross-referencing. Carroll,[5] for example, reported that abstracts of papers related to virology were found in no less than 20 sections of *Biological Abstracts*.

From the librarian's viewpoint, the purpose of an evaluation of this type is to assess and compare the practical value of particular indexing or abstracting publications as literature-searching tools. The producer of an index (which may be a library) could use this type of study for diagnostic purposes—to identify causes of failure or inefficiency and to indicate ways in which effectiveness might be improved (e.g., by a more specific vocabulary; by indexing in greater depth, that is, providing more access points per item; or by more extensive cross-referencing).

Although the procedures described in this section are similar to those in the preceding section, the purpose of the investigations is different in each case. Earlier, we were concerned with "actual" searches—how effec-

---

*A variation on this precision measure, as described in Chapter 2, is the *expected search length*.

tively a library staff performs literature-searching activities under normal operating conditions (including the use of printed indexes, if appropriate). Here, we are concerned with the evaluation of printed indexes *per se* under reasonably controlled conditions, the object being to compare the performance of different indexes and (in the case of a publisher) to determine how an index might be improved.

Some interesting studies of printed indexes have been reported in the literature, mostly from the viewpoint of coverage. Davison and Matthews[7] report on one such investigation, in which the topic "computers related to mass spectrometry," for which 183 unique references were known, was searched in 12 of the major indexes to chemistry and spectroscopy. The most interesting results were:

1. No one source located more than 40% of the known references.

2. The world's largest chemical indexes, *Referativyni Zhurnal Khimii, Chemical Abstracts,* and *Chemisches Zentralblatt,* produced only 5.5%, 24%, and 4.5% of the references, respectively.

3. The 24% retrieval from *CA* was obtained only by checking every item, in three years of the indexes, under terms indicating mass spectrometry and also terms indicating computers. This required checking approximately 5,000 items, or 10 hours of work. Direct look-up (of the association between computers and spectrometry) provided only approximately half the number of references. In other words, the precision of the search in *CA* was approximately 44/5,000, or less than 1%, while the unit cost (in time) per relevant citation retrieved was approximately 13½ minutes (44 citations found in 10 hours).

4. All the references from *Chemisches Zentralblatt* were unique to that source, because they were so out-of-date that none of the other sources covered them in the period searched.

5. Searching of *Chemical Titles* (*CT*), simulating a computer search of *CT* tapes, retrieved 11.5% of the total references found—just a little more than one-fourth of the retrieval from the best source.

This was a most interesting study that considered the problems of "findability" (recall) as well as those of coverage.

Elliott[9] compares *Psychological Abstracts* (*PA*) with *Bulletin Signaletique* (*BS*) on the basis of coverage, number and subject distribution of abstracts, and publication delay. *Psychological Abstracts* was found to be superior on all counts. Elliott concludes that, for English-speaking organizations, *BS* is only useful in complementing *PA* in coverage of European journals in medicine, the humanities, and ornithology. This investigator, however, does not consider the important aspect of findability. Perhaps it is easier to search in *BS* and, therefore, to find relevant citations at reduced cost (in search time). Moreover, Elliott makes no reference to how the publications are used. Since both tools probably are used more for retrospective searching than for current awareness, the factor of publication delay may be somewhat less important than it appears to be.

The coverage of virology literature in *Biological Abstracts* (*BA*) and in *BioResearch Index* was analyzed by Carroll.[5] Approximately 2,300 virology papers were located in a five-month span of the two indexes. The papers were drawn from 495 sources representing 44 countries. Abstracts of virology-related papers were found in no less than 20 sections of *Biological Abstracts*—other than those dealing directly with virology. This analysis of the scatter of the virology literature in *BA* is extremely pertinent to the evaluation of published indexes in general. It is very well to show that *BA* covers x% of the published literature in virology, but how much of it is actually findable by a user consulting the most likely sections or headings of the publication? Carroll's study suggests that it might be difficult to obtain high recall in many virology-related searches and that the unit cost of such searches, per relevant citation, is likely to be quite high.

Barlup[1] reports a small test on the relevancy of articles cited in *Science Citation Index*. Here "relevancy" refers to the degree to which the subject content of cited articles is similar to the subject content of the articles citing them. The authors (physicians) of 25 medical articles were sent copies of up to 10 articles that cited an earlier article they had written. They were asked to judge the relationship between the subject content of these articles and that of their own papers. Eighteen (72%) of the physicians responded. Of the 230 articles, 161 (70%) were returned. Of these, 72% were judged very closely related to the subject matter of the cited articles; 22.4% were judged slightly or indirectly related; and approximately 5% were judged not related (although approximately 18% were judged not related simply from their titles). Once again, this emphasizes the difficulty of determining relevance from titles alone. The study is very pertinent to the factors of precision and unit cost per relevant citation in searching of published indexes, although the findings are, of course, peculiar to the *Science Citation Index*.

The *Bibliography of Agriculture* has been studied comprehensively by Bourne[2,3] from the viewpoints of characteristics, extent of coverage, and overlap with other services. Checking against pertinent agricultural references in an abstract journal and in three annual reviews, Bourne discovered that the *Bibliography of Agriculture* covered only 48%–58% of the available literature relevant to the interests of agricultural researchers.

The material not covered was not fugitive literature, but was predominantly English-language, mostly from journals and conference proceedings, and much of it was of U.S. origin. A check of publication lists from the U.S. Department of Agriculture (USDA), a research laboratory, and several state agricultural experiment stations and extension services indicated a *Bibliography of Agriculture* coverage factor of 45%–74% for this type of material. On the other hand, a study of the degree of overlap between the *Bibliography of Agriculture* and 15 other major services, based on 5,000 citations, indicated that approximately 54% of the items were covered exclusively by the *Bibliography;* in fact, no single service overlaps its data base by more than 20%. In investigating and comparing time lag for inclusion of agriculture-related literature in the *Bibliography* and 11 other services, it was found that the *Bibliography of Agriculture*, on the average, published later than 8 of the 11 services. Based on a sample of 617 citations covered by both services, it was found that *Chemical Abstracts*, which includes abstracts in addition to the citation data provided by the *Bibliography of Agriculture*, published 3.7 months earlier on the average.

Bystrom[1] studied the ability to find citations on soil science and plant nutrition in four printed indexes: *Biological and Agricultural Index, Bibliography of Agriculture, Chemical Abstracts*, and *Soils and Fertilizers*. This is an interesting study because it attempts to evaluate recall, as opposed to coverage only. The approach is sound, but the sample searches reported are too few to allow any valid conclusions to be made on the relative merits of the various approaches to indexing.

Purely subjective "evaluations" of published indexes have been conducted by Drage[8] and Cluley.[6] Drage compared two methods of displaying a subject index to *Sugar Industry Abstracts*. Subscriber response to a questionnaire revealed how the publication was used, and provided user reaction to arrangement and format, subject and journal coverage, time lag, indexes, and form and content of the abstracts. Respondents also were asked to compare the utility of *Analytical Abstracts* with that of *Chemical Abstracts;* 60% indicated that they preferred the former for current-awareness purposes and 42% for retrospective-search purposes. Compared with *Chemical Abstracts*, the chief virtues of *Analytical Abstracts* were its specialized emphasis on analytical methods, the quality of the abstracts, and the ready availability of the journal, due to its modest price.

Subjective evaluations of this type, based on some form of user survey, are of value in ascertaining user attitudes or preferences toward publications. They have limited diagnostic value, however; that is, they usually contribute comparatively little to increase publication effectiveness.

The Institution of Electrical Engineers used a questionnaire to determine subjective impressions of users of printed indexes. Most of the returns were from librarians and other information specialists in British institutions, but a few also were received from technical personnel using printed indexes. The questionnaire was designed to gather data on user preferences relating to various characteristics of these indexes, as well as user assessment of the overall quality of the tools. Special emphasis was placed on the use of *Science Abstracts*, the Institution's own publication, and a related investigation involved the compilation of case studies on how the indexes to *Science Abstracts* were used under actual working conditions. These studies are described in two reports by Hall.[11,12]

The most complete group of evaluations of printed indexes is that conducted by Martyn[18] and Martyn and Slater.[19] Using comprehensive bibliographies in particular subject areas—the technique described earlier in this chapter—the coverage of various indexes was studied, as well as the ability to retrieve references through the normal use of these tools.

The various factors affecting the effectiveness of a printed index are illustrated in Figure 25. Whether or not a person elects to use an index is dependent upon the coverage it provides. Presumably, he will not attempt to make use of it if he feels that its coverage is unlikely to be adequate in the area of his current interests. Having decided to use a particular index, however, the user is faced with the task of translating his information need into a search strategy in the language of the index (i.e., he decides which terms he should search under). Usually, he will not prepare a formal search strategy before approaching the index. Nevertheless, the terms that he does search under comprise a search strategy derived heuristically. The user's ability to translate his need into the language of the index depends upon a number of factors, including: (a) his ability to express his need verbally, (b) the degree to which the vocabulary of the index matches his requirements (particularly, whether or not the vocabulary is sufficiently specific to match his precise requirements), (c) his ability to search systematically, and (d) the assistance and guidance provided by the index itself, particularly in its organization, structure, and cross-referencing.

When the user actually matches his search strategy against the index (i.e., consults a series of headings), the success or failure of the search is largely dependent on the characteristics of the indexing policy employed, particularly with regard to exhaustivity (i.e., the number of access points provided). Indexing quality and accuracy also affect performance. The searcher may not retrieve everything on skin transplantation, for example, even though he consults all the correct headings, because indexers have not always assigned these headings when they should have been

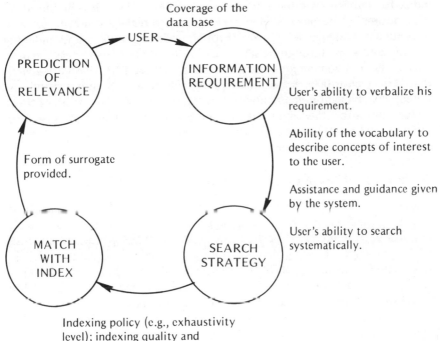

Coverage of the
data base

User's ability to verbalize his
requirement.

Ability of the vocabulary to
describe concepts of interest
to the user.

Assistance and guidance given
by the system.

User's ability to search
systematically.

Indexing policy (e.g., exhaustivity
level); indexing quality and
accuracy; semantic and syntactic
ambiguities.

Ability of the vocabulary to
describe concepts occurring
in documents.

FIGURE 25 Factors affecting the effectiveness of searches in printed indexes.

assigned. Again, the vocabulary of the index is as important in the indexing process as it is in the searching process. For example, if the vocabulary is inadequate to express all of the concepts occurring in the literature indexed, losses may result, because articles are hidden under headings the user would not normally consult.

Finally, even a searcher who consults all the correct headings may not recognize all the relevant items that appear under these headings. Whether or not he recognizes them as relevant depends largely upon the quality of the document surrogate provided.

It should be noted that the various factors affecting performance are cumulative; that is, in a search of a printed index (or a consultation of the index for current-awareness purposes), some of the relevant literature may be missed because of poor searching strategies, some because of vocabulary inadequacies, some through indexing policy and indexing quality, and some through deficiencies in the document surrogate. These various factors combined make it extremely difficult to conduct a search that will yield 100% recall (i.e., a search that will uncover all the potentially relevant items contained in the index). Moreover, all of these factors also affect the time it takes to conduct a search and, thus, govern the unit cost per relevant citation retrieved.

Evaluation of Subject Searches in the Library Catalog

A major criticism of catalog-use studies is that they tend to neglect subject searching; and when subject searching has been considered, the evaluation has been relatively superficial. A search is usually judged "successful" if the user's heading matches one appearing in the catalog or if he selects a book as the result of the search. At this level of evaluation, it is not known whether the searcher found all relevant materials or even if he found the materials that are in some sense "the best."

Clearly, the performance criteria and evaluation procedures described in this chapter are equally applicable to the evaluation of subject searches conducted in the library catalog, whether they are conducted by library staff or by users. Such an evaluation would be conducted by recording the precise topic of a search, asking the catalog user to record the headings he consults and the items he selects as likely to be relevant, recording the time spent on the search, and having one or more exhaustive parallel searches conducted as a means of estimating recall. The results of the search can then be expressed in terms of estimated recall, search time, and unit cost (in time) per relevant item found, although precision ratio or expected search length also could be used as a measure of effort.

Most importantly, this type of evaluation allows for identification of searches that have produced poor results (in terms of recall or searching time/effort) and for conducting a diagnostic analysis to determine why the failures occurred. Such an analysis could reveal defects in the catalog and could suggest methods by which the tool could be improved (e.g., provide more access points per title, more specific subject headings needed, more extensive use of see or see also references).

Evaluating the Performance of Other Information Centers

At least one further application of the evaluation criteria and procedures described in this chapter may have relevance to the librarian. With the increasing availability of computer-based information retrieval systems, many libraries, particularly industrial libraries, are purchasing various services from other information centers, especially the so-called "scientific information dissemination centers." These centers offer information services from various machine-readable data bases (e.g., *Chemical Abstracts, Engineering Index*) on a subscription basis. An individual or institution can purchase some type of information service, usually SDI but sometimes a retrospective search, directly from such a center. A number of libraries subscribe to this form of service on behalf of their own users. Several scientific information dissemination centers now exist, mostly in universities or related research institutions (e.g., Illinois Institute of Technology, University of Georgia), and some offer competing services (i.e., a number of centers offer service from the same data base).

The technical librarian may find himself in the position of having to evaluate the performance of these centers, either for provision of service or simply to assess the quality of service actually received. The criteria presented earlier in this chapter obviously are applicable to the evaluation of the performance of another information center. The criteria by which users might evaluate the performance of such an information center are listed in Table 39. This entire subject, that is, evaluation of the performance of a scientific information dissemination center, has been discussed in detail by Kuipers et al.,[13] and O'Donohue[20] has compared the performance of seven such centers in terms of the service received by one particular organization.

REFERENCES

1. Barlup, J. "Mechanization of Library Procedures in the Medium-Sized Medical Library. VII. Relevancy of Cited Articles in Citation Indexing." *Bulletin of the Medical Library Association, 57*:260–263, 1969.
2. Bourne, C. P. *Characteristics of Coverage by the Bibliography of Agriculture of the Literature Relating to Agricultural Research and Development.* Palo Alto, Calif., Information General Corp., 1969. PB 185 425.
3. Bourne, C. P. *Overlapping Coverage of Bibliography of Agriculture by 15 Other Secondary Sources.* Palo Alto, Calif., Information General Corp., 1969. PB 185 069.
4. Bystrom, M. "Agricultural Information. Can You Find It With the Index?" *Special Libraries, 59*:712–717, 1968.
5. Carroll, K. H. "An Analytical Survey of Virology Literature Reported in Two Announcement Journals." *American Documentation, 20*:234–237, 1969.
6. Cluley, H. J. "Analytical Abstracts: User Reaction Study." *Proceedings of the Society for Analytical Chemistry, 5*:217–221, 1968.
7. Davison, P. S. and Matthews, D. A. R. "Assessment of Information Services." *ASLIB Proceedings, 21*:280–283, 1969.
8. Drage, J. F. "User Preferences in Published Indexes, a Preliminary Test." *Information Scientist, 2*:111–114, 1968.

9. Elliott, C. K. "Abstracting Services in Psychology: A Comparison of *Psychological Abstracts* and *Bulletin Signaletique.*" *Library Association Record, 71*:279–280, 1969.

10. Farradane, J. and Yates-Mercer, P. A. "Retrieval Characteristics of the Index to *Metals Abstracts.*" *Journal of Documentation, 29*:295–314, 1973.

11. Hall, A. M. *Case Studies of the Use of Subject Indexes.* INSPEC Report R72/8. London, The Institution of Electrical Engineers, July 1972.

12. Hall, A. M. *User Preference in Printed Indexes.* INSPEC Report R72/7. London, The Institution of Electrical Engineers, July 1972.

13. Kuipers, J. W. et al. *Effectiveness and Cost-Effectiveness Considerations for NASIC Information Services Operations.* Bedford, Mass., QEI, Inc., 1973.

14. Lancaster, F. W. "Evaluation and Testing of Information Retrieval Systems." *In: Encyclopedia of Library and Information Science.* Edited by A. Kent and H. Lancour. Vol. 8. New York, Marcel Dekker, 1972, pp. 234–259.

15. Lancaster, F. W. *Evaluation of the MEDLARS Demand Search Service.* Bethesda, Md., National Library of Medicine, 1968.

16. Lancaster, F. W. *Information Retrieval Systems: Characteristics, Testing, and Evaluation.* New York, Wiley, 1968.

17. Lancaster, F. W. "The Evaluation of Published Indexes and Abstract Journals: Criteria and Possible Procedures." *Bulletin of the Medical Library Association, 59*:479–494, 1971.

18. Martyn, J. "Tests on Abstract Journals: Coverage, Overlap, and Indexing." *Journal of Documentation, 23*:45–70, 1967.

19. Martyn, J. and Slater, M. "Tests on Abstract Journals." *Journal of Documentation, 20*:212–235, 1964.

20. O'Donohue, C. H. "Comparison of Service Centers and Document Data Bases—A User's View." *Journal of Chemical Documentation, 13*:27–29, 1973.

21. Torr, D. V. et al. *Program of Studies on the Use of Published Indexes.* 2 Vols. Bethesda, Md., Information Systems Operation, General Electric Co., 1964.

5

Evaluation of
the Collection

Over the years, more work has been performed on the evaluation of collections—books and other materials—than on any other facet of the library. This can be partly attributed to the fact that the collection itself is relatively tangible, whereas the various library services, being intangible, are more difficult to evaluate. Much literature exists on library collections and the extent and use of these collections; and if this literature does not deal directly with evaluation as such, it is certainly of related interest.

The book collection* can be evaluated by both quantitative and qualitative methods. Line[42] and Hirsch,[26] among others, have categorized possible approaches to collection evaluation, and a comprehensive review has been made by Bonn.[5] The most obvious methods are shown in Table 41.

Size of the Collection

The absolute size of a collection is one characteristic by which it may be evaluated, in that a particular library is unlikely to function effectively if its collection is below a certain minimum size. Williams[82] stated:

There are widely accepted standards for minimum sizes of school, college, and public libraries, below which, in the judgment of professional organizations or accrediting bodies, it is impossible to provide the variety of materials required for adequate service.

*The term "book collection" is used for convenience, although the techniques described may be equally relevant to all types of library materials.

165

TABLE 41   Possible Approaches to the Evaluation of Library Collections

---

QUANTITATIVE

Absolute size of collection.

Size of collection by various methods of categorization (e.g., subject area, date, language, type of material).

Current growth rate.

Size in relation to other variables, including number of volumes per capita and number of volumes per item circulated.

Expenditures on the collection, including per capita expenditures and expenditures on the collection in relation to the total budget.

QUALITATIVE

"Impressionistic" (subjective) methods.

Evaluation against standard lists or holdings of other institutions.

USE FACTORS

Amount of collection use, as reflected in statistics of circulation and in-library use.

This statement implies that the size of a collection—for a library of a particular size and type—can be compared with some existing standard.

Collection standards do exist for public, school, college, junior college, state, and special libraries of various types. A useful review of these standards, edited by Hirsch,[27] appeared in a recent issue of *Library Trends,* and a useful bibliography has been compiled by Ottersen.[57] Examples are the "Standards for College Libraries"[71] and the "Standards for Junior College Libraries,"[72] adopted by the Association of College and Research Libraries in 1959 and 1960, respectively. At present, there are no comparable standards for university libraries in the United States, although Downs[17] has collected statistics on large university libraries with the ultimate goal of developing standards based on these statistics. This is, in fact, the normal approach to the development of standards, which are based on figures derived from libraries whose services or facilities are judged to be superior, or at least acceptable.

One possible danger, pointed out by Downs and Heussman,[18] is that: ". . . minimum standards may come to be regarded by university administrators and control boards as maximum standards, thereby impeding the growth of a given library." On the other hand, they go on to say that "There can be little doubt, however, that the overall effect of standards has been to upgrade libraries, providing substandard institutions with yardsticks by which to measure their deficiencies . . ."

Williams[82] has made the additional point that "There is normally a high correlation between the size of a library, its usefulness, and (if it is an academic library) the quality of the institution it serves." Jordan,[32] for example, claims a direct correlation between size of a college library and its ranking in terms of "academic excellence." An illustration of this correlation is shown in Table 42, which compares the range of collection size, both in absolute numbers and in volumes per undergraduate student, for the top 6% and the bottom 88% of colleges ranked by "academic excellence." More recently, Blau and Margulies[4] have shown a correlation between the size of academic libraries and the reputation of professional schools in the United States.

There are dangers, of course, in trying to compare the collections of various libraries simply on the basis of size, either absolute—total number of volumes—or in volumes per individual served. Downs[16] has pointed out an almost complete lack of uniformity in the way librarians report collection statistics. Moreover, most libraries in the United States express size in number of volumes, whereas number of unique titles held may, in fact, be a better indicator of the richness of the collection. For example, a large public library with several branches may have multiple copies of many titles (Downs mentions, as one example, a public library with 1.7 million volumes, but only 140,000 unique titles), whereas, in an academic institution, the amount of duplication is likely to be much lower.

Some standards, including those of accrediting bodies, go beyond quantitative guidelines and establish requirements for the types of mate-

TABLE 42 Correlation Between Size of Collection in College Library and Academic Excellence of Institution[32]

	Volumes in Library		Volumes in Library for Each Undergraduate Student	
	Colleges ranking 4 or over (top 6%)	Colleges ranking 1 or 0 (bottom 88%)	Colleges ranking 4 or over (top 6%)	Colleges ranking 1 or 0 (bottom 88%)
Highest library	328,000	279,000	366	187
75th percentile	165,000	60,000	185	77
Median	102,000	50,000	124	60
25th percentile	76,000	37,000	94	48
Lowest library	44,000	28,000	47	14

rials that should be included in the collection. This is more likely to be true for special libraries. The evaluation of a collection based on such standards has been discussed by Bonn.[5]

Collection size is certainly an important indicator of its utility, because, presumably, the larger the collection the greater the probability that it will be able to satisfy the information needs of its users. This assumes, of course, that the collection is appropriate (in terms of subject matter and level of treatment) to meet the needs of the population served and that it is continuing to grow. A large library that stops acquiring new publications will decline rapidly in value, except, perhaps, for purposes of historical research. This raises the question of whether absolute size is as valuable an indicator as rate of growth in measuring the potential utility of a collection.

When considering the degree to which a library satisfies the demands placed upon it, both absolute size and rate of growth must be taken into account. Percentage rate of growth alone could present a somewhat distorted picture of the quality of a collection. A library may show a high percentage rate of growth if it fails to discard obsolete items while collecting new ones. Such a library, however, is performing a great disservice to its users. In addition to creating chronic storage problems, such a policy is likely to lead to diminution in the quality of the collection. Percentage rate of growth as an indicator of the utility of a collection penalizes the library that pursues an active policy of weeding. In 1963, Piternick[58] suggested that growth in absolute number of volumes added is likely to be a much better indicator of quality than percentage increase in the size of a collection. In fact, he presented data to show that a correlation may exist between academic excellence of a university and (a) absolute size of its library in number of volumes and (b) growth rate in mean number of volumes added, but not between academic excellence and percentage rate of growth. The major data are presented in Table 43, in which academic organizations belonging to the Association of Graduate Schools are divided into three groups: (a) the top 10 universities, according to a rank-ordering prepared by Haywood Keniston and later adopted by Bernard Berelson, (b) the second 10 universities, according to the same ranking procedure, and (c) unranked institutions. As Table 43 indicates, the libraries of the top 10 universities are largest in absolute size and in number of volumes added during the period 1946–1960, but they fall below the libraries of the lower ranked institutions in their percentage growth rate.*

*A recent report by Baumol and Marcus,[3] based on statistics from 58 university libraries, indicates that, percentagewise, the smallest libraries in the group are growing much faster than the largest libraries (5.4% a year as opposed to 3.5%), indicating "regression of large and small libraries toward a common size."

TABLE 43   Library Holdings and Growth of Graduate Study Institutions[58]

Keniston-Berelson Ranking	Mean Holdings 1946 (volumes)	Mean Holdings 1960 (volumes)	Mean Additions 1946–60 (volumes)	Mean Annual Growth Rate 1946–60 (percent)	Mean Doubling Time 1946–60 (years)
Top 10	1,922,174	2,979,923	1,057,749	3.2	22.0
Second 10	811,555	1,409,364	597,809	4.0	17.7
Other AGS Members .	523,640	905,607	381,967	4.0	17.7

Clapp and Jordan[11] affirm that the adequacy of an academic library collection can be measured by the number of books it contains, but that published standards are not an appropriate basis for determining the size required for minimum adequacy. Minimum size is dependent upon many variables, including size and composition of faculty and student body, curriculum, methods of instruction, geographic location of the campus, and physical facilities. They propose a formula that might be used to assess the adequacy of academic collections. McInnis[51] has since shown that the Clapp-Jordan formula can be written as a weighted sum of several variables:

$$V = 50,750 + 100F + 12E + 12H + 335U + 3,050M + 24,500D$$

where
  F = number of faculty
  E = total number of students enrolled
  H = number of undergraduate honors students
  U = number of major undergraduate subjects
  M = master's fields offered
  D = doctoral fields offered
  V = volumes

and 50,750 is a constant, representing a minimum viable university library in number of volumes.

The formula is shown in more detail in Table 44, where the first line represents a minimum basic collection, and the succeeding lines, a series of enrichment factors. The basic collection figure of 50,750 was derived from several standard lists of basic collections for undergraduate libraries.

Clapp and Jordan, who present a similar, but somewhat simpler, formula for junior or community college libraries, are careful to point out that, "The formula presumes that even liminal or minimum adequacy can be achieved with its assistance only if all material is carefully chosen with a view to the purpose to be served, and the weeding program is as active and realistic in relation to needs as is the program of acquisition." They

TABLE 44 Formula for Estimating the Size for Liminal Adequacy of the Collections of Senior College and University Libraries[11]

(1)	Books		Periodicals		Documents	Total
	Titles (2)	Volumes (3)	Titles (4)	Volumes (5)	Volumes (6)	Volumes (7)
To a basic collection, viz.:						
1. Undergraduate library	35,000	42,000	250	3,750	5,000	50,750
Add for each of the following as indicated:						
2. Faculty member (full time equivalent)	50	60	1	15	25	100
3. Student (graduate or undergraduate in full time equivalents)	. . . .	10	. . . .	1	1	12
4. Undergraduate in honors or independent study programs	10	12	. . . .	. . . .	. . . .	12
5. Field of undergraduate concentration—"major" subject field	200	240	3	45	50	335
6. Field of graduate concentration—master's work or equivalent	2,000	2,400	10	150	500	3,050
7. Field of graduate concentration—doctoral work or equivalent	15,000	18,000	100	1,500	5,000	24,500

tested the formula on three groups: selected senior colleges, state universities, and selected junior or community colleges. Some university libraries with very large collections were found below minimum adequacy (i.e., although collections were large, the formula suggests the libraries were inadequate to support the rich and varied academic programs offered by those institutions). Five of the seven junior college libraries tested failed to meet the threshold of adequacy prescribed by the Clapp-Jordan formula, although all exceeded the basic minimum size required by the "Standards for Junior College Libraries,"[72] and some were several times larger than the minimum.

McInnis[51] an economist, attempted to verify the Clapp-Jordan formula empirically, by comparing its results with those of a regression analysis applied to library data from some leading graduate schools in the United States. He failed to do so. The regression equations generally produced higher figures for the expected number of volumes than those produced by application of the formula. In other words, minimal adequacy, as defined by the Clapp-Jordan formula, may report a low (conservative) rather than a high level of adequacy. McInnis suggests that "as a very rough, quickly computed guide to minimum levels of library size, the Clapp-Jordan formula should remain in the librarian's tool kit." He points out, however, that the formula has inherent weaknesses, a major one being that the weight for the number of doctoral fields covered by a university is so large that it exerts too strong an influence on the formula. "Doctoral field," however, is not necessarily a precise concept, and each institution will report data on fields of doctoral study in different ways. Because the formula is highly sensitive to this variable, it is important that the term "doctoral field" be precisely defined and made strictly comparable among the various institutions.

Snowball,[70] after applying the Clapp-Jordan formula at Sir George Williams University, found some evidence to support its validity for monographs, but also found evidence suggesting that it provides a low estimate for the number of periodicals needed.

The advantage of the Clapp-Jordan formula over previous formulas or standards is that it considers multiple factors affecting the required size of a collection rather than just one single factor (such as size of the student body). There is a danger, however, that the *minimal standards* established by the formula will be interpreted (by those controlling the funding of libraries) as optimum levels and, as a result, some library acquisitions may be curtailed. This was a problem faced by some of the State University of New York (SUNY) libraries, which (in 1970) found themselves in danger of having their growth restricted to the levels recommended by the formula.

This problem is discussed in detail in a report issued by the State University of New York.[73] The authors of the report clearly indicate that standards established by the formula are not only *minimal*, but are applicable only to the *threshold* period of an institution's growth. They are set at the "bread and water" level and are not appropriate to assess the adequacy of a collection in a well-established institution, a point supported by the McInnis study. The SUNY report emphasizes that:

... threshold criteria set forth in *minimal* terms are inadequate as budgeting devices for the State University of New York and . . . that minimal criteria devised in the early 1960's must be appreciably more minimal and less adequate in 1970. . . . Indeed a formula that confines itself to merely liminal levels, with no exponential factor to provide for growth beyond the threshold, should have, in theory, a built-in mechanism to keep it current and relevant.

The compilers of the SUNY report found that none of the Clapp-Jordan factors was superfluous and that "no significant growth factor was omitted from the formulas." They did, however, develop a modified formula, based on the same factors, but with changes in some of the values. This revision is shown in Table 45. Note that nearly all values have been raised above those proposed in the original formula. Particular emphasis was placed by SUNY on upgrading the formula as it relates to periodical holdings, this aspect of the Clapp-Jordan formula being regarded as especially inadequate. In addition to upgrading the Clapp-Jordan formula, the SUNY report proposed that "attainment of formula adequacy be followed by a period of exponential growth" and that the annual rate of this growth be no less than 5%, in order to keep up with newly published literature and to maintain adequacy.

A related study worth noting is that of Reichard and Orsagh,[63] who examined the expenditures and holdings of various U.S. academic libraries and related these values to size of faculty and student body. They noted that growth in collection size and library expenditures appeared to correlate strongly with faculty growth and expansion of graduate programs. Growth in undergraduate enrollment, on the other hand, appeared to exert little influence on expenditures and collection growth.

Several other formulas relating to collection size are mentioned by Bonn.[5] None of them, however, appears to have aroused the same general interest as the Clapp-Jordan formula.

Qualitative Methods

Hirsch[26] identifies two nonquantitative procedures that may be applied to the evaluation of a collection: (a) the "impressionistic" method and (b)

TABLE 45 Formula for Estimating the Size for Liminal Adequacy of SUNY University Colleges and University Centers[73]

(1)	Books		Periodicals		Documents	Total
	Titles (2)	Volumes (3)	Titles (4)	Volumes (5)	Volumes (6)	Volumes (7)
To a basic collection, viz.,						
1. Undergraduate library	50,000	60,000	1,000	15,000	5,000	80,000
Add for each of the following as indicated:						
2. Faculty member (full time equivalent)	62.5	75	3	45	25	145
3. Student (full time equivalent)	.....	10	....	1	1	12
4. Undergraduate in honors or independent study programs.............	12.5	15	....	....	.....	15
5. Field of undergraduate concentration—"major" subject field	250	300	3	45	50	395
6. Field of graduate concentration—master's work or equivalent............	2,500	3,000	20	400	500	3,900
7. Field of graduate concentration—doctoral work or equivalent............	22,500	27,000	200	6,000	5,000	38,000

the list-checking method. In the former, a collection is evaluated by one or more individuals—subject specialists, librarians, or scholars. This evaluation is entirely subjective, but it may have value if conducted by individuals with a sound knowledge of various subject areas and, more importantly, of the literature. Academic libraries in particular can rely upon the expertise of faculty members when conducting impressionistic studies of this type. The University of Chicago, for example, used 200 faculty members in the evaluation of its collections, as reported by Raney[62] in 1933. Williams[82] points out some of the advantages and limitations of this approach:

. . . fortunately there are faculty members whom the surveyor of college and university libraries can consult by means of questionnaires or interviews or both. Ideally, he can hope to base his findings on the expert opinion of men who know their subject, have a broad knowledge of its literature, have intensively used both the library he is surveying and many others, and have also kept themselves well informed of the degree to which the library is meeting the needs of their students, undergraduate and graduate. In practice, of course, the surveyor does not find such men in every subject, and the individuals he consults do not always agree. Even in the largest university there will be some important segments of the collection in which, temporarily, no one is particularly interested. If one man in a department has been depended upon to build up the relevant collections, he will probably know more about the library's holdings in his area than anyone else, but may well be unconscious of deficiencies or indifferent to them; indeed, they will be deficiencies that have developed because of his lack of interest in certain subdivisions of the subject.

Bonn[5] has reviewed other impressionistic evaluations of library collections, including several studies where faculty members from various academic departments were asked to rate the quality of the collection in their own subject areas on some type of scale. He points out that there is "a striking similarity between these rating scales and the levels or degrees of subject coverage which many libraries now specify in their acquisition policy statements." The University of Illinois Library uses four such levels (general, instructional, comprehensive, and exhaustive research), while the John Crerar Library uses five (supplementary reference, reference, research, comprehensive, and exhaustive). Bonn also suggests that opinion surveys may have certain value for the librarian, including surveys among students, the general public, and members of the library staff.

A common way of evaluating a library collection *in toto,* or in one or more specified subject areas, is to check the collection against another authority, such as the holdings of another library or the items in a subject bibliography that is accepted as complete and/or authoritative. A good example of such a checklist is *Books for College Libraries,*[6] a selected list of approximately 50,000 titles "designed to support a college teaching program that depends heavily upon the library, and to supply the necessary materials for term papers and suggested and independent outside reading." Other lists have been prepared or recommended by agencies of accreditation, and some are specifically mentioned by various library standards. Winchell's *Guide to Reference Books*[83] is frequently used as a standard for reference collections. A number of lists of "core collections" exist for various subject areas; for example, in the field of medicine, the lists of basic collections for small medical libraries compiled by Stearns and Ratcliff[74] and Brandon.[7]

For some purposes, specially prepared composite lists may be compiled. For example, in the Public Library Inquiry, as described by Leigh,[38] the fiction checklist was compiled from a number of sources: a list of best sellers from *Publishers' Weekly,* the American Library Association's "notable books of the year," lists of best books prepared by professional critics in *Nation* and *The New York Times,* and summaries of reviews appearing in *Book Review Digest.* A thorough review of lists suitable for collection evaluation is provided by Bonn.[5]

The periodical collection of a library also can be evaluated against a "standard" list, which may represent the holdings of another library, the periodicals selected for indexing or abstracting by some authoritative body (e.g., the list of journals covered by *Index Medicus* provides a guide to biomedical journals in various specific subject areas, considered most valuable by the National Library of Medicine), or the periodicals that are most frequently cited in a particular subject field. The last category appears to be particularly useful. In 1956, Brown[8] published lists of this kind for various scientific subjects, and vast quantities of citation data now are available in machine-readable form from the Institute for Scientific Information, publishers of *Science Citation Index (SCI).*

Using the *SCI* data base, Martyn and Gilchrist[46] were able to produce a list of 590 British scientific journals, ranked by the number of citations (to 1963 and 1964 issues) each received in *SCI* in 1965. It is interesting to note that the 590 journals cited were only 32% of an estimated 1,842 British scientific journals. In other words, more than two-thirds were not cited at all in the journals covered by *SCI* in 1965. It also was found that 95% of all citations were to 165 titles (9% of all the British titles and 28% of all the cited titles).

List checking is a practicable approach to evaluation of relatively small libraries or collections in fairly restricted subject areas, although, presumably, even a large collection could be checked against innumerable lists covering a broad range of subject fields. In fact, Raney[62] reports that more than 400 lists and bibliographies were used in checking the University of Chicago collections. Coale,[12] however, points out that the strengths and weaknesses of a research collection lie in printed and manuscript primary sources, as well as in the important secondary sources, and that checklists usually do not exist for most scholarly research areas:

No standard list exists of books and materials that should be in a research collection of any breadth. If there were such lists, they would probably be so lengthy that the cost of checking them against holdings would discourage their use.

Coale suggests that a large research collection should be evaluated one subject area at a time, and he describes a procedure adopted in assessing the collection of Latin-American colonial history at the Newberry Library. This technique involves the identification of a select group of scholarly books in the subject area to be studied. The bibliographies contained in these books are then checked against the library's holdings. Thus, the collection is evaluated not against some theoretical list of "best" books, but against lists of sources actually consulted by scholars writing in the field. In effect, by following this technique, the evaluator is really asking, "Could these books have been written in this library?" This method of list checking has another advantage. Because many of the items cited will be in areas peripherally related to the subject area chosen for the study, it can be used to check the strengths of the general library collection as well as in the specialized area. As Coale points out, "A library might have quite a good special collection and yet be a poor place for a scholar to work if many necessary titles tangential to his subject are lacking."

In the Newberry evaluation, bibliographies of substantial size (between 100 and 400 titles in each) were used. These bibliographies also were used to check the holdings of three other libraries, thus permitting a comparison of the Newberry collection with the other collections in the field of Spanish-American colonial history.

This type of evaluation, if the bibliographies are well-chosen, will reveal any weaknesses in the library collection, including weaknesses in coverage of particular periods, languages, or types of materials. Checking against a list of "best" books, Coale feels, is less useful, because this type of list contains only major sources that the library is likely to hold in any event. He also points out that it is possible to assess how well a library is keeping current with new acquisitions if a really authoritative bibliography exists in a particular subject area. For example, acquisitions in Spanish-American colonial history since 1936 can be checked against the Harvard *Handbook of Latin American Studies*.

Hirsch[26] mentions additional weaknesses of the list-checking approach. Lists become dated quickly. Use of standard lists may lead to conformity among collections, and the special needs of a particular clientele may be ignored. He suggests that checklists are apt to be most useful in evaluating the newer and smaller libraries and least useful in evaluating the large, well-established ones. Checklists should be very carefully selected, and specially compiled composite lists are preferable to those that are ready-made. Bonn[5] has mentioned the possibility that standard lists used to check adequacy of collections may be the very ones that were used earlier to build these collections. Their use as evaluative tools, therefore, is essentially zero.

Goldhor[22] has pointed out a further limitation in the conventional approach to list checking: The titles checked against a list in a particular subject area may represent only a small percentage of the library's total holdings in that field, and the checking operation reveals nothing about the other books held by the library. Goldhor[22,24] prefers a somewhat different approach to list checking, which he refers to as an "inductive method." This involves assessing the quality of a collection by taking a complete list of the library's holdings in a particular subject area and comparing the titles with several book-reviewing and selection tools. He points out that, "Presumably the titles held by the library which are upon multiple lists are clearly desirable, those which are included on no list are probably not desirable, and those which are on only one list are of borderline quality." Goldhor has applied his "inductive method" to several evaluations, most recently a survey of public libraries in the Minneapolis-St. Paul metropolitan area.[23]

This type of list checking seems most appropriate for public and small college libraries. It is not relevant to the evaluation of major research collections in which "uniqueness" is likely to be important; that is, a research collection may reasonably be expected to contain items not held elsewhere and not appearing on any standard lists.

McInnis,[50] another critic of the list-checking approach, maintains that few really comprehensive lists exist for any subject field and that their usefulness is limited, because the scope of a specific area, as defined by one individual or organization, may not necessarily be an appropriate definition of the scope of that subject for a particular library. Moreover, individuals may disagree as to what a particular book is really "about." Published bibliographies also may have various emphases. For example, a list compiled from a historical perspective might be of little use in evaluating a collection for its value in current research.

McInnis favors an approach to collection evaluation that is very similar to the one used by Coale; namely, that evaluation of coverage in a particular subject area need not depend on finding a single comprehensive bibliography on this subject (which probably does not exist anyway). Instead, the evaluation should be based on carefully constructed samples of bibliographic references. McInnis' approach differs from Coale's only to the extent that he emphasizes the desirability of drawing such a sample at random.

Many studies of bibliographic collections have been made using either the impressionistic or the list-checking method, or both. The literature is too extensive to summarize here. Two recent examples are the collection evaluations at the University of Colorado, Boulder, and at the State University of New York at Buffalo, reported by Webb[81] and Cassata and Dewey,[10] respectively. The Colorado study was effected solely by checking against standard bibliographies. The SUNY evaluation was conducted by library staff subject bibliographers, working in their own areas and using a variety of devices, but mostly the list-checking approach.

Evaluation of the Collection by Its Use

One obvious limitation of the methods already discussed is that they are more concerned with the collection itself than with its use. The ultimate test of the quality of a library collection, however, is the extent and mode of its use, and a large number of such evaluations have been conducted. One useful and extensive review of the literature on the statistical analysis of book use, which goes back at least to 1911, is provided by Jain.[29] This type of study is concerned with who uses the collection, for what purpose, and how much, and with which portions of the collection are most used.

Jain recognizes two major methods for obtaining samples indicative of the use of library books:

1. *The collection sample*. Selecting a sample, not necessarily random, of the total collection, and gathering information on the past use of books in this sample.
2. *The checkout sample*. Studying all books checked out from the library during a specified period of time.

The first method presupposes that the library maintains some record of how often a particular book has been borrowed—at least for a reasonable time period—generally by recording on book cards or "date labels" affixed inside the books, the date borrowed or the date on which they are due for return. There are advantages and disadvantages associated with both methods. The major pros and cons presented by Jain are shown in Table 46.

An analysis of circulation statistics, whether derived from a collection sample or a checkout sample, will reveal such information as volume of use by type of material, type of user, age of material, and seasonal variations in use. One important purpose of such an analysis is to determine which portions of the collection are most used and which are least used. These data have considerable value to the librarian, not only in collection building and collection weeding, but in making decisions on the physical accessibility of materials (which materials should be on open shelves, which in stacks, and which retired to a secondary storage area).

Circulation statistics have been included in a number of valuable studies of collection use over the years. One of the earliest was conducted by Stieg[76] at the library of Hamilton College. The analysis was based on circulation records for three consecutive academic years, and Stieg was able to derive figures to show (a) what proportion of the titles circulated in an academic year circulated X times (e.g., 74.26% of all titles circulated in 1938–1939 did so only once, 15.5% twice, and so on), (b) what proportion of the titles circulated did so in all three academic years (more than 70% of all titles circulated did so in only one of the three academic years under review), (c) the effect of publication date on circulation, and (d) the effect of subject matter on circulation.

TABLE 46 Advantages and Disadvantages of Two Methods for Sampling Book Use[29]

	Collection Sample	Checkout Sample
Can one draw inferences about the total library collection?	Yes, if sample is random	No
Can information be obtained on rate of usage of a particular group of books over a period of time?	Yes	No
Is it relatively easy to design a sampling scheme and collect data?	No	Yes
Are the problems of missing data and lack of control on the methods of recording usage histories in the past (caused by different circulation policies at different periods of time) avoided?	No	Yes

Several interesting and important studies also have been conducted at the University of Chicago and at the Yale Medical Library. Summaries of these studies follow.

Studies at the University of Chicago

Middleswort[53] investigated the use of social science and humanities books to determine which might be considered for secondary storage. On the basis of a sample of 1,234 titles drawn from the shelf list in four subject areas, he computed the average use of each title since it had been acquired by the library. He found that a book's rate of use decreases with time, and that the average use also decreases as the time lapse between publication and acquisition increases. A high positive correlation also was found between rate of circulation during the first five years after acquisition and rate of use during later years. Based on statistics of use during the first five years after acquisition, it should be possible to predict the rate of later use.

El-Sheniti[20] examined faculty use of bibliographic materials at Chicago through an analysis of 15,357 items charged out during the period May 22–26, 1956. This sample was categorized by subject distribution, departmental affiliation of borrower, and type of material borrowed.

Perhaps the best-known study of collection samples is that of Fussler and Simon,[21] whose stated objective was to answer the question, "Will any kind of statistical procedure predict with reasonable accuracy the frequencies with which groups of books with defined characteristics are likely to be used in a research library?" The major purpose of the study, and of many others of this type, was to identify books likely to be requested infrequently and, consequently, requiring less-accessible and, presumably, less-costly storage areas.

The study was based largely on systematic samples drawn from the shelf list of the University of Chicago Library in two diverse subject areas: economics and Teutonic literature and languages. For comparison purposes, smaller samples were drawn from many other subject areas. The overall sample drawn for monographs was 9,058 titles, the unit of study chosen was the *title,* and use of all copies of the title was considered. For serials, on the other hand, the study unit was the *volume,* and use of all copies of the volume was considered. For each item in the overall sample, Fussler and Simon studied records of past circulation as well as characteristics of the item itself, including language, publication date, and accession date.

For the sample drawn, the investigators studied actual use figures for the period 1954–1958. They then attempted to formulate rules that would predict the use of these items during this period under three possible conditions: (a) no record of past use is available, (b) a record of use for 5 years back is available, and (c) a record of use for 20 years back is available for most items.

In essence, they found that records of past use over a sufficiently long period provide an excellent predictor of future use. Even when such records are not available, it is possible to make certain predictions of future use based on characteristics of the books themselves—the most important predictors being age and language. For example, a rule based on language and publication date could be used to identify 25% of the economics collection likely to be used least in the future. If this rule were applied at the University of Chicago, the 25% of the economics collection retired to storage would account for only 3% of its total use. Of the 25% retired to storage, each title would have a use probability of once every 35 years on the average. The rule is a simple one to follow: Based on publication date alone, the oldest 25% of the collection would be retired; based on publication date and language, proportionally more (by publication date) would be retired from the less-used languages. For this purpose, Fussler and Simon distinguished between English, French, German, and "other." Table 47 shows retirement priorities, by age and language, in the field of economics.

It was found that prediction of use based on age and language was much more successful in the scientific disciplines than in the humanities, where use is less dependent on these factors. For example, if the same rule were used at the University of Chicago to retire 25% of the books in Teutonic languages and literature, the retired portion of the collection would account for 12% of the total use.

The accuracy with which future use can be predicted increases considerably when records of past use are available. For example, if, in addition to the rule for language and publication date, no book is sent to storage if it has been used in the preceding five years, the 25% of the economics collection with the least predicted use would account for only 2% of the total use in this subject field. The corresponding figure for the Teutonic collection is 5%. If 20-year use records are available, prediction of future use can be even more accurate, and language and age characteristics add little of value. If the 25% to be retired (in either economics or the Teutonic collection) is determined on the basis of the 25% least-used in the preceding 20 years, the retired portion of the collection would account for only 1% of the total use, and it could be expected that, on the average, each monograph would be requested only once every 100 years.

The rules, developed at the University of Chicago and based on

TABLE 47   Retirement Priorities[21]

LANGUAGE	PUBLICATION DATE
German	Pre-1904
French	Pre-1879
Other	Pre-1879
French	1879–1903
Other	1879–1903
English	Pre-1879
German	1904–1913
French	1904–1913
French	1914–1923
German	1914–1923
Other	1904–1923
French	1924–1933
German	1924–1933
English	1879–1913
French	1934–1943
German	1934–1943
Other	1924–1943
English	1914–1923

publication date and language, were later tested on random samples drawn from the collections at the University of California, Berkeley and Northwestern University. The results were similar in terms of percentage of total use represented by the 25% of titles identified for storage.

For serials, Fussler and Simon found that the most effective rule for retirement is to begin with the oldest volume of a particular serial and proceed consecutively until a volume is reached that shows a specified amount of use in a prior period of time (e.g., the last five years). This rule was more effective than the one based solely on language and age.

The study also investigated whether recorded use (through circulation records) was a good predictor of total library use, including in-library use. Responses to a questionnaire, which was inserted into the monographs and serials in the sample, revealed that recorded use appeared to be a reasonably good predictor of nonrecorded use also; that is, a group of books that averages two recorded uses every five years can be expected to average twice as many nonrecorded uses as a group of books that averages one recorded use every five years.*

---

*Later, McGrath[48] discovered a strong correlation between the subject matter of books borrowed from the library and the subject matter of books used within the library.

Studies at the Yale Medical Library

Kilgour[33] describes an analysis of the characteristics of materials circulated at the Yale Medical Library, based on a sample of 3,230 volumes—drawn from every fifth item returned by borrowers during the period of October 10, 1960–June 30, 1961. Items in the sample were categorized by type of user, type of materials (journals, books), and date of publication. The rate of circulation was strongly related to date of publication (see Figure 26): 79% of all items circulated (2,652/3,230) were published during the 12 years immediately preceding the conduct of the survey.

A study to identify a core of biomedical journals capable of satisfying 75% of all current demands was conducted at the medical libraries of Yale and Columbia and reported by Kilgour and Fleming.[35] Cancelled charge slips for journal issues published during a designated 42-month period were analyzed. These circulation data were collected for one year at Yale and for six months at Columbia. It was discovered that, although Columbia received more than 2,000 journals and Yale more than 1,500, a core of 262 journals supplied 80% of the total usage of journals published during the period 1959 to mid-1962. In fact, slightly more than 50% of the demand in both libraries was satisfied by as few as 67 journals.

The results from the Yale component of this study were compared with the results of an earlier (1962) study reported by Kilgour.[34] In 1962, an analysis of cancelled charge slips for a shorter period of time (approximately three months) was used to rank the 104 most-used journals published during 1956–1960. The first 37 journals on the list represented 49% of the usage, and the first 86 journals 73%. These figures differ from those for the Yale component of the 1964 study as reported by Kilgour and Fleming[35] (69 out of 1,551 journals supplied 50% of the use). In attempting to explain why 37 journals contributed 49% of the use in the 1962 study, while 69 journals were necessary to supply 50% of the use in the 1964 investigation, the authors suggested that some type of saturation effect may have existed for the heavily used titles. The rate of use of the most popular titles, virtually to maximum capacity, remains relatively constant over a period of time (unless duplicate copies are added to satisfy higher demand). The less-used materials, however, accumulate additional loans with the passage of time; the implication being that the shorter the period for which circulation records are analyzed, the lesser the number of journals that will contribute a fixed percentage of the total usage. Conversely, the longer the circulation period studied, the greater the number of journals that will contribute to this fixed percentage of usage.

In other words, sixty-nine Yale titles supplied 50 percent of use in one year as opposed to thirty-seven in three months, not so much because the heavily used

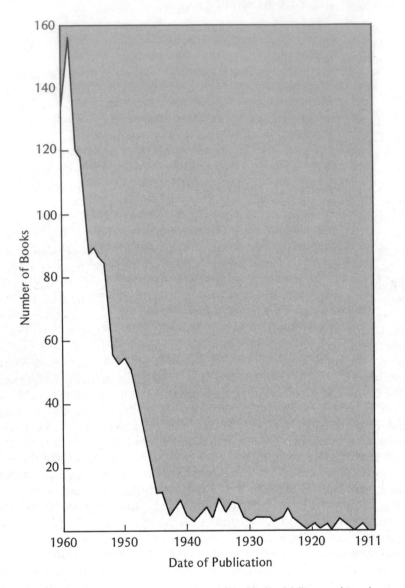

FIGURE 26   Books borrowed from Yale Medical Library plotted by date of publication.[33]

titles were more heavily used during a year, but rather because the little-used titles accumulated more loans over a year and thereby depressed the 50 percent level.

Another study on the use of medical books, also conducted at Yale, is reported by Raisig et al.[61] A total of 430 interviews was conducted with faculty members and postdoctoral fellows on the day after they had returned books to the library, to determine type and age of materials borrowed, purposes for which borrowed, and how users learned of the existence of the particular books borrowed. The survey disclosed that approximately 60% of all items circulated had been published during the preceding five years and approximately 80% during the preceding decade.

Similar studies of circulation patterns in specific libraries, covering both books and periodicals, have been conducted elsewhere. Kovacs,[36] for example, at the Downstate Medical Center Library of the State University of New York, was able to produce a ranked list of journals by number of circulations, and to show the distribution of book and journal circulations by date of publication and by specific subject area. A very substantial study of demands for medical literature, as reflected in the interlibrary loan (ILL) activity of the National Library of Medicine, was reported by Kurth[37] in 1962. It covered the calendar year 1959, and involved 77,698 ILL requests from 1,780 libraries in the United States and abroad. Kurth was able to show the demand distribution over these libraries (80% of the demand came from 20% of the libraries), including distribution by type of library and by geographic area; to show distribution by date of publication; and to produce a list of biomedical journals ranked by number of requests generated.

Relative Use Method

Jain[28,29,30,31] proposes a "relative use" method for estimating book use. The procedure uses both collection and circulation samples and is, according to Jain, more effective than using either one individually. To study "relative use," it is necessary to draw samples from (a) the total collection (S), (b) monographs borrowed for home use (H), and (c) monographs used within the library (I). Each of these samples is then divided into subsets by certain preestablished characteristics: age, language, subject, year of acquisition, and so on. Finally, the expected use of each of these subsets, based on size alone, is compared with the actual recorded use. (For example, Jain found that in the chemistry library at Purdue University, 11.9% of the collection was acquired prior to 1935, but the checkout sample indicated that only 2% of the usage could be attributed to materials acquired before 1935.) In this type of analysis, only relative use, not absolute numbers, is important. The relative use, R, for any particular group of books, i, may be defined as

$$R_i = \% \text{ relative use of group } i = \frac{H_i + I_i}{S_i} \times 100,$$

where H_i is the number of monographs from group i borrowed during a specified period, I_i is the number of monographs from group i used in the library during the same period, and S_i is the total number of monographs from group i in the collection sample. The statistics are entirely relative. The proportions will vary, depending on the size of the samples taken from the collection, from the books on loan, and so on. The subsets having the lowest R_i (relative-use factor), however, are those least important from the point of view of usage. According to Jain, "A sample of check-outs for home use collected during a relatively short period of time along with a sample of the total collection is more reliable than the past usage data for a shelf list sample for studying home use of monographs." When Jain applied his formula at the Purdue University Library, he drew a large sample from the collection by taking a 20% systematic sample from the shelf list after a random start. The checkout sample was drawn during a specified period in the spring of 1966. Concurrently, a sample for in-library use was derived by examining all books left on tables. This procedure, as Jain himself points out, has certain limitations. Not all books left on tables have actually been used, while not all books that have been used are left on tables (some used items will have been reshelved, and some items will have been used at the shelf itself).

Last Circulation Date

Trueswell[77,78,79] mentions some of the problems involved in basing use predictions on records of past circulation. He points out that one way of predicting future use (used by Fussler and Simon) is:

. . . to examine the total number of times each book in the library (or in a sample) has circulated (if this information were available) and to rank the books according to the number of circulations, including a factor about the distribution of range of use dates. This would require a book card or record of all transactions for each volume which in general would be rather difficult to obtain. This difficulty occurs primarily because the circulation data for the highly used books fill up a book card rather rapidly and a given book, although used considerably, may have only a few circulation entries on the new book card. Some approaches to measuring circulation and book use have been made by the application of this method but difficulties were encountered in collecting data.

He describes an alternative procedure for predicting future use when complete records of past use are not available, his objective being to identify a "core" collection of heavily used items that should be made most accessible in the library. He maintains that, "There is a predictable optimum number of volumes for a library's core collection that will satisfy a given percent of user circulation requirements."

Trueswell's procedure is based only on the last recorded circulation date. The book cards for each volume borrowed during a specified period of time are examined, and the last circulation date for each volume (i.e., the date immediately preceding the present checkout) is recorded. These data are then plotted in the form of a cumulative frequency distribution; that is, "percentage of circulation having a last circulation date (LCD) within the cumulative time period" versus "specified time period" (see Figure 27).

As depicted in Figure 27, nearly 90% of the volumes had last circulation dates within the preceding 12-month period; that is, 90% of the books had circulated at least once during the past 12 months, 50% within the preceding 3 months, and 10% within the past month.

Figure 28 presents the data in a slightly different way, based on items that had *not* previously circulated during the cumulative time period under consideration (36 months in this case). For example, 10% of the sample had not circulated during the past 12 months and approximately 3% had not circulated during the past 36 months. In other words, 97% of the books in

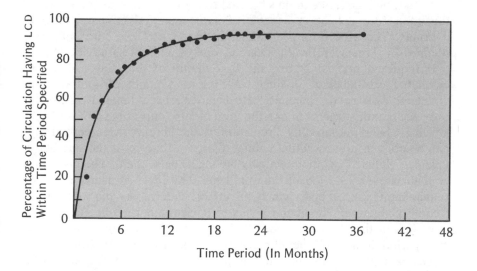

FIGURE 27 Distribution of book use by last circulation date method.[78]

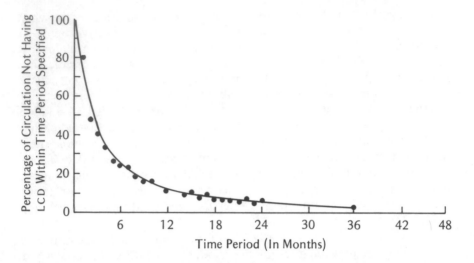

FIGURE 28   Distribution of book use by last circulation date method.[78]

the sample had been charged out at least once during the past 36 months. If the "core collection" was defined as the set of books previously charged out during the past 36 months, it could be expected to satisfy 97% of the current circulation needs.

Trueswell's method can thus be used to estimate the size and composition of a core collection capable of satisfying a fixed percentage of demands. The procedure for estimating the size of the core collection (defined by Trueswell, in this case, as one capable of satisfying 99% of user requirements) is: During the first month of the study, all books circulated are "labeled" in some way; the next month, 90% of all items circulated will need "labeling" (10% having been labeled during the previous month's transactions); the third month, only some 50% will need labeling. Using the monthly circulation by the library, these percentages can be converted into actual volume figures to arrive at the number of volumes "labeled" without actually having to mark them. The process is continued over a period of time until the 99% level of user circulation requirements is reached, which, in effect, determines the size of the "core" collection. The actual books forming the core collection can be identified in the stacks, because their last circulation date is within the time period defined by the 99 percentile point in Figure 27. Books in the stacks having a last circulation date prior to a given cutoff point could, according to Trueswell, be removed and placed in limited-access storage.

Trueswell has applied these techniques at the Deering Library and the Technological Institute Library at Northwestern University (the data in Figures 27 and 28 are from the latter). A core collection at the Deering Library was predicted to be approximately 40% of the library's holdings and, at the Technological Institute, approximately 25% of the holdings.

Trueswell[80] also applied his procedure to the Goodell Library at the University of Massachusetts and to the Mount Holyoke College library, and he found a similar distribution in the percentage of the collection that accounted for a given percentage of the total usage.

Other Studies

Using statistics of past circulation, Morse[54] has illustrated how mathematical models can be used to predict future demand for books, and has applied these models to data available from the Science Library at MIT. The models can be used to predict, for example, the probable future rate of demand for those portions of the collection retired to a less-accessible storage area.

A novel approach to predicting which books in a university collection are likely to be most-used has been described by McGrath.[49] In his "classified course technique," course descriptions in the university catalog are classified by the bibliographic classification scheme being used at the institution. This results in a series of departmental subject "profiles" and an overall university profile. Using three independent data samples, McGrath attempted to show that books with class numbers matching the institutional profile were more likely to be used than books not matching the profile.

If the profile is insignificant, circulation of books matching the profile and circulation of books not matching the profile should be roughly in proportion to the proportion of these two groups in the collection as a whole. To prove the hypothesis, one must show that the proportion of circulation from books matching the profile is greater than the expected circulation from this subset when its size is compared to that of the complete collection. Based on data collected at the University of Southwestern Louisiana, McGrath was able to show that books matching the institutional profile were (a) more likely to be removed from the shelves, (b) after being removed from the shelves, were more likely to be charged out than left on tables, and (c) were more likely than not to be charged out.

The major analysis of McGrath's study was based on an 11-month circulation sample; the key data are summarized in Table 48. The total collection consisted of 172,029 volumes, of which 129,883 matched the

TABLE 48   Distribution of Book Use by Match and Nonmatch with University Course Profile[49]

	Charged Out		Not Charged		Total
	Actual	Expected	Actual	Expected	
Match	53,333	42,905	76,550	86,977	129,883
Nonmatch	3,495	13,922	38,651	28,223	42,146
Total	56,828		115,201		172,029

institutional profile and 42,146 did not. A total of 56,828 volumes (approximately 33% of the complete collection) were circulated during the 11-month period. If "profile matching" has no influence on circulation, one would expect that approximately 33% of each set (matching and nonmatching) would be borrowed. Actually, matching items were borrowed at a ratio of 53,333/129,883, approximately 41%, while the non-matching items were borrowed at a ratio of 3,495/42,146, or approximately 8.3%. These data were confirmed by similar data from the South Dakota School of Mines and Technology. The other parts of the hypothesis (relating to the rate of removal of books from the shelves and the rate of borrowing books thus removed) also were proved in McGrath's study.

In 1956, McClellan[47] described a system of collection control used at the Tottenham Public Libraries (London). An important element in this collection control was a "count," conducted on a specified day of each month, which showed—for each of 150 subject categories—how many books were out on loan and how many were on the shelves. These monthly data were used to indicate trends in the use of the collection, to reveal subject areas in which the library needed to acquire more materials, and to establish priorities for revising the collection (by, for example, discarding obsolete and other little-used items) in various subject areas.

A theoretical study by Sinha[69] in 1971 presents a model which shows, for given budget and space constraints, how many books the library should hold and what the date span of these materials should be, in each subject area, in order to maximize use. The model can be used to predict the need to acquire more materials in a particular area, or it can suggest the need to weed out some of the older materials in specific sections of the collection to make space for more recent acquisitions.

One reason that studies of collection use based on items circulated are much more common than studies based on use within the library is that they are more easily conducted. A recent book by Daiute and Gorman,[15] however, presents a detailed account of procedures that can be used to study in-library book use by interviewing library users. The data gathered from these interviews can be correlated with data on characteristics of library users contained in a machine-readable data base. The techniques described have been tested at the Rider College library in Trenton, New Jersey.

All of the aforementioned studies were designed to determine which parts of a library's collection are likely to be most-used and which least-used. The major objective of this type of analysis is to provide data to aid the library manager in identifying collection weaknesses (e.g., by revealing subject areas in which usage is low as related to the number of users having a potential interest in these subjects) and in deciding which materials to discard or, in the case of a large research library, which materials to relegate to a secondary storage area. Decisions on which materials should be retired to secondary storage can be based on age, on observed rates of use, or on a combination of these criteria. Existing evidence indicates that retirement decisions based on usage are more sound than those based on age alone. Retirement rules derived from age or use criteria also can be modified in various ways, depending upon the type of materials involved. For example, retirement criteria may be applied more stringently to certain subject areas, or to certain languages, than to others.

Leimkuhler and Cooper[40] have pointed out, however, that in a large research library, the size of the active (i.e., nondepository) portion of a collection cannot remain constant over a long period. If it does, eventually demands on the depository collection will exceed demands on the "active" collection. Table 49 illustrates a situation in which the total collection and the rate of obsolescence are growing exponentially, but the active collection remains constant, and retirement is based on age of materials. The depository also grows exponentially, and retirement age is reduced annually. The fraction of total library use from the depository also would grow exponentially.* In the situation depicted in Table 49, where the growth and obsolescence rates are fixed at 0.05,† demand from the depository would exceed demand from the "active" collection

*Some justification for this exponential model is provided by statistics available from Purdue University libraries since 1925. These statistics (see Figure 29) show a steady increase of approximately 6% per annum in both total holdings and new acquisitions. Circulation has more or less paralleled this rate of growth; however, at any one time, the total number of items on loan is considerably less than the size of the collection: the number of books "inactive" in a year is very large and increasing steadily.

†Data presented by Jain[28] suggest that average circulation declines at a fairly steady rate of 6% per annum with each year since acquisition, and at a rate of approximately 4.5% per annum with each year after publication.

TABLE 49   Depository Size and Usage When the Active Collection Is Held at a Fixed Level and Both Growth Rate and Obsolescence Rate Are 5% a Year[40]

Year After Start of Depository, t	Relative Size of Depository, m_t	Relative Usage of Depository, w_t	Retirement Age, d_t
1	0.05	0.003	60 yrs.
5	0.12	0.01	42
10	0.39	0.15	19
15	0.53	0.28	13
20	0.63	0.40	9
25	0.73	0.53	6
50	0.92	0.85	2

after approximately 25 years. After 50 years, 92% of the total collection would be retired to storage, and the fixed-size active collection would satisfy only 15% of the total demands. Leimkuhler and Cooper point out that:

It is interesting to observe the delayed effect on the usage of the depository as compared with rapid initial growth of the precentage of volumes in the depository. The size of the depository is only dependent on the growth rate of the collection, while the use of the depository is dependent on both the growth rate and the obsolescence rate. The values in Table [49] hold for the case where an age rule is used and the rates are equal to 0.05; but the pattern would be much the same for other rates and selection rules. In the long run the depository would eclipse the active collection.

Although, as the authors point out, "it is unlikely that the simple exponential model provides a sufficient explanation of the actual patterns of inactivity of library materials," it is clear that the size of an "active" or "core" collection cannot be allowed to remain constant, but must be adjusted upwards to ensure that the core can always satisfy a fixed percentage of the total demands placed on the library.

Effect of Accessibility

Raffel and Shishko[60] have made a comparison of various "weeding" (retirement) criteria from the viewpoint of both effectiveness of the criteria and cost of implementing a weeding policy. They based their investigation on circulation data and dates of publication and acquisition.

Their assumption was that there will be some loss of circulation associated with the storage of books in less-expensive, but inconvenient, locations (i.e., some users want a book only if it is immediately available and will not wait for its recovery from storage). Because new books are added to a collection each year, however, and because the use of books declines systematically with age (see Figure 30), they concluded that "the

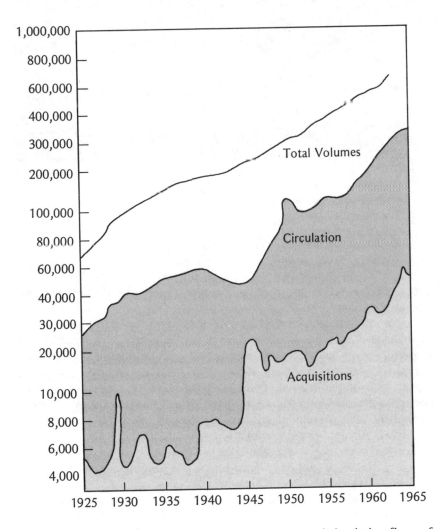

FIGURE 29 Growth of collection, acquisition rate, and circulation figures for Purdue University libraries, 1925–1965.[40]

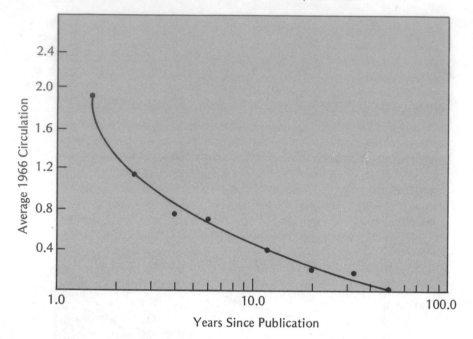

FIGURE 30   Average 1966 circulation of a book as a function of x, the number of years since its publication.[60]

number of books stored inexpensively can rise each year without lowering aggregate benefits."

Using a random sample of 412 books selected from MIT stacks, Raffel and Shishko identified 188 that were in the collection in January 1963. For this sample, they calculated the number of circulations that would have been "lost" during the years 1964 – 1967, based on three retirement criteria: date of publication, date of acquisition, and circulation data. These data are shown in Figure 31, which plots the percentage of books removed by each retirement criterion against the percentage of circulations lost had this criterion been used. For example, if the circulation criterion had been used to retire 70% of the collection, approximately 40% of the circulations would have been lost. (The assumption here is rather simplistic—that circulation of a particular book will be "lost" if it is stored inconveniently. This analysis appears *not* to take into account that a book badly needed will be requested from storage, and that a substitute may be found for a book not available in the library.)

In comparison, if the acquisition-date criterion had been used to retire

70% of the collection, approximately 60% of the circulation would have been lost. The "foreknowledge" curve shows the best possible retirement policy, resulting in only a 10% circulation loss with 70% of the collection retired.

The Raffel and Shishko analysis also indicates that retirement on the basis of circulation data is likely to be more effective than retirement on the basis of either publication or acquisition date (which turn out to be quite similar in performance). Another consideration, however, is the cost of implementing a particular retirement policy. Some associated cost factors are:

1. *Publication Date Weeding.* This is likely to be least expensive, because it can be done *en masse* from catalog cards or the books themselves. The catalog cards need not be altered. Instead, a general notice can be posted prominently in the catalog area (e.g., "All books published prior to 1940 are located off the immediate premises.").

2. *Acquisition Date Weeding.* This will be more expensive, because it requires examination of records other than catalog cards (which usually

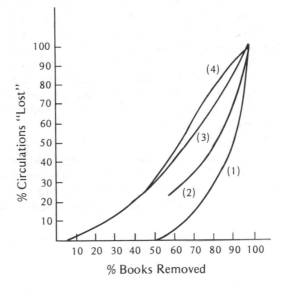

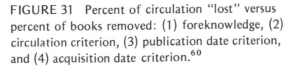

FIGURE 31   Percent of circulation "lost" versus percent of books removed: (1) foreknowledge, (2) circulation criterion, (3) publication date criterion, and (4) acquisition date criterion.[60]

do not show acquisition date) and, more importantly, because it will require modification of catalog cards to show which items are stored away from the library.

3. *Circulation Date Weeding.* This is likely to be most expensive. It requires the conduct of some type of circulation analysis, the examination of date labels, and the changing of catalog cards. Raffel and Shishko estimate that it would cost approximately $0.80 to $1.00 per volume retired, whereas retirement on the basis of publication date would likely cost somewhere in the range of $0.40 per volume.

The authors go on to suggest that, balancing costs against benefits (or inconveniences), publication date weeding may be the most cost-effective approach, at least for science materials.

Lister[44] has developed models to show costs associated with the retirement of materials to storage on the basis of age and use statistics. He demonstrates that, for books stored in a compact form in less-accessible storage areas, storage cost per volume is reduced; but the cost per circulation is increased, especially if some form of cost penalty is assessed for the delay and inconvenience caused to users. The "least-cost decision rules" are very sensitive to changes in unit circulation costs: As cost per circulation for items stored goes up, the library's overall savings from compact storage are drastically reduced. When Lister's cost models were applied empirically to three departmental libraries at Purdue University, it was found that retirement on the basis of usage was more efficient than retirement on the basis of age. Lister's models show, however, that significant cost savings would occur only if a substantial proportion of the total collection (up to 60%) were stored in compact form. Lister's work has been summarized by Andrews.[1]

Simon[68] also has studied the economics of book storage under conditions imposing cost penalties for time delays and other inconvenience factors. His cost penalty has three components: (a) cost of retrieving an item from the storage area, (b) cost associated with patron inconvenience, and (c) cost due to loss of circulations caused by stored books not being available for browsing.

Useful review articles on weeding criteria have been written by Cooper[13] and Seymour.[66,67] Cooper's article describes some procedures used at the Chemistry Library of Columbia University, including an application of Trueswell's "last circulation date" criterion.

It is important to note that the various circulation studies described in this chapter make the assumption that future use of books can be predicted from present rates of use, a claim made by Middleswort[53] in 1951. Newhouse and Alexander,[56] two economists who undertook a cost-benefit analysis of the Beverly Hills Public Library, support this assumption in the following terms:

It is plausible to suppose that the proportion of books t years old which leave the collection each year is relatively constant over time. In other words, we can assume that, on the average, demand for a new book in a certain class t years from now can be represented by demand today for a book in that class that is t years old.

Line and Sandison,[43] however, take a diametrically opposite view and claim that, "no existing studies can be used to predict future usage." They base this claim largely on the difference between "synchronous" and "diachronous" decay of the literature, referred to in more detail in Chapter 13.

It also should be noted that, while several of the techniques discussed in this chapter are intended to retire complete groups of materials to storage (by date, subject, language, or some combination of these), usage indicators may create exceptions to general rules; that is, a particular book will not be discarded or retired to storage if it has been used above some threshold level, even though it falls within a general category of materials identified as prime candidates for retirement. Moreover, it is not universally accepted that materials can be retired to storage systematically on the basis of a formula or routine practice, and not all retirement programs operate on such bases.

One of the most comprehensive programs of this type, the Yale Selective Book Retirement Program, designed to retire approximately 60,000 items each year, is based largely on volume-by-volume weeding, treating each book on its own merit. As reported by Ash,[2] only certain types of materials can be retired *en bloc*, and these generally are within a particular subject area (e.g., dissertations in economics). General learned-society serial publications, it was found, also can be retired on the basis of age, providing that certain serials are withheld from the general retirement plan on the basis of usage or other factors. According to Rouse,[64] the Yale program has retired almost a quarter of a million volumes to storage and transferred more than 50,000 to other campus libraries.

The extent to which various portions of a book collection will be used, as revealed by a number of the studies mentioned in this chapter, is dependent upon a number of factors, including age of materials and subject area. Physical accessibility is another factor influencing rate of use; that is, all other things being equal, the most accessible materials are likely to be used proportionately more than the materials that are less conveniently located. Likewise, demand for portions of the collection or for particular kinds of materials may be stimulated by "highlighting" these items—placing them in a "prime" location.

Mueller[55] conducted a study of public libraries in six suburban communities (of varying sizes) in the Chicago area, primarily to determine whether "new" books were used more frequently than "old" books. The study revealed that, in three of the libraries, new titles were used substantially more often than old titles. No significant differences, however, were observed in the other three libraries. Apparently, in the first group of libraries, factors other than mere age of books were exerting strong influences on demand. In these libraries, special emphasis had been placed on the display of new titles (e.g., via a "new book shelf"), and a shorter circulation period had been allowed for these, which in itself would tend to increase the number of circulations occurring during a year. Mueller points out that a librarian has the ability to shape patterns of use by providing differing levels of accessibility to various portions of the collection.

Goldhor[25] studied the effect of "prime location" on the circulation of 110 selected titles in two medium-sized public libraries in Illinois. The rate of circulation for these titles, when observed over a six-month period, was found to be much the same in the two libraries. During a second six-month period, the 110 titles were placed on special display near the circulation desk in one of the two libraries. The use of the selected titles increased significantly in this library.

More on Storage

A major portion of this chapter has been concerned with evaluating a collection to determine which items are most-used and which are least-used, with the ultimate objective of optimizing storage of the collection. Optimization is achieved by storing the most-used portion of a collection in the most-accessible and convenient location and by storing lesser used portions in progressively less-convenient and less-accessible locations. For example, in a university library, the most-used books and serials would be on open shelves, less-used items might be stored in bookstacks located in the library building, and least-used materials might be stored in an off-campus depository or warehouse. Such a depository could be owned by the university itself or might be a cooperative depository (e.g., the Center for Research Libraries) in which little-used research materials from a number of libraries are stored and organized. The assumption is, of course, that prime storage space on campus is more expensive than off-campus storage space. Some penalties associated with off-campus storage are (a) the delay associated with retrieving a volume from storage when it is needed and (b) the actual cost of this retrieval. Depending upon the location of the depository, this could involve mailing fees, messenger time, telephone charges, expenses for picking up the item by car, or other costs of this kind.

Another cost factor must be considered in the storage of less-used materials. The volumes on open shelves must be arranged in a systematic way, usually by the classification scheme adopted by the library, to allow for browsing and to permit the user to find a particular item easily once its shelf location has been determined through the catalog. But materials in bookstacks that are accessible only to members of the library staff, and particularly those in remote storage areas, do not need to be stored by any type of subject arrangement. Indeed, it may be uneconomical and inefficient to do so. Instead, these materials may be stored "compactly" in other ways.

Metcalf[52] identifies a number of possible "compact" shelving methods, including storage by size, date of acquisition, arranging the books on their fore-edges, using unconventional shelving or shelving arrangements, or various combinations of these.

A useful review of "conventional" methods of compact storage was made by Lopez;[45] another, on methods incorporating mechanical retrieval devices, by Schriefer and Mostecky;[65] and a third, on the possibilities of microform for saving space, by Stevens.[75] Data from the Yale Compact Storage Plan, as reported by Ash,[2] indicated that, in compact storage, books could be stored for as little as $0.42 each, whereas the cost for storage on conventional shelving was $1.68 per volume. Although space is conserved by all compact-storage techniques, there may be an added cost if mechanical and mobile shelving units are used, and these costs may, in fact, offset much, if not all, of the gain derived from saving space.

A recent study of compact storage was made by Ellsworth,[19] who analyzed 12 storage systems to determine their cost and economy of space in housing a collection of half a million volumes. He reported that, while conventional bookstacks can store only 15 volumes per square foot, the Randtriever (a system in which books are stored in containers and retrieved mechanically) can store as many as 147. On the other hand, this device is expensive, with an associated cost of $1.42 per volume for inaugurating the program. In contrast, the Yale system of arrangement by size and shelving on fore-edges costs from $0.40 to $0.50 per volume.*

*Ellsworth's 1969 figures indicate a per-volume cost of $0.49 for the Yale system and $1.08 for the Randtriever, when only costs of the building and shelving are taken into consideration. When all compact storage costs for inaugurating a storage program are considered (including land, changing of records, and transfer to storage), the costs per volume range from $1.13 for the Yale system to $1.44 for expansion of conventional shelving to $1.69 for the Randtriever. Ellsworth suggests, however, that the "comparative annual costs parallel the comparative initial costs."

The most efficient storage system from the viewpoint of space, then, is not necessarily the least expensive. In fact, a system using mechanical retrieval devices may be highly compact but, overall, quite expensive. Ellsworth also points out that costs associated with the alteration of records, the retrieval of books from storage, and the inconvenience to library users may offset most, if not all, economies in actual space occupied.

Raffel and Shishko[60] provide another useful analysis of storage alternatives. Table 50 compares a number of these storage alternatives for library materials that are used frequently, moderately, and infrequently. Costs of storage per volume, per year, for each alternative, are related to possible benefits or inconvenience factors. Based on figures derived for MIT in 1968, costs were calculated on the basis of space requirements, land, construction, building maintenance, and storage equipment (conventional shelving and compact shelving). The total cost per volume per year is "the sum of the annual maintenance cost per volume, the uniform annual building and storage equipment cost per volume, and the annual interest charges on the cost of lands used for book storage per volume."

For a "moderate use" collection, compact storage halves the annual storage costs per volume from approximately $0.28 to $0.14. The necessity to weed the collection periodically, however, and perhaps to provide some retrieval mechanism, may reduce the net savings on storage to around 10%–20%. In general, the authors point out that alternative storage devices were not a particularly attractive way of saving money at MIT. The best alternative saved approximately 15% of the current annual expenditure for the storage of nonreserve books—only 6.4% of the library's annual budget. The potential saving, therefore, was only 15% of 6%, or approximately 1% of the total budget.

Raffel and Shishko also point out that off-campus compact storage, at MIT at least, offered little economy over on-campus compact storage (a savings of only $0.015 per volume per year). At MIT, with 250,000 volumes compactly stored off-campus, the saving would be only $3,750 per year, which probably would not be enough to offset the cost of retrieval from storage when needed, in addition to the associated inconvenience factors.

Book shelving models developed at Purdue University have been discussed by Leimkuhler,[39] Cox,[14] Leimkuhler and Cox,[41] and Raffel,[59] with particular reference to shelving by book height. They point out that relatively efficient storage can be achieved by using as few as three to five different shelf heights and that, by shelving books on their fore-edges, economical storage can be achieved with only two shelf heights. Raffel[59] shows, however, that if all books were stored by size on their fore-edge, the best that could be achieved would be to double shelf capacity. It

TABLE 50   Cost/Volume Associated with Various Storage Alternatives[60]

Storage Alternative	Benefits	Cost/Volume/Year
Infrequent use:		
1. Open access, conventional storage, on campus.	Browsing possible.	$0.2269
2. Open access, conventional storage, off campus.	Browsing possible only for those willing or able to travel off campus (presumably for special projects or papers). Retrieval system necessary, with delay incurred.	0.1992
3. Closed access, compact storage, off campus.	Browsing impossible. Retrieval system necessary, with delay incurred.	0.0752
Moderate use:		
1. Open access, conventional storage, on campus.	Browsing possible.	0.2825
2. Closed access, conventional storage, on campus.	Browsing possible but discouraged, except for special projects.	0.2581
3. Open access, conventional storage, off campus.	Browsing possible for those willing to travel off campus. Retrieval system necessary, with delay incurred.	0.2509
4. Closed access, conventional storage, off campus.	Browsing possible only under very special circumstances. Retrieval system necessary, with delay incurred.	0.2293
5. Closed access, compact storage, on campus.	Browsing impossible, but retrieval delay short.	0.1360
6. Closed access, compact storage, off campus.	Browsing impossible, retrieval necessary, with delay incurred.	0.1213
Heavy use:		
1. Open access, conventional storage, on campus.	Easy browsing possible.	0.3474

should be noted, however, that the Yale system of compact storage, with 22-inch aisles between stacks (as described by Ash), claims to store four and one-half times as many books in the same space as conventional shelving. Ellsworth also quotes figures for the Yale system of arrangement: 64 volumes per square foot, as opposed to 15 volumes using conventional shelving.

Buckland et al.[9] have analyzed storage costs in relation to the total library budget for acquisition and storage. Table 51 shows the effect of storage costs at two hypothetical special libraries in the field of petroleum, one located in an urban area where real estate is expensive and the other in a lower cost rural area. With comparable budgets for acquisition and storage, the rural library will be able to acquire more journal titles and retain them for longer periods, the net result being that it will be able to satisfy a greater proportion of demands from its own collection.

This chapter has considered various possible approaches to the evaluation of collections of bibliographic materials. Ultimately, however, a library collection must be evaluated in terms of the proportion of all demands it is able to satisfy. If a collection is sufficiently large, is well-chosen in relation to the needs of the community served, is accessible, and is updated and weeded, it should be capable of satisfying the great majority of legitimate demands (both known-item and subject-related requests) placed upon it. In Chapter 2, several studies that have measured failure rates in libraries were noted, including the important element of "collection failures." Chapter 6 will further identify procedures that can be used to measure the ability of a library to supply particular materials to users when the need for them arises.

TABLE 51   Comparison of Storage Costs for City Library and Rural Library[9]

	City library	Rural library
Assumptions		
Annual acquisitions cost	£5 per title	£5 per title
Annual storage costs	£0.125 per volume	£0.033 per volume
Requests received	2,000 per annum	2,000 per annum
Conclusions		
If annual budget £1,000		
Titles taken	140	175
Retention period	18 years	22 years
Volumes in stock	2,520	3,850
Requests satisfied	76%	80%
If annual budget £1,500		
Titles taken	205	260
Retention period	18 years	23 years
Volumes in stock	3,690	5,980
Requests satisfied	83%	88%

REFERENCES

1. Andrews, T. "The Role of Departmental Libraries in Operations Research Studies in a University Library. Part 1. Selection for Storage Problems." *Special Libraries,* 58:519–524, 1968.
2. Ash, L. *Yale's Selective Book Retirement Program.* Hamden, Conn., Archon Books, 1963.
3. Baumol, W. J. and Marcus, M. *Economics of Academic Libraries.* Washington, D.C., American Council of Education, 1973.
4. Blau, P. M. and Margulies, R. Z. "The Reputations of American Professional Schools." *Change,* 6:42–47, 1974–1975.
5. Bonn, G. S. "Evaluation of the Collection." *Library Trends,* 22:265–304, 1974.
6. *Books for College Libraries.* Chicago, American Library Association, 1967.
7. Brandon, A. N. "Selected List of Books and Journals for the Small Library." *Bulletin of the Medical Library Association,* 61:179–200, 1973.
8. Brown, C. H. *Scientific Serials.* Chicago, Association of College and Reference Libraries, 1956.
9. Buckland, M. K. et al. *Systems Analysis of a University Library.* Lancaster, Eng., University of Lancaster Library, 1970.
10. Cassata, M. B. and Dewey, G. L. "The Evaluation of a University Library Collection: Some Guidelines." *Library Resources and Technical Services,* 13:450–457, 1969.
11. Clapp, V. W. and Jordan, R. T. "Quantitative Criteria for Adequacy of Academic Library Collections." *College and Research Libraries,* 26:371–380, 1965.
12. Coale, R. P. "Evaluation of a Research Library Collection: Latin-American Colonial History at the Newberry." *Library Quarterly,* 35:173–184, 1965.
13. Cooper, M. "Criteria for Weeding of Collections." *Library Resources and Technical Services,* 12:339–351, 1968.
14. Cox, J. G. *Optimum Storage of Library Material.* Lafayette, Ind., Purdue University Libraries, 1964.
15. Daiute, R. J. and Gorman, K. A. *Library Operations Research.* Dobbs Ferry, N.Y., Oceana Publications, 1974.
16. Downs, R. B. "Uniform Statistics for Library Holdings." *Library Quarterly,* 16:63–69, 1946.
17. Downs, R. B. *University Library Statistics.* Washington, D.C., Association of Research Libraries, 1969.
18. Downs, R. B. and Heussman, J. W. "Standards for University Libraries." *College and Research Libraries,* 31:28–35, 1970.
19. Ellsworth, R. *The Economics of Compact Storage.* Metuchen, N.J., Scarecrow Press, 1969.
20. El-Sheniti, E. S. "The University Library and the Scholar: A Study of the Recorded Faculty Use of a Large University Library." Doctoral Dissertation. Chicago, Graduate Library School, University of Chicago, 1960.
21. Fussler, H. H. and Simon, J. L. *Patterns in the Use of Books in Large Research Libraries.* Chicago, University of Chicago Press, 1969.
22. Goldhor, H. "Analysis of an Inductive Method of Evaluating the Book Collection of a Public Library." *Libri,* 23:6–17, 1973.
23. Goldhor, H. *A Plan for the Development of Public Library Service in the Minneapolis-St. Paul Metropolitan Area.* St. Paul, Minn., Library Division, State Department of Education, 1967.
24. Goldhor, H. "Are the Best Books the Most Read?" *Library Quarterly,* 29:251–255, 1959.

25. Goldhor, H. "The Effect of Prime Display Location on Public Library Circulation of Selected Adult Titles." *Library Quarterly, 42*:371–389, 1972.
26. Hirsch, R. "Evaluation of Book Collections." *In: Library Evaluation*. Edited by W. S. Yenawine. Syracuse, N.Y., Syracuse University Press, 1959, pp. 7–20.
27. Hirsch, F. E., ed. "Standards for Libraries." *Library Trends, 21*, 1972.
28. Jain, A. K. *A Sampled Data Study of Book Usage in the Purdue University Libraries.* Lafayette, Ind., Purdue University, 1965.
29. Jain, A. K. *Report on a Statistical Study of Book Use.* Lafayette, Ind., School of Industrial Engineering, Purdue University, 1967.
30. Jain, A. K. "Sampling and Data Collection Methods for a Book-Use Study." *Library Quarterly, 39*:245–252, 1969.
31. Jain, A. K. "Sampling and Short-Period Usage in the Purdue Library." *College and Research Libraries, 27*:211–218, 1966.
32. Jordan, R. T. "Library Characteristics of Colleges Ranking High in Academic Excellence." *College and Research Libraries, 24*:369–376, 1963.
33. Kilgour, F. G. "Recorded Use of Books in the Yale Medical Library." *American Documentation, 12*:266–269, 1961.
34. Kilgour, F. G. "Use of Medical and Biological Journals in the Yale Medical Library." *Bulletin of the Medical Library Association, 50*:429–449, 1962.
35. Kilgour, F. G. and Fleming, T. P. "Moderately and Heavily Used Biomedical Journals." *Bulletin of the Medical Library Association, 52*:234–241, 1964.
36. Kovacs, H. "Analysis of One Year's Circulation at the Downstate Medical Center Library." *Bulletin of the Medical Library Association, 54*:42–47, 1966.
37. Kurth, W. H. *Survey of the Interlibrary Loan Operations of the National Library of Medicine.* Washington, D.C., DHEW, Public Health Service, 1962.
38. Leigh, R. D. "The Public Library Inquiry's Sampling of Library Holdings of Books and Periodicals." *Library Quarterly, 21*:157–172, 1951.
39. Leimkuhler, F. F. "On Information Storage Models." *In: Planning Library Services: Proceedings of a Research Seminar Held at the University of Lancaster, 9–11 July 1969.* Session 1, Paper 2. Edited by A. G. Mackenzie and I. M. Stuart. Lancaster, Eng., University of Lancaster Library, 1969.
40. Leimkuhler, F. F. and Cooper, M. D. "Analytical Models for Library Planning." *Journal of the American Society for Information Science, 22*:390–398, 1971.
41. Leimkuhler, F. F. and Cox, J. G. "Compact Book Storage in Libraries." *Operations Research, 12*:419–427, 1964.
42. Line, M. B. *Library Surveys.* Hamden, Conn., Archon Books, 1967.
43. Line, M. B. and Sandison, A. "'Obsolescence' and Changes in the Use of Literature with Time." *Journal of Documentation, 30*:283–350, 1974.
44. Lister, W. C. "Least Cost Decision Rules for the Selection of Library Materials for Compact Storage." Doctoral Dissertation. Lafayette, Ind., School of Industrial Engineering, Purdue University, 1967. PB 174 441.
45. Lopez, M. D. "Compact Book Storage: Solutions Utilizing Conventional Methods." *Library Trends, 19*:352–361, 1971.
46. Martyn, J. and Gilchrist, A. *An Evaluation of British Scientific Journals.* ASLIB Occasional Publication No. 1. London, ASLIB, 1968.
47. McClellan, A. W. "New Concepts of Service." *Library Association Record, 58*:299–305, 1956.
48. McGrath, W. E. "Correlating the Subjects of Books Taken Out of and Books Used Within an Open-Stack Library." *College and Research Libraries, 32*:280–285, 1971.
49. McGrath, W. E. "The Significance of Books Used According to a Classified Profile of Academic Departments." *College and Research Libraries, 33*:212–219, 1972.

50. McInnis, R. M. "Research Collections: An Approach to the Assessment of Quality." *IPLO Quarterly, 13*:13–22, 1971.
51. McInnis, R. M. "The Formula Approach to Library Size: An Empirical Study of Its Efficiency in Evaluating Research Libraries." *College and Research Libraries, 33*:190–198, 1972.
52. Metcalf, K. D. *Planning Academic and Research Library Buildings.* New York, McGraw-Hill, 1965, pp. 157–165.
53. Middlesworth, L. E. "A Study of Book Use in the University of Chicago Library." Master's Thesis. Chicago, Graduate Library School, University of Chicago, 1951.
54. Morse, P. M. *Library Effectiveness: A Systems Approach.* Cambridge, Mass., MIT Press, 1968.
55. Mueller, E. "Are New Books Read More Than Old Ones?" *Library Quarterly, 35*:166–172, 1965.
56. Newhouse, J. P. and Alexander, A. J. *An Economic Analysis of Public Library Services.* Lexington, Mass., Lexington Books, 1972.
57. Otterson, B. "A Bibliography on Standards for Evaluating Libraries." *College and Research Libraries, 32*:127–144, 1971.
58. Piternick, G. "Library Growth and Academic Quality." *College and Research Libraries, 24*:223–229, 1963.
59. Raffel, J. A. "Compact Book Storage Models." Master's Thesis. Lafayette, Ind., Purdue University, 1963.
60. Raffel, J. A. and Shishko, R. *Systematic Analysis of University Libraries.* Cambridge, Mass., MIT Press, 1969.
61. Raisig, L. M. et al. "How Biomedical Investigators Use Library Books." *Bulletin of the Medical Library Association, 54*:104–107, 1966.
62. Raney, M. L. *The University Libraries.* Chicago, University of Chicago Press, 1933.
63. Reichard, E. W. and Orsagh, T. J. "Holdings and Expenditures of U.S. Academic Libraries: An Evaluation Technique." *College and Research Libraries, 27*:478–487, 1966.
64. Rouse, R. "Within-Library Solutions to Book Space Problems." *Library Trends, 19*:299–310, 1971.
65. Schriefer, K. and Mostecky, I. "Compact Book Storage: Mechanization Systems." *Library Trends, 19*:362–378, 1971.
66. Seymour, C. A. "Weeding the Collection: A Review of Research on Identifying Obsolete Stock. Part 1. Monographs." *Libri, 22*:137–148, 1972.
67. Seymour, C. A. "Weeding the Collection: A Review of Research on Identifying Obsolete Stock. Part 2. Serials." *Libri, 22*:183–189, 1972.
68. Simon, J. L. "How Many Books Should Be Stored Where? An Economic Analysis." *College and Research Libraries, 28*:92–103, 1967.
69. Sinha, B. K. "Operations Research in Controlled Acquisition and Weeding of Library Collections." Doctoral Dissertation. Philadelphia, University of Pennsylvania, 1971.
70. Snowball, G. J. "Letter to the Editor." *College and Research Libraries, 33*:487–489, 1972.
71. "Standards for College Libraries." Prepared by the Association of College and Research Libraries. *College and Research Libraries, 20*:274–280, 1959.
72. "Standards for Junior College Libraries." Prepared by the Association of College and Research Libraries. *College and Research Libraries, 21*:200–206, 1960.
73. State University of New York. Prepared by Associates for Library Services, and Chancellor's Advisory Committee on Libraries. *Proposals for the Growth of Library Collections of the State University of New York: A Formula for Liminal Adequacy, with Recommendations for Growth Beyond.* Albany, N.Y., 1970.

74. Stearns, N. S. and Ratcliff, W. W. "An Integrated Health-Science Core Library for Physicians, Nurses and Allied Health Practitioners in Community Hospitals." *New England Journal of Medicine, 283*:1489–1498, 1970.
75. Stevens, R. E. "The Microform Revolution." *Library Trends, 19*:379–395, 1971.
76. Stieg, L. "A Technique for Evaluating the College Library Book Collection." *Library Quarterly, 13*:34–44, 1943.
77. Trueswell, R. W. "A Quantitative Measure of User Circulation Requirements and Its Possible Effect on Stack Thinning and Multiple Copy Determination." *American Documentation, 16*:20–25, 1965.
78. Trueswell, R. W. "Determining the Optimal Number of Volumes for a Library's Core Collection." *Libri, 16*:49–60, 1966.
79. Trueswell, R. W. "Two Characteristics of Circulation and Their Effect on the Implementation of Mechanized Circulation Control Systems." *College and Research Libraries, 25*:285–291, 1964.
80. Trueswell, R. W. "User Circulation Satisfaction vs. Size of Holdings at Three Academic Libraries." *College and Research Libraries, 30*:204–213, 1969.
81. Webb, W. "Project CoED: A University Library Collection Evaluation and Development Program." *Library Resources and Technical Services, 13*:457–462, 1969.
82. Williams, E. E. "Surveying Library Collections." *In: Library Surveys*. Edited by M. F. Tauber and I. R. Stephens. New York, Columbia University Press, 1967, pp. 23–45.
83. Winchell, C. M. *Guide to Reference Books*. 8th Edition. Chicago, American Library Association, 1967. *Supplements*.

6

Evaluation of
Document Delivery
Capabilities

As stated previously, the principal criterion by which a library collection is judged is whether or not it satisfies the demands placed upon it or, more precisely, what proportion of the demands it is able to satisfy; in other words, its ability to provide documents required by library users. This may be referred to as *document delivery capability*. When evaluating such capabilities, the primary concerns should be how *many* requests can be satisfied and (since, presumably, through interlibrary cooperation virtually any request for published materials can be filled eventually) how *long* it takes to satisfy various requests.

Buckland[7] uses the term *satisfaction level* when referring to the criterion of whether or not a reader can find a particular book on the shelves when he wants it. Clearly, the larger the collection of titles held, the more demands it is likely to satisfy. But other factors may influence satisfaction level, and three "critical" ones are identified by Buckland:

1. The number of copies held.
2. The frequency with which a book is sought (i.e., its popularity).
3. The length of time it is off the shelves when being used.

A library's document delivery capability is governed, then, not only by the number of titles in its collection, but also by the number of copies that are available—particularly of the most-used titles—and by the loan period established.

The document delivery capability, unlike many other facets of library operation, is relatively easy to measure in quantitative terms, and a number of surveys have indeed measured the ability of a library to provide needed documents. As early as 1934, for example, Gaskill et al.[19] reported on the use of the library at Iowa State College. Interviews with 1,042 students disclosed that 87 (8%) were unable to locate the materials they were seeking when they came to the library. An analysis of all failures revealed that 12% were due to collection inadequacies and 60% to books being checked out by other users. In the study of the Science Library at MIT, reported by Bush et al.[12] in 1956, it was found that the library was able to supply approximately 85% of the books and 93% of the periodicals requested by users, an overall success rate of approximately 89%. Although effectiveness varied among types of users and types of materials, it never fell below 70%, with ability to supply biology journals receiving the lowest score. Bush et al. also investigated reasons for inability to supply needed materials, and reported that the major cause was items being out on loan at the time they were requested.

The most extensive investigation of the document delivery capability of libraries was undertaken by the Institute for the Advancement of Medical Communications (IAMC) for the National Library of Medicine. It has been reported by Orr et al.,[35] Orr and Schless,[34] and Pizer and Cain.[40] A related paper by Pings[38] discusses techniques that might be used to monitor and measure document delivery service within the Regional Medical Library environment. The *document delivery test* (DDT), used by IAMC in its investigation, is a simple, effective method of measuring the ability of a library to supply documents. It measures both the adequacy of a collection and the speed with which the library can supply documents, both from its own holdings and from outside sources. The test was devised to evaluate the strengths of collections and the quality of service in U.S. medical libraries. The DDT sample consisted of 300 citations, drawn at random from a much larger pool of items cited in a sample of recent papers in biomedicine. It covered a broad range in terms of date, source, language, and type of materials (although the majority of citations were to biomedical journals, some were to monographs and other bibliographic forms).

The test was administered to medical libraries by the project staff of IAMC, who simulated library users. The IAMC staff members had no special knowledge of the libraries they were testing, and the library staff themselves were unaware that the test was taking place. The scope of the evaluation is illustrated in Table 52; the data sheet completed by the

TABLE 52   Parameters of the Document Delivery Test

1. Not in library (coverage)

2. In library. Time to deliver
   $<10^1$ (10 minutes)
   10^1 to 10^2 (10 minutes to 2 hours)
   10^2 to 10^3 (2 hours to one day)
   10^3 to 10^4 (one day to one week)
   $>10^4$ (over one week)

3. Borrowing, estimated. From last 50 ILL requests.

investigator for each item in the sample is shown in Figure 32. Each item in the sample of 300 was checked in the catalogs of the library to determine whether or not it was included in the library collection (section 1 in Figure 32), thus measuring the *coverage* of the collection (i.e., proportion of items actually held by the library).

The next step was to determine how quickly items held in the collection could be obtained. Eighteen possible search outcomes were identified (see sections 2–6 in Figure 32): the item may be immediately available on the open shelves; it may be shelved in some less-accessible location; it may be on loan or at the bindery, with an estimated return date (or estimated delivery time [EDT]) several days or weeks away; it may be missing completely; and so on. Each of these possible search outcomes was translated into a standard speed code representing five points on an exponential scale (see Table 52).* For example, an item found on the open shelves at the first attempt and without staff help received the best possible score ($<10^1$) on the exponential scale. For an item not held by the library being evaluated, an estimate was made of how long it would take to borrow it from another library. This estimate was based on statistics of how long it had taken to satisfy the last 50 interlibrary loans handled by the library (for this phase of the evaluation, the cooperation of the library involved is clearly required, and the study can no longer be unobtrusive).

Through administration of the document delivery test, it is possible to develop a library *capability index* (CI), which varies from a maximum score of 100 to a minimum of 0. In the unlikely event that a library were to hold all items in the test sample, with all items being present on open shelves when sought, the library would receive a score of 100. The test has been applied to 92 medical school libraries in the United States (see Orr and Schless[34]). The percentage of test items owned by these libraries

---

*Evans and Borko[18] have suggested that a more simplified method of scoring (i.e., one using fewer categories) would produce the same results.

DOCUMENT DELIVERY DATA SHEET

Author(s) or Editor(s) (Books only) /	Journal or book title

Volume /	Pages /	Date

Institutional source of citation:	Sample number	Case number

1.
In medical library's collection?   (CIRCLE ONE)   No 1 → STOP   Yes 2

2.
On immediate premises?   (CIRCLE ONE)   No 1   (SPECIFY)   Yes 2
Storage site _____   (E.D.T. _____)
→ STOP

3.
On shelves?   (CIRCLE ONE)   No 1   Yes 2 → STOP

4.   (CIRCLE ONE)
Off-shelf status   E.D.T.   Circulation 4   Can't locate in 1st search X

Bindery	1	(_____)	
In process	2	(available? Y N)	
In storage	3	(_____)	
Special location	5	(mediated? Y N_____)	
To be shelved	6		
Recorded as missing	7		
Other known status	8	(_____)	

(SPECIFY _____)
→ STOP

5.   (CIRCLE ONE)   **6.**
Circulation status   Loan period   Result of second search

Reserve	1		(_____)
Inter-library loan	2		
Faculty	3	(Recall? Y N)	(_____)
Students	4	(Recall? Y N)	(_____)
Other	5	(Recall? Y N)	(_____)

On shelf	1
Can't locate	2
Other	3

(SPECIFY) _____

(SPECIFY) _____
→ STOP   → STOP

COMMENTS: (e.g. location tool problems)

FIGURE 32   Document delivery data sheet.[35]

varied from a low of 57% to a high of 97% (average = 82.9%, median = 85.2%). The capability index of these libraries varied from a low of 49 to a high of 94.

It is possible to administer the test, with a sample of 300 citations, in approximately four hours. With a sample of this size, one can be 95% confident that the CI for a library will not vary ± 5 points on repeated tests with different samples, unless the capability of the library changes between tests.

Penner[37] has described the development of a similar document delivery test, in the field of library and information science, and its application to two library school libraries, using a sample of 296 citations. In this case, however, it took approximately nine hours to administer the test.

Procedures very similar to the DDT, to assess the ability of a library to supply bibliographic materials needed by users, were developed and tested by De Prospo et al.[13] The probability that a user will find a particular bibliographic item when needed is the product of the probability that the library owns the item and that the item is on the shelves. Probability is expressed by the number of successful outcomes in each 100 attempts. A probability of 0.41 means that 41 of each 100 attempts to find a particular item will be successful. To test the ability of public libraries to provide needed items, the investigators formed the following three probability samples:

1. *Recently published books.* A sample of 500 titles drawn from the *American Book Publishing Record* for the years 1966–1970 (BPR sample).

2. *Periodicals.* A sample of 80 citations to periodical articles published during the years 1966–1970, drawn from printed indexes commonly held by public libraries.

3. *Titles known to be in the library's collection.* A sample of 500 citations drawn from the shelflist of the library being evaluated.

These samples can be used to determine the probability that a user will be able to find a needed book or periodical article in a particular library. In the case of the BPR sample, the library's catalog is checked to determine the "probability of ownership," Pr(O). For example, if a library owned 325 of the books in the sample, the Pr(O) would be 0.65. When the library shelves are searched for the titles owned, an "availability of books owned probability," Pr(B), can be calculated. A Pr(B) of 0.40 means that a user has a 40% probability of finding an owned item on the shelves when he needs it; in other words, 130 of the 325 items held by the library will be found on the shelves when a search is made. When the Pr(O) is multiplied by the Pr(B), the result is a new probability, Pr(A), the probability of availability. In the aforementioned example, the Pr(A) of the library is 0.65 × 0.40, or 0.26. This means that, in this hypothetical library, a user has 26 chances out of 100 to find a particular recently published book.

The BPR sample was applied by De Prospo and his colleagues to a group of 20 U.S. public libraries of varying sizes. In this group, the Pr(O) ranged from a low of 0.08 to a high of 0.58, while the Pr(B) ranged from 0.55 to 0.81. The Pr(A) varied from less than 0.10 to approximately 0.60. As might be expected, the Pr(A) correlated directly with the size of the library (0.27 for large libraries, 0.18 for those in the medium-size range, and 0.08 for the small ones), although the probability of an owned book being on the shelf, Pr(B), was greatest in the medium-sized libraries.

The Pr(O) for the sample of periodical articles is calculated in exactly the same way as for the BPR sample. The "probability of ownership," Pr(O), multiplied by the "probability of availability of articles owned," Pr(C), provides the overall "probability of availability," Pr(A), for periodical articles. In the public libraries surveyed, great variations in PR(O) were encountered, ranging from approximately 0.10 to 0.95. If a library did own a particular periodical, however, the probability of the user being able to find a specific article was high—9 chances out of 10. The overall availability, Pr(A), in the 20 libraries varied from a high of 0.95 to a low of 0.09, these probabilities being directly related to the size of the library.

The third sample—consisting of 500 citations drawn from items known to be held by a library—is used to determine the probability that an owned item will be available (i.e., on the shelf) when needed. The "shelf availability probability," Pr(S), represents the proportion of the 500 titles drawn from the library's shelflist that are found on the shelves when a search is made. In the public libraries tested, this probability ranged from 0.58 to 0.89; the best chance of success was in the medium-sized libraries.

The ability of a library (University of California at Berkeley) to satisfy the document delivery demands generated by an SDI service has been studied by Bourne and Robinson.[2] Twenty-three SDI printouts generated by the Center for Information Services at UCLA, representing 13 users of the service at Berkeley, were used in the study. Of the 680 citations contained in these printouts, 89.7% were held by the library at Berkeley and 85.4% were immediately available on the shelves; that is, 76.6% of the 680 citations sought were immediately available.

Line [27] has pointed out that studies assessing a library's services by the number of demands satisfied are performing only part of an evaluation of document delivery capabilities. Librarians also should be concerned with why users do not come to the library to find bibliographic materials when the need arises. Line describes an attempt to identify a sample of bibliographic materials needed by members of the staff at Bath University, England, and to determine what proportion of the materials actually was available in the university library. On two separate occasions, members of the university's academic staff were asked to record bibliographic details of items they would like to see at the time they encountered the reference to each item. On the first occasion, they were asked to record those references they encountered on a given day; in the second instance, they were asked to record the first 12 references (to materials they would like to see) that they encountered in a given month. The data-gathering form used on the second occasion is shown in Figure 33. A total of 60 individuals (out of a possible 250) returned 356 usable forms.

Of the 356 references recorded in the study, 70 required no follow-up: respondents had seen them on the library shelves or in journals they themselves received. For the majority of the remaining items, information was available to indicate whether they actually were held by the library and whether they were immediately available when needed (i.e., on the shelves). Line reports that the total availability of items for which information was available was 45%, and the figure for immediate availability was 36%. Availability varied with the purpose for which the material was wanted (41% for research requirements and 54% for teaching requirements) and with the type of material wanted. The level of availability was lower for books (35%) than for journals (48%), and it was extremely low (17%) for reports. Commenting on the surprisingly low availability figures achieved in this study, Line suggests that they may be biased. In particular, he suggests that, of the staff members who chose to participate, a disproportionate number might have been dissatisfied with the service in the past, and that other participants might have recorded only those items likely to be difficult to locate, thus the really common (and therefore most available) items might have been omitted from the sample.

The results of the first survey were closely paralleled, however, by the results of a second survey conducted with 45 selected individuals known to be sympathetic to the aims of the study. Each was given 20 cards on which to record brief information about the next 20 references encountered, and the action taken on each (see Figure 34). Of the 900 cards thus circulated, 437 were returned by 29 individuals. The major results of this survey are summarized by Line as follows:

Of the 437 items wanted, 261 were actually obtained, 115 were requested on inter-library loan, 9 were requested as offprints, and 21 were ordered for the library: for 406 items (93%), therefore, successful action, or action likely to be successful, was taken. For the remaining 31, search was either not undertaken, or abandoned. Of the 270 items sought in Bath University Library, 180 (67%) were found; Bath University Library therefore provided 41% of all the items wanted, and 45% of the items for which search was not abandoned. These results are similar to those of the previous survey, where immediate local availability was 36% (a further 9% being in stock but not available at the time).

Bath University Library was tried first for 270 (64%) of the 437 items wanted; in 71 (17%) of cases, inter-library loan was tried first, presumably because the item

AVAILABILITY SURVEY, 1968–69.

For library use only

All references to printed material that you come across which you would like to see personally, *and* all actual printed items of interest to you that you come across for the first time (i.e. without having a prior reference to them), should be recorded, *each on a separate form.*

1-5   Name: _____ School: _____ Date: _____
7-8

1 2 3 4 5

6.   1 2 3
     4 5 6
     7 8 9
     . . X

9,10   Item (brief details): _____

7-8

11.   Wanted in connection with: (tick boxes as appropriate)

Research on contract ☐
Personal research ☐
Teaching ☐
Other purposes ☐
    please name: _____

9.   1 2 3
     4 5 6
     7 8 9
     . . X

10.   1 2 .
      . . X

12.   Estimated importance of reference (please ring appropriate number on the rating scale below)

(least important) 1 2 3 4 5 (very important)

11.   1 2 3
      4 5 .
      . . X

13.   Source of reference: (tick relevant box)

Reference in another book or periodical

your own or a colleague's ☐
belonging to Bath University Library ☐
belonging to another library ☐
Abstracting or indexing journal ☐
Bibliography ☐
Library catalogue ☐
Personal (orally or by correspondence) ☐
Item actually seen while browsing or
    searching in Bath University library ☐
    elsewhere ☐
        state where: _____ ☐

12.   1 2 3
      4 5 .
      . . X

13.   1 2 3

      4 5 6

      7 8 9
      . . X

14.   Other source ☐
        please specify: _____

14.   1 2 3
      4 5 6
      . . X

PLEASE TURN OVER

FIGURE 33   Form used in survey of availability of library materials at Bath University.[27]

Action taken

Please tick *all* cells applicable: e.g. if you check Bath
University Library and fail to find it, and then apply on interlibrary loan, three cells should be ticked.

		Action				
			If taken:			
		Taken	Successful	Unsuccessful		
	Bath University Library					
15.	Check branch library				15.	1 2 3
	Check main catalogue					4 5 6
	Consult item					7 8 9 X
16.	Borrow item				16.	1 2 3
17.	Other Library				17.	
	please name: _____					1 2 3
	visit in person					4 5 6
	borrow personally by post					7 8 9
18.	Inter-library loan application	(to be completed by Library)			18.	1 2 3
	Order copy for University Library					4 5 6
	Order personal copy from bookshop					7 8 9 X
19.	Other action				19.	1 2 3
	please specify: _____					
	No action					7 X

20.	Date of completion: _____	20.	Y X 0
	Please retain this form until you have taken all the action you propose to take on this particular item. When it is completed, please return to the University Librarian, Northgate House.		1 2 3 4 5 6 7 8 9

FIGURE 33   (Continued)

AVAILABILITY SURVEY 1969	For Library use only
Please record each reference you come across or use on a separate card. 1-5. Name: _____ School: _____	1 ☐ 2 ☐ 3 ☐ 4 ☐ 5 ☐

6.   Nature of item:
   Book   ☐
   Periodical   ☐
   Report   ☐
   Other   ☐
      please give details:
      _____
	6.1.
	2
	3
	4
	5
	. X

7. Date of publication of item: _____	7.1 2 3
	   4 5 6
	   7 8 9
	   . . X

8-9.   Source of reference: (tick one box only)
   Already known to be in Bath University Library   ☐
   Reference in another book or periodical
      your own or a colleague's   ☐
      belonging to Bath University Library   ☐
      belonging to another library   ☐
   Abstracting or indexing journal   ☐
   Bibliography   ☐
   Library catalogue   ☐
   Personal (orally or by correspondence)   ☐
   Items actually seen while browsing or searching
      in Bath University Library   ☐
      elsewhere   ☐
         state where _____
   Other source   ☐
      please specify _____
                              TURN OVER
	8.1
	
	2
	3
	4
	5
	6
	7
	8 X
	
	9.1
	2
	3
	4 5 6
	. . X

FIGURE 34   Data-gathering form for material availability study at Bath University library.[27]

	For Library use only
PLEASE COMPLETE OTHER SIDE FIRST	
10. Action taken:	10. 1 2 3
Please state the actions taken on this item <u>in the</u>	4 5 6
<u>order in which you take them.</u>	7 8 .
	. . X

	Action*	Results†	
1			11.
2			12.
3			13.
4			14.
5			15.
6			16.
7			17.

*Key to Actions

Bath Univ. Library	U
Other library	L = [state which]
Inter-library loan request	I
Own copy	O
Borrow copy from colleague	B
Purchase for self	P
Any other action	A = [state]
No (further) action	N

†Key to Results

√ = Successful
X = Unsuccessful
NIS = Not in stock
NA = In stock but not } U & L only
   available

Date: _____	18.

AFTER COMPLETION, PLEASE RETURN TO
THE UNIVERSITY LIBRARIAN, NORTHGATE HOUSE

FIGURE 34 (Continued)

was known or believed not to be in the University Library. In a few of these cases, the individual may have been mistaken (although an inter-library loan request would normally be checked by the library staff, the card would have been filled in by the respondent before checking). Some of the other items on which other actions were taken (other library, borrow from colleague, own copy, ask for offprint) may also have been in Bath University Library. The 41% of items actually found in Bath University Library is almost certainly rather lower than the proportion of items actually in the library.

Much the commonest second action taken was to apply for an inter-library loan: of the 75 items on which second action was taken, 46 (61%) were pursued in this way. Twelve items were ordered for the library, 6 were borrowed from a colleague (one attempted borrowing failed—the only failure among 'second actions'), and 5 were bought by the respondent for himself. Five other items were followed up in various ways.

Urquhart and Schofield[45,46] describe a survey method designed to measure availability of materials, in which library users record details of books that are not available at the time they are needed. The method, which has been applied at four university libraries in the United Kingdom, was developed by the Library Management Research Unit of Cambridge University Library, and it is intended to answer the following questions:

1. Which particular books are in such heavy demand that they are often unavailable?
2. How successful are readers at finding the books they are looking for?
3. What are the reasons for their failure?
4. What steps can be taken to reduce their chances of failure?

The survey method was applied at the Cambridge University Library during two separate periods (9 weeks and 13 weeks, respectively) in the autumn of 1969 and spring of 1970. Library users cooperated by filling out a colored slip, noting identifying data for any items they sought on the open shelves but were unable to find. They then placed the completed slips on the shelf at the point where the sought items should have been. The "status" of the library user (faculty; MA; first-, second-, or third-year undergraduate) also was recorded in the survey. All books consulted in the library were reshelved by members of the staff and matched with the "shelf slips" at this point, and the latter were removed. When a book was returned to circulation status from outside the library (e.g., returned from the bindery or by a borrower), a different kind of slip was placed inside the book. The "book slip" recorded where the book had been and, in the case of an item out on loan, the status of the borrower. When the book was returned to the shelves, the "book slip" was matched with the "shelf slip," if one existed (i.e., if a user had sought the book while it was absent from the shelves). At the end of the survey period, any slips remaining on the shelves were checked to determine why they remained (e.g., book still missing, slip misfiled, or slip left on shelf in error after the book had been returned).

Because the survey was conducted at the end of an academic term, when all items on loan should have been returned to the library, it was theoretically possible to match all shelf slips with the appropriate book slips. Through these procedures, the investigators were able to obtain a broad picture of the shelf availability of library holdings sought by users and to determine where items were located at the time they were needed. Interviews with 1,000 users at Cambridge during the two survey periods indicated that 67% had cooperated fully in the study.

Results of the Cambridge study are shown in Table 53. Reasons for unavailability of materials are very similar for both survey periods. Approximately 30% of the books sought, but not found, were in use in the library at the time, and a further 50% were out on loan. Note that this table does not express percentage of success. There is no way of determining from these data how many successes occurred (i.e., cases in which the user was able to find the item sought on the shelves). The investigators were concerned only with the number of failures and the reasons for such failures. This survey technique also ignores collection failures (i.e., when items needed are not held by the library).

The investigators did, however, attempt to relate failure rate to success rate in terms of the number of items borrowed. During the two test

TABLE 53   Results of Two Surveys of Materials Availability at Cambridge University[45]

	No. of Slips		% of Total Failures	
Causes of Failure	Autumn 1969	Spring 1970	Autumn 1969	Spring 1970
MA borrowing	934	1,675	27.9	26.9
BA borrowing	} 966	407	} 28.9	6.5
3rd-year borrowing		1,279		20.6
Internal use*	954	1,896	28.5	30.5
Re-labelling and re-binding	21	60	0.6	1.0
Missing books	90	124	2.7	2.0
Overdue books	19	38	0.6	0.6
Unaccounted for	116	355	3.5	5.7
Incorrect copying of class marks	141	176	4.2	2.8
Looking in the wrong place	44	104	1.3	1.7
Unknown (book found with slip on shelf)	62	106	1.9	1.7
TOTALS	3,347	6,220		

*Books consulted within the library, but not borrowed.

periods, 41,747 items were borrowed. Concurrently, 5,261 failures were recorded. Since only 67% of the users cooperated in the study, however, it is reasonable to assume that only two-thirds of the "failures" were represented in these figures. When the investigators weighted the results of the spring 1970 term to account for this, they discovered that the failure rate varied from one out of four (i.e., three items borrowed for every four sought) to one out of eight, depending on the status of the user. Note, however, that this appears to bias the results against the library. Successes are measured only in terms of items borrowed, while failures are measured in terms of all items sought (whether for borrowing or in-library use). Presumably there were many other successes during this period (i.e., cases in which the user discovered an item and used it in the library) that are not represented in these ratios.

Another attempt to estimate failure rates was made by counting the number of volumes reshelved on three floors of the library during a two-week period and relating this figure (which is assumed to represent total use of library materials) to the one for failures to find sought materials on these floors. The failure rate varied from a low of 7% to a high of 25%, depending largely on the floor involved (each floor represented different subject areas).

By dating a sample of the shelf slips, it also was possible to estimate "waiting time" (i.e., the period between the time a book is looked for, but not found, and the time it is returned to the shelves). Waiting time could then be related to type of use (in-library or outside) and, in the case of items used away from the library, to the status of the borrower.

A further analysis was conducted for the purpose of relating failures by status of library users to status of users causing the failures (e.g., what proportion of all failures encountered by third-year undergraduates was caused by other third-year undergraduates using the sought materials, and what proportion was caused by other categories of library users).

One of the most important results of this survey was the ability to identify specific titles that caused multiple failures. Books sought unsuccessfully on more than one occasion accounted for 46% of total failures during the first survey period and for 60% during the second. Put differently, approximately 500 books among the 500,000 on open shelves accounted for nearly half of the failures. Moreover, approximately half the failures to find parts of periodicals were accounted for by only 40 periodical titles. Clearly, this technique can be used to identify items in great demand. If additional copies of a relatively small number of titles are purchased, it should be possible to reduce the failure rate (or, conversely, increase the rate of success) considerably, providing, of course, that the same titles are sought term after term. This assumption is not an obvious one in an academic environment, where student reading is likely to be tied closely to course offerings and reading lists that may change drastically from one year to the next. The Cambridge study, however, indicated that the more times a book was sought unsuccessfully during one term, the more likely it was to be sought unsuccessfully during another.

As a result of the survey in the Cambridge University library, the investigators recommended the purchase of extra copies of selected items and suggested that, to increase accessibility, specific changes be made in policies relating to the reservation of materials, the length of time materials could be used in the library, and the loan period for materials from heavily used sections of the collection. The total cost of administering the survey was a modest £205.

Urquhart and Schofield[46] describe how the survey was applied at the libraries of three other British universities: Bradford, Sussex, and Glasgow. The procedure was slightly modified at these institutions: the shelf slips recorded failures to locate books on particular subjects, as well as failures to locate particular known items; the survey was based on a complete academic term; and interviews were conducted with a random sample of readers, as they were leaving the library, during a two-week period of peak use. These users filled out a questionnaire designed to collect details on types of users, subject areas of the searches, how many books or other items they were looking for, how many they found, how many additional books they consulted, how many items they were borrowing, how many failure slips they had completed, number of missing items for which an adequate substitute was found, intended action in the case of a failure, and the effect of the failure on their work.

The causes of failures encountered in the three libraries, based on an analysis of the shelf slips, is shown in Table 54. The category "reader failure" covers those readers who failed to find an item actually present on the shelves (i.e., the user looked in the wrong place). Library B had a very high "on loan" failure rate, because it acquires no duplicate copies, and borrowers are able to retain books until requested by another reader. In contrast, the other two libraries do purchase duplicates and have less-liberal loan periods.

A high proportion of the failures in libraries A and C were due to "missing items," but no explanation was given for these high rates, which appear excessive. The results of the intensive questionnaire surveys in the three libraries are presented in Table 55. Failure rate (i.e., failure to find an item sought) varies from a low of 32% in library C (where much of the use is in the library) to a high of 48.7% in library A. In libraries A and B, data on the various materials relate only to books; in library C, however, journals also are represented in the figures.

TABLE 54   Reasons for Unavailability of Materials in Three University Libraries[46]

Cause of failure %	Library A (books only)	Library B (books only)	Library C Books	Periodicals
Not in stock	2.3	3.8	10.3	10.2
On loan	29.9	66.4	47.5	13.5
to students		} 49.7	31.9	11.3
to postgrads	Mainly students		9.9	0.8
to staff		11.5	5.8	1.5
other		5.2	—	—
Missing (at least one copy)	20.5	6.9	19.2	11.3
all copies	3.6		10.0	11.3
not all copies	17.5		9.2	—
At binders or photocopiers	0.2	2.6	0.4	15.4*
Reader failure	28.9	12.0	13.4	25.1
Other	0.5	—	2.3	5.6
Unaccounted for (probably in use in library)	16.5	6.0	6.5	19.2
Queries	—	2.3	0.4	—
Total	100.0	100.0	100.0	100.3
Total Number of slips	4,334	2,408	527	

*This figure included cases where the periodical had been reserved before sending to the binders.

Table 56 depicts the follow-up action that a user proposed to take in the event of a failure. These categories are not mutually exclusive; and the percentages do not add up to 100, because a user might have indicated more than one intended action. Intended action depends heavily on local situations and policies. Because Library A has duplicate copies of popular titles, as well as a policy of short loans, the probability of finding a missing item on a second visit is high, and a large number of users, 69.2%, indicated they would try again later. Presumably, also, the category "try another library" is dependent on the local availability of other resources.

Table 57 illustrates the users' subjective assessments of the effects of failure on their work. Failure rates by subject and by user status also were studied, and some sample results from these analyses are shown in Tables 58 and 59.

Urquhart and Schofield[45] suggest a number of possible applications for the results of this type of study:

1. As an indication to administrators of library deficiencies, and the effect of these deficiencies on the academic program of the university,

TABLE 55   Main Results of Intensive Surveys in Three Libraries[46]

	Library A	B	C*
Total number of forms completed	1,823	859	154
Total number completed by readers using library books	1,442	658	139
% forms correctly completed	77	82.5	89
% failure rate for books looked for	48.7	39.3	32
% of cases of failure where substitutes were found	15.3	22.1	13.7
Ratio of in-library to ex-library use	1.64:1	6.7:1	11.2:1
Ratio of number of books found by browsing to number of specific books looked for and found	0.55:1	0.55:1	1.62:1
Apparent co-operation rate in filling in failure slips	1 in 6.5	1 in 7.3	1 in 5

*Library c had the highest ratio of in-library use to borrowing, and the highest browsing ratio, but the results here are not comparable because the questionnaire in Library c included items other than books.

with the object of obtaining improved funding to allow remedy of these defects.

2. To indicate priorities for the librarian.

3. To indicate subject areas of weakness.

4. To indicate need for changes in library policy (e.g., loan periods, duplication of titles).

5. To indicate specific titles in great demand.

A somewhat similar approach was used in a survey conducted at the University of Lancaster library and reported by Buckland et al.[8] to measure availability of materials. All users visiting on a particular day were asked to complete a questionnaire that captured details on charac-

TABLE 56   Follow-up Action After Shelf Failure[46]

Total number of readers failing	Library A 692	Library B 274	Library C 51
No action	15.3%	10.2%	13.7%
Come back later	69.2%	37.2%	29.4%
Reservation	11.1%	13.9%	9.8%
Try another library	16.3%	39.8%	17.6%
Try Reading Room or reserve collection	16.2%	25.2%	*
Find substitute	25.3%	22.6%	7.8%
Borrow from friend	23.7%	13.1%	7.8%
Buy	14.5%	8.0%	0%
Consult member of staff (either teaching or library)	19.5%	16.4%	33.3%

*No reading room or reserve collection.

TABLE 57　Effect of Failure on a Reader's Work[46]

Effect of failure	Library A	Library B	Library C
Vital	7.1% ⎫	⎧ ⎫	⎧ ⎫
Serious	7.1% ⎬ =36.9%	⎨37.2%⎬	⎨15.7%⎬
Important	22.7% ⎭	⎩ ⎭	⎩ ⎭
Useful	9.4% ⎫	⎧ ⎫	⎧23.5%⎫
Delay	19.2% ⎬ =28.6%	⎨24.1%⎬	⎨11.8%⎬ =35.3%
No effect	17.5%	22.3%	31.4%
No answer	17.0%	16.4%	17.6%

teristics of the user, type of library use, and degree of success achieved in finding sought items. A total of 563 completed questionnaires were placed in a box at the library exit; the box was emptied every 15 minutes. Items not found by users were immediately checked to determine their location. Thus, although the location of an item at the exact moment a user looked for it could not be established, it could be determined a few minutes later. The largest category of unavailable items was that of "already out on loan"; but substantial numbers were found in such categories as "on the shelves, but not located by the user," and "at the bindery," among others. To improve accessibility, the library undertook a number of corrective measures, including the adoption of a differential loan period (discussed later in this chapter), the installation of an antitheft device, and improved binding procedures.

A recent study by Mavor and Vaughan[29] revealed that the Hamline University library was able to supply approximately 43%–51% of the materials needed by faculty and students to support the work of 30 courses. These figures were based on a sample of approximately 2,000 documents.

TABLE 58　Failure Rates for Individual Books by Subject[46]

Library A		Library B		Library C	
Subject	*% Failure*	*Subject*	*% Failure*	*Subject*	*% Failure*
History	36.7	Geography and		Chemistry	19.0
Sociology	54.0	Chemistry	38.0	Engineering	40.0
Physics	57.2	Social Science	56.0	Physics	24.0
		Language and		Other Science	
		Literature	36.0	subjects	39.0
		Biological			
		Science,			
		Medicine,			
		Agriculture	33.0		

TABLE 59   Failure Rates by Type of User (Library A Only)[46]

Type of user	% Failure
Academic staff	30.1
Non-academic staff	26.3
Postgraduate	45.8
Undergraduate	50.3
Other (e.g., students from outside bodies)	56.2
Average	48.7

Somewhat related to the evaluation of document delivery is the investigation of how long it takes an individual library user to find a call number for a known item in the catalog and then to locate the item itself on the shelves. A limited investigation of such activities in a large academic library was undertaken by Jestes,[23] using techniques of systems analysis. By means of flowcharting, together with estimates of time and costs, Jestes was able to identify inefficiencies in the existing mode of operation and to suggest various alternative approaches that could save the time of library users.

Factors Influencing Availability of Materials

Several important factors that influence the availability of bibliographic materials, such as size of the collection (number of unique titles held), amount of duplication of popular titles, and loan period, were discussed earlier in this chapter. Collection size and other factors relating to the quality and appropriateness of the collection were discussed in Chapter 5. Investigations also have been conducted on the need for duplicate copies and the influence of the loan period on accessibility of bibliographic materials, and these will be considered here.

Buckland,[7] reporting on analyses conducted by the Library Research Unit at the University of Lancaster, compares the strategies of (a) providing more duplicate copies and (b) reducing loan periods. For the individual borrower, long loan periods are convenient; they are inconvenient, however, for everyone else. The provision of duplicate copies is convenient for library users, but is expensive, and it uses up funds that could be spent in other ways, including the addition of new titles. Moreover, any decision relating to loan periods is complicated by the fact that some books (comparatively, a small proportion of the total collection) will be in great demand, and others will be needed infrequently. While there is no reason to establish a short loan policy for less-used items, such a policy would be beneficial for materials in great demand. Unfortunately, some effort is required to identify those items likely to be in great demand.

A possible alternative to duplication of copies and reduction of loan periods would be to establish an efficient procedure that would allow for reservation of materials and for recall from circulation when requested by another reader. This is not always a good substitute: it does not help the user who needs a particular item immediately nor the user who is browsing on the shelves in a particular subject area. For the browser, it is important that the shelves display a wide selection of available materials, including books that are current and in some sense regarded as "best." Unfortunately, as pointed out by Buckland[7] and again by Buckland and Hindle,[9] the danger is that the browser will be faced with some "collection bias"—the most popular books, which may be the highest quality or most useful works, are likely to be absent from the shelves, while the books in least demand will be present.* Other aspects to be considered in any decision are of an administrative or "political" nature. Some policies will be easier to administer than others, and some will be more popular than others among portions of the user population and/or, in the case of an academic institution, among the university administration.

Buckland points out the complicated relationships that exist between loan and duplication policies. At Lancaster, an analysis was conducted to relate the factors of loan period, copies available, and popularity of particular items to user satisfaction level. The important relationships among these various factors are presented by Buckland as follows:

(a) For any given loan period, the chances of a reader finding on the shelves a copy of the book he seeks varies inversely with the popularity. The greater the popularity, the lower the satisfaction level; the less the popularity, the higher the satisfaction level (see Figure 35).

(b) For any given popularity, the length of the loan period and the satisfaction level are inversely related. The longer the loan period, the lower the satisfaction level; the shorter the loan period, the higher the satisfaction level (see Figure 36).

(c) For any given satisfaction level, the popularity and the length of the loan period are necessarily also inversely related. The greater the popularity, the shorter the loan period has to be; the less the popularity, the longer the loan period can be (see Figure 37).

(d) Increasing the number of copies available, like shortening the length of loan

---

*It is important to note that collection bias relates to the demand for particular books, but not necessarily to the quality of these books. It is obvious that the books most in demand in a particular subject field are those least likely to be present on the shelves. It is not clear, however, that the books most in demand are necessarily "the best." Goldhor,[20] for example, was able to show (in one subject area, in one public library) that the best books (in this case, those reviewed most favorably) were not borrowed significantly more often than the others.

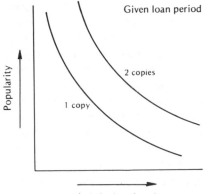

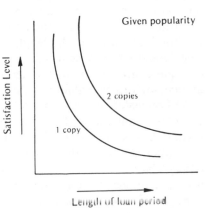

FIGURE 35 Satisfaction level as influenced by duplication rate and popularity.[7]

FIGURE 36 Loan period related to satisfaction level and duplication rate.[7]

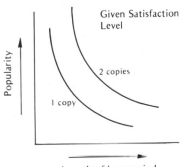

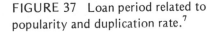

FIGURE 37 Loan period related to popularity and duplication rate.[7]

periods, increases satisfaction level. To this extent, it is an alternative strategy. The relationship can be seen in Figures 35–37 by comparing the curve for one copy with the curve for two copies.

Buckland proposes that "the cardinal rule of library stock control is that both the loan period and the duplication policy should be related to the level of demand for the title and to each other." Circulation data collected from a number of universities showed that there is a strong tendency for a borrower to keep a book until it is due for return, and that the frequency with which the items are renewed by borrowers appears to be little influenced by the length of the loan period.* These findings led Buckland to the conclusion that "the librarian has, in his ability to determine official loan periods, a powerful and precise control device for influencing the availability of the books in his library."

At Lancaster, calculations relating to satisfaction level were made by computer simulations. The data manipulated consisted of statistics on the various levels of demand for portions of the collection (estimated from circulation data) and the effect on availability, for each level of demand, of any given combinations of (a) length of loan, (b) amount of in-library use, (c) number of copies, and (d) probability that a reader will reserve an item not immediately available on the shelves. With these data, it was possible to estimate the satisfaction level that the library would provide, which was estimated to be 60% in 1967–1968 for the University of Lancaster library; that is, a user seeking an item on the open shelves would find it 6 out of 10 times. By extension, these estimates can be used to calculate the probable effects on satisfaction level of changes made to loan and duplication policies. Table 60 shows estimated satisfaction level for books at five levels of demand (popularity) when loan period and number of copies are varied.

It also is possible to calculate the probable effect of these changes on "collection bias." It was estimated at Lancaster that approximately 45% of the most-used and most-recommended titles were not available on the open shelves at any one time (a collection bias of 45%). Brophy et al.[4] have defined collection bias as the percentage of the 10% most popular books that are absent from the shelves. As shown in Figure 38, collection bias increases with the length of the loan period.

TABLE 60   Estimated Satisfaction Level (%) for Varying Levels of Popularity, Loan Period, and Duplication Rate[7]

Official Loan Period	Number of Copies	Estimated Satisfaction Level for Books at Each of Five Levels of Popularity				
		A	B	C	D	E
5 weeks	1	52	62	72	82	97
5 weeks	2	84	91	97	99	100
1 week	1	90	94	98	99	100

*Elsewhere, Brophy et al.[4] have pointed out that "no matter how long the loan period may be, a book will not actually be used for more than about ten hours *on average*."

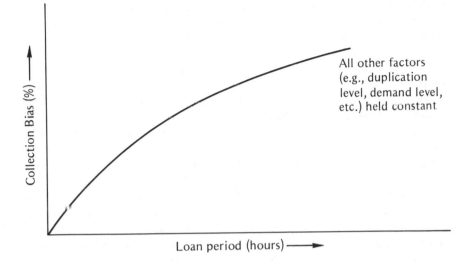

FIGURE 38   Relationship between collection bias and loan period.[4]

Three possible actions were identified by Buckland[7] that could raise satisfaction level from 60% to 80% on the average and, at the same time, reduce collection bias to 20% or less:

A. No change in loan policies but enough systematic duplication to achieve the desired standards. Estimated cost of duplication £10,000–£15,000 ($24,000–$36,000) initially and £2,000 ($4,800) recurrently.

B. Staff and graduate students, four return dates a year; undergraduates, two weeks; renewals permitted. Although traditional, policies based on the status of the borrower are rather inefficient from the point of view of stock control—and, arguably, inequitable. This particular policy would have achieved an estimated satisfaction level of 73 percent and a collection bias of 32 percent.

C. A variable loan policy, whereby the most popular books are subject to a shorter loan period regardless of the status of the borrower. Numerous permutations are possible. One was that about 10 percent of the stock should be subject to a one-week loan period, the rest would have four return dates a year. This was expected to raise satisfaction level to 86 percent and reduce collection bias to 8 percent.

After these alternatives were carefully weighed, the third—variable loan period—was eventually adopted, and the 10% of the collection most-used was made available for loan periods of one week only. The most-used portion of the collection was identified by clerical staff, who examined the date labels of 70,000 volumes in two and one-half days at a total cost of approximately $264, plus supervision. The change to a variable loan policy led to a "dramatic increase" in library use. It was reported that borrowing from open shelves increased by 200% in two years, although the user population increased by only 40% during that period. This suggests that a "self-reinforcing" situation occurs: Demand for library service increases when users find they can locate needed books on the shelves.

The study at the University of Lancaster has been summarized in some detail, because it is a particularly good example of the application of operations research techniques to studies of document availability and how availability can be increased. The work at Lancaster also is discussed by Buckland and Woodburn[10] and by Buckland et al.[8] A more complete discussion is given in a recent book by Buckland.[5]

A number of other studies have been conducted to determine the need for duplication of titles or the need to vary loan periods. Burkhalter and Race,[11] for example, consider the effect of loan-period variations on library costs and on user satisfaction. Newhouse and Alexander,[33] in an analysis of the Beverly Hills Public Library, estimated that a circulation period of two weeks satisfies approximately two-thirds of all requests for specific titles. If the circulation period were increased to three weeks, "satisfaction level" would drop to approximately 60%, and to approximately 55% for a four-week loan period. In other words, assuming that most users keep a book for the full loan period (which has been shown to be generally true), a three-week loan period would decrease circulation by 10% and a four-week loan period by 20%. Note, however, that this assumption makes no allowance for "browsing," which might result in a user finding an acceptable alternative (perhaps better or more appropriate in the case of a nonfiction title) to the book he sought when he came to the library.

The subject of loan period and its effect on document delivery capabilities also has been studied by Goyal.[21] In his model, which relates specifically to periodicals, user satisfaction is a function of three variables: loan period, probability of finding an item on the shelf when needed, and expected time before an item is returned to the shelf. For a given demand rate and for a given value of the other two variables, an optimal loan period—one that maximizes the probability of user satisfaction—can be calculated.

Bommer[1] has developed mathematical models to predict circulation demand for titles in a particular subject area as a function of rate of circulation and of measures of teaching and research activity within a university. The models are intended to predict the number of new titles that will be required in a particular subject area, the number of duplicate titles that will be needed, and the number of copies to be placed on reserve, the objective being to maximize use of library materials for each dollar expended. The models take into account the number of both faculty and students working in particular subject areas, the rate of obsolescence of materials, and a factor of diminishing returns, based on the concept that, although use of the collection in a particular subject area increases with an increasing number of titles, the incremental use of each additional title is successively smaller. As in the Lancaster studies, Bommer uses the probability of demand and the extent of duplication, as well as the probability of an item being on the shelf at any one time, as factors determining circulation per title. A model, based on these probabilities, can yield estimates of mean demand rate for items held by the library as functions of mean circulation rate, rate of duplication, and mean loan period. The difference between mean demand rate and mean circulation rate indicates the extent to which demands for items held by the library are not satisfied. Bommer applied his models to data derived at the Lippincott Library of the University of Pennsylvania.

Morse[30] has presented sophisticated mathematical models for estimating circulation demand and for studying the effects of both loan period and duplication policies on the ability of a library to satisfy this demand. He has applied these models to records of past circulation, drawn from samples of books in and circulation files of the Science Library at MIT (i.e., both "collection samples" and "check-out samples" in Jain's terminology).

Data are gathered (for various subject fields of the collection) on the mean yearly circulation per book, the mean number of books on loan at any one time, the mean number of reservations per book, the mean number of reservation cards on hand at any one time, and the fraction of books on loan that are overdue. These data determine the mean loan period, which is the mean fraction of a year that a book is off the shelf for a single circulation. The mean loan period for a book, multiplied by the number of times it circulates per year, yields the fraction of the year that the book is not available in the library. Mean loan period, together with a figure representing the fraction of users who reserve a book when they are unable to find it in the library, are two important variables when deciding whether a particular title should be duplicated and by how many copies.

Simmons[43] discusses an analysis of several years of circulation records available from an automated circulation system at the library of the University of British Columbia, with the objective of identifying the most-used books in the collection. This analysis resulted in the purchase of more than 2,000 additional copies of such titles. Simmons points out that the decision to purchase duplicate copies of a title was based on a number of considerations, including (a) the number of users who borrowed it, (b) the number of days it was off the shelf and unavailable for loan, and (c) the number of times it was requested during a specified period, as evidenced by the number of reservations (holds) made.

Dougherty[14] has described an innovative document delivery service introduced at the University of Colorado. In response to a telephone call from a member of the faculty or other staff member, the university library staff will retrieve an item from the stacks, check it out, and deliver it to the office of the requester. The goal is one-day delivery. During the first year of operation, 69% of all items requested were delivered in one working day; 12% were delivered later (an overall success rate of 81%); 5% were requests for noncirculating items; 8% were not owned by the library, but were requested on interlibrary loan; 2% were on order, but not yet received; and 4% were missing items. During the first 18 months of operation, more than one-third of the faculty had used the service at least once, and many were found to be repeat users. Faculty response was very favorable, and more than half of those using the service reported that it had altered their library use patterns. The total cost of the service was reported to be $9,500; and Dougherty feels that, if savings in time of faculty members is considered, it is easily justified in terms of cost-effectiveness. A somewhat similar service is offered by Ohio State University Libraries, and by a number of other academic libraries.

Doughtery and Blomquist[15] have described, in some detail, a study in which they measured faculty attitudes towards library service in two academic institutions—one (Ohio State University) with a document delivery service of the type described above, and the other (Syracuse University) without such a service. The Ohio users, who were very positive in their assessment of the document delivery service, exhibited a more favorable attitude toward the library than did the Syracuse users. In contrast, the Syracuse faculty, having no experience with such a service, were quite negative concerning its value.

In the conduct of this study, Dougherty and Blomquist developed two useful measures relating to document delivery. The first of these, *expectation rate* (ER), is a value, on a 10-point scale, by which a library user expresses his expectation of being able to successfully retrieve a particular document from the library when needed. An ER of 10, for example, would indicate that a user is completely confident of being able to retrieve a particular item. This rate is actually a measure of confidence in the library. The second measure is the *document exposure index* (DEI), which measures the extent to which departmental libraries match an individual's profile of interest. Suppose, for example, that a faculty member's area of specialization and interest is measurement and evaluation in education. If he uses only the education library on campus and this library holds approximately 80% of all the material in the library system that matches his interests, then the DEI for this individual would be 80%. If, in addition to the education library, he began to use the psychology library, his DEI might increase to, say, 85%.

Lubans et al.[28] have described the use of computer-based circulation data in administrative decision making at the University of Colorado Libraries, Boulder. Listings were generated to show items most frequently used, distribution of library use by academic department or major, distribution of use by subject, and so on. The authors conclude that a mechanized circulation system can yield data useful in book selection, budget allocation, and surveying of user characteristics. Grant[22] also reported on the use of a computer-based circulation system to identify books that should be purchased in multiple copies.

A study of a library's ability to supply journal volumes or parts is discussed by Piternick.[39] The investigation was conducted at the Woodward Biomedical Library at the University of British Columbia. During a 12-day period in 1971, users of this library were asked to complete a form each time they failed to find a journal they were seeking. A total of 370 failures was reported. Of these, 100 (27%) failed because the journals were not held by the library or because issues were not yet received. In 66 cases (18%), the item sought was at the bindery; in 34 cases (9%), it was being used in the library; and in only 64 cases (17%), the item was out on loan. In 41 cases (11%), the sought item was actually present, but the user had been unable to find it. Piternick points out that the 64 journals already on loan when required by users constituted only 4.7% of a total of 1,373 journals circulated during the period, and that circulation was not as great a contributor to failures as might have been supposed. In her opinion, the results of this survey did not warrant the introduction of more restrictive circulation policies for journals; attention should be concentrated instead on some of the other problems encountered.

Decisions involving alternative strategies relating to the improvement of accessibility should take into account both cost-effectiveness and effectiveness considerations. Leimkuhler and Cooper[26] have pointed out that:

Duplication of popular items increases the availability of the items but actually decreases the circulation rate per volume of the library. While duplicates may be acquired at less cost than original items, because they have already been catalogued, it is unlikely that this reduction in cost is sufficient to prevent duplication from increasing the average cost per use for the collection.

Elsewhere, Leimkuhler[25] has presented a queuing model to show the effect of duplication on circulation. Essentially, this model indicates that two copies of a title can never succeed in doubling the circulation rate per title. Assume that a single copy of a title is off the shelf (i.e., in circulation) for one-half of the year. The availability rate, therefore, is 0.5. According to the model, the addition of a second copy will increase its availability to 0.8, and circulation will increase by only 60%. Although availability has increased considerably, the overall average circulation rate for the title has dropped 20%. Thus, the cost per circulation for this title can be said to increase as a result of duplication. The model also indicates that duplication at two branch locations produces a lower rate of circulation and a reduced level of availability per title than duplication at a single location.

The timeliness of document delivery has been addressed in an interesting study by Reisman et al.[41] Using the Delphi technique, the investigators derive "utility curves," which show the effect (on value to the user) of delays in delivery of materials via interlibrary loan and other library operations.

One very important aspect of document delivery has not been discussed explicitly in this chapter, namely, document delivery via interlibrary loans (ILL). While interlibrary lending is of great importance in the field of library service, and increasing attention is now being paid to the development of regional and national networks for ILL, the criteria and methods for its evaluation are relatively straightforward. The success of any ILL activity can presumably be measured in terms of (a) the proportion of ILL requests satisfied and (b) the time it takes to satisfy these requests (range, median, mean).

From a cost-effectiveness viewpoint, the primary concern is how much it costs to satisfy a particular request. Alternative network configurations can and should be evaluated against two criteria: speed of delivery and unit cost per request satisfied. The evaluation of ILL activities is relatively easy, because the evaluation criteria are both simple and unequivocal (a request either is satisfied within a particular time period or it is not). Moreover, it is not difficult to determine if a request is satisfied and to produce an aggregate performance score. It is necessary, of course, to maintain accurate records,* in order to determine success rates and response times; but, at least for the purposes of macroevaluation, no special evaluation methodology need be developed. The accurate *costing* of ILL transactions is more difficult; but, again, it is largely a matter of keeping very accurate figures for a representative sample of all transactions.

The evaluation of document delivery via ILL is far less difficult than the evaluation of document delivery from the shelves of a particular library, because, in the former, a written record exists of all demands, while, in

*Unfortunately, not all libraries maintain adequate records of ILL transactions. Furthermore, the types of records maintained vary widely among libraries.

the latter, no such record is available unless a special survey is undertaken for a specified period.

Some aspects of the evaluation of ILL, however, are not so straightforward. One reason for this is that it would be valuable to go beyond response time to determine what proportion of all items had arrived in time to be useful to the individuals requesting them. Some indication of this could be derived, perhaps, by counting ILL requests that are cancelled by their initiators, as well as cases where items are borrowed but not collected by the requesters. It would be more useful, however, to undertake a survey to determine the actual impact of ILL delays on library users; that is, to determine, for a sample of requests, whether delays in delivery reduced the value of the material to the requester. It probably would be necessary to use some form of scale, ranging from:

Arrived in good time. No effect at all on its value to me.

to

Work completed. Material no longer needed.

It also would be valuable to know something about the hidden mass of the iceberg: the number of ILL requests that are not made. This would involve identifying and counting the cases in which a library user needs a particular item, cannot find it in the library, and fails to request it (because he is unaware of ILL service, because he suspects that it would take too long, or for some other reason). It is very difficult to obtain this type of data, or even to estimate the number of cases; but it is important, because, as Line pointed out, library performance should be evaluated in terms of user needs (latent demands) as well as actual demands made.

Microevaluation of ILL activities, of course, would require more than the counting of successes and failures. It would involve an analysis of the failures (both absolute failures and failures due to unacceptable response time), categorization of failures, and an attempt to determine why they occurred. This necessitates the identification of factors affecting the success rate, for a particular system or network. Thomson[44] has mentioned several factors that are likely to be of importance:

1. Size of the libraries involved.
2. Distance between libraries.
3. Characteristics of materials requested, including date and form of publication.
4. How carefully, if at all, the citation was verified.
5. The presence or absence of union lists in the region.

The evaluation of ILL activities also has been addressed by Duggan,[16] Braude and Holt,[3] Warner,[47] Nelson Associates,[31,32] Ellis et al.,[17] and Kaushik,[24] among others. A study of costs is presented in a book by Palmour et al.[36] Rouse et al.[42] have listed variables affecting costs and have described a mathematical model of an ILL network suitable for use in analytical, simulation, and evaluation activities.

This chapter has described a number of possible approaches that can be used to determine the ability of a particular library to deliver the documents needed by library users. It also has identified and discussed some major factors affecting document delivery capabilities. Two major approaches to the evaluation of document delivery have been identified:

1. The use of some type of citation pool from which a sample of citations is drawn and used to test the document delivery capabilities of a number of libraries.

2. The use of some type of survey, wherein actual needs of a sample of library users are identified, and the library is tested on its ability to satisfy these needs.

The first approach is a useful technique for comparing the document delivery capabilities of a number of libraries. Its value and validity are entirely dependent upon the representativeness of the citation sample. Although the actual test may use a relatively small set of citations (e.g., 300), it must be drawn completely at random from a much larger pool of citations. The easier part of the problem is to ensure that the sample is representative of some universe of citations (e.g., in a particular subject field). The more difficult part is to ensure that the sample is representative of the actual needs of library users—a basic assumption of the document delivery test as used by Orr and by DeProspo. This point is emphasized also by Buckland,[6] who mentions a second assumption; namely, "that searching by professional librarians from another library approximates the search behavior of researchers who are not professional librarians." In this sense, the DDT must be regarded as a test of optimum capabilities—the ability of the library to deliver documents, assuming that (a) the user can locate the correct call number from the catalog and (b) the user is able to find the correct place on the shelves where a particular item should appear. Buckland favors tests based on actual records of demand rather than tests based on general samples. In particular, he is somewhat critical of the type of general sample proposed in the DeProspo study. Another limitation of the document delivery test is that, while it is simple to apply, the scoring system becomes quite complicated when the test is attempted in a large library system (e.g., a university library system comprising a main library and multiple departmental libraries).

To evaluate the document delivery capabilities of a single library, a survey of the type used by Urquhart and Schofield is preferred to the use of some "standard" document delivery test, although the former is clearly more difficult to administer. There can be no doubt with this kind of study that the test is based on the real demands of users. The DDT, as first used by Orr et al., is a useful tool for macroevaluation. It produces a numerical score that indicates the performance level of a particular library. The survey method used by Urquhart and Schofield is more suitable for microevaluation, because it is able to pinpoint the specific weaknesses of a particular library and to suggest ways in which the performance of the library may best be improved. It assumes, however, that user demands do accurately reflect user needs. It could be argued that a DDT, based on a carefully derived sample, because not limited by demands actually made, is more likely to provide an evaluation of the performance of a library against the needs of a user group (latent as well as actual demands).

REFERENCES

1. Bommer, M. "The Development of a Management System for Effective Decision Making and Planning in a University Library." Doctoral Dissertation. Philadelphia, University of Pennsylvania, 1971. ED 071 727.
2. Bourne, C. P. and Robinson, J. *SDI Citation Checking as a Measure of the Performance of Library Document Delivery Systems.* Berkeley, Institute of Library Research, University of California, 1973. ED 082 774.
3. Braude, R. M. and Holt, N. "Cost Performance Analysis of TWX-Mediated Interlibrary Loans in a Medium-Sized Center Library." *Bulletin of the Medical Library Association,* 59:65–70, 1971.
4. Brophy, P. et al. *The Library Management Game: A Report on a Research Project.* Lancaster, Eng., University of Lancaster Library, 1972.
5. Buckland, M. K. *Book Availability and the Library User.* New York, Pergamon Press, 1975.
6. Buckland, M. K. "The Management of Libraries and Information Centers." *In: Annual Review of Information Science and Technology.* Edited by C. Cuadra. Vol. 9. Washington, D.C., American Society for Information Science, 1974, pp. 335–379.
7. Buckland, M. K. "An Operations Research Study of a Variable Loan and Duplication Policy at the University of Lancaster." *Library Quarterly,* 42:97–106, 1972.
8. Buckland, M. K. et al. *Systems Analysis of a University Library: Final Report on a Research Project.* University of Lancaster Library Occasional Papers, No. 4. Lancaster, Eng., University of Lancaster Library, 1970, pp. 29–55.
9. Buckland, M. K. and Hindle, A. "Loan Policies, Duplication and Availability." *In: Planning Library Services.* Edited by A. G. Mackenzie and I. M. Stuart. University of Lancaster Library Occasional Papers, No. 3. Lancaster, Eng., University of Lancaster Library, 1969.
10. Buckland, M. K. and Woodburn, I. "An Analytical Study of Library Book Duplication and Availability." *Information Storage and Retrieval,* 5:69–79, 1969.

11. Burkhalter, B. R. and Race, P. A. "An Analysis of Renewals, Overdues, and Other Factors Influencing the Optimal Charge-Out Period." *In: Case Studies in Systems Analysis in a University Library*. Edited by B. R. Burkhalter. Metuchen, N.J., Scarecrow Press, 1968, pp. 11–33.

12. Bush, G. C. et al. "Attendance and Use of the Science Library at M.I.T." *American Documentation, 7*:87–109, 1956.

13. DeProspo, E. R. et al. *Performance Measures for Public Libraries*. Chicago, Public Library Association, 1973.

14. Dougherty, R. M. "The Evaluation of Campus Library Document Delivery Service." *College and Research Libraries, 34*:29–39, 1973.

15. Dougherty, R. M. and Blomquist, L. L. *Improving Access to Library Resources: The Influence of Organization of Library Collections, and of User Attitudes Toward Innovative Services*. Metuchen, N. J., Scarecrow Press, 1974.

16. Duggan, M. "Library Network Analysis and Planning (LIB-NAT)." *Journal of Library Automation, 2*(3):157–175, 1969.

17. Ellis, R. et al. *NIL: A Study of Unfilled Interlibrary Loan Requests in the NYSILL System*. Washington, D.C. ERIC, 1970. ED 047 766.

18. Evans, G. E. and Borko, H. *Effectiveness Criteria for Medical Libraries. Final Report*. Los Angeles, Institute of Library Research, University of California, 1970. ED 057 813.

19. Gaskill, H. V. et al. "An Analytical Study of the Use of a College Library." *Library Quarterly, 4*:564–587, 1934.

20. Goldhor, H. "Are the Best Books the Most Read?" *Library Quarterly, 29*:251–255, 1959.

21. Goyal, S. K. "Application of Operational Research to Problem of Determining Appropriate Loan Period for Periodicals." *Libri, 20*:94–100, 1970.

22. Grant, R. S. "Predicting the Need for Multiple Copies of Books," *Journal of Library Automation, 4*:64–71, 1971.

23. Jestes, E. C. "An Example of Systems Analysis: Locating a Book in a Reference Room." *Special Libraries, 59*:722–728, 1968.

24. Kaushik, B. L. "A Case History and Analysis of Inter-Library Loan Service in the IIT Delhi Library." *Annals of Library Science and Documentation, 19*(2):52–71, 1972.

25. Leimkuhler, F. F. "Systems Analysis in University Libraries." *College and Research Libraries, 27*:13–18, 1966.

26. Leimkuhler, F. F. and Cooper, M. D. "Analytical Models for Library Planning." *Journal of the American Society for Information Science, 22*:390–398, 1971.

27. Line, M. B. "The Ability of a University Library to Provide Books Wanted by Researchers." *Journal of Librarianship, 5*:37–51, 1973.

28. Lubans, J., Sr. et al. *A Study With Computer-Based Circulation Data of the Non-Use and Use of a Large Academic Library*. Boulder, Colo., University of Colorado Libraries, 1973.

29. Mavor, A. S. and Vaughan, W. S., Jr. *Development and Implementation of a Curriculum-Based Information Support System for Hamline University*. Landover, Md., Whittenburg, Vaughan Associates, Inc., 1974.

30. Morse, P. M. *Library Effectiveness: A Systems Approach*. Cambridge, Mass., MIT Press, 1968.

31. Nelson Associates, Inc. *An Evaluation of the New York State Library's NYSILL Pilot Program*. New York, 1968, 150 pp.

32. Nelson Associates, Inc. *Interlibrary Loan in New York State*. New York, 1969.

33. Newhouse, J. P. and Alexander, A. J. *An Economic Analysis of Public Library Services.* Lexington, Mass., Lexington Books, 1972.
34. Orr, R. H. and Schless, A. P. "Document Delivery Capabilities of Major Biomedical Libraries in 1968: Results of a National Survey Employing Standardized Tests." *Bulletin of the Medical Library Association, 60*:382–422, 1972.
35. Orr, R. H. et al. "Development of Methodologic Tools for Planning and Managing Library Services." *Bulletin of the Medical Library Association, 56*:235–267, 1968.
36. Palmour, V. E. et al. *A Study of the Characteristics, Costs and Magnitude of Interlibrary Loans in Academic Libraries.* Westport, Conn., Greenwood Publishing Co., 1972.
37. Penner, R. J. "Measuring a Library's Capability." *Journal of Education for Librarianship, 13*:17–30, 1972.
38. Pings, V. M. "Monitoring and Measuring Document Delivery Service." *In: Papers and Reports of the Kentucky-Ohio-Michigan Regional Medical Library, Issue 2.* Detroit, Regional Medical Library, Wayne State University, 1969.
39. Piternick, A. B. "Measurement of Journal Availability in a Biomedical Library." *Bulletin of the Medical Library Association, 60*:534–542, 1972.
40. Pizer, I. H. and Cain, A. M. "Objective Tests of Library Performance." *Special Libraries, 59*:704–711, 1968.
41. Reisman, A. et al. "Timeliness of Library Materials Delivery: A Set of Priorities." *Socio-Economic Planning Sciences, 6*:145–152, 1972.
42. Rouse, W. B. et al. *A Mathematical Model of the Illinois Interlibrary Loan Network.* Urbana, Ill., Coordinated Science Laboratory, University of Illinois, 1975.
43. Simmons, P. "Improving Collections Through Computer Analysis of Circulation Records in a University Library." *Proceedings of the American Society for Information Science, 7*:59–63, 1970.
44. Thomson, S. K. *Interlibrary Loan Involving Academic Libraries.* ACRL Monograph No. 32. Chicago, American Library Association, 1970.
45. Urquhart, J. A. and Schofield, J. L. "Measuring Readers' Failure at the Shelf." *Journal of Documentation, 27*:273–276, 1971.
46. Urquhart, J. A. and Schofield, J. L. "Measuring Readers' Failure at the Shelf in Three University Libraries." *Journal of Documentation, 28*:233–241, 1972.
47. Warner, E. S. "A Tentative Analytical Approach to the Determination of Interlibrary Loan Network Effectiveness." *College and Research Libraries, 32*(3):217–221, 1971.

7

The Range and Scope of Library Services

One valid way to evaluate a library is by studying the range and scope of services it provides. It is difficult, however, to determine the precise service policies of a particular library without following some form of standardized procedure. It also is impossible to compare the policies of several libraries unless each has been examined according to the same standard procedure. Orr et al.[4] have standardized a method for producing a detailed inventory of library services which covers the entire spectrum of user services and accommodates a wide range of related policies.

The inventory is compiled via a highly structured interview with the director of a library, using a detailed checklist of the various services offered to users and the library's stated policies with regard to these services (see Table 61 for the broad categorization of user services from which the checklist was constructed).

A detailed interview guide is used to explicate the checklist, and each interviewer strictly follows and asks the questions exactly as they appear therein. The questions are presented in a yes/no branching form, similar to a flowchart used in systems analysis (see Figure 39 for the portion of the interview guide that relates to the provision of facsimiles). On the basis of the library director's answers to the questions, the interviewer checks

TABLE 61   Categorization of Library User Services[4]

LIBRARY SERVICES CLASSIFIED BY USER-FUNCTION SERVED

I. DOCUMENT SERVICES—providing documents* for which user has correct bibliographic descriptions (citations)
    A. *Making documents available for temporary use*
        1. On one-time basis
        2. On continuing basis (e.g., routine specified journal titles)
    B. *Supplying user with personal copies of documents*
        1. Originals (ordering for user)
        2. Facsimile copies

II. CITATION SERVICES—providing citations to documents
    A. *On one-time basis*
        1. Providing correct citations when user has incomplete or inaccurate bibliographic descriptions ("verification")
        2. Providing citations to documents relevant to user specified subjects
            (a) Sample bibliographies (e.g., "several recent papers")
            (b) Exhaustive bibliographies
            (c) Critical bibliographies (selected for "merit")
    B. *On continuing basis*
        1. General alerting services (e.g., current journal shelves, monthly acquisitions list)
        2. Specific alerting services
            (a) Relevant to user-specified subjects or tailored to interests of user groups
            (b) Tailored to user's individual interests.

III. ANSWER SERVICES—providing *specific* information to answer user's questions
    A. *Simple facts* (e.g., address, spelling of name)
    B. *Simple summaries* (e.g., biographical sketch prepared from multiple sources)
    C. *Complex facts* (e.g., compilation of conflicting data)
    D. *State-of-the-art summaries or critical reviews*

IV. WORK-SPACE SERVICES—providing space equipped for user to "work"† within library
    A. *Work involving library materials*
    B. *Other work*

V. INSTRUCTION AND CONSULTATION SERVICES
    A. *Formal and informal instruction in library-related subjects*
    B. *Helping with user's personal information system*
    C. *Exhibits*

VI. ADJUNCT SERVICES
    A. *Translations*
    B. *Editing*
    C. *Non-print media and equipment* (e.g., films, sound recordings)
    D. *Special services* (e.g., preparation of illustrations)

---

*The term "document" as used here and elsewhere in this article refers to a discrete bibliographic unit of recorded information, regardless of its type or form; it can be a journal article, book, reprint, technical report, etc., or a facsimile copy of any of these types of documents.

†"Work" is defined very broadly to include any user activity the library accommodates as a matter of policy, e.g., it may provide rooms for group discussions.

SECTION 16

Types of Service Provided for Supplying Facsimile Copies

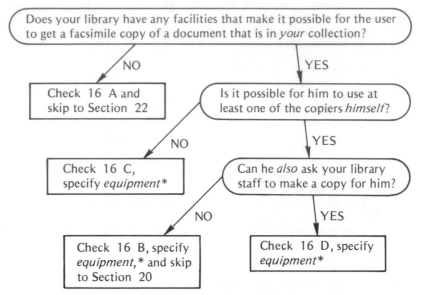

Does your library have any facilities that make it possible for the user to get a facsimile copy of a document that is in *your* collection?

NO

Check 16 A and skip to Section 22

YES

Is it possible for him to use at least one of the copiers *himself*?

NO

Check 16 C, specify *equipment**

YES

Can he *also* ask your library staff to make a copy for him?

NO

Check 16 B, specify *equipment,** and skip to Section 20

YES

Check 16 D, specify *equipment**

*It is important to specify whether equipment capable of reproducing *half-tones* and *bound* volumes is available.

FIGURE 39 Portion of interview guide used in studying range and scope of services.[4]

the appropriate boxes on the accompanying checklist. The interview guide also contains additional information that the interviewer is to seek from the library director (e.g., the "specify equipment" in Figure 39), including details on matters that might affect the user's time, effort, or expense. Further examples from the interview guide, relating to various document services, are shown in Figures 40 through 47. The complete ·survey instrument consists of 54 sections.

This standardized inventory of library services was developed by Orr et al. at the Institute for the Advancement of Medical Communication (IAMC), under contract with the National Library of Medicine and, in 1968, was used by the University City Science Center in the conduct of a national survey of academic medical libraries. The required interview with the library director takes approximately two hours to complete. An obvious advantage of this inventory approach is that it allows the range and scope of the services offered by various libraries to be compared in a

SECTION (1)
DOCUMENT SERVICES

Means of Obtaining Documents When User Is at Library

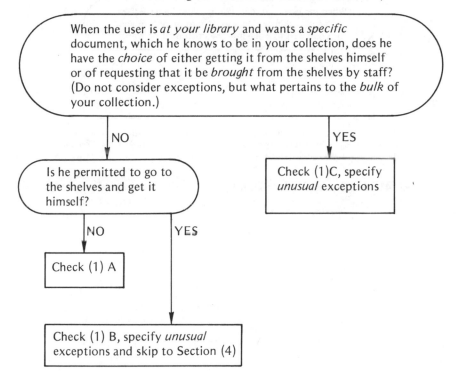

When the user is *at your library* and wants a *specific* document, which he knows to be in your collection, does he have the *choice* of either getting it from the shelves himself or of requesting that it be *brought* from the shelves by staff? (Do not consider exceptions, but what pertains to the *bulk* of your collection.)

NO

YES

Is he permitted to go to the shelves and get it himself?

Check (1)C, specify *unusual* exceptions

NO

YES

Check (1) A

Check (1) B, specify *unusual* exceptions and skip to Section (4)

NOTE: Check (1) A *only* if *most* of the stacks are closed to the given category of user. Checking (1) B for a given user category indicates that the *only* way a user in that category can obtain *most* of documents in the collection is by going to the shelves himself. Even where a self-service *only* policy is followed, exceptions are commonly made for documents in special locations (e.g., locked shelves) or in storage. It is not necessary to note such exceptions *when they are common to most libraries.*

FIGURE 40   Further example from interview guide used in studying range and scope of services.[4]

completely standardized way. The inventory was quite sensitive to differences among academic libraries (see Figure 48 for a summary of copying policies in six academic medical libraries participating in the IAMC field trials), and application of the procedures was found to stimulate analysis and reappraisal of policies by the libraries surveyed.

The inventory has a value beyond pure description and comparison. By

SECTION (2)
DOCUMENT SERVICES

Requests for Staff Delivery of Documents When User Is at Library

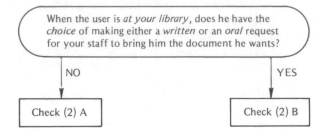

NOTE: A check in (2) A will be interpreted as meaning that *only* written requests are accepted- the possibility that *only* oral requests are accepted was considered unlikely. If this should be the case, check (2) A and *specify* this unusual policy.

FIGURE 41   Further example from interview guide used in studying range and scope of services.[4]

SECTION (3)
DOCUMENT SERVICES

Delivery of Documents to Locations Within Library

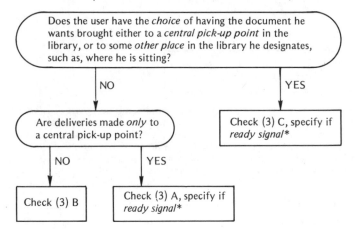

*Ready signal: A display system that enables the user to see from a distance his document is ready for him to pick-up.

NOTE: Checking (3) B means that deliveries within the library are made *only* to a seat location or a carrel, etc., as contrasted to a central pick-up point.

FIGURE 42   Further example from interview guide used in studying range and scope of services.[4]

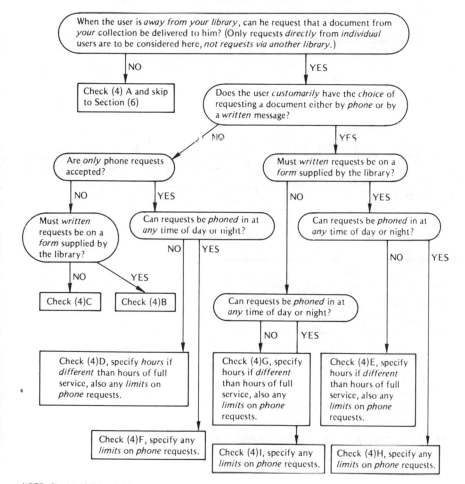

SECTION (4)
DOCUMENT SERVICES

Requests for Documents When User Is Away From Library

When the user is *away from your library*, can he request that a document from *your* collection be delivered to him? (Only requests *directly* from *individual* users are to be considered here, *not requests via another library*.)

NO — Check (4) A and skip to Section (6)

YES — Does the user *customarily* have the *choice* of requesting a document either by *phone* or by a *written* message?

NO — Are *only* phone requests accepted?

YES — Must *written* requests be on a *form* supplied by the library?

Must *written* requests be on a *form* supplied by the library?

Can requests be *phoned* in at *any* time of day or night?

Can requests be *phoned* in at *any* time of day or night?

Check (4)C

Check (4)B

Can requests be *phoned* in at *any* time of day or night?

Check (4)D, specify *hours* if *different* than hours of full service, also any *limits* on *phone* requests.

Check (4)G, specify hours if *different* than hours of full service, also any *limits* on *phone* requests.

Check (4)E, specify hours if *different* than hours of full service, also any *limits* on *phone* requests.

Check (4)F, specify any *limits* on *phone* requests.

Check (4)I, specify any *limits* on *phone* requests.

Check (4)H, specify *limits* on *phone* requests.

NOTE: Checking (4) B or (4) C means that the library does not *customarily* accept *phone* requests directly from its users. Checking (4) D or (4) F means that it does not *customarily* accept *written* requests.

FIGURE 43 Further example from interview guide used in studying range and scope of services.[4]

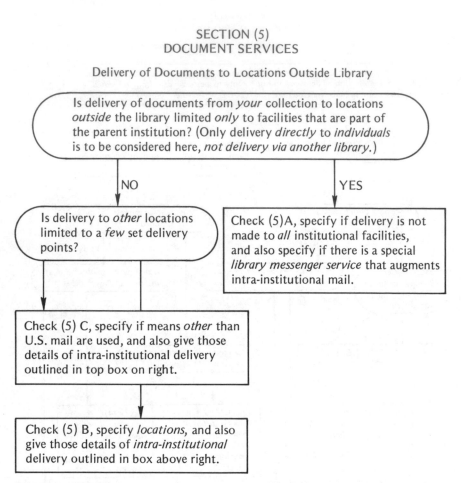

SECTION (5)
DOCUMENT SERVICES

Delivery of Documents to Locations Outside Library

Is delivery of documents from *your* collection to locations *outside* the library limited *only* to facilities that are part of the parent institution? (Only delivery *directly* to *individuals* is to be considered here, *not delivery via another library*.)

NO | YES

Is delivery to *other* locations limited to a *few* set delivery points?

Check (5)A, specify if delivery is not made to *all* institutional facilities, and also specify if there is a special *library messenger service* that augments intra-institutional mail.

Check (5) C, specify if means *other* than U.S. mail are used, and also give those details of intra-institutional delivery outlined in top box on right.

Check (5) B, specify *locations*, and also give those details of *intra-institutional* delivery outlined in box above right.

NOTE: Checking (5) C means that documents are delivered to *any* address the user designates. The possibility that a library delivers documents *only* to *extra-institutional* locations has been ignored. If this is the case, check (5) B or (5) C, as appropriate, and specify this unusual policy.

FIGURE 44 Further example from interview guide used in studying range and scope of services.[4]

SECTION (6)
DOCUMENT SERVICES

Reservation and Notification

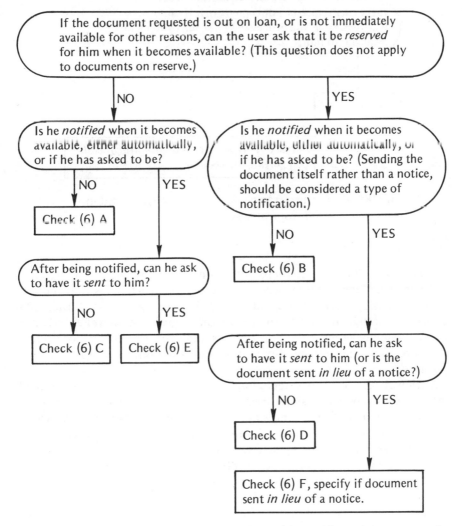

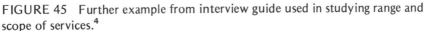

FIGURE 45   Further example from interview guide used in studying range and scope of services.[4]

SECTION (7)
DOCUMENT SERVICES

Availability of "In Process" Documents

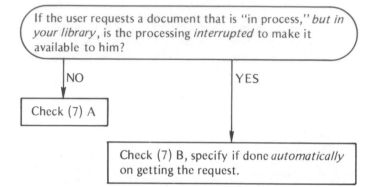

If the user requests a document that is "in process," *but in your library*, is the processing *interrupted* to make it available to him?

NO

YES

Check (7) A

Check (7) B, specify if done *automatically* on getting the request.

FIGURE 46   Further example from interview guide used in studying range and scope of services.[4]

compelling a librarian to focus attention on the services and related policies of his organization, weaknesses and inconsistencies that require correction may become evident. According to Orr et al.,[4] the data collected through the inventory technique "give a comprehensive but detailed picture of what the library does and does not offer to, or do for, its users, including any significant differences in policy for different user groups."

Although the inventory technique was developed for use by trained interviewers in biomedical libraries, it also has been applied to other types of libraries and has been found suitable for use by librarians in "interviewing themselves"; that is, the instrument can be self-administered; therefore, it is usable in a library self-survey.

Orr et al.[4] also report on experiments using techniques for weighting the categorical data obtained in the inventory, to develop some type of quantitative score that would reflect the range and scope of the services provided by various libraries. Before the inventory can be used to produce a quantitative score, numerical weights must be assigned to each broad category of service (document services, citation services, answer services) and these weights also must be divided among the various service alternatives in each category—the weights reflecting some judgment on the value and/or benefits of the service options. The experiments

SECTION (8)
DOCUMENT SERVICES

Circulation of Serials

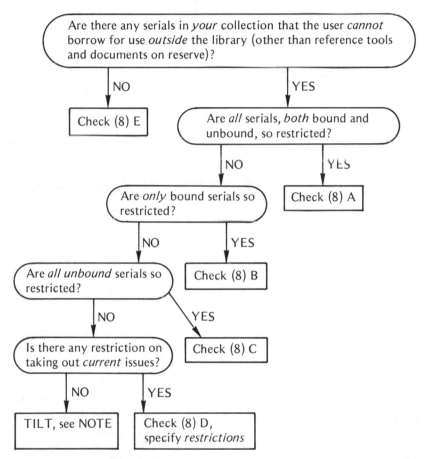

NOTE: Here, as elsewhere, when a question tree leads to TILT, it means that some dichotomy has either broken down or has been misunderstood. Often this can be remedied by starting down the tree again and clearing up yes-no choices either by more explanation or by specifying the exceptions that caused the difficulty. For example, in this tree, TILT might be reached if the only serials not circulated were specific titles or specific volumes. In this case the difficulty could be handled by checking (8) E, and specifying the exceptions.

FIGURE 47 Further example from interview guide used in studying range and scope of services.[4]

	Library A	Library B	Library C	Library D	Library E	Library F
6. Facsimile Copies at *User's Option*						
a. Types of Service						
(1) No copying facilities						X
(2) Self-service only	X					
(3) Staff-mediated service only			X	X		
(4) Choice of self- or staff-mediated service		X			X	

FIGURE 48 Summary of copying service available at six academic medical libraries.[4]

in weighting used three separate groups: 8 undergraduates studying administrative processes, 4 library school students, and 15 hospital librarians. The subjects were asked to weight the various service alternatives, according to their judgment of the importance of the alternatives, and to express their weightings by the allocation of "points." Each was given 1,000 points to allocate in this way. The weight assigned to a particular service policy was viewed as a "score" that a library would earn if it claimed this policy. An "ideal" library would be able to earn all 1,000 points. Table 62 shows, at the broad category level, how these various groups weighted the services covered by the inventory. The potential utility of using this method for comparing the services of a number of libraries is demonstrated in Table 63: Six academic medical libraries are compared, using a weighting scheme established by averaging the point allocations of two practising medical librarians. It is clear that the resulting index of library performance is highly sensitive to the weighting method adopted, and Table 63 should be regarded merely as demonstrating the application of the technique, using the "optimal" point allocation shown in the first column and applying it to the six libraries.

The IAMC investigators also report on the development of another inventory, which covers the services offered by a library to other

TABLE 62   Results of Trials of Weighting Method with Different Groups[4]

Services	8 Undergraduate Students			4 Library Students			15 Hospital Librarians			All Groups*		
	(1) Mean Number Points Allotted	(2) Average Deviation from Mean	(3) Index of Disagreement	(4) Mean Number Points Allotted	(5) Average Deviation from Mean	(6) Index of Disagreement	(7) Mean Number Points Allotted	(8) Average Deviation from Mean	(9) Index of Disagreement	(10) Overall Mean	(11) Average Deviation from Mean	(12) Index of Disagreement
Document Services	420	38	9	390	40	10	450	82	18	420	20	5
Citation Services	230	22	10	230	62	27	280	61	22	250	23	9
Answer Services	88	16	18	120	39	32	110	64	58	110	11	10
Instruction and Consultation Services	61	18	30	65	29	45	61	25	41	62	2	3
Work-Space Services	130	63	48	110	46	42	47	21	45	95	33	35
Adjunct Services	68	26	38	85	34	40	48	28	58	67	13	19

Columns (1), (4), (7), and (10) may not total exactly 1000 points because of rounding errors. All values are rounded to 2 significant figures or nearest whole number.

Index of Disagreement = [Average Deviation from Mean ÷ Mean No. Points Allotted] × 100.

*Here the mean for each group is treated as a single "observation," and the average deviation from the mean reflects variation among the 3 groups.

TABLE 63   Demonstration Scoring of Inventory Data for Six Academic Medical Libraries Relative to "Optimal" Library[4]

Services	"Optimal" Library Points Allotted	Library A		Library B		Library C		Library D		Library E		Library F	
		Points Earned	Relative Score	Points Earned	Relative Score	Points Earned	Relative Score	Points Earned	Relative Score	Points Earned	Relative Score	Points Earned	Relative Score
Document Services	524	212	40%	382	73%	296	56%	394	75%	394	75%	192	37%
Citation Services	285	243	85%	119	42%	243	85%	184	65%	142	50%	236	83%
Answer Services	82	75	91%	75	91%	68	83%	75	91%	59	72%	59	72%
Other Services†	109	50	46%	29	27%	62	57%	68	62%	23	21%	46	42%
All Services	1000	580	58%	605	60%	669	67%	721	72%	618	62%	533	53%

Relative Score =[Points Earned ÷ Points Allotted for "Optimal" Library] × 100.

*The values in this column were obtained by averaging the number of points allotted by two of the authors (V.P. and I.P.).

†Here "Other Services" includes "Work-Space Services," "Instruction and Consultation Services," and "Adjunct Services."

libraries; that is, it is an "inventory of interlibrary services." In addition to covering the obvious area of interlibrary loan, this inventory includes such activities as cataloging and binding for other libraries, exchange services, maintenance of union lists, and the provision of training and management services.

A comprehensive survey of service policies in Indiana libraries was conducted in 1969 by Olson,[3] a former member of the IAMC study team. The object of the survey was to "describe and evalute the prevailing pattern of service policies in Indiana libraries, including academic, public, school, and special libraries and information centers." Olson developed an expanded, modified interview guide of the type used in the IAMC study. It was designed for use in a mail survey, and was self-administered by Indiana librarians participating in the survey. A sample page from the questionnaire is shown in Figure 49. The questionnaire was mailed to all academic libraries (excluding departmental libraries), to all special and public libraries, and to a sample of school libraries in the state. The overall response rate was well over 50%. The data collected were weighted on the basis of "value preferences of groups of Indiana librarians from all types of libraries surveyed," using the method reported earlier by Orr et al.;[4] namely, the allocation of 1,000 points among the various service options. Three weightings were developed: one by a group of public librarians, one by a group of academic librarians, and one by a group of school librarians. Figure 50 shows how the 1,000 points were allocated to the broad service categories by the three groups. A points allocation made by one special librarian is included for comparison purposes. Note that the academic and school librarians placed greater emphasis on access to materials and less emphasis on question-answering services than did the public librarians. Table 64 shows how closely the policies of each type of library match the service policies of an "ideal" library (1,000 point score) of the same type.

Olson's survey instrument proved to be highly discriminating, because it revealed a wide range of performance levels among libraries of a particular type. For example, some small public libraries scored as low as 9%, while others scored as high as 63%. In some instances, small public libraries achieved higher scores than their larger counterparts. Olson's survey includes much data on the detailed policies of Indiana libraries with regard to circulation of materials in the collection, provision of bibliographic citations, answer services, user instruction and educational programs, user relations, "wherewithal" (hours available, space available, and other factors affecting use of the library's resources), and other

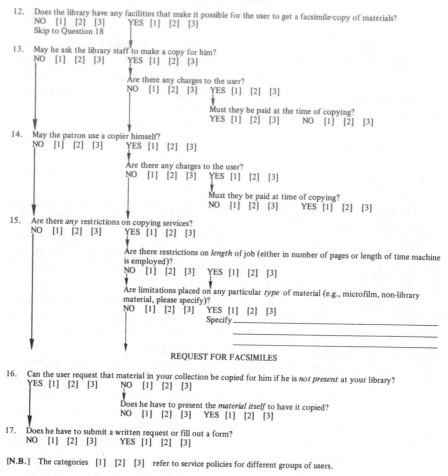

FACSIMILE COPYING

12. Does the library have any facilities that make it possible for the user to get a facsimile-copy of materials?
NO [1] [2] [3]   YES [1] [2] [3]
Skip to Question 18

13. May he ask the library staff to make a copy for him?
NO [1] [2] [3]   YES [1] [2] [3]

Are there any charges to the user?
NO [1] [2] [3]   YES [1] [2] [3]

Must they be paid at the time of copying?
YES [1] [2] [3]   NO [1] [2] [3]

14. May the patron use a copier himself?
NO [1] [2] [3]   YES [1] [2] [3]

Are there any charges to the user?
NO [1] [2] [3]   YES [1] [2] [3]

Must they be paid at time of copying?
NO [1] [2] [3]   YES [1] [2] [3]

15. Are there *any* restrictions on copying services?
NO [1] [2] [3]   YES [1] [2] [3]

Are there restrictions on *length* of job (either in number of pages or length of time machine is employed)?
NO [1] [2] [3]   YES [1] [2] [3]

Are limitations placed on any particular *type* of material (e.g., microfilm, non-library material, please specify)?
NO [1] [2] [3]   YES [1] [2] [3]
Specify _____
_____
_____

REQUEST FOR FACSIMILES

16. Can the user request that material in your collection be copied for him if he is *not present* at your library?
YES [1] [2] [3]   NO [1] [2] [3]

Does he have to present the *material itself* to have it copied?
NO [1] [2] [3]   YES [1] [2] [3]

17. Does he have to submit a written request or fill out a form?
NO [1] [2] [3]   YES [1] [2] [3]

[N.B.] The categories [1] [2] [3] refer to service policies for different groups of users.

FIGURE 49 Sample page from questionnaire used in survey of Indiana libraries.[3]

special services. The data are worth studying, and provide a good example of how the standard inventory technique can be applied to a large group of libraries, and the ability of this technique to discriminate among libraries and to rank them by overall service score.

One limitation of the inventory approach, as developed by IAMC and used by Olson, is that it reflects only the librarian's weighting of

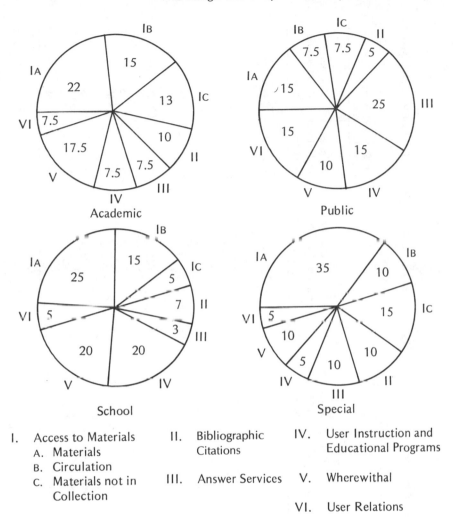

FIGURE 50   Distribution of 1,000 points among major service policy categories for academic, public, school, and special libraries.[3]

services and perception of library policies. Presumably, somewhat different results would be achieved if the weighting were established by a group of library users and if the users' perceptions of library policies were recorded.

A more user-oriented approach to the evaluation of library services was used by Loertscher[2] in evaluating the services provided by school media

TABLE 64   Match of Scores of Indiana Libraries with Optimal Service Policies of Ideal Library: Total Scores for All Service Policies[3]

	Maximum Score (Points) for "Ideal" Library	Median % of Maximum Score	Mean % of Maximum Score	Confidence Interval of Mean	Range of Individual Library Scores	
					Minimum % of Maximum Score	Maximum % of Maximum Score
SCHOOL LIBRARIES						
Elementary, Total	1000	38%	39%	*	12%	85%
By Enrollment						
251–500	1000	36	36	± 4%	12	57
501–700	1000	47	48	± 7	20	79
Over 700	1000	33	38	± 6	12	67
Middle	1000	52	50	± 4	18	83
High	1000	47	49	± 2	13	85
PUBLIC LIBRARIES						
Central, Total	1000	40	39	*	9	78
By Population						
Under 4,000	1000	32	31	± 2	9	63
4,000–9,999	1000	41	40	± 3	13	60
10,000–29,999	1000	44	42	± 3	23	58
Over 30,000	1000	57	58	± 4	34	78
Branches	1000	42	42	± 3	9	73
ACADEMIC LIBRARIES	1000	51	51	± 2	30	68

*Not Computed

centers. The evaluation was made by the users of the service (i.e., teachers). Teachers participating in the study (nine schools were represented in this phase) were presented with a list of 64 services that a media center might provide. For each service, the teacher was asked to indicate how often the media center in his school provided this service, using the scale:

> 3 = Regularly, as the need arises
> 2 = Occasionally
> 1 = Rarely or never
> X = Don't know or doesn't apply

This technique permitted the ranking of services in order of the degree to which they were provided at the institutions surveyed (or, at least, the degree to which they were provided according to the perceptions of the users). A service that all users record as regularly provided would receive the perfect score of 3. The higher the score achieved by a particular service, the more agreement there would be among respondents that this service was regularly provided by the media centers they used. Loertscher also had users rate—again on a three point scale—the quality of the services provided. He further studied the services of the media center from the staff viewpoint, asking each staff member to (a) judge the importance of each service and (b) indicate how frequently each service was provided. Loertscher was then able to compare the users' perception of the quality of services provided with the perceptions of the suppliers of this service. Some sample data obtained from both media staff and teachers are presented in Table 65. All of these tabulations are based on a maximum possible score of 3.

Although some recent uses of the inventory technique as a means of evaluating library service have been emphasized, the technique is not, in fact, a new one. An example of an earlier study was Smith's[5] checklist of adult services to assess the scope of adult education activities offered by public libraries. The checklist was used to determine which of 37 services a particular public library provided, the reasons why certain services were not provided, and the types of service offered to various categories of users (adult education agencies and community groups of various types). The means by which libraries provide these services also were investigated.

Theoretically, the methods described in this chapter could be used by an individual library user or a group of users to evaluate the services provided by a particular institution. It is unlikely, however, that library users would be sufficiently motivated to undertake a systematic survey of

TABLE 65 Sample of Data from Survey of Services Offered by Media Centers in Indiana High Schools: Mean Responses and Rankings by All Media Staffs and Teachers[2]

Service number and description	1 Importance of services as perceived by media staffs in 40 schools		2 Frequency of services given (received)						3 Satisfaction rating of the teachers in 9 schools	
			(a) By the media staffs in 40 schools		(b) By the media staffs in 9 schools		(c) By the teachers in 9 schools			
	Mean	Rank	Mean	Rank	Mean	Rank	Mean	Rank	Mean	Rank
14. Makes media center facilities readily accessible to groups or individual students upon teacher request.	2.92	7	2.88	5	2.88	6	2.61	3	2.47	5
15. Plans with teachers to correct students' problems in finding and utilizing resource materials through classroom or individualized instruction.	2.61	25	2.30	24	2.16	31	1.88	28	2.07	31

MAKING TEACHERS AWARE OF SERVICES AND MATERIALS

16. Informs teachers about new equipment acquired by the media center.	2.92	5	2.82	8	2.80	9	2.45	7	2.46	8
17. Informs teachers about new materials acquired by the media center.	2.98	1	2.88	3	2.88	5	2.55	5	2.57	1
18. Informs and reminds teachers about services offered by the media center.	2.82	10	2.64	10	2.58	13	2.21	16	2.33	13
19. Orients new teachers to media center services.	2.92	6	2.58	14	2.50	14	1.95	24	2.33	15
20. Provides information about services and materials available to teachers from other libraries and media centers in the area.	2.36	52	2.12	34	1.96	46	1.72	41	1.93	49

Note: This is an example of the data collected by Loertscher.[2] Each mean score is on a 3-point scale. Each column presents mean score for a particular service and the rank of this service when the services are ordered on the basis of mean score.

this type. These procedures, then, are most likely to be used by librarians for assessing their own services or for comparing the services of a number of libraries.

Consumer publications in the United States have not as yet involved themselves in the possibility of evaluating libraries from the consumer's point of view. It is interesting to note, however, that, in 1969, the British consumer publication *What?* presented a feature on "how to test your library." This feature was subsequently reprinted in the library litera- ture.[1] The publishers of *What?* (National Suggestions Centre Ltd.) provided a checklist by which a user might assess the services of a public library (shown in Table 66). Members of the *What?* research panel also assessed their own public libraries, using a 14-point scale reflecting various services and characteristics of the libraries. Points were awarded according to the scheme illustrated in Table 67. Table 68 shows how 35 public libraries in Britain—some municipal and some county—scored on the *What?* consumer scale. Note the wide variations in performance: from a high score of 13 to a low of 4. Although librarians, with some justification, might regard this method of weighting as superficial, it represents a serious attempt on the part of a group of consumers to identify criteria (important to them) for judging the quality of the services offered by a public library. As such, it is rare, if not unique, and cannot be dismissed lightly.

TABLE 66   Checklist by Which a User Might Assess the Services of a Public Library[1]

---

1. Is the library in an easily accessible place in the town? Is there parking space? Can mothers with babies, and disabled people get to the shelves?
2. How many tickets are you allowed? Six is generous, anything below four too little.
3. Can you borrow records?
4. How long are you allowed for reading? Two weeks is usual, three generous.
5. How long does the library keep books you order after they have notified you they are in? Books should not be sent back immediately if you don't claim them at once.
6. How much does it cost to reserve a book? The cost of notifying you by postcard is all it should cost.
7. Is there a separate readers' advice desk and does anyone have time to sit at it?
8. Does the library publish lists of books it has recently bought?
9. Are there tables and chairs near the shelves? Can you find a chair in the reference section or are they all taken by students?
10. Are the catalogues readily available and does someone explain how to use them?
11. How often does the book stock change? How long is it since there was a new book in on your special subject?
12. How old are the reference books?

In conclusion, the *What?* researchers have this to suggest to the library patron: "If your library falls short on any of our criteria, this suggests that you should be asking some awkward questions. There may be a perfectly good explanation, but libraries will not improve unless the public makes its wants known."

TABLE 67   Point Allocation for Assessment of Public Library[1]

Distance		Proportion of qualified staff	
Within 1 mile of reader's home	2 points	40 per cent	2 points
Over 1 mile, under 3	1 point	20–40 per cent	1 point
Over 3 miles	0 point	Under 20 per cent	0 point
Opening hours per week		*Cost of ordering books*	
Over 60	3 points	Free	3 points
40–60	2 points	4d.	2 points
Under 40	1 point	6d.	1 point
Under 30	0 point	Over 6d.	0 point
Reference books in stock			
Over 5 000	3 points	*Readers' Advice Desk*	1 point
1 000–5 000	2 points		
100–1 000	1 point	*Maximum possible points*	14
Under 100	0 point		

REFERENCES

1. "How to Test Your Library." *Library Association Record,* 72:49–52, 1970.
2. Loertscher, D. V. "Media Center Services to Teachers in Indiana Senior High Schools 1972–1973." Doctoral Dissertation. Bloomington, Ind., Graduate Library School, Indiana University, 1973.
3. Olson, E. E. *Survey of User Service Policies in Indiana Libraries and Information Centers.* Indiana Library Studies No. 10. Bloomington, Ind., Indiana State Library, 1970.
4. Orr, R. H. et al. "Development of Methodologic Tools for Planning and Managing Library Services. III. Standardized Inventories of Library Services." *Bulletin of the Medical Library Association,* 56:380–403, 1968.
5. Smith, H. L. *Adult Education Activities in Public Libraries.* Chicago, American Library Association, 1954.

TABLE 68   Consumer Rating of 35 Public Libraries[1]

Authority and Library	Distance	Hours	Reference books	Readers advice	Staff	Cost	Total (max. 14)
Berkshire County Council High St., Abingdon, Berks.	0	2	1	0	0	2	5
Bristol City and County Central Library, College Green	1	3	3	1	2	1	11
Bucks. County Council Broadway, Chesham	1	2	1	1	1	2	8
Cheshire County Council Upton Village Hall, Upton Heath 1	2	1	0	0	0	2	5
Chorley Corporation Avondale Road, Chorley, Lancs.	2	2	1	0	1	1	7
Colchester Borough Shewell Road, Colchester, Essex	2	3	3	1	0	2	11
Cornwall County Council Carlyon Road, St. Austell. North Gate, Launceston	0 0	2 1	2 0	1 0	1 2	2 2	8 5
Derby Corporation Central Library, The Wandwick Sitwell Street, Spondar	0 2	2 2	3 0	1 0	1 1	2 2	9 7
Dorset County Council Central, Dorchester	0	2	2	1	1	3	9
Eccles Corporation Central Library, Church Street	2	2	2	1	1	2	10
Essex County Council High Street, Maldon	1	1	1	1	2	2	8
Fife County Council Church Square, St. Andrews	2	2	3	0	1	1	9
Forfar Town Council Meffan Institute, Forfar, Angus	1	2	2	0	0	3	8
Glasgow Corporation Cardonald District, Mosspark Drive	2	2	0	0	1	0	5
Gloucester County Council City Library, Brunswick Road	2	2	3	1	1	1	10
Gloucester Corporation The Steep, Wotton under Edge	0	1	0	0	2	2	5
Halesowen Corporation Hayley Street, Halesowen, Worcs.	2	1	2	0	1	3	9

TABLE 68 (Continued)

Authority and Library	Distance	Hours	Reference books	Readers advice	Staff	Cost	Total (max. 14)
Hertfordshire County Council							
Combe St., Hemel Hempstead	1	2	2	1	1	2	9
Sparrows Herne, Bushey Heath	2	2	1	1	2	2	10
Hillingdon Borough Council							
Potter Street, Northwood Hills	2	2	1	1	2	2	10
Hove Corporation							
Church Road, Hove	2	2	2	1	1	0	8
Leicester Corporation							
Westcote Branch, Narborough Rd.	2	3	0	0	1	1	7
Lichfield Corporation							
Bird Street, Lichfield	1	1	2	1	1	1	7
Malvern Urban District Council							
Graham Road, Malvern, Worcs.	0	2	2	1	1	1	7
Manchester Corporation							
Hulme District Library	2	3	3	1	1	0	10
Northampton County Council							
Central Library, Abington Street	2	3	3	1	1	3	13
Rutland County							
Oakham, Rutland	2	1	1	0	0	3	7
Sevenoaks Urban District							
The Drive, Sevenoaks	0	2	2	0	1	0	5
Sheffield Corporation							
Surrey Street, Sheffield	1	3	3	1	1	2	11
Solihull Corporation							
Ulleries Road, Solihull	2	2	1	0	1	0	6
Somerset County Council							
Linden Road, Clevedon	2	2	1	0	1	0	6
Surrey County Council							
West Byfleet Branch Library	2	1	1	0	1	0	5
Walsall Corporation							
Central Library, Walsall	0	2	3	1	2	2	10
Warwickshire County							
Kineton Road, Wellesbourne	2	1	1	0	2	3	9
Wiltshire County							
Hill Street, Trowbridge	2	2	3	1	1	1	10
Yorks, N.R. County Council							
College Square, Stokesley	0	1	0	0	0	3	4

8

Evaluation of Technical Services

The evaluation of technical services, as compared to other types of evaluation, presents a somewhat different set of problems. Technical services, as such, cannot be evaluated directly in terms of user satisfaction. Although users could conceivably be asked their opinions about technical processing (e.g., "Are you conscious of significant delays between the publication of a book or a periodical issue and its appearance on the library shelves?"), this type of subjective survey is likely to be of limited utility. It is obvious, however, that the results of various technical processes are being evaluated when an attempt is made to measure the performance of certain public services or tools. For example, the evaluation of a card catalog, if properly conducted, would in part be an evaluation of the cataloging policies and practices of a particular library.

As mentioned in Chapter 1, technical services can be evaluated, theoretically at least, from two viewpoints: (a) their internal efficiency and (b) their long-range effect on the public services of the library. A reasonable amount of work has been performed on the internal efficiency of technical services, particularly in the last 10 years, and is well-covered in the literature. Only a few of the major studies will be discussed here.

Time and Cost Factors

In measuring the efficiency (as opposed to effectiveness) of an operation, cost and productivity factors are of paramount importance. Applied to library technical services, the measurement of efficiency must consider the time and cost of processing an item from the time it is ordered to the time it reaches the shelves (both staff time consumed in the various steps involved, which is the major component in processing costs, and the time elapsing from date of either ordering or receipt of an item to the date of its appearance on the shelves) and the productivity of the staff (how many items a staff member can order, check in, accession, catalog, classify, and so on, in a specified period of time).

A number of studies on technical processing costs have already been published. Examples are the analyses by MacQuarrie,[7] covering a group of libraries in Southern California, and by Wynar et al.[17] at the University of Denver Libraries. Discussions of cost analysis techniques also are available, a notable one being that of Brutcher et al.[1] A detailed discussion of procedures for determining "labour costs per unit of output," with some sample figures from British libraries, is presented by Smith and Schofield.[9] While several of the published studies appear to be very thorough and complete, cost analyses of this type generally have two basic limitations: (a) although many data are presented, it is not always clear how these data were derived, and it is thus impossible for a second investigator to duplicate the methodology to obtain truly comparable data for a second institution or group of institutions, and (b) directly related to the first point, there are no generally accepted standards for what should be measured in these cost studies and for how the costs should be derived and presented.

The need for standardizing the conduct of cost analyses has been emphasized in two papers by Tuttle (formerly Welch).[11,14] In her review paper of 1970, Tuttle[11] points out that "these studies have not been standardized and their results systematized to produce useful units of measure for comparison purposes." She goes on to review some of the more important cost studies and to describe progress made to date toward the development of standards. Spencer[10] has described an approach to the measurement of unit costs in libraries. She uses a random alarm device to sample the working time of personnel, thereby deriving unit costs for interlibrary loans and photocopying services.

A figure of obvious interest to library managers is the *unit cost* of processing a book from the time it is ordered to the time it actually reaches the shelves and is available for use. Although such unit cost figures—sometimes broken down to show costs involved in each processing step—have been made available by a number of libraries, they are of limited value for interlibrary comparisons. Unless the cost figures were obtained in exactly the same way, processing costs cannot be compared. Providing that a library holds its own methodology constant, however, the unit cost figure should be useful for internal purposes—to reflect changes in processing costs over time or, more importantly perhaps, to measure the effect of making changes in library procedures with the object of improving overall efficiency.

Another method of presenting technical processing costs is the TSCORE (Technical Services Cost Ratio), which relates the costs of technical processing to the costs of purchasing library materials. As described by Tuttle,[12] the TSCORE of a library is obtained by dividing the total salary expenditure for technical processing activities during a specified period by the total amount spent on the purchase of materials during the same period. In other words, the TSCORE indicates the cost of technical processing for each dollar expended on the purchase of materials. For example, if a library spends $250,000 a year for purchase of materials and $110,000 a year in salaries associated with technical services, the TSCORE would be $110/250, or $0.44; that is, the library spends $0.44 in technical processing salaries for every dollar it spends to purchase materials. The TSCORE includes all costs incurred from the time an item is ordered (with the exception of selection costs) until it is made available on the library shelves.

Welch[14] reports on a survey of 10 university libraries in which the TSCORE varied from a low of $0.45 to a high of $1.00. In this sample, the TSCORE varied directly with the size of the library. On the other hand, in a group of 12 large public libraries, an inverse relationship was found between the TSCORE and the size of the book fund (i.e., the larger the book fund the less it cost to process a book into the collection). No similar relationships were discernible in a sample of eight smaller public libraries.

A TSCORE has the same utility and limitations as a unit cost figure. It may be used for comparisons within a library and, with the caveats previously mentioned, it may be used to compare costs in different libraries.

It is clear that processing costs are directly related to processing time, and a few investigators have recorded the times involved in various operations under stopwatch conditions. Notable among these studies are those of Voos[13] and Leonard et al.,[6] the latter computing the times involved in 76 different tasks. A useful bibliography of time, cost, and management studies of technical processing has been compiled by Dougherty and Leonard.[4]

Efficiency of Operations

Although some libraries have put a great deal of effort into streamlining their technical services, with the objective of increasing efficiency and reducing costs, it is likely that considerable improvements could be made in many institutions. Martyn,[8] referring to an investigation reported by Butterworth,[2] has highlighted the inefficiencies that may exist:

The acquisition procedures of two university libraries were examined. I shall not repeat the whole study, but the following bit of routine was typical of both libraries' operations. Books received in one library, after a routine which checked everything on the invoice except the price (and then passed the invoice to the bursar, who checked it all again anyway—except the price), were given to two senior cataloguers, who passed them on to their four subordinates. The bibliographical details were then assembled and checked (as they had already been on the original request form, which had been discarded). Then the books were classified and catalogued, and the cataloguing subsequently checked against BNB; if the classification differed, BNB was assumed to be at fault. The senior cataloguers then checked their subordinates' work. In total the output per head of these six professionals was five books per day, and they did nothing else but catalogue. In other parts of the routine, all the paperwork of ordering was gone through before the catalogue was checked to see whether the required book was already in stock or not. Various ledgers such as a "Library Purchases Register" and "Departmental Order Record" were kept, although they had no function whatsoever. The same information was recorded separately a number of times, and the same job done again at various stages of the routine. As Butterworth points out, this sort of picture "draws the reader's attention to the fallacy of presuming that industrious, intelligent and even dedicated people will eliminate wasteful effort so that they can concentrate on the creative aspect of their work."

Although Butterworth was writing about two British university libraries, there is no reason to suppose that similar examples of inefficiency do not exist on the American library scene.

A great deal can be done to improve the efficiency of library operations by subjecting them to close scrutiny through readily available techniques from industrial engineering, operations research, and management science. Applicable techniques include procedures as simple as flowcharting (to reveal duplication of effort and suboptimum sequences of tasks) and time and motion studies. The application of these and other techniques to libraries has been described by Dougherty and Heinritz[3] and in a compilation edited by Lancaster.[5]

A substantial study of methodologies for the evaluation of library services, including a comprehensive bibliography, was prepared by Wessel et al.[16] as part of the ATLIS (Army Technical Library Improvement Studies) program. This study, which also is described in condensed and partial form by Wessel,[15] discusses a number of techniques that might be applied profitably to the evaluation of library technical services.

One analytical technique described by Wessel et al. is known as SCORE (Service Components Reliability and Efficiency Analysis). Its objective is to determine the success probability of a particular operation or service and its mean cost. In applying SCORE, each library activity is broken down into a sequence of events, so that each event is dependent on the successful completion of the one immediately preceding it. During a particular time period, careful records are maintained on the times and costs involved in each event and on the degree of success achieved. The sum of data gathered on each event in a complete operation yields overall time and cost figures, as well as an indication of the probability that the operation will be completed successfully. The technique can be used to identify problem areas (i.e., events that have low success rates in relation to other events, events that are most costly, events that are most time-consuming) and thus has diagnostic value. Such highlighting of problem areas may lead to modifications in the procedures used by the library in order to increase effectiveness (i.e., raise the probability that an operation will be completed successfully) or efficiency (i.e., reduce time or costs), and the librarian can apply the SCORE technique at a later time to gauge the effects of changes made.

A second analytical technique is SCOUT (Service Components Utility Analysis), which is designed to determine whether a library is allocating its resources to best advantage in terms of services provided to users. SCOUT involves the identification of all significant operations performed by the library and the recording of manhours spent per week in each operation. Each operation is assigned a value or weight representing the relative contribution this operation is calculated to make in satisfying user needs. The object of SCOUT is to identify discrepancies between the resources allocated to various operations and the calculated overall value of the operation (i.e., situations in which expenditure on an operation is high, but value of the operation is low in comparison). Again, the technique can be used to estimate the effect of making changes to library operations (e.g., increasing or decreasing manhours assigned to a particular function). It is clear that the value of this technique depends entirely on how successfully one can weight various library operations in terms of their relative utility in meeting user needs. Such weighting is not easy and must eventually be based on subjective criteria. Wessel and his colleagues do, however, suggest methods that might be used to develop a weighting scheme in which subjectivity is reduced.

Wessel's third technique, CORE (Correlation, Regression, and Effectiveness Analysis), is used to identify libraries that, within a particular group of institutions, deviate most from the norm, from the standpoint of the cost or time involved in a particular operation. For example, if unit cataloging costs for a group of libraries are determined, it might be possible to identify a few libraries whose costs are unusually high or low in relation to the group as a whole. Both groups should be examined to determine the reasons for these variations and to establish, if possible, whether any relationship exists between cataloging cost and cataloging quality. The technique may be used to identify optimum (most cost-effective) operations that could be used as models for other libraries. It also might be used as a means of arriving at performance standards. CORE, of course, will work only if the method used to gather time and cost data is held constant from library to library. It also is dependent on the ability to measure the "quality" of an operation or service.

GAME (Group Attainment and Methods Analysis) is a technique that analyzes an operation systematically to identify unnecessary steps, to arrange necessary steps into an optimum sequence, to standardize work methods, and to develop standards for the time that should be spent on each step.

The Wessel study, although somewhat difficult to digest *in toto,* is an important one. Although frequently overlooked by librarians, it contains a useful discussion on the purpose of evaluation in libraries and on performance criteria, as well as a description of a number of potentially valuable evaluation techniques.

Effect of Technical Services on Public Services

Much of the work performed on the evaluation of technical services in libraries has emphasized the internal efficiency of these operations (i.e., time and cost factors). Attempts to analyze the quality of technical services are almost nonexistent,* and very little has been done to evaluate the operations of a technical services department to determine the effect these operations will have on the public services provided by the library. Yet, in the long run, technical operations must be evaluated to determine their eventual impact on library services. It is not meaningful to evaluate cataloging, for example, except in terms of effectiveness of results; that is, how effective is the catalog as a finding tool? Although some catalog use studies have been conducted, they are relatively rare. Very few libraries have attempted to evaluate their own catalogs diagnostically—to

---

*Even such "internal" quality studies as investigations of the consistency of classification and subject cataloging (intercataloger and intracataloger consistency) are generally lacking.

discover failures and imperfections, to identify ways of reducing these failures, to improve utility of the catalog, and to assess the effect of proposed changes on cataloging costs.

Although a library manager may know that substantial delays in technical processing can occur from the time a book is ordered until the time it becomes available to users, he is unlikely to know precisely how significant these delays are in public service operations. Only by catalog use studies, document delivery tests, and similar investigations of public services will it be possible to determine the long-range effect of technical services on the public services provided. More studies of this type are needed to indicate, for example, what proportion of all sought items are unavailable at the time they are required because of processing delays (e.g., on order, but not yet received; received, but not yet cataloged; unavailable, at the bindery; and so on).

While studies of the internal efficiency of technical services are worthwhile, a complete evaluation of technical services also must take into account longer range effects. It is unwise to base an evaluation solely on internal efficiency, because maximum internal efficiency is not always compatible with maximum effectiveness. If changes are proposed in technical service activities, the librarian must know not only what effect these changes will have on costs and productivity, but also what effect, if any, the changes will have on the quality of the services provided; that is, a true cost-effectiveness evaluation is needed. Because the value of a typical book (as measured by the number of uses it will receive) tends to be at its highest level immediately after it has been published and tends to taper off considerably and rapidly thereafter, anything the librarian can do to speed the availability of books is likely to be beneficial. It may be more expensive, for one reason or another, to take certain steps to reduce processing delays (e.g., original cataloging as opposed to waiting for cataloging data from another source), but if these steps reduce user "failures" and decrease the unit cost per circulation of an item, they may be amply justified on cost-effectiveness grounds. Because a library is a fairly complex system, the librarian must be aware that a change made in one activity may have repercussions that will affect, perhaps adversely, a number of other activities. He must, therefore, attempt to assess the effect of a proposed alteration to a processing activity from a long-range (i.e., effect on other activities and on services provided) as well as a short-range (e.g., reduction in processing costs) viewpoint.

In general, cost reduction at the input stage of any operation will frequently lead to increased output costs. An obvious example would be cataloging economies derived through reduction in the number of access points provided (number of subject headings per item or number of cross-references). This could be expected to increase the rate of searching failures and might very well increase average searching time (it lowers the overall probability that a user will find what he is seeking on his first attempt). Input costs versus output costs are discussed further in Chapter 13.

REFERENCES

1. Brutcher, C. et al. "Cost Accounting for the Library." *Library Resources and Technical Services, 8*:413–431, 1964.
2. Butterworth, J. *Productivity Now*. Oxford, Pergamon Press, 1969.
3. Dougherty, R. M. and Heinritz, F. J. *Scientific Management of Library Operations*. New York, Scarecrow Press, 1966.
4. Dougherty, R. M. and Leonard, L. E. *Management and Costs of Technical Processes: A Bibliographical Review, 1876–1969*. Metuchen, N. J., Scarecrow Press, 1970.
5. Lancaster, F. W., ed. "Systems Design and Analysis for Libraries." *Library Trends, 21*, 1973.
6. Leonard, L. E. et al. *Centralized Book Processing: A Feasibility Study Based on Colorado Academic Libraries*. New York, Scarecrow Press, 1969.
7. MacQuarrie, C. "Cost Survey: Cost of Ordering, Cataloging and Preparations in Southern California Libraries." *Library Resources and Technical Services, 6*:337–350, 1962.
8. Martyn, J. "Evaluation of Information Handling Systems." *ASLIB Proceedings, 21*:317–324, 1969.
9. Smith, G. C. K. and Schofield, J. L. "Administrative Effectiveness: Time and Costs of Library Operations." *Journal of Librarianship, 3*:245–266, 1971.
10. Spencer, C. C. "Random Time Sampling with Self-Observation for Library Cost Studies: Unit Costs of Interlibrary Loans and Photocopies at a Regional Medical Library." *Journal of the American Society for Information Science, 22*:153–160, 1971.
11. Tuttle, H. W. "Standards for Technical Service Cost Studies." *Advances in Librarianship*. Vol. 1. Edited by M. J. Voigt. New York, Academic Press, 1970, pp. 95–111.
12. Tuttle, H. W. "TSCORE: The Technical Services Cost Ratio." *Southeastern Librarian, 19*:15–25, 1969.
13. Voos, H. *Standard Times for Certain Clerical Activities in Technical Processing*. Dover, N. J., Technical Information Branch, Picatinny Arsenal, 1964.
14. Welch, H. M. "Technical Service Costs, Statistics, and Standards." *Library Resources and Technical Services, 11*:436–442, 1967.
15. Wessel, C. J. "Criteria for Evaluating Technical Library Effectiveness." *ASLIB Proceedings, 20*:455–481, 1968.
16. Wessel, C. J. et al. *Criteria for Evaluating the Effectiveness of Library Operations and Services*. Washington, D.C., Thompson Co., *Phase 1. ATLIS Report No. 10*, 1967, AD 649 468; *Phase 2. ATLIS Report No. 19*, 1968, AD 676 188; *Phase 3. ATLIS Report No. 21, 1969*, AD 682 758.
17. Wynar, B. S. et al. "Cost Analysis in a Technical Services Division." *Library Resources and Technical Services, 7*:312–326, 1963.

9

Evaluation of Automated Systems in Libraries

During the last decade, a considerable amount of activity has taken place in the field of library automation; that is, the application of computers and related data-processing devices to the technical processes and routine "housekeeping" functions of libraries. A large number of libraries in the United States and elsewhere are now using computers for such operations as circulation control, ordering and acquisition, cataloging, production of catalog cards or printed catalogs, and checking-in of serial publications. A variety of automated systems—minicomputers as well as larger computer configurations—are being used by many types of libraries: national, university, college (including junior and community colleges), public, and school library systems. Some function in an off-line, batch-processing mode, while others operate on-line. Some libraries (e.g., at Bochum University) are highly automated, while others have applied automation to only one operation. A recent development of major importance has been cooperation among libraries in automation activities, both through the establishment of networks (of the State University of New York, Ohio College Library Center, and the Scandinavian LIBRIS types) and through the use of cooperative processing centers (e.g., the Massachusetts Central Library Processing Service and the College Bibliocentre in Ontario). The state of library automation has been reviewed several times, notably by Hayes and Becker[3] and in the *Annual Review of Information Science and Technology*. This chapter will consider criteria by which such systems might be evaluated.

The reference to evaluation criteria by which systems *might* be evaluated is deliberate. A review of the literature on library automation reveals that discussions on evaluation of automated systems are practically nonexistent. If librarians have evaluated the results of their automation activities in a serious and systematic way, they certainly have not written about them.

As with other library activities, an automated system may be evaluated at various levels. Presumably, the *effectiveness* of the system should be evaluated through factors such as accuracy, volume of transactions handled, and speed of processing. Another type of evaluation would involve comparing the performance of an automated system with that of the manual system it replaced. An automated system may be judged cost-effective if it performs either at the same level of effectiveness as the manual system, but at reduced cost, or at a higher level of effectiveness at a cost comparable to that of the manual system. Unfortunately, the situation usually is not this simple. Frequently the automated system provides capabilities that are almost impossible for the manual system to provide. Thus, an important element in the evaluation will be some form of cost-benefit analysis involving identification of the benefits associated with the automated system. If the automated system is more expensive than the manual system, the question then is whether the system benefits outweigh the costs. In the long run, the objectives of automation should be to increase the capabilities and/or effectiveness of the library, and, ultimately, to increase accessibility/exposure per dollar of expenditure.

Some of the major potential advantages of automating any kind of operation are listed in Table 69. It is worthwhile considering these in more detail, with special reference to their applicability in a library situation.

Improved productivity. This is an important objective of automation in industry, where repetitive tasks performed by human operators can be handled more quickly and accurately by computers. Improved productivity also may be relevant in the bibliographic environment. For example, a computer-based information retrieval system makes it possible to conduct many searches simultaneously. This can be achieved through an off-line,

TABLE 69 · Possible Reasons for Mechanization

1. Improve productivity	6. Increase range and depth of service
2. Reduce staff	7. Facilitate cooperation
3. Improve control	8. By-products
4. Reduce error	9. Improve dissemination
5. Improve speed	10. Reduce unit cost of operation

batch-processing mode, or by allowing many users simultaneous access to a data base from remote on-line terminals (in a typical month, several thousand searches are conducted throughout the United States by means of the MEDLINE system of the National Library of Medicine). In the case of a circulation-control system, improved productivity is demonstrated if the automated system can handle greater volumes of circulation than the manual system without increasing the number of staff involved in this activity. Alternatively, productivity improves if the automated system handles the same volume of circulation with fewer staff members.

Staff reduction. An obvious example of reducing the need for human operators through automation has been demonstrated by the change to automatic switching/direct dialing in the telephone system. Automation in libraries also may reduce the need for staff (e.g., self-charging circulation systems) or may reduce the number of persons needed to perform a particular function (as in shared cataloging operations conducted through on-line terminals). It should be recognized, however, that a reduction in staff is not always made with the objective of reducing costs. Under certain conditions, a process may be automated as a matter of expediency or necessity, for example, when qualified staff are not available. Moreover, in some organizations—government agencies in particular—it is much easier to obtain money for equipment or contract work than to obtain authorization to increase personnel levels. Also, because the idea of "automation" carries a certain amount of glamour, automation projects may attract funds that would not be made available for other purposes. While some librarians have been able to obtain substantial funding for automation projects, it is unlikely that these funds would have been made available to employ more staff.

Two related factors are important when considering automation. First, computer costs are declining and will continue to decline for some time, whereas staff salaries and related costs will continue to rise. An automated operation that today may be more expensive than a manual one is likely to be less expensive in the near future. The second point is that automation may free professional or semiprofessional staff from routine clerical tasks and allow them to devote their time to more productive activities.

Improved control. Automation can improve overall control in large recording and inventory operations, such as an airline reservation system or circulation control in a large library system with multiple branches.

Error reduction. Automated systems can operate with a high degree of accuracy. This is why they are used in such critical activities as air traffic control, monitoring of space missions, and monitoring vital functions of patients in hospitals. Because of high levels of accuracy, computers also may be applied to quality control activities in industry and the operation of information systems (e.g., checking the validity of terms in indexing records and the validity of both terms and logic in search strategies). Automated systems may do more than reduce error. They may facilitate the simple and rapid correction of errors once detected (this would be particularly true of on-line input operations) and may compensate for certain human errors or for incomplete or inaccurate information (e.g., misspelled or incomplete authors and titles).

Improved speed. Automation also can facilitate the rapid handling of transactions and allow for up-to-date file maintenance. Some good examples of systems having these characteristics are airline reservations and inventory control in industry. In libraries, on-line circulation systems could speed the processes of charging books in and discharging them and indicate almost immediately the location of a particular book. Similarly, an on-line system for the retrieval of data or bibliographic references is capable of providing a very rapid response to a critical request.

Increased range and depth of service. Another objective of automation is to provide capabilities that would be too costly or difficult, if not impossible, to provide in a manual system. A computer-based index or catalog can provide far more access points to a particular item than it would be possible to provide conveniently and economically in a card catalog or printed index. The computer-based information retrieval system can easily handle highly complex search strategies, involving large numbers of terms in complex logical relationships, that would be virtually impossible to deal with manually. An on-line circulation system or catalog allows a book to be accessed by "unconventional" approaches, as suggested in the Chicago study on requirements for future catalogs. These types of systems also can generate, on a routine basis, records useful to the librarian, but tedious and time-consuming to obtain from a manual system (e.g., breakdowns on circulation of books in various subject areas, on the characteristics of users, on the length of time books are held by users, and so on). The automated system can produce calculations and correlations rapidly on all data collected (e.g., distribution of circulation by subject or age of material) and can present these data in tabular printout or in the form of plots on a video display.

Facilitation of cooperation. There is little doubt that an important benefit of automating library activities is the contribution that automation can make in promoting interlibrary cooperation. Such cooperation is facilitated by the availability of machine-readable data bases, which allow for the efficient exchange and sharing of bibliographic records, and by telecommunications systems, which virtually eliminate the significance of physical separation of institutions. Automation facilitates the establishment of cooperative processing centers and networks, thereby reducing duplication of effort, and provides strong incentives for standardization.

By-products and fringe benefits. Most automated systems will provide valuable by-products and fringe benefits. Once a machine-readable record has been prepared for one purpose, it is advantageous and economical to use it for other purposes. Many large, multipurpose information systems produce several products from a single input operation. If a machine-readable data base is formed to produce a printed index or abstracting publication, this file can be manipulated by computer to provide retrospective searching, dissemination, and related capabilities and services. Sometimes other types of fringe benefits may result. For example, an efficient on-line system, by providing better overall control of circulation and location, may reduce the need for providing duplicate copies of titles in departmental libraries within a university system.

Efficient dissemination. Machine-readable data bases, even large ones, can be exchanged and disseminated efficiently. It would be exceedingly difficult to make such large data bases widely available in conventional printed form.

Reduced unit costs. Through one or more of the aforementioned benefits, the unit cost of a particular operation may be reduced.

Note that some of the advantages are long-term and relate to improved or expanded capabilities, while others are short-term and affect the quality or efficiency of the operation. Cost-effectiveness and cost-benefit considerations are both represented in Table 69.

Automation does not necessarily reduce costs, although it may if libraries are able to join together in a cooperative enterprise. Moreover, as mentioned earlier, cost-wise, automated procedures are becoming increasingly competitive with manual procedures. A relatively new development is the minicomputer, which puts an in-house data-processing capability within the reach of even small libraries. If an automation project cannot be justified from the cost standpoint (that it is cheaper than the equivalent manual operation), it may be justifiable in some other way (improved effectiveness or gaining of additional capabilities).

Perhaps the most articulate opponent of library automation is Ellsworth Mason.[5,6] He has been severely critical of libraries in the United States for embarking on expensive automation projects while budgets for personnel and books remain static or are being reduced. He views automation projects as public relations gimmicks that, unlike other library activities, have been largely free from cost challenge and justification.

While Mason's criticisms are based primarily on cost considerations, without apparent concern for the potential impact of automation on the effectiveness of operations or benefits to the librarian in the form of new capabilities, much of his criticism appears valid. He points out that thorough cost analyses usually are lacking in libraries, both for automated systems and the manual systems they replace. Realistic cost analysis is needed to compare one system with another. Such an analysis must include all applicable costs—everything required to produce the end product. Table 70 lists the major categories under which costs need to be considered. When all cost elements are identified and summed (capital expenditures being amortized over a period of years), they may be reduced to *unit costs per operation;* that is, per item acquired, per item circulated. This would allow for a comparison of costs between automated and manual procedures, as well as for the observation of fluctuating unit costs with volume of use, time, and so on.

A complete cost analysis of a particular operation will involve:

1. The identification, perhaps by flowcharting, of all the detailed steps involved in the operation.
2. The identification of all equipment used in each step.
3. The calculation of unit costs for each step, sampled over a reasonable time period, and based on accurate production statistics, costs of staff time, and costs of equipment utilization.

This type of detailed cost analysis for library automation has rarely been conducted or, at least, the results have rarely appeared in print. One exception is the detailed cost analysis of the LOLITA on-line acquisition system at Oregon State University produced by Auld and Baker.[1] Sample data from this system are shown in Tables 71–73. Table 71 identifies each step (operation) in the system, showing for each the volumes, times, storage requirements, and computer costs; Table 72 gives a more complete analysis of traffic, times, and costs; and Table 73 summarizes costs

TABLE 70   Major Categories of Costs of Library Operations

1. Staff salaries
2. Materials costs
3. Equipment purchase/rental
4. Space requirements
5. Maintenance
6. Computer time
7. Programming
8. Contractor services
9. Staff training

TABLE 71 Volumes, Times, Storage Requirements, and Computer Costs for Each Step in an On-line Acquisitions System[1]

Operation	Computer cost per operation	Wall clock time per operation (in seconds)	CPU time per operation (in seconds)	Average traffic (users) for sample	Storage increase per operation (in characters)	Total number of operations for the year
1. Search for main entry	$.045	19.9	.441	24.7	none	5,368
2. Input P.O., HELD, GIFT	.153	124.1	1.026	23.0	738	16,964
3. Prepare P.O. form file, update vendor data, P.O. accounting	.014	batch	.147	NA	494	16,964
4. Print P.O. form	.039	batch	.097	NA	none	16,964
5. Input P.O. invoice	.075	55.4	.539	20.9	218	14,403
6. Input TF invoice	.022	26.0	.092	26.1	84	9,293
7. Invoice accounting (P.O. or TF) and list invoice for audit	.0057	batch	.047	NA	128	23,696
8. Input catalog data for P.O., remove P.O. from on-order/in-process file	.114	61.8	.940	22.5	313	10,810

for each step on an annual basis. This type of detailed cost analysis is the exception rather than the rule in library automation.

Automated procedures in libraries most likely will be cost-effective where either a basic machine record, once created, can be used for many different purposes (order, acquisition, catalog, circulation, binding) and/or the cost of development and maintenance can be shared by several institutions, for example, a network or a cooperative processing center. Unfortunately, it is difficult to compare manual and automated systems on the basis of cost alone. Although it is relatively easy to derive costs for an existing manual system, it can be rather difficult to accurately predict the costs of a projected automated system. Once the automated system is installed, however, accurate cost figures can be derived for its operation; but these cost figures may not be strictly comparable with the cost figures for the manual system, because the new system may have changed the method of operation and/or the range and scope of services offered. Thus, one might be comparing the costs of two different systems, one providing greater benefits than the other. Another problem is that, once an automated system is installed, it is likely that no good cost or efficiency

TABLE 72   Sample Analysis of Traffic, Times, and Costs for an On-line Acquisitions System[1]

Operation	Sample		Wall Clock Time (seconds)		CPU Time/Op (seconds)		Traffic		Cost/Op	
	No. of items	Ses-sions	Min.	Max.	Min.	Max.	Min.	Max.	Min.	Max.
1. Search for main entry	4524	50	8.6	180.0	.259	5.852	10	55	$.025	$.590
2. Input P.O., HELD, GIFT	813	15	94.8	175.2	.673	1.497	6	41	.109	.217
3. Prepare P.O. form file, update vendor data, P.O. accounting	1312	7	BATCH	BATCH	.122	.295	NA	NA	.011	.032
4. Print P.O. form	1048	3	BATCH	BATCH	.092	.102	NA	NA	.038	.040
5. Input P.O. invoice	1029	10	42.9	94.1	.373	.743	4	34	.059	.103
6. Input TF invoice	2361	10	19.8	41.4	.072	.113	14	47	.018	.042
7. Invoice accounting (P.O. or TF) and list invoice for audit	5517	5	BATCH	BATCH	.042	.064	NA	NA	.0049	.0068
8. Input catalog data for P.O., remove P.O. from on-order/in-process file	1042	15	40.8	108.0	.671	1.270	7	42	.090	.153

TABLE 73   Annual Costs for Each Processing Step in an On-line
Acquisitions System[1]

| | Computer | | | |
Operation	Unit	Annual	Personnel	Total
1. Search for main entry	$.045	$ 241.56	$.015	$.060
2. Input P.O., HELD, GIFT	.153	2,595.49	.080	.233
3. Prepare P.O. form file, update vendor data, P.O. accounting	.014	237.50	none	.014
4. Print P.O. form	.039	661.60	none	.039
5. Input P.O. invoice	.075	1,080.23	.036	.111
6. Input TF invoice	.022	204.45	.016	.038
7. Invoice accounting (P.O. or TF) and list invoice for audit	.0057	135.07	none	.0057
8. Input catalog data for P.O., remove P.O. from on-order/in-process file	.114	1,232.34	.040	.154
Total		$6,388.24		

figures will be found for the manual system it replaced. A typical complaint is that voiced by Hunt:[4] "No costing was ever carried out on the manual system as it existed before the introduction of the computer."

Before the effectiveness of any system—manual or automated— designed for a particular library operation can be evaluated, a list of performance criteria for the system (requirements that the system should be capable of satisfying) must be prepared. Table 74 gives an example of requirements for a circulation system. Once these are identified, a particular system, existing or projected, can be evaluated in terms of its ability to meet the requirements. When considering a change to automation, its advantages and disadvantages in terms of increased effectiveness and additional capabilities must be weighed.

Possible disadvantages might include the following:

1. Dependence on a computer that may not be completely under library control.*

2. Possible dependence on nonlibrary staff for design, development, and maintenance.

3. In the case of a batch-processing system, updating of files is not up-to-the-minute (e.g., circulation files may be updated only once every

---

*A great potential advantage of minicomputers is that they are inexpensive enough to be purchased outright by even relatively small libraries.

TABLE 74   Example of Performance Criteria for a Circulation System

1. Charging/discharging rapid.
2. Minimal error.
3. Easy to understand. Training minimized.
4. Should indicate rapidly and unequivocally

    a. particular book—who has
    b. particular user—what they have
    c. date borrowed/due for return.

5. Should permit reservation and recall.
6. Should allow renewal.
7. Statistics: Volume, User Patterns, Book Patterns.
8. Record on use of each book.
9. Economical to install and operate.

24 hours), therefore, certain records may be unavailable when they are needed.

4. Record format may be dictated by data-processing requirements, possibly leading to compromises.

5. A system not fully under library control may not be stable. Changes in hardware are likely to lead to system changes, creating the need for reprogramming. This can be both expensive and disruptive to library operations.

6. The initial cost of planning, designing, and installing the system may be high.

7. Unless the system has adequate "back-up" capability, it may not be sufficiently reliable for certain types of library operations; that is, there must be an efficient form of back-up to provide for times when the computer is "down" for maintenance purposes.

8. "Human factors" also must be taken into account. In the case of an on-line system, there can be problems, among staff as well as library users, in adapting to a completely different mode of operation.

When a librarian considers the desirability of replacing an existing manual system with an automated system, he must develop a "profit and loss" sheet, showing the features that favor one system over the other or are common to both. Such a profit-and-loss sheet, as presented by Cox and Balmforth,[2] is shown in Figure 51. The decision of whether or not to automate also should be based on longer term considerations. As previously indicated, an automated system that today is more costly than a manual system may be less costly in a few years time.

To reiterate, the decision to automate any library operation must

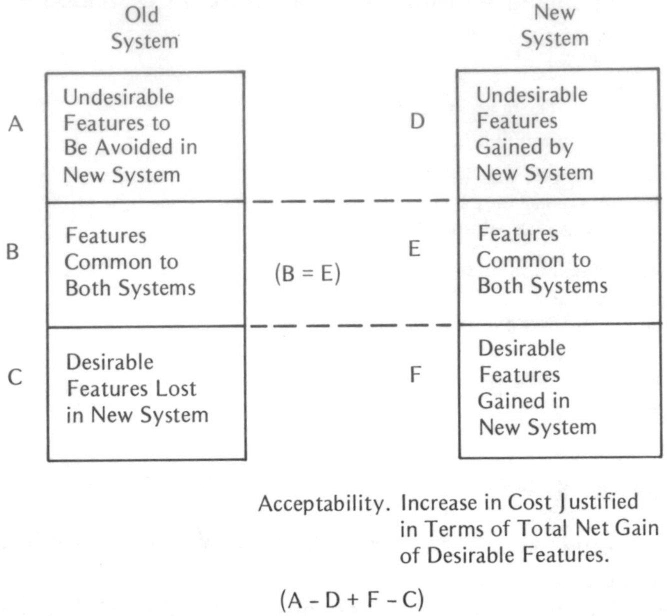
Old System
New System
A
Undesirable Features to Be Avoided in New System
D
Undesirable Features Gained by New System
B
Features Common to Both Systems
(B = E)
E
Features Common to Both Systems
C
Desirable Features Lost in New System
F
Desirable Features Gained in New System
Acceptability. Increase in Cost Justified in Terms of Total Net Gain of Desirable Features.
(A - D + F - C)

FIGURE 51 Profit and loss sheet to compare two different systems.[2]

consider the effect of automation on the performance (effectiveness) of the system and the capabilities (benefits) of the system, as well as the costs. Tables 75–79 depict some possible benefit and effectiveness considerations relating to a number of library operations to which automation might be applied.

TABLE 75 Benefit and Effectiveness Considerations for a Circulation Control System

Benefits:

1. Improved accuracy and control.
2. Speed of charging/discharging.
3. Economy of staff. Productivity.
4. New records that can be maintained (circulation patterns).
5. Integration into a multipurpose system (ordering, catalog, circulation, binding).
6. Secondary benefits; for example, reduction in the number of duplicate copies needed.

Benefits must be balanced against costs, the unit cost per circulation, now and projected in the future.

Effectiveness: evaluated in terms of accuracy and speed.

TABLE 76   Benefit and Effectiveness Considerations for an Interlibrary Loan System

Benefits:

1. Improved accuracy and control.
2. Speed of processing.
3. Productivity (volume of loans) increased per staff member involved.
4. Statistics more complete and accurate.
5. Paper and paper handling reduced.

Benefits must be balanced against costs to lending and borrowing institutions.

Effectiveness: evaluated in terms of speed of service and accuracy of transactions.

TABLE 77   Benefit and Effectiveness Considerations for an On-line Catalog

Benefits:

1. More current through on-line entry.
2. Library cooperation (shared cataloging) facilitated through telecommunications and machine-readable data bases.
3. Depth of subject cataloging can be increased economically.
4. More access points can be provided efficiently and economically.
5. "Nonconventional" approaches to retrieval can be used (e.g., color, language, size, date).
6. Multiple, simultaneous access to very large files from remote locations is possible.
7. Items can be searched for by combinations of characteristics (e.g., author and publisher).
8. Truncated "search keys" allow a search to be conducted with incomplete or inaccurate author/title information.

Benefits must be balanced against unit cost per item entered and against catalog maintenance costs.

Effectiveness: evaluated against user success in finding entries by author, title, subject, or other approaches, as well as time taken to conduct a search.

TABLE 78   Benefit and Effectiveness Considerations for a Computer-Produced Printed Catalog

---

Benefits:

1. Improved accessibility through

   (a) multiple locations
   (b) increased access points.

2. Facilitation of other operations (e.g., interlibrary lending).
3. By-products from the machine-readable record (e.g., special subject bibliographies).
4. Updating and distribution improved.

Benefits must be balanced against cost per item input, cost per catalog printed, maintenance costs.

Effectiveness: evaluated in terms of user success in finding sought entries, ease of use, speed of use.

TABLE 79   Benefit and Effectiveness Considerations for an Automated Library Network

---

Overall costs in building and maintaining the network must be balanced against the benefits to participating libraries, *which can be great:*

1. Makes automation technically and economically feasible in even small institutions.
2. Sharing of expensive computer resources:

   (a) facilitates use to optimum capacity
   (b) improves efficiency of machine use.

3. Ability and willingness of libraries to cooperate and share increases.
4. Standardization is promoted.
5. Provides improved management controls and data for decision making; for example, book selection may be improved by knowing how many copies already exist in a region and how much they are used.
6. Duplication of materials and effort may be reduced through:

   (a) improved interlibrary loan procedures
   (b) cooperative acquisition policies
   (c) cooperative cataloging.

7. Individual libraries may have improved control over acquisitions, circulation, and other procedures.

Effectiveness: evaluated against a wide range of quality and time considerations, depending on which activities are automated within the network.

Summary and Conclusion

Various approaches to evaluation of an automated library system are possible:

1. *Evaluation against system objectives.* Objectives for a particular library operation must be carefully defined. The automated system should be examined to determine how many of the objectives it meets, how well, and in what time frame.

2. *Cost evaluation.* Unit costs per item acquired, cataloged, circulated, and so on, should be used to compare various systems, as well as to balance against system benefits.

3. *Quantitative evaluation.* The most obvious among a number of possible quantitative considerations is the effect of automation on the number of transactions that can be handled in a specified time; another is its effect on the volume of use. Automated systems have the capability of increasing library use (i.e., increasing exposure or accessibility). Some possible ways of achieving this are:

(a) Wide distribution of printed catalogs and bibliographies.

(b) More efficient acquisition procedures.

(c) More efficient cataloging procedures. (Note: more efficient technical processes increase exposure/accessibility by getting materials to the public faster and cheaper.)

(d) More access points in the machine catalog, especially an on-line catalog.

(e) More effective use of the catalog through more access points and built-in redundancy to compensate for common human errors.

(f) Improved recordkeeping (e.g., by knowing where a particular copy is at any time).

(g) Cooperative processing in acquisitions, cataloging, etc., reduces unit costs and number of duplicates required, thus freeing more money for book collection and public services.

4. *Qualitative evaluation.* The following are some possible qualitative considerations, and are mentioned only as examples.

(a) Is the automated system more accurate? Are there fewer errors? This can be determined by sampling and quality control procedures.

(b) *Findability.* Does the automated system increase findability of items? The on-line catalog/circulation system should increase findability by providing more access points, by error compensation techniques, and by built-in instructional features.

(c) *Improved reference capabilities*. A library network can increase the reference capabilities of even small institutions by making vast bibliographic resources available through remote terminals. The reference capabilities of a library can be evaluated before and after joining such a network.

(d) *Document delivery capability* can be assessed by various techniques discussed in Chapter 6. Certainly automation could lead to greatly improved delivery capabilities, especially if it takes the form of participation in a network. Such networking allows more efficient sharing of bibliographic resources, and, with on-line linkage, each library's collection is an extension of the collections of the other libraries in the system; the resources of *each* library are increased. Interlibrary lending also may be improved by mechanized procedures, and on-line searching systems may eventually interface with random-access microfiche stores or with digital stores to permit rapid, remote access to full text.

Cost factors are always of paramount importance. All managers of programs and services attempt to accomplish as much as possible with the money available to them. Before automating any operation, a librarian must ask himself whether or not the action will result, in the short or long run, in improved accessibility/exposure per dollar of expenditure.

This chapter has considered various possible approaches to the evaluation of automated systems in libraries. One further consideration of great importance is how an automated system can contribute to the measurement and evaluation of library services in general.

In the 1970s, the movement is toward development of integrated on-line systems; that is, systems that serve multiple library functions, including ordering and acquisition, cataloging, and circulation control, among others. Multipurpose library systems of this type exist, in embryo at least, in such activities as the on-line circulation system at Ohio State University, the Ohio College Library Center, the Scandinavian LIBRIS system, and the BALLOTS project at Stanford University. With an integrated on-line system, it is possible to perform many studies of the types discussed in this book by using continuous automatic monitoring procedures. Visualize a system that is both an on-line library catalog and a circulation control system. Routinely, such a system can yield comprehensive analyses of circulation patterns, catalog use, and document delivery capabilities. By on-line monitoring and analysis of the results of such an operation, one can determine (on a continuous basis) what people are looking for, whether they find an entry for the item they are seeking, why they miss entries that actually exist, and whether the book they are seeking is available (on the shelf) at the time it is needed.

The completely integrated on-line system could provide valuable data on user needs that have been difficult to collect in the past. It could identify:

1. Inadequacies in the collection by subject, and specific items that are sought, but lacking.
2. Needs for additional copies of books.
3. Problems encountered in the use of a catalog, and search approaches used, to determine what additional entries, types of entries, or features are needed.

In other words, the integrated on-line system will allow continuous objective analysis of performance, whereas, in existing manual operations, such analyses can be done only on a one-time or "spot check" basis. Not only can an on-line system be designed to collect data needed for evaluation purposes, but, by the incorporation of programs for computation and data reduction, it can conduct analyses and correlations, presenting the results in the form of tables or graphs (on-line display or printed form) to keep management informed on the performance, failures, and limitations of the library. Automated systems, when more widespread, will permit continuous monitoring and quality control of library operations, activities which, in the present manual service environment, require special effort to perform.

REFERENCES

1. Auld, L. and Baker, R. "LOLITA: An On-Line Book Order and Fund Accounting System." *In: Proceedings of the 1972 Clinic on Library Applications of Data Processing.* Edited by F. W. Lancaster. Urbana, Ill., Graduate School of Library Science, University of Illinois, 1972, pp. 29–53.
2. Cox, N. S. M. and Balmforth, C. K. "Some Notes on Costs and Benefits." *In: Interface: Library Automation with Special Reference to Computing Activity.* Cambridge, Mass., MIT Press, 1971, pp. 216–223.
3. Hayes, R. M. and Becker, J. *Handbook of Data Processing for Libraries.* New York, Wiley, 1970.
4. Hunt, C. J. "Evaluating the Performance of a Computerized Library System: The Acquisitions System in Manchester University Library." *In: The Art of the Librarian.* Edited by A. Jeffreys. Newcastle upon Tyne, Oriel Press, 1973, pp. 58–71.
5. Mason, E. "Automation, or Russian Roulette?" *In: Proceedings of the 1972 Clinic on Library Applications of Data Processing.* Edited by F. W. Lancaster. Urbana, Ill., Graduate School of Library Science, University of Illinois, 1972, pp. 138–156.
6. Mason, E. "The Great Gas Bubble Prick't; or Computers Revealed—by a Gentleman of Quality." *College and Research Libraries, 32*:183–196, 1971.

10

The Relevance of Standards to the Evaluation of Library Services

This chapter will focus on the possible utility of standards in the evaluation of library services. For information on the various surveys of library standards that have been conducted, consult the references and supplementary bibliography at the end of this chapter.

Standards are essential to the successful conduct of many activities, especially manufacturing, maintenance, and engineering operations. They have potential value in virtually all fields, and libraries are no exception. Library standards, however, have been described in a variety of adverse ways, including "unenforceable guidelines," "debatable terms," "platitudes," and "ambiguous generalities," to name a few. In light of existing standards, it is little wonder they have been referred to in derogatory terms.

Library standards differ markedly from industrial and engineering standards, because they usually are regarded as models to be followed rather than as enforceable codes. The South African Library Association,[15] for example, has pointed out in its standards for public libraries that there are many interpretations of the purpose for such standards: "Standards may be interpreted variously as the pattern of an ideal, a model procedure, a measure for appraisal, a stimulus for future development and improvement and as an instrument to assist decision and action not only by librarians themselves but by laymen concerned indirectly with the institution, planning and administration of public library services." If

288

this statement accurately reflects what library standards should be, then existing standards are inadequate.

Hamburg et al.[9] are critical of library standards on the grounds that they are concerned almost exclusively with measuring *inputs* to the library rather than measuring *outputs* or benefits to the users. They cite the 1966 *Minimum Standards for Public Library Systems* (Public Library Association) as an example. They go on to explain how the standards of today fail:

1. They are descriptive in nature, making evaluation difficult.
2. Quantitative objectives are formed by arbitrary value judgments.
3. They emphasize evaluating the input to libraries rather than output to users.
4. They discourage progress, in that "meeting the standards" implies adequacy.

They also suggest that library objectives have not been defined with sufficient preciseness and clarity so that "suitable performance measures" can be derived for them. Consequently, library standards can only be descriptive (e.g., descriptions relating to "proper" management) or quantitative (relating to minimum levels, usually in terms of input to the library). Hirsch[10] has pointed out that "we need clearly defined, carefully reasoned, unequivocal standards for our libraries. This is no time for platitudes and ambiguous generalities."

Wallace[18] has identified four major types of library standards: accreditation, personnel, diagnostic or benchmark, and projective. Each category has its own characteristics, problems, and, in some cases, disadvantages for those adopting standards. Accreditation standards are minima—set by an outside agency—which must be met before "benefits" can be received. The complaint voiced against this type of standard is that the minima may come to be accepted as the maxima and may be detrimental to long-term goals. It is feared that this type of standard may be misinterpreted and, hence, misapplied by those responsible for funding libraries, thereby inhibiting the growth of an institution. This problem was discussed in Chapter 5 in relation to the Clapp-Jordan formula.

Personnel standards are indirect in that they relate to the staff of a library, but not directly to its services or objectives; although, quite obviously, the services of a library are only as good as the staff that provides them. The employment of personnel is governed by these standards, and they cover such things as certification, hours of employment, vacations, and promotions.

Diagnostic standards furnish a quantitative basis ("benchmark") for comparison, and are based on models of conditions present in libraries that are assumed to be in some sense "good." They are used especially in library self-evaluations. Because they represent existing conditions, these standards are valid and beneficial only when constantly updated and revised.

Projective standards are designed to provide guidelines for the development of library service—"blueprints for the future." They are more service oriented, and their purpose is to depict library service as it should be rather than how it is. Such standards frequently are controversial, and many consider them to be unrealistic, impossible, and unenforceable. Nevertheless, projective standards are necessary if library service is to improve.

The following are examples of differing needs that the various types of standards are designed to meet.

1. The establishment of a preliminary goal for a new institution or the specification of minimum requirements for the purpose of accreditation (minimal standards).

2. The assurance of an adequate staff in the library and that working conditions are favorable (personnel standards).

3. The specification of normative practices or accepted guidelines, beyond the minimal level, in order to furnish a method of comparison with other institutions for self-evaluation (diagnostic standards).

4. The specification of long-range goals for future development (projective standards).

Regardless of type, there are definite requirements that must be met when formulating standards. Without these, standards have little real value or meaning. Some requirements for meaningful standards include:

1. *Research* and the compilation of statistics in the areas being standardized, perhaps the most urgent and basic of all needs in the development of standards.

2. *Measurability*, to provide a basis for evaluation and evaluative judgment. A service or other activity must be measurable in order to determine if the function in question "meets the standard."

3. The standard must be clearly defined and *definable* so that it conveys the same meaning to all who read it.

4. *Appropriateness* to the institution or service to be evaluated is essential.

5. *Authoritativeness*, which bases the standard on practices and research, not on assumptions or prejudices.

6. In order to be effective, the standard must be *realistic*. Otherwise, it will be ignored and result in wasted effort.

Because each institution wants to retain its individuality, it is surprising that any standards exist. This desire to retain individuality poses a very real problem in the formulation of standards, which is compounded by strong differences in interpretation of the meaning and purpose of standards by librarians, administrators, committee members, and others. This divergence is evident in the history of library standards.

Some History

As described by Wallace,[17] the first attempt by a national organization to create some standards was the authorization, in 1917, by the American Library Association (ALA), "to take up the question of standardization of libraries and librarians. . . ." The committee never really succeeded in this task, and, finally, in 1923, recommended that its function be changed to that of a committee on library service. This committee's action was more or less representative of the problems and ultimate fate of many committees to follow.

Public library standards in the United States date back to 1933, when a two-page document called for a few essential minima of service. By 1943, public library standards had grown to a 92-page statement of qualitative and quantitative measures. In comparison, a statement in 1956 represented something of a retreat. In fact, this statement de-emphasized *standards* (especially quantitative standards) and stressed *principles* of service. The 1956 standards did, however, introduce a very important consideration: the need to view individual libraries as members of larger systems rather than in complete isolation. The subject of standards for public libraries was one of considerable interest during the period 1955–1965, but the product of this decade, the 1966 standards, was a comparatively minor revision of the already outdated standards of 1956. As Martin[11] has pointed out, rather than growing toward the 1970s, this statement saddled the profession with standards that were formed essentially two decades ago.

Until the late 1920s, individual academic librarians were the instigators and authors of statements of what a college library should be, both in qualitative and quantitative terms. In 1928, the Carnegie Corporation, which was administering a substantial program of grants to libraries, discovered that no accepted standards existed for college libraries and set out to write some. The Carnegie standards were regarded as quite sound, but they did not receive wide acknowledgement.

The first attempt in this area by ALA was a document, issued in 1929, relating to budgets, classification, and compensation plans for academic libraries. The College and Reference Section of ALA suggested minimum standards for college libraries in 1930. In 1934, as discussed by Brown,[3] the North Central Association, a body of accreditation, stated that: (a) an effective college must have a good library, and (b) the functions of the college library should be defined entirely by the educational program of the institution. ALA, in 1943, adopted a set of classification and pay plans for college libraries prepared by the Subcommittee on Budgets, Compensation, and Schemes of Services for Libraries Connected with Universities, Colleges, and Teacher Training Institutions of the ALA Salaries, Staff, and Tenure Board. In 1957, ALA instructed its Committee on Standards to prepare a new document for college libraries, which the Association of College and Research Libraries (ACRL) approved in 1959. According to Brown,[3] the 1959 standards introduced two important measures relating to the adequacy of college libraries: (a) the annual expenditure for the library, expressed as a percentage of total expenditures for all educational and general purposes, and (b) the number of volumes in the collection (a basic figure plus a supplementary figure related to college enrollment). In 1968, ACRL asked its Committee on Standards and Accreditation to rework the ALA "Standards for College Libraries." By 1971, this committee had prepared an entirely new set of standards, "Guidelines for College Libraries," but ACRL withheld its approval of this document; its major criticisms of the document related to the absence of quantitative standards and to the vagueness of the "guidelines" themselves. At present, a reconstituted ACRL committee is proceeding with further revisions of the college library standards.

If college libraries are in a temporary state of limbo on standards, university libraries are even worse off. As Watkins[19] has pointed out: "At present, no official statement of general standards for university libraries has been made either by the Association of Research Libraries or the Association of College and Research Libraries, the two bodies which might be expected to make such a statement." Standards for university libraries, however, have been produced in Great Britain, Canada, and Germany. A definite need for such standards does exist, as a guide to required levels of financial support, if for no other reason. For disbursement of both state and federal funds, some professionally established norms are essential, particularly in the area of collection size and rate of growth. University administrators fear that if acceptable standards are not produced by the profession itself, other, less-qualified bodies may establish standards on which levels of funding for university libraries may be based.

As described by Watkins, an ACRL Committee on Standards met in 1967 to consider the feasibility of establishing standards for university libraries and appointed an ACRL Ad Hoc Committee to Consider Possible University Library Standards. A joint meeting of ACRL and ARL (Association of Research Libraries) was held in Boston, Massachusetts, which resulted in a recommendation for a joint committee of ACRL and ARL to develop university library standards. The committee, ARL-ACRL Joint Committee on University Library Standards, was appointed early in 1968. Its first product was *University Library Statistics,*[7] a compilation of quantitative data from 50 leading universities. This document, as described by Downs and Heussman,[8] was intended to present data on existing practices from which standards could eventually be derived. The standards themselves still do not exist, although certain "criteria for judging excellence in university libraries," based on these statistics, have been produced.

Standards for junior college libraries have been in existence since 1929. These standards, consisting of quantitative statements emanating from the American Council on Education (ACE) and the American Association of Junior Colleges (AAJC), were minimal and restricting. The Junior College Round Table of ALA prepared, in 1930, a preliminary statement of quantitative standards, and a revised statement was finally approved by ALA in 1932. The foundations for the present junior college library standards were laid in 1953, when the Junior College Libraries Section of ALA voted to establish a committee to form evaluative standards for junior college libraries. These standards were approved in 1956 by the Junior College Libraries Section, but were not published until 1960, when they were issued in modified form by ACRL. According to Wallace,[16] these standards represented the first attempt at a national statement of what a two-year college must provide in the way of library service.

Subsequently, ALA and AAJC appointed an Ad Hoc Subcommittee on the Revision of the Junior College Library Standards to examine the 1960 standards and determine the need for revision. The subcommittee met in 1967 and presented a preliminary revised draft in 1968. The final draft, known as "AAJC-ACRL Guidelines for Two-Year College Library Learning Resources Centers," was finally approved in 1972, and replaced the 1960 standards. Again, according to Wallace,[16] it was felt that "standards" was too strong a term, as this implies something "measurable, enforceable, and directly related to library goals." A "guideline," on the other hand, "suggested a level of performance for self-evaluation." Quantitative measures, too, were rejected, because it was felt that adequate research had not been completed to support existing statistics. In this situation, as in others, standards were replaced by guidelines and quantitative measures by vague qualifications.

No pretense at completeness has been made in this overview of the history of library standards; nor has any reference been made to library standards in individual states, to standards adopted by bodies of accreditation, to standards relating to libraries in a specialized category (e.g., prison libraries or medical libraries), or to the standards situation outside the United States. Only some of the more important milestones at the national level have been mentioned.

The Value of Standards

Much has been written on present standards. Some writers have attempted to defend their weaknesses, some have dismissed them as mere quasi-guidelines, and others have attempted to suggest criteria for future improvement. Library standards have certainly been the source of considerable controversy.

Concerning public library standards, Martin[11] comments: ". . . the existing standards for public libraries tend more to indicate what can be achieved rather than what should be achieved." He continues by saying that standards have reflected only a general sense of what public libraries are for, not a focused viewpoint. As for the future, he concludes that a new sense of direction is needed—not a revision or updating of current standards, but a totally new outlook directed toward the future. Burkhalter[4] seems to agree with Martin's opinion on public library standards: "A major problem is the vagueness of many of the standards; it would be impossible to tell whether a particular library has lived up to them. . . . At best, they provide dimensions of service and organization which the library and its manager can use as guidelines. . . ."

Wheeler[20] offers an explanation for the inadequacy of public library standards: "They do not spring from any deep 'scientific' research, but since the beginning have only been empirical." He suggests that, to be fair and acceptable, standards must be based on a compromise between current actual averages and current results of successful (but not "miraculous") performances of the better libraries. He admits that raising the standards does not guarantee improved quality or performance; however, setting lower standards poses a serious threat to all library service, especially that of the more progressive libraries.

Much healthy criticism has been leveled at the present standards for college libraries, a major one being that these standards do not provide a solid quantitative basis for funding. In times of tight budgets, it is increasingly important to have reliable quantitative standards by which to judge how much funding is needed and why. Clapp and Jordan[6] summarize it well: "When . . . standardizing authorities omit or refuse to set standards in quantitative terms, the budgeting and appropriating authorities, who cannot avoid quantitative bases for their decisions, are compelled to adopt measures which, though perhaps having the virtue of simplicity, may be essentially irrelevant."

There are excuses for forming guidelines rather than establishing standards in university as well as college libraries. Downs and Heussman[8] suggest two: (a) there is a great deal of diversity among institutions and, in the case of universities, in the very definition of what a university should be, and (b) there is a fear that minimum standards will be accepted as maximum standards, thus impeding growth and expansion. Chicorel[5] expands on the second of these by commenting that growth in population and in knowledge cannot be built into standards such as the number of volumes and the money spent for library materials and services. Brown[3] also suggests that it is because of growth and change in a rapidly expanding world that concrete, quantitative standards must be prescribed and met. Standards frequently must be revised to reflect changing needs. She reasons that the present guidelines ". . . allow so much latitude to the individual institution that they are ineffective in establishing a common goal for college libraries or for influencing a cost-conscious college administration."

Bailey[2] summarizes some criticisms of college library standards: they are set too high; they should be regarded as guidelines only; and they need to be more qualitative. He points out that half the four-year colleges presently do not meet the existing standards on collections and expenditures. Meder[12] concurs that standards should be improved, but they should be stated in terms of quality "norms" and a description of excellence. He feels that quantitative standards will not, in the long run, produce good libraries. The starting point for effective standards lies in the objectives of libraries themselves; to be valuable, they must be directly related to the resources and objectives of the institution: "In a sense, professional librarianship has found its life by losing it and achieved true success by emphasizing the spirit of quality and service rather than the letter of quantitative measures."

Standards for college and university libraries, then, must be based on more than size of institution or number of books in a collection. They must relate to the goals and objectives of the institution. As Hamburg et al.[9] emphasized, outputs (i.e., services) as well as inputs need to be considered. Myers[14] states it somewhat differently: "The present standards and quantitative measurements which are used to evaluate libraries do not measure library effectiveness."

The same criticisms, more or less, have been leveled at standards for junior college libraries. If standards are to improve quality, the extent to which libraries meet the standards must be susceptible to precise measurement. Yet, the 1960 standards,[1] for example, include statements that are not at all susceptible to precise measurement: "Collection: The holdings of the junior college library should include a generous amount of carefully chosen works. Budget: should be determined in relation to the total budget of the institution. Staff: The library should have a broadly educated and well qualified staff. . . ." Vague statements such as these cannot be used as a basis of precise measurement; they do not provide criteria by which library services may be evaluated and, indeed, on the surface, have little real practical value.

Many problems, of course, are involved in developing standards for junior college or other types of libraries. Each institution is different, serving different audiences and having different requirements. For evaluation purposes, standards should be precise, quantifiable, and measurable. On the other hand, there is the danger that precise, quantifiable standards would serve to equalize all institutions. They would tend to "generalize" libraries, but would not take into account differences attributable to peculiar local conditions. Standards that might help one library to improve may have a stultifying effect on another.

No mention has been made here about standards for special libraries. Such standards do exist, but they present the biggest problem of all. The very concept of special library standards is paradoxical: the word "special" implies uniqueness, and the word "standard" implies generality. Because special libraries, as a group, are so heterogeneous, any attempt to define common elements inevitably leads to meaningless generalities. Special libraries have widely differing objectives and use a variety of means to achieve their objectives. It is inconceivable that a set of standards could be derived that would apply equally to all of them. Standards for special libraries have been referred to as "meaningless platitudes" by Moon[13] and as nothing more than "recommended practices" by others.

In summary, library standards have a tendency to be guidelines rather than true enforceable standards of the type that govern engineering and manufacturing operations. Present standards are largely based on current practices at existing institutions that, in some sense, are considered "good." They emphasize inputs rather than outputs (services). Also, the great diversity among libraries makes it extremely difficult, and even dangerous, to attempt development of precise, quantifiable standards. Consequently, library standards as they now exist, while having some value as procedural guidelines or in establishing absolute minimal requirements for various types of libraries,* are too general and imprecise

---

*Downs and Heussman[8] have stated: "There can be little doubt, however, that the overall effect of standards has been to upgrade libraries, providing substandard institutions with yardsticks by which to measure their deficiencies."

to be used in the detailed evaluation of library services. Perhaps what is needed is standards by which individual institutions can evaluate their own performances in relation to the needs of their user populations; that is, standards or guidelines are needed for conducting the type of evaluative studies discussed in this book.

REFERENCES ·

1. Association of College and Research Libraries, Committee on Standards. "Standards for Junior College Libraries." *College and Research Libraries, 21*:200–207, 1960.
2. Bailey, G. M. "The Role of the Standards." *Drexel Library Quarterly, 2*:207–212, 1966.
3. Brown, H. M. "College Library Standards." *Library Trends, 21*:204–218, 1972.
4. Burkhalter, B. R. "Systems Management in the Library Field." *In: Quantitative Methods in Librarianship: Standards, Research, Management.* Edited by I. Hoadley and A. Clark. Westport, Conn., Greenwood Press, 1973, pp. 3–17.
5. Chicorel, M. "Statistics and Standards for College and University Libraries." *College and Research Libraries, 27*:19–22, 51, 1966.
6. Clapp, V. W. and Jordan, R. T. "Quantitative Criteria for Adequacy of Academic Library Collections." *College and Research Libraries, 26*:371–380, 1965.
7. Downs, R. B. and Heussman, J. W. *University Library Statistics.* Washington, D.C., Association of Research Libraries, 1969.
8. Downs, R. B. and Heussman, J. W. "Standards for University Libraries." *College and Research Libraries, 31*:28–35, 1970.
9. Hamburg, M. et al. *Library Planning and Decision-Making Systems.* Cambridge, Mass., MIT Press, 1974.
10. Hirsch, F. E. "Introduction: Why Do We Need Standards?" *Library Trends, 21*:159–163, 1972.
11. Martin, L. A. "Standards for Public Libraries." *Library Trends, 21*:164–177, 1972.
12. Meder, A. "Accrediting Agencies and the Standards." *Drexel Library Quarterly, 2*:213–219, 1966.
13. Moon, E. E. "Standards for Everything." *Library Journal, 90*:209, 1965.
14. Myers, R. E. "Library Self-Evaluation." *In: Quantitative Methods in Librarianship: Standards, Research, Management.* Edited by I. Hoadley and A. Clark. Westport, Conn., Greenwood Press, 1973, pp. 61–65.
15. South African Library Association. *Revised Standards for South African Public Libraries.* Cape Town, South Africa, 1966.
16. Wallace, J. O. "Two-year College Library Standards." *Library Trends, 21*:219–232, 1972.
17. Wallace, J. O. "History and Philosophy of Library Standards." *In: Quantitative Methods in Librarianship: Standards, Research, Management.* Edited by I. Hoadley and A. Clark. Westport, Conn., Greenwood Press, 1973, pp. 39–56.
18. Wallace, J. O. "Practical Meaning of Library Standards." *In: Quantitative Methods in Librarianship: Standards, Research, Management.* Edited by I. Hoadley and A. Clark. Westport, Conn., Greenwood Press, 1973, pp. 31–38.
19. Watkins, D. R. "Standards for University Libraries." *Library Trends, 21*:190–203, 1972.
20. Wheeler, J. L. "What Good Are Public Library Standards?" *Library Journal, 95*:455–462, 1970.

BIBLIOGRAPHY ON LIBRARY STANDARDS

American Library Association. Coordinating Committee on Revision of Public Library Standards. *Public Library Service: A Guide to Evaluation with Minimum Standards.* Chicago, American Library Association, 1956.

Association of College and Research Libraries. Committee on Standards. "Standards for College Libraries." *College and Research Libraries, 20*:274–280, 1959.

Association of College and Research Libraries. Committee on Standards. "Standards for Junior College Libraries." *College and Research Libraries, 21*:200–206, 1960.

Carnovsky, L. "Public Library Surveys and Evaluations." *Library Quarterly, 25*:23–36, 1955.

"Guidelines for Establishing Junior College Libraries." *College and Research Libraries, 24*:501–505, 1963.

Harling, E. B. "Possibility of Quantitative Standards for University Book Collections." *In: Quantitative Methods in Librarianship: Standards, Research, Management.* Edited by I. Hoadley and A. Clark. Westport, Conn., Greenwood Press, 1973, pp. 57–60.

Hirsch, F. E. "New College Library Standards." *Library Journal, 84*:1994–1996, 1959.

Hirsch, F. E. "New Standards to Strengthen College Libraries." *ALA Bulletin, 53*:679–682, 1959.

Hirsch, F. E. "Evaluation Trends." *Library Trends, 14*:191–202, 1965.

Hirsch, F. E. "Raising the Standards: College Libraries." *Drexel Library Quarterly, 2*:199–201, 1966.

Humphreys, K. W. "Standards in University Libraries." *Libri, 20*:144–155, 1970.

Johnson, B. L. "The New Junior College Library Standards." *ALA Bulletin, 55*:155–160, 1961.

Jones, F. T. "The Regional Accrediting Association and the Standard for College Libraries." *College and Research Libraries, 22*:271–274, 1961.

Lohmann, O. "Efforts for International Standardization in Libraries." *Library Trends, 21*:330–353, 1972.

Lombardi, J. "Standards at the Grass Roots." *ALA Bulletin, 60*:377–379, 1966.

Murray, F. B. "Canadian Library Standards." *Library Trends, 21*:298–311, 1972.

Norris, E. D. "Establishing Standards." *Special Libraries, 51*:229–231, 1960.

Orne, J. "Standards in Library Technology." *Library Trends, 21*:286–297, 1972.

Ottersen, S. "A Bibliography on Standards for Evaluating Libraries." *College and Research Libraries, 32*:127–144, 1971.

Parker, W. W. "College Library Standards and the Future." *College and Research Libraries, 19*:257–264, 1958.

Ploch, R. A. "A Model for Library Standards." *In: Quantitative Methods in Librarianship: Standards, Research, Management.* Edited by I. Hoadley and A. Clark. Westport, Conn., Greenwood Press, 1973, pp. 66–68.

Public Library Association. Standards Committee. *Minimum Standards for Public Library Systems, 1966.* Chicago, American Library Association, 1967.

Special Library Association. Professional Standards Committee. "Objectives and Standards for Special Libraries." *Special Libraries, 55*:672–680, 1964.

Special Library Association. "Appraisals of 'Objectives and Standards for Special Libraries.'" *Special Libraries, 56*:197–201, 1965.

Wasserman, P. "Measuring Performance in a Special Library—Problems and Prospects." *Special Libraries, 49*:377–382, 1958.

11

Library Surveys

Over the years, libraries have been the subject of some type of examination by library administrators, users, and staff. The survey is one means by which to critically examine a library and the services it offers. McDiarmid[30] states simply: "The library survey may be defined as the careful, critical and factual analysis of library conditions." Lyle[28] goes one step further and includes in his definition (at least by implication) the library user: ". . . a library survey is a specialized type of investigation whose goal is the improvement of library service." Since the ultimate justification for the library is the service it offers, all library surveys must obviously include the user in their scrutiny and evaluation. A survey, then, should consider how well the library meets user needs and should be directly related to stated goals and objectives. In this sense, a library survey becomes a use study, which Tobin[45] defines as: ". . . any study which deals with the use of the library, in any or all of its aspects, by its patrons or its staff." A library survey, as discussed in this chapter and defined by Line,[27] is "a systematic collection of data concerning libraries, their activities, operations, staff, use and users, at a given time or over a given period."

The purpose of conducting a survey varies according to the goals and objectives of the institution, the particular problems encountered, or the specific questions concerning the library's activities that its managers would like to have answered. Basically, one of the primary objectives of a library survey is to determine if the library is, indeed, fulfilling the purpose for which it was established. On a more mundane level, the reasons for engaging in a survey might be to accumulate data on a particular problem, to discover means of overcoming deficiencies, to confirm an assumption, or merely to provide general information. Ford[17] suggests that, in relation to the users themselves, a survey might be conducted to explain "observed phenomena," predict behavior, or even control behavior by manipulating conditions. Tauber and Stephens[44] indicate that the basic aims of a survey should be evaluation of the effectiveness of the services provided, determination of the extent to which user needs are satisfied, and identification of ways in which service might be improved.

Regardless of purpose or goal, certain qualities are essential in any survey. The most important criterion is that the objective be clearly defined. All facts or data relevant to the institution being surveyed must be collected, organized, and analyzed *in light of the desired goals*. It also is important that interpretations be logical, intelligent, and realistic, and that they provide the foundation for future improvements. In short, according to McDiarmid,[30] ". . . the survey should never be considered the end but merely a means to an end—achievement of the library's social purpose. . . . It is when each fact is analyzed, compared with other items and applied to the problems at hand that the survey achieves its real aim, the basis of future action and a more effective library program."

To achieve individual objectives, various types of surveys can be conducted by any given library, agency, or individual: A mass survey covers many aspects and a number of institutions; a general survey, perhaps the most common type of library survey, is an intensive study of one particular institution; a special-aspect survey covers one or more facets of an individual library, for example, a survey of technical services or reference departments; and a research survey concentrates on one special phase or activity in a number of institutions, for example, the collections of medical libraries. Within these categories, surveys can be further classified as descriptive or analytical. Past library surveys generally have been descriptive in nature; they have merely presented data in tabular or narrative form. Analytical surveys attempt to delve deeper into this data to identify patterns of behavior or, possibly, to determine cause-and-effect relationships. The distinction between the two lies in the aims of the individual surveys rather than in the methods used. The scope of library surveys has been well presented by Line,[27] and a useful critique is given by Goldhor.[18]

Surveys can be conducted either from within the library (self-survey) or by an "outsider." The self-survey involves a study—possibly continuous—of the organization, its facilities and services, and routines by the library administration and staff. Three elements are involved in a self-survey: a clear understanding and statement of the library's purpose; a comprehensive study of the library's community; and a thorough and objective analysis of the data, with a list of recommendations to improve or update policies or procedures in the light of intended purpose (Bonn).[9] According to Tauber,[40] self-surveys are designed to "blueprint the course of action for the future."

Surveys undertaken by "outsiders" are commissioned by librarians themselves or by administrative bodies to focus on critical problems, perhaps those that the library administration has been unable to solve. Among those classified as "outsiders" are: library associations, nonlibrary associations, institutions (federal or state governments, departments, or agencies), commercial organizations, foundations, library school accrediting agencies, and personal consultants or surveyors (Tauber).[39] The outside survey has two obvious advantages: (a) it may be undertaken by an organization or an individual having greater expertise in survey work than anyone on the staff of a particular library, and (b) the library administration may be more willing to act on recommendations of an outside consultant. The outside survey also may be more "objective."

A very important consideration, obviously, is the technique used to gather data for the study. The method selected must take into consideration the information required; the time, money, and staff available; and the probability of cooperation by the survey audience. Depending on the method chosen, the end result may be either scientific or purely impressionistic in nature. The technique can vary from individual observation and diary-keeping to a detailed and intricate operations-research study. Other devices may include questionnaires; interviews; historical, descriptive, experimental, and documentary analyses; checklists; visits, statistics, and records; comparisons with existing standards; or any combination of these. Regardless of the technique used, the problem, as Wasserman[46] puts it, "is less one of attaining the right answers than it is of asking the right questions."

Many library surveys are less than perfect. Inadequate sampling, lack of uniformity in statistics used for comparisons, limited availability of funds, and inconclusiveness of results are problems that frequently occur. Methodological defects are particularly prevalent. Comparisons of libraries are made on inadequate bases, because data are gathered and presented in different ways. Vague or inappropriate goals also contribute to the limitations of many surveys. Because of such defects, the survey may produce no firm recommendations or recommendations that inspire little confidence.

If well-executed, however, the library survey can produce useful results: a clearer understanding of the library program; improved policies, staff conditions, and operations; increased library support; and greater library use. Wilson[50] cites several cases in which, following a survey, funding was increased, new programs were developed, or changes were made in existing operations.

Some History

Library surveys date back at least to 1876, when a study of facts and statistics on the public library in America was reported in *Public Libraries in the United States*. In 1919, *A Survey of Libraries in the United States*[37] was conducted "to present an accurate description of the most generally prevailing forms of practice. . . ." More than 3,000 libraries were sent questionnaires, but no attempt was made to evaluate or comment on the replies (a response rate of 49.5% was achieved). The survey did, however, yield useful statistics on existing library practices in the early 1920s.

The Public Library Inquiry (1949–1952) was an undertaking of unparalleled size, comprising 19 projects reported in 10 volumes. The general report, by Leigh,[25] whose major purpose was to "analyze on a nationwide scale a sociocultural institution and an entire occupational group," summarized the conclusions of the separate studies. Among the achievements claimed by this survey were improved library services, improved status of the profession, clarification of the purpose of libraries, and an explanation to the public of what the library does and where it is going. According to Lyle[28] ". . . the survey has contributed to the movement toward a scientific evaluation of libraries and their services."

In general, library surveys are becoming less purely descriptive and more analytical or evaluative. Surveys conducted in the last two decades more likely studied the library user, patterns of library use, and degree to which user needs were satisfied. The changing emphasis perhaps can be best illustrated by some selected statements of purposes for library surveys, arranged in chronological sequence:

1. "To make a careful and comprehensive study of the entire library situation." [Wilson et al.,[49] 1948]
2. "The report attempts to tell what the public library actually does." [Berelson,[8] 1949]
3. "An appraisal in sociological, cultural, and human terms of the extent to which the libraries are achieving their objectives." [Leigh,[25] 1950]
4. "An assessment of the public library's actual and potential contribution to American society." [Leigh,[25] 1950]

5. To determine ". . . the adequacy of the University Libraries for present and possible future programs of the University." [Tauber,[43] 1958]

6. "What are attitudes of undergraduates toward the library?" [Purdue,[32] 1964]

7. To determine ". . . for what kinds of people are public libraries provided." To determine ". . . the nature of the public that they are serving or failing to serve." [Groombridge,[19] 1964]

8. "Gather information about (a) the nature of individuals who use the library, (b) the ways in which they make use of its facilities, (c) their opinions about the library and its services." [Behling and Cudd,[7] 1967]

9. "Provide a library service program that will reach all the people." [Martin,[31] 1969]

10. "An attempt to discover patterns of use, 'attitudes,' and level of awareness faculty and students demonstrate toward the services offered to them." [Burns,[12] 1973]

Methods used in conducting library surveys have been quite varied. Most have used questionnaires as a major source of data. Personal visits, checklists, statistics, correspondence, and interviews also have been used in various combinations. The results are impossible to compare, because of the lack of uniformity involved in the survey methods and in the questionnaires themselves. Consequently, general conclusions cannot be drawn from the many surveys that have been conducted.

Following are some conclusions from library surveys that illustrate the types of findings associated with such studies:

1. ". . . the libraries have been maintained during the past 40 years at a substandard level of financial support and administrative efficiency." [Wilson,[49] 1948]

2. ". . . the public library's clientele is a self-selected minority with special characteristics . . . comprising . . . the younger, better schooled, culturally alert members of the community." [Berelson,[8] 1949]

3. ". . . the general public has little knowledge about the public library and its services and seems to regard the public library as a fine thing for a community to have—for other people to use." [Berelson,[8] 1949]

4. "The university libraries of Australia . . . still represent by overseas standards considerably less than those essential for the kind of development of collections that teaching staff and students require." [Tauber,[41] 1962]

5. "73.8% of 1,627 students possess strongly favorable attitudes toward Purdue University Libraries." [Purdue,[32] 1964]

6. "Chicago Public Library is too institution-oriented and not enough people-oriented." [Martin,[31] 1969]

7. "General lack of awareness among some users." [Leonard et al.,[26] 1969]

Erickson[15] conducted a follow-up study of surveys performed in college and university libraries to determine the percentage of recommendations that were eventually adopted. As shown in Table 80, of the 775 recommendations made, more than two-thirds had an effect of some kind: 60% were largely or totally carried out, and 10% to a lesser degree. Only in 15% of the cases did the surveys have no influence in the achievement of recommendations. In another study, Erickson[16] produced further evidence to demonstrate the value of surveys. An example is given in correspondence from Swank relating to a study conducted at Stanford: "The survey did set forth a program which in large part was promptly effected. There is no question about results, whether direct or indirect, and there is no doubt that the survey was an effective instrument in helping to bring about those results."

The Literature on Library Surveys

A considerable number of library surveys have been conducted, many more than could possibly be reviewed here. In fact, several rather comprehensive reviews and bibliographies already exist, which will be reviewed here.

Tobin[45] notes that the term "use studies" did not appear as a heading in *Library Literature* until 1960, when nine titles were listed. In the period 1960–1973, some 477 entries appeared. Two major types of studies appear among these: (a) comprehensive surveys of the use of a library in its entirety, and (b) the use of library materials. Studies of complete user communities are conducted far more frequently than studies of particular user groups, and library nonusers have rarely been studied. The majority of studies have been restricted to a single library, and approximately 75% of these to a specific aspect of their use.

Barber[4] reviews surveys of library use by scientists. Twenty studies were compared to determine how information was found, how materials and the catalog were used, and how assistance was sought. It was concluded that scientists have no clearcut opinions on the best method for acquiring information. They tend, however, to go first to colleagues (informal channels of information), avoiding libraries and other formal information sources and eschewing librarians and other information professionals.

In "Review of User Studies,"[33] 450 use studies were examined; only 58

TABLE 80 Summary of Recommendations Made in Twelve College and University Library Surveys[15]

Recommendations	Govt., Organ., and Admin.		Technical Services		Readers' Services		Integration and Cooperation		Library Building		Resources for Study and Research		Library Personnel		Financial Admin.		Total	
	No.	Per cent	No.	Per cent	No.	Per cent	No.	Per cent	No.	Per cent	No.	Per cent	No.	Per cent	No.	Per cent	No.	Per cent
Achieved:																		
completely	59	40.4	59	40.2	60	50.4	12	22.7	24	31.6	5	8.2	22	21.4	28	40.0	269	34.7
to a large degree	23	15.7	30	20.4	22	18.5	10	18.7	23	30.3	28	45.9	33	32.0	16	22.9	185	23.9
to a small degree	13	8.9	14	9.5	5	4.2	6	11.3	3	3.9	15	24.6	18	17.5	3	4.3	77	9.9
In operation at time of survey	2	1.4	4	2.7	2	1.7	4	7.6	—	—	1	1.6	1	0.9	5	7.1	19	2.5
Not ascertainable	1	0.7	—	—	—	—	3	5.7	—	—	1	1.6	—	—	1	1.4	6	0.8
Not applicable	—	—	—	—	—	—	1	1.9	3	3.9	—	—	—	—	—	—	4	0.5
Not achieved	48	32.9	40	27.2	30	25.2	17	32.1	23	30.3	11	18.1	29	28.2	17	24.3	215	27.7
Total recommendations	146	100.0	147	100.0	119	100.0	53	100.0	76	100.0	61	100.0	103	100.0	70	100.0	775	100.0
Librarian:																		
agreed with recommendation	131	89.7	123	83.7	98	82.4	45	84.9	52	68.4	53	86.9	90	87.4	62	88.6	654	84.4
disagreed with recommendation	12	8.2	14	9.5	14	11.8	6	11.3	15	19.8	4	6.5	8	7.8	2	2.9	75	9.7
agreed with reservations	3	2.1	10	6.8	6	5.0	1	1.9	7	9.2	2	3.3	5	4.8	1	1.4	35	4.5
Not ascertainable	—	—	—	—	1	0.8	1	1.9	2	2.6	2	3.3	—	—	5	7.1	11	1.4

were judged of sufficient quality to be analyzed. Survey findings are presented, together with their implications for developing and improving library and information services. It was discovered that: people expend as little energy as possible in pursuing a particular goal; behavior exhibits resistance to change; many users are totally unaware of existing information sources; users often disapprove of the quality of service provided by libraries; and collections are sometimes inadequate. The conclusions of this report are that, because of the methodologies used, the studies had little to offer for the development and improvement of information systems.

Weinstock et al.[47] arrived at the same conclusion. They analyzed and critiqued studies on the use of biomedical information sources and concluded that existing studies did not provide sufficient information for the design of a national biomedical information system. While the results of the studies indicated types of needs and users, they offered no direct guidance for the planning of libraries and information systems. Deficiencies of the studies included: insufficient detail for comparison of users studies; unrepresentative samples; lack of distinction between expressed and unexpressed needs; omitted areas of investigation; and little comparability among various studies.

The public library scene offers little more. Wight[48] sampled public library surveys "representative of chief decades" and found the approach most frequently used by libraries was a comparison of their activities and resources with ALA standards; the second method related services and resources to other libraries of similar size; and the third involved comparison of collections with standard bibliographies. These methods were drawn from actual surveys conducted from the 1930s to the 1960s. The primary shortcoming of the surveys was lack of a central objective or purpose to which the studies could be applied. Without clear objectives, many of the surveys produced little of practical value to the efficient management of libraries. As Wight succinctly summarizes, "On the basis of this sharply limited evidence it may be tentatively hypothesized that the general public library survey of single public libraries has made little contribution to a substantial body of theoretical knowledge about the management of the American public library."

In an overview of studies conducted from 1966 to 1970, Wood[51] concluded that the self-administered questionnaire, with accompanying interview, is used most frequently for the study of information transfer, while the counting of citations or analysis of loan records is used most often in the study of literature use. He did indicate, however, that some improvements had occurred. Samples had been chosen more scientifically, more thought had been given to questions asked, and results had been analyzed with greater statistical sophistication. On the other hand, response rates frequently were low, and results had only very local applicability and could rarely be generalized.

There are some very useful bibliographies of use studies. Atkins[2] compiled a bibliography of public, academic, and school library surveys, including studies of the use and nonuse of resources. The bibliography, consisting of 70 pages of completely annotated and indexed citations, covers studies conducted in the United Kingdom and North America since 1950.

Bunge[10] lists public library surveys and plans from 1944 to 1964, which give an indication of the present status of statewide library planning and provide guidance to those involved in such planning. This project updates one conducted by Ridgway[34] in 1950.

Davis and Bailey[18] compiled an exhaustive bibliography of use studies, including the areas of humanities and social science, but with major emphasis on engineering. More than 430 annotated entries are given, complete with background information, report summary, and conclusions and/or recommendations made. An update is provided by DeWeese,[14] who lists 547 use studies, including those cited by Davis and Bailey.

A bibliography of book use studies was compiled by Jain.[20] More than 80 studies of this type are listed, as well as studies dealing with how and for what purpose the library is used. Various types of libraries and methodologies used are included. Rike[35] cites some 130 annotated statewide library surveys published between January 1, 1956 and December 31, 1967. Background information, summaries of the surveys, and recommendations are given. A specialized bibliography, prepared by Jonikas,[21] includes more than 280 surveys of the public library community or public library use. This project was sponsored by the American Library Association's Office of Adult Education.

Useful bibliographies also appear at the end of many articles on "survey of surveys." Burns[12] lists more than 50 references to use studies; the Auerbach Corporation[3] published a 676-item bibliography; and Weinstock et al.[47] cite more than 90 use studies in their report. It is readily apparent that user surveys have received much attention, especially in the last 20 years. Other useful surveys, all including bibliographies, have been prepared by Bates,[6] Slater, [36] Tauber,[42] Lancaster,[24] and Zaremba.[52]

Value and Limitations of Library Surveys

Armstrong[1] feels that library surveys will provide a measure of the kinds of service users want and what they actually receive. In fact, he believes that measurements obtained in user surveys are so important that every library should conduct one every few years: "Measurement is essential and no other available technique comes as near to measuring the actual library product as the user survey." Lyle[28] also recognizes the value of the survey method: "Indeed, the library survey could not have survived unless it had made a substantial contribution to the improvement of libraries and librarianship." McCarthy and Howder,[29] on the other hand, cast some doubt on the present use of surveys: "As a device for rationalizing and strengthening campus library services and collections, the survey has proved itself. One might conclude that the heyday of its usefulness has passed."

Other writers have concluded that user studies, in general, are largely a waste of time. Taube,[38] for example, refers to "the generally accepted failure of use studies." He also states that past user studies have had "zero value" and future studies, conducted in a similar way, have an "expectation of zero value" as direct guides to the design of information services. Goldhor[18] criticizes the survey on several counts: subjectivity, poor methodology, and meaningless comparison. He contends that continuous appraisal, not a one-time review, is needed: "Theoretically a general survey is nothing else than an inferior substitute for the administrative machine of current appraisal and review of operations."

Criticisms have been leveled at library surveys, or user studies in general, by many other writers. Some of the major criticisms are:

1. Vague and/or varying methods of measurement. (Auerbach,[3] Barnes,[5] Bunge,[11] Burns,[12] Ford,[17] Goldhor,[18] "Review of User Studies,"[33] Weinstock et al.[47])
2. Lack of valid ways to relate or compare data from different surveys. (Auerbach,[3] Barnes,[5] Bunge,[11] Ford,[17] Goldhor,[18] Weinstock et al.[47])
3. Lack of scientific approach to design. (Ford,[17] Goldhor,[18] Taube[38])
4. Lack of detail in information reported. (Auerbach,[3] Bunge[11])

McCarthy and Howder[29] conjecture that the general library survey, at least in universities, will be used less frequently in the future. They believe that the general survey will be replaced by more specialized studies, and that "more sophisticated analyses and evaluations . . . may be required in order to effect the improvements which the general survey has brought to many libraries in the past 35 years."

As in the previous chapter, no attempt has been made at a comprehensive review of the literature of library surveys. Instead, a guide to some of the more important literature on library surveys, especially the reviews, bibliographies, and critiques, has been presented.

The design of library surveys has been well covered by Line.[27] It is clear that the library survey, if it is to produce results of any value, must be carefully designed according to procedures that are well-established in social science research. Samples must be scientifically derived, and all proposed approaches to the gathering of data must be critically examined to determine their validity and reliability. Appropriate statistical procedures must be applied in the analysis and interpretation of the survey results. A very useful summary of sampling procedures and other techniques of experimental design, specifically related to library and information services, is presented in the book by King and Bryant.[23] The need for sophisticated statistical analysis is, however, questioned by Kee.[22] He suggests that even an "imperfect" survey can produce valuable results.

A well-conducted library survey can produce a considerable number of data that are of potential value in the evaluation of library services. This is especially true if the survey goes beyond purely quantitative data on volumes and types of use, and general characteristics of the users, and attempts to assess the degree to which the library services meet the needs of the community served. Preferably, the survey should incorporate some of the techniques for measuring the performance of various services that have been described in this book. At the very minimum, however, a well-conducted survey can provide a useful indication of how satisfied the users are with the services provided, and can identify areas of dissatisfaction which may require closer examination through more sophisticated microevaluative techniques.

REFERENCES

1. Armstrong, C. M. "Measurement and Evaluation of the Public Library." *In: Research Methods in Librarianship: Measurement and Evaluation.* Edited by H. Goldhor. Urbana, Ill., Graduate School of Library Science, University of Illinois, 1968, pp. 15–24.
2. Atkins, P. *Bibliography on Use Studies of Public and Academic Libraries 1950– November 1970.* Library and Information Bulletin No. 14. London, The Library Association, 1971.
3. Auerbach Corporation. *DOD User Needs Study—Phase 1.* Tech. Mem. 1151-TR-3. Philadelphia, 1965.
4. Barber, S. A. "A Critical Review of the Survey of Scientists' Use of Libraries." *In: The Provision and Use of Library and Documentation Services.* Edited by W. L. Saunders. Oxford, Eng., Pergamon Press, 1966, pp. 145–179.
5. Barnes, R. C. M. "Information Use Studies. Part II. Comparison of Some Recent Surveys." *Journal of Documentation,* 21:169–176, 1965.

6. Bates, M. *User Studies: A Review for Librarians and Information Scientists*. Washington, D.C., Office of Education, 1971. ED 247 738.
7. Behling, O. and Cudd, K. "A Library Looks at Itself." *College and Research Libraries*, 28:416–422, 1967.
8. Berelson, B. *The Library's Public*. New York, Columbia University Press, 1949.
9. Bonn, G. S. "Library Self-Surveys." *Library and Information Science*, 9:115–121, 1971.
10. Bunge, C. A. "Statewide Public Library Surveys and Plans, 1944–64." *ALA Bulletin*, 59:364–374, 1965.
11. Bunge, C. A. "Statewide Library Surveys and Plans: Development of the Concept and Some Recent Patterns." *Library Quarterly*, 36:25–37, 1966.
12. Burns, R. W. *A Survey of User Attitudes Toward Selected Services Offered by the Colorado State University Libraries*. Fort Collins, Colo., Colorado State University Libraries, 1973. ED 086 261.
13. Davis, R. A. and Bailey, C. A. *Bibliography of User Studies*. Philadelphia, Drexel Institute of Technology, 1964.
14. DeWeese, L. C. "A Bibliography of Library Use Studies." *In: A Statistical Study of Book Use*. By A. K. Jain. Lafayette, Ind., Purdue University, 1967.
15. Erickson, E. W. *College and University Library Surveys, 1938–1952*. ACRL Monograph No. 25. Chicago, American Library Association, 1961.
16. Erickson, E. W. "The Library Survey: Its Value, Effectiveness and Use as an Instrument of Administration." *In: Library Surveys*. Edited by M. F. Tauber and I. R. Stephens. New York, Columbia University Press, 1967, pp. 231–244.
17. Ford, G. "Progress in Documentation: Research in User Behavior in University Libraries." *Journal of Documentation*, 29:85–106, 1973.
18. Goldhor, H. "A Critique of the Library Survey." *Illinois Libraries*, 32:609–612, 1950.
19. Groombridge, B. *The Londoner and His Library*. London, The Research Institute for Consumer Affairs, 1964.
20. Jain, A. K. *A Statistical Study of Book Use*. Lafayette, Ind., Purdue University, 1967.
21. Jonikas, P. *Bibliography of Public Library Surveys Contained in the Collections of the University of Chicago Library and the Headquarters Library of the A.L.A.* Chicago, American Library Association, 1958.
22. Kee, W. A. "Must Library Surveys Be Classics in Statistics?" *Special Libraries*, 51:433–436, 1960.
23. King, D. W. and Bryant, E. C. *The Evaluation of Information Services and Products*. Washington, D.C., Information Resources Press, 1971.
24. Lancaster, F. W. "Assessment of the Technical Information Requirements of Users." *In: Contemporary Problems in Technical Library and Information Center Management: A State of the Art*. Edited by A. Rees. Washington, D.C., American Society for Information Science, 1974, pp. 59–85.
25. Leigh, R. D. *The Public Library in the United States: The General Report of the Public Library Inquiry*. New York, Columbia University Press, 1950.
26. Leonard, L. E. et al. *Centralized Book Processing: A Feasibility Study Based on Colorado Academic Libraries*. Metuchen, N.J., Scarecrow Press, 1969.
27. Line, M. B. *Library Surveys*. Hampden, Conn., Archon Books, 1967.
28. Lyle, G. R. "An Exploration into the Origins and Evaluation of the Library Survey." *In: Library Surveys*. Edited by M. F. Tauber and I. R. Stephens. New York, Columbia University Press, 1967, pp. 3–22.
29. McCarthy, S. A. and Howder, M. L. "Library Surveys." *In: Research Librarianship: Essays in Honor of Robert B. Downs*. Edited by J. Orne. New York, R. R. Bowker, 1971, pp. 129–140.

30. McDiarmid, E. W. *The Library Survey; Problems and Methods.* Chicago, American Library Association, 1940.
31. Martin, L. A. *Library Response to Urban Change: A Study of the Chicago Public Library.* Chicago, American Library Association, 1969.
32. *Purdue University Libraries Attitude Survey, 1959–1960.* Lafayette, Ind., Purdue University Libraries Staff Association, 1964.
33. "Review of User Studies." *In: Recommendations for National Document Handling Systems in Science and Technology.* Appendix A, Volume 2, Section 8. Santa Monica, Calif., System Development Corporation, 1965.
34. Ridgway, H. A. "State Plans and Surveys of Public Library Service." *ALA Bulletin,* 44:463–468, 1950.
35. Rike, G. E. *Statewide Library Surveys and Development Plans: An Annotated Bibliography, 1956–1967.* Springfield, Ill., Illinois State Library, 1968.
36. Slater, M. "User and Library Surveys." *In: British Librarianship and Information Science, 1966–1970.* Edited by H. W. Whatley. London, The Library Association, 1972, pp. 232–256.
37. *A Survey of Libraries in the United States,* Vols. 1–4. Chicago, American Library Association, 1926.
38. Taube, M. "An Evaluation of 'Use Studies' of Scientific Information." *In: Emerging Solutions for Mechanizing the Storage and Retrieval of Information.* (Studies on Coordinate Indexing, Vol. 5.) Washington, D.C., Documentation, Inc., 1959, pp. 46–71.
39. Tauber, M. F. "A Survey of Library Surveys." *Library Journal,* 86:1351–1357, 1961.
40. Tauber, M. F. "Management Improvements in Libraries: Surveys by Librarians." *College and Research Libraries,* 15:188–196, 1954.
41. Tauber, M. F. *Resources of Australian Libraries.* 3 Vols. Canberra, Australian Advisory Council on Bibliographical Services, 1962.
42. Tauber, M. F. "Survey Method in Approaching Library Problems." *Library Trends,* 13:15–30, 1964.
43. Tauber, M. F. et al. *The Columbia University Libraries: A Report on Present and Future Needs.* New York, Columbia University Press, 1958.
44. Tauber, M. F. and Stephens, I. R., eds. *Library Surveys.* New York, Columbia University Press, 1967.
45. Tobin, J. C. "A Study of Library 'Use Studies.'" *Information Storage and Retrieval,* 10:101–113, 1974.
46. Wasserman, P. "Measuring Performance in a Special Library—Problems and Prospects." *Special Libraries,* 49:377–382, 1958.
47. Weinstock, M. J. et al. "User Practices Based on a Review of User Studies." *In: A Recommended Design for the United States Medical Library and Information System.* Vol. 2. Washington, D.C., Herner and Company, 1966. Section V, pp. 1–56.
48. Wight, E. A. "The Contribution of the Public Library Survey." *Library Quarterly,* 38:293–300, 1968.
49. Wilson, L. R. et al. *Report of a Survey of the Libraries of Cornell University for the Library Board of Cornell University.* New York, Cornell University Press, 1948.
50. Wilson, L. R. "The University Library Survey: Its Results." *College and Research Libraries,* 8:368–375, 1947.
51. Wood, D. N. "User Studies: A Review of the Literature from 1966–1970." *ASLIB Proceedings,* 23:11–23, 1971.
52. Zaremba, E. "Public Library Surveys." *Drexel Library Quarterly,* 7:48–55, 1971.

12

Effect of Physical Accessibility and Ease of Use

One criterion by which a user will judge any type of service is the amount of effort he must expend in order to use it. Ease of use, then, is a major factor in the selection of an information source, as it is in the selection of other types of service. In 1960, Mooers[23] promulgated this fact in Mooers' Law: "An information retrieval system will tend *not* to be used whenever it is more painful and troublesome for a customer to have information than for him not to have it."

The extent to which the services of any library or information center are used is likely to be heavily influenced by considerations of effort. The librarian, theoretically at least, has some power to influence use by reducing the amount of effort needed to use the services offered. Ease-of-use factors include physical accessibility (e.g., where the library is located and where various portions of the collection are stored) and "intellectual" accessibility (e.g., how well a collection is cataloged or indexed, how easy the catalog is to use, how clearly the shelves are signposted), as well as miscellaneous accessibility factors governed by library policies (e.g., which books may circulate and for how long, how many books may be borrowed at one time, and so on). Although several of these questions are touched upon elsewhere in this book, it may be worthwhile to mention here some of the major studies that have addressed the "ease of use" problem as it affects libraries and information centers.

Evidence suggests that perceived ease of use may be the major criterion considered in selecting an information source and the overriding factor influencing whether or not a particular information service is used. In fact, some studies have shown that ease of use is ranked ahead of quantity or quality of information expected from a particular source. This was the finding, for example, of Rosenberg's[28] questionnaire survey of 96 professionals in industrial and government organizations. A very similar finding was made by Allen and Gerstberger[2] in 1967. Their study, which investigated criteria by which engineers select a source of information when faced with a particular problem-solving situation, attempted to establish empirical support for a model of information-seeking behavior proposed earlier by Allen.[1] According to Allen's model, selection of an information source is based almost exclusively on accessibility, the most accessible source (channel) being chosen first; considerations of quality and reliability are secondary, although these factors are important in influencing the degree to which the user is willing to accept information supplied from a particular source. The Allen and Gerstberger study found empirical support for Allen's model. Specifically, they concluded that:

1. Accessibility is the single most important determinant of the overall extent to which an information channel is used.

2. Both accessibility and perceived technical quality influence the choice of first source.

3. Perception of accessibility is influenced by experience. The more experience an engineer has with a channel, the more accessible he perceives it to be.

4. The rate at which ideas are accepted or rejected is related to the perceived quality of the information provided by a channel. Engineers thus use technical quality as the criterion in a filtering process which compensates, in part, for the neglect of technical quality considerations when selecting an information channel.

These findings have important implications for the librarian, as the investigators are quick to point out:

Improving the quality or performance of a particular information service will not, in and of itself, lead to increased use of the service. More investment in library holdings, for example, will be wasted unless at the same time we make this material more accessible to the user. Engineers won't simply be attracted to the library by improvements in the quality or quantity of the material contained there. The library must, in a sense, come to them.

Dougherty and Blomquist[8] have suggested that, in an academic environment also, many researchers attach greater importance to the accessibility of collections than to the comprehensiveness of collections. A different type of study, but related to the subject of accessibility, was undertaken by Ennis.[9] His report deals with adult book reading and contains a rather complete analysis of the effect that book availability has on reading patterns.

Although it might be true that recent studies have drawn attention to the importance of accessibility as a determinant of use, the effect of accessibility has been discussed in the professional literature for many years. Waples[33] pointed out, in 1932, how reading is influenced by the accessibility of materials, and that physical accessibility, bibliographic accessibility, and intellectual accessibility ("readability") all are important. He states that "accessibility and readability in combination virtually determine what the general reader reads."

Fussler[10] also has recognized the importance of physical accessibility in determining the extent to which library services will be used. His 1950 paper discusses factors affecting accessibility and mentions procedures whereby libraries may improve overall levels of accessibility to bibliographic materials. Hertz and Rubenstein[14] also have discussed physical accessibility as a factor influencing the use of published literature.

One of the most complete studies to determine the effect of accessibility on the use of literature was conducted by Soper.[31] It was based on an analysis of citations appearing in samples of recent scholarly articles in science, the social sciences, and the humanities. For each source cited in a particular article, Soper attempted to determine where the source was physically located at the time the article was written (i.e., in the author's personal collection, in an office or departmental collection, in the library of the author's institution, in another library in the same town, or available only through a source outside the town in which the author lived and worked). Soper hypothesized that citation patterns would be directly related to the physical accessibility of materials: the more physically accessible a source, the more likely that it would be cited. This hypothesis was supported by the data collected from 178 respondents and 5,175 references. Approximately 59% of all references cited in Soper's sample were located in the personal collections of the authors, approximately 26% in their institutional libraries, and approximately 10% in geographically less-accessible libraries. In general, the more accessible a source, the greater the likelihood that it would be cited. Respondents indicated that they preferred to use their personal collections rather than university or other libraries, because their personal collections were more accessible and were arranged to reflect their own specific interests. The material that a scholar or research scientist felt was most important to his work was likely to be in his own collection, even though it also may have appeared in a nearby library. Respondents tended to be negative in their attitudes toward libraries, judging them difficult to use and "generally unpleasant to work in." Ninety-eight percent of all Soper's respondents maintained some type of personal collection, and the tendency to maintain such a collection appeared unrelated to the size or excellence of the respondent's institutional library (i.e., personal collections were maintained even when the institutional library was highly rated).

Soper's findings strongly support hypotheses made earlier by Woodburn,[36] who concluded that bibliographic materials exist at various levels of accessibility: personal collections, departmental collections, university libraries, and less-accessible libraries. The most cost-effective system for any individual will be one in which the most-used materials are in his own collection, the materials used less frequently will be in a departmental collection, and so on, the least-often needed materials being least accessible (e.g., through interlibrary loan). Woodburn suggests that an individual having access to a comprehensive personal or departmental collection will not be inclined to visit the university library.

The Physical Accessibility of Libraries

Two major aspects of physical accessibility affect the use of libraries: (a) the location of the library itself, and (b) the location of its collections (what proportions are on open shelves, in immediately accessible stacks, or in remote storage areas). A third accessibility factor relates to the number of hours a library is open. Accessibility can be increased or decreased by changing the hours of service.

A small amount of literature exists on where to locate libraries, with a view toward maximizing their accessibility and use. Much of this literature relates to the siting of public libraries. Neale,[24] for example, reported on how distance affected the use of public library branches. Her study was based on data collected from two branches of the Chicago Public Library, and she was able to show how usage declines as distance from the branch increases. Her data also indicate that students and professional people are willing to travel farther than other categories of potential users, and that men will travel farther than women. Other studies to determine the relationship between library use and distance or travel time have been conducted by Berelson,[3] Bundy,[4] Monat,[22] and Ulveling.[32] A detailed analysis of the geographic distribution of users of selected branches of the Chicago Public Library was made by Schlipf,[29] who concludes that:

. . . library patrons are strongly influenced by distance in both their choice of branch library and in the degree to which they use that library. If properly constructed, a map dividing the city into branch library "service areas" on the bases of simple geographic proximity is a remarkably good predictor of library use patterns. . . . Library use declines rapidly as distance from the nearest branch or bookmobile stop increases.

Factors influencing the location of library buildings also have been presented by Wheeler,[34,35] Hills,[15] Holt,[16] and Garrison,[11] among others.

A more recent analysis concerning the successful location of public branch libraries was made by Coughlin et al.[5] They found that the social and economic level of area residents was the most important factor influencing the use of a public library branch. The collection of the library was a secondary consideration, and location near a school or shopping center was a less-important variable. The radius of the "market area" of a library (defined as the area in which 80% of the users reside) was found to range from 0.5 to 1.85 miles for adults and somewhat less for children and teenagers. This radius was lowest in areas of low socioeconomic status. Roberts[27] describes how a "law of retail gravitation"—used by market researchers in establishing optimum sites for retail outlets—may be applied to the selection of public library sites.

Osborn,[25] a statistician and a worker in the field of town planning, discusses the location of the public library in relation to other town facilities.

A useful discussion on limited accessibility provided by conventional public library services is included in a recent book by Jordan.[18]

Although public libraries have special problems because of the comparatively large geographic areas they serve, the effect of physical accessibility on library use is not exclusive to such libraries. Indeed, where on campus a university or college library is located can have a considerable influence on its use; and Slater[30] has shown that the precise location of an industrial library within a particular building complex is likely to exert considerable influence on the type and amount of its use. In fact, the extent to which an individual uses any library is at least partly dependent upon the distance between the library and his home or office.

The Physical Accessibility of Materials

A second aspect of physical accessibility relates to the location of the library's collections. The more accessible that materials are made within a particular library, the more likely that they will be used. Thus, the librarian can exert influence on the use of certain portions of the collection by changing their locations. A librarian who recognizes the importance of physical accessibility will attempt to arrange the collection so the portions that appear to be in greatest demand will be most accessible (i.e., placed on open shelves), while other portions of the collection, presumed to be in lesser demand, will be relegated to less-accessible storage areas, including controlled-access stacks and off-site storage locations. While it may be possible to obtain a book from the stacks or from a warehouse rapidly, it may appear to the user that such a book is less accessible than it actually is and certainly less accessible than the books appearing on open shelves. It is important, of course, that studies of the relationship between physical accessibility and use should be carefully controlled to distinguish cause from effect. From a set of empirical data, it might be concluded that the selection of journals on open shelves is good, because these are the most heavily used. The obvious alternative, however, is that they are used most because they are the most accessible. It is possible that a different set of journals on open shelves would have received greater use.

In Chapter 5, mention was made of a study by Goldhor,[12] which showed how a librarian might increase the use of a particular group of books by placing them in a prime location. This study was conducted in two public libraries.

Harris[13] has shown how the physical location of portions of a collection can influence the use of materials in an academic library. Under controlled conditions, portions of an academic collection were made more accessible, both in physical location and reduction of formal barriers to use, resulting in a measurable increase in the use of these materials. One group of materials was a reserve book collection. In a second case, a group of library materials was moved to a lounge area, away from the formal library setting.

Pings,[26] in a study of an engineering library, found that browsing* was important to users, and that the physical arrangement of materials can exert a considerable influence on how the collection is used.

Other recent studies have produced further evidence to substantiate the importance of ease of use in the selection of sources of information. Lancaster,[20] in an investigation of information-seeking behavior in the neurosciences, found ease of use to be a major consideration in the selection of a current-awareness publication. He determined that professionals in the neurosciences have a strong tendency to acquire needed journal articles by writing to the authors for reprints. This method of acquiring needed scientific material, as opposed to the use of libraries, was preferred by many of the several hundred respondents in this survey, presumably because of ease-of-use considerations. To obtain a photocopy

---

*A rather complete study of browsing and the need for classified open-shelf collections to facilitate browsing has been made by Hyman.[17]

from a library usually involves a visit to the library (and perhaps a certain amount of "red tape"), whereas a professional can request a reprint without leaving his desk. This also is one of the reasons why *Current Contents* ranks extremely high as a source for keeping current with the scientific literature. Not only is it comprehensive and compact, but it also provides addresses of authors; and the publisher guarantees that it can provide a tearsheet of any article represented in the publication. Respondents in this survey indicated overwhelmingly that a current-awareness source must provide addresses of authors to facilitate requests for reprints. Lancaster points out that published current-awareness tools provide only one part of an efficient alerting service. Such publications stimulate a demand for a document delivery system that also is easy to use. The publisher of a current-awareness bulletin should be prepared to provide such a backup capability for document delivery, allowing the subscriber to request any item by filling in a simple order card.

The convenience of having materials close at hand or of having such materials delivered directly to home or office is undoubtedly an important consideration for many people. It explains, at least in part, the importance attached to personal collections, the popularity of SDI (Selective Dissemination of Information) and other "directed" services, and the popularity of any service that allows materials to be ordered without having to personally visit the institution, however close it may be. This also explains the increasing growth of mail order merchandising and the recent interest in "books by mail" programs.[19] The importance of "direct access and delivery" in library service of the future, as well as some of the problems involved, has been well presented by Jordan.[18]

The value of a document delivery service that avoids the necessity for making a personal visit to a library was recognized by Dougherty.[7] He describes such a service introduced at the University of Colorado, in which a faculty or staff member may order needed materials by telephone. In this service, the library staff will retrieve an item from the stacks, charge it out, and have it delivered to the office of the requester. The goal of the service is one-day delivery, and, in fact, approximately 69% of all items requested during the first year were delivered within a single working day. Dougherty reports that during the first 18 months, the service had been used by more than 33% of the faculty. More than half of those who used the service reported that it had altered their own patterns of library use. Dougherty maintains that this service, which costs approximately $9,500 a year to implement, is clearly justified from the cost-effectiveness standpoint because of the time it saves for faculty and staff members.

An even more ambitious and convenient service has been inaugurated experimentally at Hamline University, and is described by Mavor and Vaughan.[21] Members of the library staff work with individual faculty members to determine which bibliographic materials appear to be most valuable in support of particular courses. The librarian is considered a partner of the professor in the planning of courses, and accepts the responsibility for conducting appropriate literature searches and of acquiring all materials needed by faculty and students for use in the course, whether or not these materials are immediately available at Hamline.

Although the major emphasis of this chapter has been on physical accessibility, it is important to recognize that there are several different levels of accessibility that will affect the use or nonuse of information services. These levels have been clearly identified by Dervin.[6]

1. *Societal accessibility.* Society must perceive the need to provide certain types of information and must allocate the resources necessary to satisfy these needs.

2. *Institutional accessibility.* Appropriate organizations for the provision of information must exist and must be able and willing to make needed information available to a particular individual.

3. *Physical accessibility.* The individual must have ready access to the information sources and to the resources they provide.

4. *Psychological accessibility.* The individual must be able to recognize his need for information, be willing to seek this information, and be able to convey the need to a second person (the information specialist), when necessary.

5. *Intellectual accessibility.* The individual must be intellectually capable of using the information provided—perhaps to evaluate it in terms of its applicability to his own needs.

It is quite evident that the "principle of least effort," as enunciated clearly by Zipf,[37] governs the use made of libraries and other sources of information and is, in fact, a major determinant of their use. It is important that the librarian recognize this phenomenon, and that it be carefully taken into account in the planning of library buildings, in the allocation of storage space, and, perhaps most importantly, in the planning of new and innovative services.

REFERENCES

1. Allen, T. J. *Managing the Flow of Scientific and Technological Information.* Cambridge, Mass., Sloan School of Management, Massachusetts Institute of Technology, 1966. PB 174 440.

2. Allen, T. J. and Gerstberger, P. G. *Criteria for Selection of an Information Source.* Cambridge, Mass., Sloan School of Management, Massachusetts Institute of Technology, 1967. Another version appears in *Journal of Applied Psychology, 52*:272–279, 1968.
3. Berelson, B. *The Library's Public.* New York, Columbia University Press, 1949, pp. 40–46.
4. Bundy, M. L. *Metropolitan Public Library Users: A Report of a Survey of Adult Library Use in the Maryland Baltimore-Washington Metropolitan Area.* College Park, Md., School of Library and Information Services, University of Maryland, 1968.
5. Coughlin, R. E. et al. *Urban Analysis for Branch Library System Planning.* Westport, Conn., Greenwood Press, 1972.
6. Dervin, B. *The Information Needs of Urban Residents: A Conceptual Context, 1973.* Baltimore, Md., Baltimore Regional Planning Council, 1973.
7. Dougherty, R. M. "The Evaluation of Campus Library Document Delivery Service." *College and Research Libraries, 34*:29–39, 1973.
8. Dougherty, R. M. and Blomquist, L. L. *Improving Access to Library Resources: The Influence of Organization of Library Collections, and of User Attitudes Toward Innovative Services.* Metuchen, N. J., Scarecrow Press, 1974.
9. Ennis, P. H. *Adult Book Reading in the United States: A Preliminary Report.* Report No. 105. Chicago, National Opinion Research Center, 1965.
10. Fussler, H. H. "The Problems of Physical Accessibility." *In: Bibliographic Organization: Papers Presented Before the 15th Annual Conference of the Graduate Library School, July 24–29, 1950.* Edited by J. H. Shera and M. E. Egan. Chicago, University of Chicago Press, 1951, pp. 163–186.
11. Garrison, G. "Some Recent Public Library Branch Location Studies by City Planners." *Library Quarterly, 36:*151–155, 1966.
12. Goldhor, H. "The Effect of Prime Display Location on Public Library Circulation of Selected Adult Titles." *Library Quarterly, 42*:371–389, 1972.
13. Harris, I. W. "The Influence of Accessibility on Academic Library Use." Doctoral Dissertation. New Brunswick, N. J., Rutgers, The State University, 1966.
14. Hertz, D. B. and Rubenstein, A. H. *Team Research.* New York, Department of Industrial Engineering, Columbia University, 1953.
15. Hills, T. S. "On Location of Library Buildings." *In: Library Buildings: Innovation for Changing Needs: Proceedings of the Library Buildings Institute, San Francisco, 1967.* Edited by A. F. Trezza. Chicago, American Library Association, 1972, pp. 155–159.
16. Holt, R. M. "Criteria for Selecting a Location for a Central Library Building." Paper presented at the American Library Association Preconference Institute, St. Paul, Minn., 1954.
17. Hyman, R. J. *Access to Library Collections.* Metuchen, N. J., Scarecrow Press, 1972.
18. Jordan, R. T. *Tomorrow's Library: Direct Access and Delivery,* New York, R. R. Bowker, 1970.
19. Kim, C. H. and Sexton, I. M. *Conference on Books by Mail Service: A Report.* Terre Haute, Ind., Department of Library Science, Indiana State University, 1973.
20. Lancaster, F. W. "A Study of Current Awareness Publications in the Neurosciences." *Journal of Documentation, 30*:255–272, 1974.
21. Mavor, A. S. and Vaughan, W. S., Jr. *Development and Implementation of a Curriculum-Based Information Support System for Hamline University.* Landover, Md., Whittenburg, Vaughan Associates, Inc., 1974.
22. Monat, W. R. *The Public Library and Its Community: A Study of the Impact of Library Services in Five Pennsylvania Cities.* State College, Pa., Institute of Public Administration, Pennsylvania State University, 1967.

23. Mooers, C. N. "Mooers' Law or Why Some Retrieval Systems Are Used and Others Are Not." *American Documentation, 11*:ii, 1960.
24. Neale, D. L. "Study of the Relation Between Distance from the Public Library Branch and Its Use." Master's Thesis. Chicago, Graduate Library School, University of Chicago, 1950.
25. Osborn, E. "The Location of Public Libraries in Urban Areas." *Journal of Librarianship, 3*:237–244, 1971.
26. Pings, V. "A Study of the Use of Materials Circulated from an Engineering Library, March to May 1956." *American Documentation, 18*:178–184, 1967.
27. Roberts, R. G. "Reilly's Law: The Law of Retail Gravitation." *Library Association Record, 68*:390–391, 1966.
28. Rosenberg, V. *The Application of Psychometric Techniques to Determine the Attitudes of Individuals Toward Information Seeking.* Bethlehem, Pa., Center for the Information Sciences, Lehigh University, 1966. Another version appears in *Information Storage and Retrieval, 3*:119–127, 1967.
29. Schlipf, F. A. "The Geographical Distribution of Urban Public Library Use and Its Relationship to the Location of Branch Libraries." Doctoral Dissertation. Chicago, Graduate Library School, University of Chicago, 1973.
30. Slater, M. "Types of Use and User in Industrial Libraries: Some Impressions." *Journal of Documentation, 19*:12–18, 1963.
31. Soper, M. E. "The Relationships Between Personal Collections and the Selection of Cited References." Doctoral Dissertation. Urbana, Ill., Graduate School of Library Science, University of Illinois, 1972.
32. Ulveling, R. A. "Administration of Branch Systems." *In: Current Issues in Library Administration: Papers Presented Before the Library Institute at the University of Chicago, August 1–2, 1938.* Edited by C. B. Joeckel. Chicago, University of Chicago Press, 1939, pp. 135–162.
33. Waples, D. "The Relation of Subject Interests to Actual Reading." *Library Quarterly, 2*:42–70, 1932.
34. Wheeler, J. L. *The Effective Location of Public Library Buildings.* Occasional Papers No. 52. Urbana, Ill., Graduate School of Library Science, University of Illinois, 1958.
35. Wheeler, J. L. *A Reconsideration of the Strategic Location for Public Library Buildings.* Occasional Papers No. 85. Urbana, Ill., Graduate School of Library Science, University of Illinois, 1967.
36. Woodburn, I. "A Mathematical Model of a Hierarchical Library System." *In: Planning Library Services: Proceedings of a Research Seminar Held at University of Lancaster, 9–11 July 1969.* Session 3. Edited by A. G. Mackenzie and I. M. Stuart. Lancaster, Eng., University of Lancaster Library, 1969.
37. Zipf, G. K. *Human Behavior and the Principle of Least Effort.* Cambridge, Mass., Addison-Wesley, 1949.

13

Cost-Performance-Benefits Considerations

As stated in Chapter 1, any type of service, including library service, can be evaluated from several possible viewpoints:

1. How well the service is satisfying its objectives, which usually means how well it is satisfying the demands placed upon it. This is an evaluation of the effectiveness of the service.
2. How efficiently (in terms of costs) it is satisfying its objectives. This is cost-effectiveness evaluation.
3. Whether the service justifies its existence (i.e., the worth of the service). Evaluating worth is concerned with cost-benefit relationships.

Cost-effectiveness, then, is the relationship between level of performance (effectiveness) and the costs involved in achieving this level. Several alternative methods may be used to obtain a particular performance level (e.g., a particular document delivery score). The least expensive alternative is the most cost-effective. Cost-benefits refers to the relationship between the benefits of a particular product or service and the cost of providing it. Generally, it is more difficult to measure benefits than performance (effectiveness), except that, in a commercial sense, benefits equate with return on investment. The expression "cost-performance-benefits" relates to the entire spectrum of costs, performance (level of effectiveness), and benefits.

The cost of library service is measured in terms of input of resources (funds). Under costs, both the costs that are relatively fixed (e.g., cost of acquiring and housing the collection) and those that are relatively variable need to be considered. There are two kinds of variable costs:

1. The variable cost that is a function of the number of transactions. For example, if the number of books circulated each year is increased, the unit cost per circulation will be reduced by X dollars; that is, the cost of purchasing library materials is allocated to an increased number of uses of these materials.

2. The variable cost that is a function of alternative modes of operation. For example, it is possible to achieve a particular level of performance in document delivery by alternative strategies, the most important being the purchase of additional copies and the variation of loan periods.

Several possible approaches to measuring the performance or effectiveness of various facets of library service have already been mentioned, including:

1. The ability of the library to deliver a particular item when it is needed.

2. The ability of the catalog and the shelf arrangement to disclose the holdings of particular items or of materials on particular subjects.

3. The ability of reference staff to answer questions completely and accurately.

4. The speed with which a particular item can be located when needed.

5. The speed with which a reference inquiry can be answered or a literature search conducted and the results presented to the library user.

6. The amount of effort that the user must himself expend in exploiting the services of the library (including factors of physical accessibility of the library and its collections, the size and quality of the library staff, and the way in which the collections are cataloged, indexed, shelved, and signposted).

Note that these measures bear a similarity to the performance criteria for information retrieval systems, first presented in Chapter 1 and discussed in greater detail in Chapter 4.

The benefits of library service are extremely difficult to measure, a point that was first made in Chapter 1. Most published "goals and objectives" statements for library service relate to supposed ultimate benefits (e.g., improved level of education, better use of leisure time, a more "aware" and socially responsible citizenry), but these are virtually impossible to measure. Some, more tangible, criteria for measuring the benefits of libraries and other information services include:

1. Cost savings through the use of the service as compared with the costs of obtaining needed information or documents from other sources.

2. Avoidance of loss of productivity (e.g., of students, faculty, research workers) that would result if information sources were not readily available.

3. Improved decision making or reduction in the level of personnel required to make decisions.

4. Avoidance of duplication or waste of research and development effort which either has been done before or has been proved infeasible by earlier investigators.

5. Stimulation of invention or productivity by making widely available the literature on current developments in a particular field.

These benefit measures relate more clearly to industrial libraries and to libraries whose major role lies in the support of research than they do to public libraries or even to the majority of academic libraries. The first two factors in the above list have been discussed by Mueller,[63] and the third by McDonough[61] (in relation to management information systems). Martyn[58] has presented impressive figures on the cost of unintentional duplication of scientific research in the United Kingdom. Cooper[28] reports some revealing figures on savings in research time as a result of disseminating research communications through the Information Exchange Groups of the National Institutes of Health. Examples of new products or new applications of existing ones, developed as a result of stimulus from information services, are cited by Arthur D. Little, Inc.[1] in a program evaluation of the State Technical Services. Similar examples are documented in the records of the Small Business Administration. Under certain circumstances, then, it may be possible to express the benefits of various types of information services in tangible terms (e.g., in dollar or time savings), although this is not easy to do. For other types of service (e.g., in the public, school, or college library), it is virtually impossible to measure the benefits in any tangible terms.

Although an attempt was made earlier in this chapter to present a firm distinction between cost-effectiveness and cost-benefit considerations, these terms tend to be used rather loosely, and the relationship between cost and effectiveness may be difficult to distinguish from the relationship between cost and benefits. Suppose, for example, that the loan period is reduced on certain books known to be in great demand. An immediate benefit of such action is in the reduction of costs, because the availability of the titles is improved without having to purchase additional copies and the unit cost per circulation is reduced. This action also has a definite influence on the effectiveness of the service, because satisfaction level is likely to increase and collection bias to decrease. Such action, then, may have immediate observable internal benefits (in terms of reduced costs to achieve a particular level of service); it will have a long-range influence on the *effectiveness* of the service; and it may have an even longer range influence on the *benefits* of the service to users (which should be reflected in increased use of the library and reduced costs for units of service). Obviously, then, cost, performance, and benefits are very closely interrelated and cannot be completely separated. Figure 52 attempts to illustrate these interrelationships for three library activities.

Mason[60] and Magson[57] both have presented techniques that might be used to evaluate the benefits of library service. The article by Magson, in particular, offers a detailed discussion of this subject. Both authors attempt to arrive at a "benefit" figure for a particular library activity by comparing the cost of the activity with an alternative approach in order to achieve the same results. One alternative could involve elimination of a certain activity, with library users having to obtain the particular service elsewhere. The measure of "benefit" is the savings associated with the present service as compared to the costs of the alternative method of achieving the same results. A cost-benefit analysis also was attempted by Rosenberg,[74] who took a sampling of the services offered by an industrial library and derived figures to show the time saved by the engineering staff because of their existence. An approach to an economic theory of the library has been suggested by Buckland.[21]

A cost-effectiveness analysis seeks to increase the value received (effectiveness) for the resources expended (cost). The cost-effectiveness of a library operation can be improved in one of two ways:

1. Maintaining the present performance level (e.g., in terms of document delivery capabilities and response time) while reducing the costs of operating the system.

2. Holding operating costs constant while raising the average performance level.

As described by Hitch and McKean[39] in a completely different context, five basic steps are involved in a cost-effectiveness analysis.

1. Defining the objectives that must be attained.
2. Identifying alternative methods of meeting the objectives.
3. Determining the costs of the various alternatives.
4. Establishing one or more models that relate the costs of each

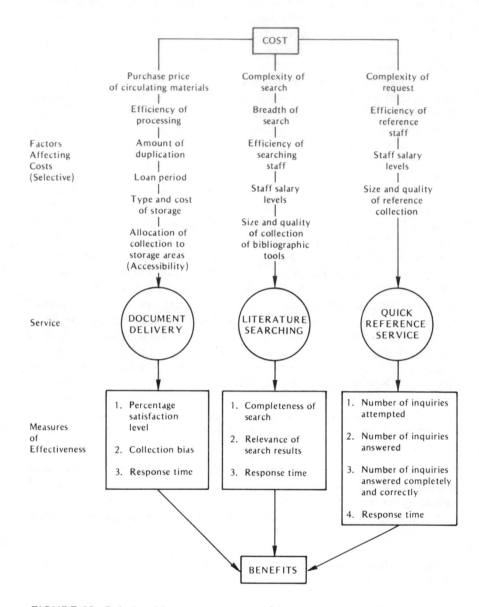

FIGURE 52   Relationships among costs, performance, and benefits of library service.

alternative to an assessment of the extent to which each could assist in attaining these objectives. The model used may take the form of mathematical equations, a computer program, or merely a complete verbal description of the situation.

5. Establishing a criterion for ranking the alternatives in order of desirability, and choosing the most promising. The criterion provides a method of weighing estimated costs against estimated effectiveness. The structure of the cost-effectiveness analysis program is illustrated in Figure 53, which is an adaptation of a figure presented in another context by Quade.[70]

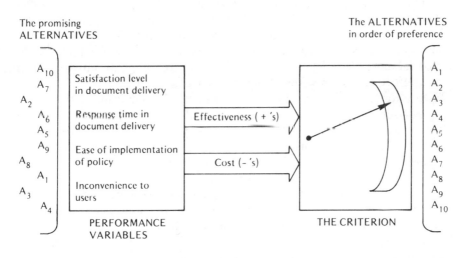

FIGURE 53   Structure of a cost-effectiveness analysis, after Quade.[70]

The cost-effectiveness analysis of a library service involves a study of payoff factors, trade-offs, break-even points, and diminishing returns.

The remainder of this chapter will concentrate on the relationship between the cost of library service and its effectiveness (i.e., how well it responds to the demands placed upon it). Occasionally, however, cost-benefit considerations may appear.

The Law of Scattering

A cost-effectiveness analysis involves the optimum allocation of resources to provide the best possible service with available funds; in other words, with *payoff* or *return on investment*. Various cost-effectiveness analyses have been mentioned throughout this book, the most notable perhaps involving the identification of library materials that will be most used (e.g., a group of serials in a particular subject area that is likely to satisfy X percent of all demands) and those that are likely to be least-used (thereby becoming prime candidates for discarding from the collection or at least withdrawing to less-accessible and less-costly storage areas).

Two empirical relationships, sometimes referred to as "laws," are extremely relevant to the cost-effectiveness analysis of library service. These relationships, which have been discussed in detail in the professional literature, are "Bradford's Law of Scattering" and the "Zipfian distribution." Fairthorne[31] refers to both as "empirical hyperbolic distributions." Because the distributions indicate payoff factors for various library policies, particularly the yield (in use) per dollar invested (in bibliographic materials or services), they are of great importance in cost-effectiveness analyses of library services.

Bradford first described his "law" in an article[8] published in 1934; then, in 1948, provided more detail in his book *Documentation.*[7] In searching for journal articles in two subject fields, lubrication and applied geophysics, Bradford discovered that a comparatively small number of "core" journals in these fields yielded a high proportion of all the relevant papers. Beyond this nucleus of high-yield core journals, he identified "zones" of less-productive journals, each zone providing reduced yield as increased numbers of marginally productive journals were added. Bradford identified three zones of scatter in the two subject areas he was working with. His data for applied geophysics are summarized in Table 81, wherein column A lists the number of journals; column B, number of references yielded by journals in column A; column C, the cumulative sum of journals; column D, the cumulative sum of references; and column E, the common logarithms of numbers in column C. At one extreme of this distribution, the first two journals listed yield 179 of the 1,332 total references. At the other extreme, 169 journals yield a single reference each. A total of 326 journals supplied 1,332 references.

A comparison of dispersion in the two areas of Bradford's study, showing the three zones he identified for each subject, is given in Table 82. For applied geophysics he divided the journals into the three zones as follows:

1. Those producing more than four references in a year. Nine sources in this zone yielded 429 references.
2. Those producing more than one, but not more than four, a year. In this zone, 59 sources produced 499 references.

TABLE 81   Bradford's Data on Scatter of the Literature of Applied Geophysics[7]

A	B	C	D	E
1	93	1	93	0.000
1	86	2	179	0.301
1	56	3	235	0.477
1	48	4	283	0.602
1	46	5	329	0.699
1	35	6	364	0.778
1	28	7	392	0.845
1	20	8	412	0.903
1	17	9	429	0.954
4	16	13	493	1.114
1	15	14	508	1.146
5	14	19	578	1.279
1	12	20	590	1.301
2	11	22	612	1.342
5	10	27	662	1.431
3	9	30	689	1.477
8	8	38	753	1.580
7	7	45	802	1.653
11	6	56	868	1.748
12	5	68	928	1.833
17	4	85	996	1.929
23	3	108	1,065	2.033
49	2	157	1,163	2.196
169	1	326	1,332	2.513

3. Those producing one or less a year. In this zone, 258 sources produced a total of 404 references.

One of the most explicit descriptions of the law of scattering is that presented by Brookes:[11]

If a large collection of papers is ranked in order of decreasing productivity of papers relevant to a given topic, three zones can be marked off—such that each zone produces one-third of the total of relevant papers. The first, the nuclear zone, contains a small number of highly productive journals, say n_1; the second zone contains a larger number of moderately productive journals, say n_2; and the outer zone a still larger number of journals of low productivity, say n_3. The law of scatter states that

$$n_1:n_2:n_3 = 1:a:a^2$$

where a is a constant.

TABLE 82   Bradford's Data on Scatter for Two Fields[50]

Grouping by yield	Applied geophysics		Lubrication	
(zones)	Journals	References	Journals	References
1	9	429	8	110
2	59	499	29	133
3	258	404	127	152

In Bradford's data, the value of a was found to be approximately 5. Following this law, as pointed out by Brookes, a collection of 248 journals might yield 660 papers relevant to a particular topic during a specified time period. If the set of journals is divided into Bradford's three zones of decreasing yield per journal—each zone contributing approximately the same number of relevant papers (in this case 220)—the nuclear zone might contain 8 highly productive journals, the second zone 40 (8×5) journals of moderate productivity, and the third zone the residue of 200 (8×5^2) journals of low productivity.

Vickery[85] restated the law of scattering more precisely, and showed that it should apply not only to three zones but, with the value of a suitably modified, to any number of zones into which a collection of journals is divided. He also showed that the logarithms of the cumulative total of journal titles, plotted against the cumulative total of relevant articles yielded, will produce a curve of the type represented in Figure 54. Based on an analysis of 1,600 items borrowed by an industrial library from outside sources, Vickery was able to show that the scatter of periodical references actually read by scientists was similar to the scatter by source identified by Bradford. In Figure 54, Vickery's data (curve A) is plotted beside Bradford's data (curves B and C).

Stevens[78] compared the dispersion or scattering phenomenon in eight subject areas and concluded that scatter occurred least in pure science, more in technology, and most in the humanities. Leimkuhler,[50] however, cast doubts on the validity of this conclusion. The Stevens data, as presented by Leimkuhler, are shown in Table 83. When applied to the data in Tables 82 and 83, the ratios between zones 2 and 1 and zones 3 and 2 vary from approximately 2 to 7 (the a value of Bradford's scattering equation). As previously mentioned, Bradford suggested an a value of 5 as a representative number for his data.

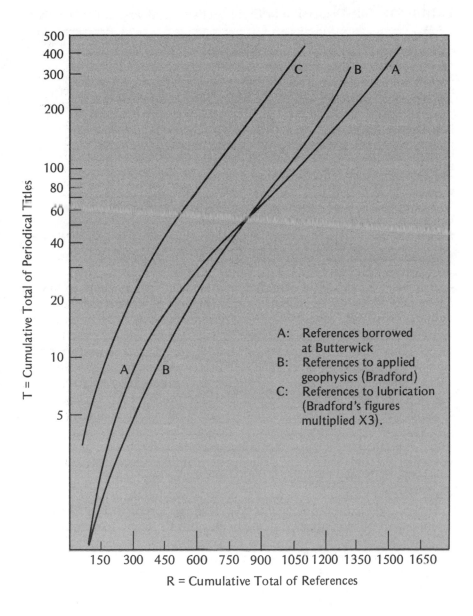

FIGURE 54   The scatter of literature when cumulative total of references is plotted against cumulative total of periodicals contributing.[85]

TABLE 83   Title Dispersion in Eight Studies Summarized by Stevens*

		No. of journals† with % of references			
Subject field	Number of references	25%	50%	75%	100%
Chemistry	3,633	2	7	24	247
Chemistry	1,085	1	5	19	131
Biochemistry	17,198	3	12	56	851
Physics	1,279	1	3	17	134
Electrical engineering	17,991	3	9	39	—
Radio engineering	1,506	2	8	20	—
Chemical engineering	21,728	3	23	—	—
U.S. history	452	14	54	149	259

*Reproduced from Leimkuhler.[50]
†Journals are counted in order of decreasing productivity.

Brookes[12,19] has pointed out that each subject field is likely to have a "long tail" of journals that contribute only one or two papers a year to the subject. This "tail" may consist of approximately half of all contributing journals. When journals are plotted by yield—where $R(1)$ is the total of relevant papers in the journal ranked 1, $R(2)$ the total of relevant papers in the journal ranked 2, and $R(n)$ the total of relevant papers in the first n of ranked journals—against the total number of journals known to contribute (n) on semilogarithmic graph paper, "the graph will be found to begin with a rising curve which runs, sooner or later, into a surprisingly smooth straight line." Brookes[10] refers to this as the "Bradford-Zipf bibliograph," and points out that this bibliograph is useful because, if enough data are collected to allow the straight line plot to be reached, it is possible to predict the end of the line (i.e., to estimate the total number of journals contributing in some way to a particular subject field).

Groos[37] applied the Bradford distribution to more than 20,000 physics citations. He found that application of Bradford's linear distribution was effective for the highly and moderately productive journals, but that at some point on the long tail of the distribution, the curve falls away from its linear form. Brookes[11] later referred to this as the "Groos droop," pointing out that this aberration is reduced as new journals containing relevant citations are found. He suggested that the Groos phenomenon may reflect an incomplete literature search.

Other investigators, working in various subject areas, have demonstrated the Bradford scattering phenomenon; for example, Cole's[26,27] study of literature use within the petroleum industry. Cole's data are presented in Table 84 and Figure 55, in which the cumulative number of references (*RT*) is plotted against the logarithm of the cumulative number of titles contributing these references. The straight line that results is derived from three sets of data: those of Boig and Loftman[5] (point A), those of Cole himself (point B), and those of Bernal[4] (point C). Bernal's data are derived from a variety of scientific subjects, while the other two sets are from the petroleum literature. In Figure 56, these data are presented in a slightly different way. The cumulative fraction of references (*R/RT*) is plotted against the logarithm of the cumulative fraction of titles (*T/TT*). (As Cole points out, for any collection of *RT* references derived from *TT* titles, *R* is the total number of references derived from the *T* most productive titles and *R/RT* and *T/TT* are the cumulative fractions of references and titles respectively. Thus, as an illustration from Table 84, Cole's data for the petroleum literature show that 12.7% of the journals contributed approximately 61% of all the references.)

To demonstrate the practical utility of Bradford's law, Cole showed that, in a petroleum library having space for approximately 2,000 volumes

TABLE 84   Scatter of the Literature on Petroleum Technology[26]

Titles	Cumulation of titles (T)	Refs. per title	Cumulation of refs. (R)	T/TT	R/RT
1	1	122	122	0.005	0.135
1	2	51	173	0.010	0.191
1	3	43	216	0.015	0.239
2	5	29	274	0.025	0.303
1	6	26	300	0.030	0.332
1	7	24	324	0.036	0.359
2	9	20	364	0.046	0.403
2	11	17	398	0.056	0.441
1	12	16	414	0.061	0.458
1	13	15	429	0.066	0.475
2	15	14	457	0.076	0.506
1	16	11	468	0.081	0.518
1	17	10	478	0.086	0.529
8	25	9	550	0.127	0.608
5	30	8	590	0.152	0.653
2	32	7	604	0.162	0.668
9	41	5	649	0.208	0.718
14	55	4	705	0.279	0.780
14	69	3	747	0.350	0.827
28	97	2	803	0.492	0.889
100	197 (TT)	1	903 (RT)	1.0	1.0

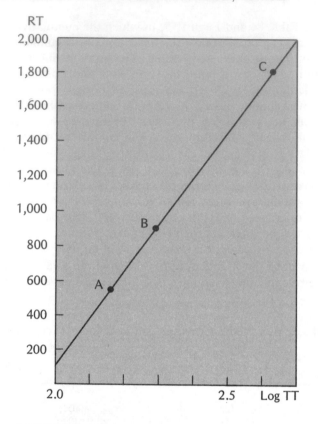

FIGURE 55   Literature scatter derived from studies
by Boig and Loftman (A), Cole (B), and Bernal (C).[26]

of periodicals, some 190 titles, retained for approximately 11 years each,
would provide optimum utilization of the space available. Such a collection would likely satisfy approximately 75% of all demands.

Brookes[18] presented a quantitative method for finding the optimum set
of periodicals capable of providing a specified level of literature coverage
in any well-defined scientific field. Like Cole, he based his procedure on a
combination of the law of scatter and the law of obsolescence. Several
other authors, including Strain[79] and Basile and Smith,[2] have described
procedures used by particular libraries to determine which periodical
titles should be held, and for how long, to satisfy a specified level of
demand.

Cezairliyan et al.[25] reported on their experiences in searching for papers on thermophysical properties. A total of 9,810 papers—from 1,282 journals—was identified for the period 1940–1958. When these journals were ranked by productivity, 51% of the 9,810 references were found in the top 50 journals (3.9% of the 1,282).

Hockings[40] applied the Bradford distribution to a collection of periodicals held by a multidisciplinary industrial research library. Periodical use was determined through an analysis of sources cited in technical reports written by staff members of the laboratory served during a three-year period of productivity, 1970–1972. The total size of the periodical set used was approximately 420, and this was constant for each of the three years. During the three years covered, 94%, 91%, and 93% of all citations were found in a group of 142 periodicals, and 92%, 85%, and 88% of all citations

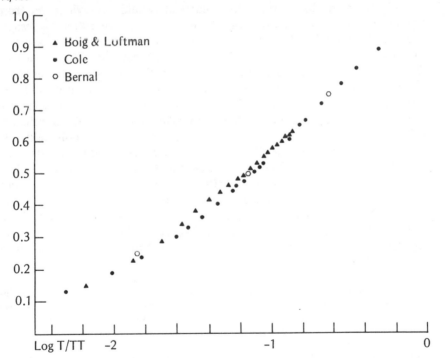

FIGURE 56   The data of Figure 55 when cumulative fraction of references (R/RT) is plotted against the logarithm of the cumulative fraction of titles (T/TT).[26]

were found in a group of 82 periodicals. The annual aging factor for the literature was estimated to be 0.806, or a half-life* of 3.2 years. The average annual aging factor was used to develop the following retention policy for the 142 high-yield journals: the periodical ranked 50 should be held for 10 years; and the periodical ranked 10 for 18 years. This retention policy would satisfy 90% of the demand for journals, as measured by citations in the technical reports of 1970 (opposed to 94% if no discard policy were applied to the 142 titles); but the policy had an uneven impact on the various scientific disciplines covered. Hockings concluded that a single aging factor is not well suited to the development of a discard policy in a multidisciplinary library.

The Bradford law has been demonstrated primarily in the distribution of sources cited in the literature of a particular subject field.† Other studies, including those of Vickery[85] and several investigations at the Yale Medical Library,[43,44,45] indicate that the distribution also holds true for the sources actually used by the workers in a particular field (as evidenced from figures for circulation or interlibrary loans). Studies of collection usage, such as those by Fussler and Simon[32] and Trueswell,[80,81,82] suggest that this pattern of usage is equally relevant for materials other than journals. Leith[51] has shown that the distribution also applies to journal references in the personal collection of a scientist in the field of radiation and cell biology. He suggests that the "core" journals in a particular subject field are likely to yield no more than approximately 55% of all relevant references; that is, a scientist who scans the core journals in his field only is likely to miss approximately 45% of the articles relevant to his interests.

Goffman and Morris[35] point out that the "nucleus" of journals in a particular subject field is rather arbitrarily defined, because "it depends on the number of articles chosen to effect the division of periodicals into zones." The size of a nucleus (core collection) will vary from field to field, depending upon the extent of subject dispersion. Periodicals falling into the first zone, however, will always be those with the highest payoff or rate of return.

---

*A number of investigators, including Burton and Kebler,[24] have referred to the obsolescence of literature in terms of "half-life," this half-life being the time during which one-half of the literature currently active (i.e., used) was published. A half-life of 3.5 implies that 50% of all sources demanded were published within the past 42 months. The term "half-life" also has been used with somewhat different meanings in the literature (e.g., the time after publication during which one-half the uses of a particular item are made). The distinction between the two uses of the term reflects the distinction between synchronous and diachronous decay, as discussed later in this chapter.

†It should be noted that each investigator may use a different mathematical formulation of the Bradford distribution. As Wilkinson[87] has shown, Bradford himself presented his law in two ways, one graphical and one verbal, and these are not mathematically identical.

Goffman and Morris also have observed the Bradford distribution in the circulation pattern of periodicals in a library. Data derived from the Allen Memorial Medical Library in Cleveland, Ohio, for the month of March 1968, are presented in Table 85, and are divided into eight zones of decreasing yield in Table 86. The authors point out:

The minimum nucleus of journals circulated during March 1968 consisted of eleven titles that were borrowed 113 times, followed by sixteen periodicals circulating 108 times, twenty-one journals 107 times, and so on. Consequently, successive zones of periodicals circulating about the same number of times formed the approximate geometric series $1:(1.4):(1.4)^2: \ldots (1.4)$.[7] It is interesting to note that half the circulation for this month was accounted for by only seventy-six journals.

TABLE 85 Distribution of Journal Circulation in a Particular Month in One Medical Library[35]

No. of journals	Circulation per journal	No. of journals	Circulation per journal
1	18	12	6
1	12	15	5
2	11	28	4
1	10	36	3
3	9	75	2
7	8	186	1
4	7		

TABLE 86 The Data of Table 85 Presented as Bradford Zones[35]

Zone	Time circulated	No. of journals	Bradford constant (n)
1	113	11	—
2	108	16	1.5
3	107	21	1.3
4	110	28	1.3
5	110	38	1.4
6	110	55	1.4
7	109	93	1.7
8	109	109	1.2
	876	371	Average 1.4

They further suggest that the same phenomenon exists for the distribution of users of library services, and they present data to substantiate this claim; that is, a relatively small number of users may account for a high percentage of the total use of a library's services. If the users and their subject interests can be identified, the journals with the highest yield for the particular subjects could be added to the "minimal core" identified on the basis of circulation figures.

A valuable analysis of periodical literature use in the social sciences, as measured by demands made on the National Lending Library (NLL) in England, was conducted by Wood and Bower.[90] The analysis was based on all requests received by NLL during a four-week period in 1968: 684 different serial titles in the social sciences, of which 64 were identified as titles not held by the library. In Figure 57, the cumulative percentage of total requests is plotted against the number of titles requested. The same data are presented in Table 87. While 620 titles are needed to satisfy 100% of the demand, approximately 56% can be satisfied by 116 titles, and 20.3% of the demand by as few as 17. Distribution of demand by age of materials is shown in Figure 58, wherein the 1968 plot is superimposed on plots of data derived from two earlier studies conducted at NLL, one based on science and technology serials (1963) and the other on medical serials (1967). In the NLL study, the "half-life" of social science periodicals was approximately three and one-half years.

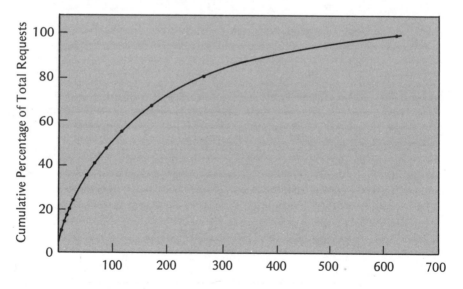

FIGURE 57   Cumulative percentage of NLL requests in the social sciences plotted against number of titles requested.[90]

TABLE 87   Distribution of Requests for Social
Science Periodicals[90]

No. of times used	No. of titles	Cum. % of total requests
40	1	2.5
35	1	4.7
31	1	6.6
26	1	8.2
19	2	10.6
18	1	11.8
17	1	12.8
16	1	13.8
15	1	14.8
14	3	17.4
13	1	18.2
12	1	19.0
11	2	20.3
10	6	24.1
9	8	28.6
8	6	31.6
7	8	35.1
6	17	41.5
5	21	48.0
4	32	56.1
3	56	66.1
2	97	78.2
1	352	100.0

A question worth considering at this point is whether citation counts are more or less useful than analyses of actual library usage for purposes of identifying a core of highly productive sources, or whether both techniques will yield essentially the same ranked list of sources in a particular subject field. Bourne[6] points out some differences between the two approaches and some problems that each presents. An obvious difference is that citations rarely are made to recently published materials (e.g., published one month earlier), whereas library circulation records will include such sources. Another difference is that the user population represented by the citation counting method (i.e., authors) may be different from that in a typical library. Although some systematic differences in results might be expected from the two procedures, Bourne feels that data thus far collected supports the view that "there is no obvious difference in the results obtained by the two techniques."

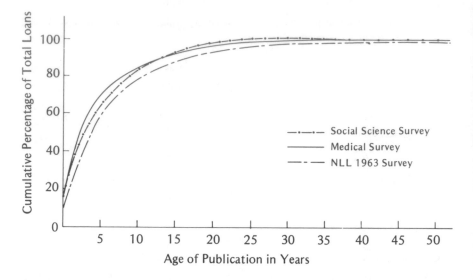

FIGURE 58   Distribution of requests for social science periodicals by age.[90]

This viewpoint, however, is not shared by all investigators. Earle and Vickery,[30] for example, derived literature-use patterns in the social sciences, based on citation counts, that were somewhat different from those derived in an analysis of requests made to the National Lending Library for social science periodicals and reported by Wood and Bower.[90] The major difference noted was in the age of materials used. The half-life of social science journals was three and one-half years in the NLL study, nine years for social science literature as a whole, and six years for journal literature in the citation study. Earle and Vickery suggest that neither citation counts nor loan demands alone may be adequate indicators of the value of sources, as both may have built-in biases, and that two or more such indicators used jointly might provide a far more accurate picture. As mentioned by Bourne, citations do not necessarily reflect current demand. The citations appearing in a particular paper may have been collected by the author over a period of years (as reported by Soper,[77] there is evidence to suggest that a large proportion of all items cited by an author appear in his personal files); in any event, they relate to a use period that may have occurred several months or even years prior to the date of publication.

Elsewhere, Vickery[86] has compared various types of indicators of the "value" of periodicals. Five such indicators were used to rank British science and technology periodicals:

1. The Martyn and Gilchrist[59] survey, based on citation data derived from the *Science Citation Index* (which ranked *Nature* in the first position).
2. A survey based on a sample of sources cited by British authors only (which placed *Lancet* at the top of the list).
3. A survey of loan requests received at NLL (which placed *Chemical and Process Engineering* at the top of the rankings).
4. An analysis of titles most held by a sample of British libraries (which placed *Philosophical Transactions* at the top of the list).
5. An analysis based on the number of items published during one year in each source (which ranked *Nature* first).

Vickery addresses possible biases in the various approaches. A limitation of all citation counts is that the items cited by an author may represent only a small percentage of all items read. Moreover, citation studies based on the *Science Citation Index* are drawn from a limited set of source journals (which are not necessarily representative of all science and technology journals published in the world), and citations appearing in nonjournal sources (e.g., books, technical reports) are not included. A major limitation of the use of requests to NLL as an indicator of demand is that they represent demands only for items not available to the requester locally (i.e., in his local library). Moreover, as pointed out by Vickery, the total distribution of the use of sources in a particular subject field is not necessarily completely reflected in demands made to libraries. Numbers 4 and 5 of the indicators of value listed above were considered very dubious in terms of actual use or demand for these sources.

Vickery discovered that, if the first 89 journal titles in each of the five lists are considered, 225 different titles occur; and only 12 of these titles are common to all five lists. This again emphasizes the desirability of using more than one indicator to determine total use of the literature in a particular field.

Line et al.[53] have reported on another type of literature-usage study. They set out to determine whether or not a Bradford type of distribution also applies to the citation of individual articles within a particular journal; that is, "Do a comparatively small number of articles in a particular journal account for a very large percentage of all references to that journal?" An affirmative answer to this question could have important implications for both librarians and publishers. Published volumes of "most cited articles" from particular journals could reduce the need for a library to maintain complete back files of certain titles and for publishers to maintain large inventories of back issues of their periodicals.

The preliminary test involved three scientific journals in different disciplines, and was restricted to an analysis of self-citation patterns (i.e., citations in a particular journal to earlier papers published in the same journal), although a check was made to determine whether the pattern of self-citation resembled that of citations from outside sources. In general, the results revealed that a few journal articles are cited quite frequently, while others are cited infrequently or not at all. The authors suggest that 10% of the journal articles might account for between 50% and 75% of all citations to that journal, which results might justify the publishing of volumes of "key papers." When the analysis was extended over a period of time, however, no great consistency in article citations was observed. The papers most cited in one particular year may not be those most heavily cited in another year, even one relatively close in time. Some articles were cited more often with the passage of time, while others were cited less. As stated by Line et al. "Some articles decay, while others mature." It is, therefore, impossible to identify the real "key" papers until some years after they have been published.

Parenthetically, it is worth remembering that the use of citation analysis to determine the importance of various journals has a long history, predating Bradford. Pioneers in this field were Gross and Gross,[38] who, in 1927, used citations in the *Journal of the American Chemical Society* to determine the most frequently cited journals in chemistry. Many citation analyses have been conducted since then. In 1944, Brodman[9] attempted to check the validity of citation analysis in the evaluation of journals. If the importance of a journal is strongly correlated with frequency of citation, she reasoned, then there should be some correlation between a list of journals cited most frequently and those judged most important by a group of specialists in the subject area. She was able to find little correlation of this kind for physiology journals. In a follow-up study, Postell[67] discovered that, while there was little correlation between the list of journals submitted by Brodman's subject specialists and the list of journals cited most frequently in physiology, the former list did resemble fairly closely a list of journals most used in a medical library.

Raisig,[72] in 1962, expressed confidence in the citation-analysis procedure as a way of evaluating journals, but he pointed out that, in a study of this kind, the citation sample must not be drawn from a single journal, as was the case in the studies by Gross and Gross and several others. Instead, the sample must be drawn at random from a broad base of journals. Moreover, any ranking of journals on the basis of citation must be based not on simple citation frequency, but on *citation density** (i.e.,

*Garfield[33] uses the term *impact factor*.

the number of citations relative to the number of articles published). Raisig was strongly critical of the comparison conducted by Brodman on the grounds that her "opinion sample" represented the views of only a very limited group and could not be considered random. Using a wide range of journals, from which citations were drawn at random, Raisig[73] produced a ranked list of biomedical journals on the basis of citation density.

Until the 1960s, citation counting was a laborious and tedious manual procedure. Today it is possible to conduct citation studies less painfully by using the machine-readable data bases of the Institute for Scientific Information (*Science Citation Index* and *Social Science Citation Index*). Garfield[33] has described the use of these data bases in journal evaluation. Using citations from the *Science Citation Index* during the last quarter of 1969, he showed that 152 journals accounted for 50% of all citations and 767 journals for 75%. He concluded that a relatively small number of journals could satisfy a high proportion of all demands in a typical science library. In 1973, the Institute for Scientific Information announced a Journal Citations Reports (JCR) service, which identifies the 1,000 journals that have received the most citations during a specified time period. For each of these journals, JCR shows: the number of citations it received, from which journals, and the age of the articles cited; and how many times the journal cited other journals, which journals, and the age of the articles cited.

In a recent article, Bell[3] compared citation lists in medicine with other indicators of the value of medical journals. She produced a core list of medical journals on the basis of the number of medical libraries holding these journals. A sample of 40 medical school libraries was used, and journals held by 60% or more of these were selected to form the ranked list. There were 852 qualifiers. A core of 369 titles subscribed to by 90%–100% of the libraries surveyed was identified (63 titles were held by all 40 libraries). She then compared her top-ranking journals with the top-ranking titles in three other lists: those of Raisig[73] and Garfield, and the journals contributing the most citations to MEDLINE off-line printouts during a three-month period. She found little agreement among the rankings.

Zipf's Law

The related Zipfian distribution was first described by Zipf in 1935[91] and more completely in 1949.[92] His work was concerned with the use of words in natural-language text. He found that, when a large collection of text is analyzed, a comparatively small number of words occur very frequently and account for a large proportion of all the word occurrences in the text. When the cumulative percentage of total word usage is plotted against the cumulative percentage of words contributing to this usage, a characteristic hyperbolic distribution—which has become known as a Zipfian distribution—results. In the hypothetical, but typical, example (Figure 59), 90% of all the word usage in a particular text collection is accounted for by approximately 20% of all the unique words occurring in the text.

It is clear that the Zipfian distribution is very similar to the Bradford distribution. If, instead of using a logarithmic scale, the cumulative percentage of usage of journals in a particular subject field is plotted against the percentage of journals contributing to this usage (in rank order

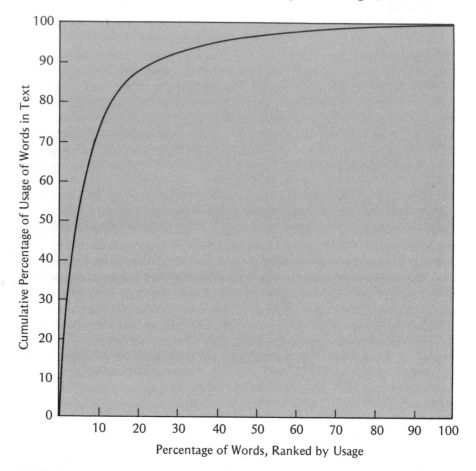

FIGURE 59   Zipfian distribution for the use of words in text.

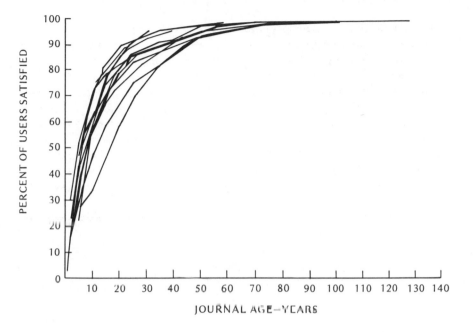

FIGURE 60 Distribution of journal use by age in chemistry.[6]

by amount of usage), the results would be similar to the characteristic Zipfian distribution of Figure 59. The distributions of use or demand by source and by age of materials, as shown in Figures 57–58 and 60–62, also are essentially Zipfian. Leimkuhler[50] has stated that Zipf's law and Bradford's law are "essentially just two different ways of looking at the same thing," and Brookes[11] claims that the two distributions are nearly identical. It is not clear who first noticed the similarity between these distributions, although Kendall[41] may have been the first to do so in print.

Zipf's law, like Bradford's, is one of diminishing returns. Zipf found that his distribution fits a wide range of languages and texts. In fact, he extended the application beyond language; he viewed his law as a "principle of least effort," and showed this principle to be generally applicable to a wide range of activities in which a choice is made from a finite number of possibilities. Whenever choices are made over a period of time from a finite number of competing "elements," a relatively small number of the elements is likely to account for a very high proportion of all selections made (i.e., few elements contribute much of the usage, and when all contributing elements are plotted—in ranked order—against total usage, the hyperbolic distribution of Figure 59 will result). Fairthorne[31]

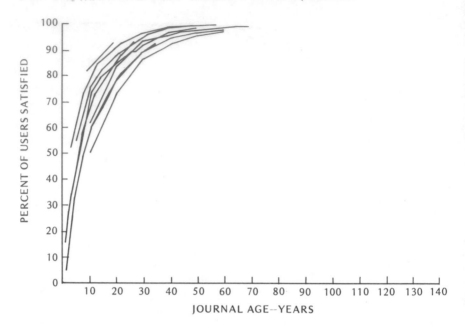

FIGURE 61   Distribution of journal use by age in medicine.[6]

reviews a number of applications, bibliographic and nonbibliographic, in which distribution of use has been shown to follow a Zipfian pattern.

The Bradford-Zipf empirical hyperbolic distributions, as illustrated, govern a wide range of activities relevant to the provision of library services, including the dispersion of bibliographic references among contributing sources, the use of periodicals or books within a library, and, possibly, the use of library services over the entire user population. Lotka,[55] as early as 1926, showed that this type of distribution also appears to be true for the productivity of authors, when they are ranked by the number of articles they write. Lotka's findings were derived from the fields of physics and chemistry. More recently, Murphy[64] has produced some evidence to suggest that Lotka's law also may hold true in the humanities.

As depicted elsewhere by Lancaster,[49] the use of index terms selected by indexers from a controlled vocabulary appears to follow a Zipfian distribution. Lancaster[48] also has shown that this distribution holds true for the retrieval of bibliographic references from sources included in a mechanized information retrieval system. Figure 63 shows the distribution of 1,387 journals contributing 6,491 citations selected at random from a much larger set of citations retrieved in 302 MEDLARS searches. From this plot, it can be seen that, while 1,387 separate journals were needed to account for the total number of citations in the sample, approximately 10% of these journals accounted for 50% of all citations retrieved. This curve would indeed be a more dramatic one if the approximately 1,000 journals indexed by the National Library of Medicine, but not making a single appearance among 6,491 retrieved citations, were included in the plot. Brookes[12] has shown a similar distribution for the total number of sources contributing to a comprehensive MEDLARS search on muscle fibers.

Although he does not specifically mention Zipf, Trueswell[83] has demonstrated that the Zipfian distribution appears to hold true for circulation of books and periodicals in libraries. He presents curves from public, academic, and special libraries which illustrate the similarity of distribution when percentage of total circulations is plotted against percentage of holdings contributing to the circulations. Figure 64 shows the curve for the Air Force Cambridge Research Laboratory. Trueswell refers to this distribution as an "80/20 rule." He points out that, in business and

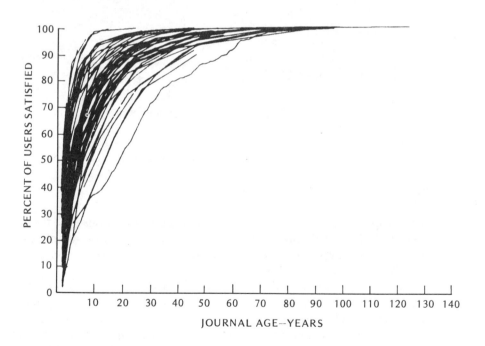

FIGURE 62 Distribution of journal use by age for science and technology as a whole.[6]

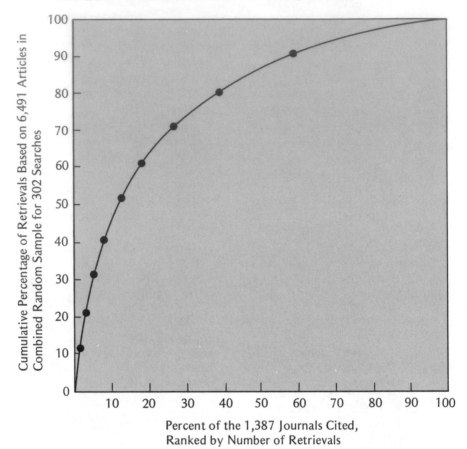

Percent of the 1,387 Journals Cited,
Ranked by Number of Retrievals

FIGURE 63   Distribution of sources contributing references to searches in a computer-based retrieval system.

industry, approximately 80% of the activity of a warehouse is from approximately 20% of the items stored there. The 80/20 rule also applies to libraries, where approximately 80% of the circulation is from approximately 20% of the total collection.

Brookes[12,16,17] has applied the Bradford-Zipf distribution to a number of practical library problems, including the relationship between service provided by branch libraries and by a main library.[17] He developed a model that considers the probabilities that a user will visit a branch library before visiting the main library, that he will visit the main library first, that he will be satisfied at one or the other, and the relative costs to the user in visiting one or the other. The Bradford-Zipf law can be used, in this kind of model, to determine the minimum viable collection for a branch library. In another application, Brookes[12] applied a similar analysis to determine the optimum distribution of periodicals within a library system comprising a central library and a number of branches for the purpose of minimizing both purchase and user cost factors. Elsewhere, he[16] extends his analysis to a three-level hierarchical system consisting of local, regional, and central libraries.

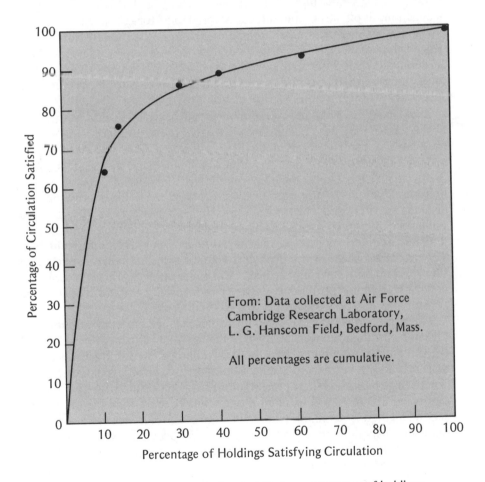

FIGURE 64 Percentage of circulation satisfied vs. percentage of holdings satisfying circulation.[80]

Rate of Obsolescence

Laws of diminishing returns are extremely important for the operation of efficient library services. Because librarians operate on limited budgets, it is important that their funds be allocated in the most efficient way possible; that is, they must purchase materials likely to receive the most use in relation to funds expended, and they must allocate their prime storage space to those items that are likely to be most-used. Studies of the distribution of use or the demand for bibliographic materials—likely to be of the Bradford-Zipf hyperbolic type—can aid in decisions relating to acquisition, duplication, and allocation of prime storage space. A related law of diminishing returns, examined in Chapter 5, is the law of obsolescence, which indicates that, as a document becomes older, its use is likely to diminish. This law also governs decisions relating to the weeding (discarding) of materials and the selection of materials for retirement to a secondary storage area or storage medium.

Buckland[20] has presented preliminary data suggesting that scatter and obsolescence may be closely related; that is, literature with wide scatter may have a comparatively long life, while literature that is compact becomes obsolete more quickly. Brookes[19] has suggested that obsolescence and scatter both may be related to the rate of growth of the literature. The faster the literature (of a particular field) is growing, the less the scatter and the more rapid the obsolescence. Krauze and Hillinger[47] attempted to produce a comprehensive theoretical model of the dynamic interactions involved in literature growth and citation behavior. The model is based on the probability $P(t,x)$—that a paper published at time (t) contains a reference to a specific paper published (x) years earlier, and shows that this probability decays exponentially with the elapsed time (x) and also decreases with the size of the literature.

There are two ways of studying the obsolescence or decay of published literature through citation analysis. One method is to take a sample of current literature and determine how the sources cited in this sample are distributed with respect to publication date. It can be expected that, all other things being equal, volume of citations will decline with age; that is, the recent literature will be cited proportionally more than the older. The second method is to examine how the number of references to a sample of published papers declines with age. To undertake this type of analysis, citation of these papers must be observed over a considerable period of time. Line et al.[53] refer to the first of these measures as *synchronous* decay and to the second as *diachronous*. They point out that virtually all studies of obsolescence have observed synchronous decay, but that the more complex diachronous situation has hardly been explored. Also, it is not certain that the synchronous situation can be used to predict the diachronous situation, although this assumption is frequently made for the purposes of decision making in libraries.

The subject is further discussed in detail in an excellent review article by Line and Sandison.[54] The distinction between synchronous and diachronous decay can be applied to the measurement of the use of library materials, as well as to the measurement of citations. To revert to the terms first introduced in Chapter 5, synchronous studies of library use are based on checkout samples, while diachronous studies are based on collection samples. It is the contention of Line and Sandison that these two approaches might give somewhat different results and, in fact, that there is nothing to substantiate that either procedure will accurately predict future use.

The half life figure for obsolescence is derived on the basis of citations to the literature. It is clear, however, that a count of citations to particular volumes of a journal is influenced by the number of articles published in each. Because most journals increase in size (i.e., publish more articles each year), the more recent volumes will attract more citations because there are more papers to be cited. This growth element must be considered in a true picture of obsolescence.

Line[52] describes a technique for eliminating the literature growth element to obtain a half-life figure that reflects only the rate of decay of journals. The technique involves the identification of a "median citation age" or "apparent half-life," which is defined as "the time within which half the citations in a citation study occur." If the annual growth rate of literature in a subject field is known, the median citation age can be used to produce a "corrected" half-life reflecting real obsolescence. Line makes the assumption that the increase in the number of references due to the growth of the literature is counterbalanced by a higher apparent obsolescence rate, resulting in a utility factor that is constant from year to year.

Brookes,[15] however, has criticized this technique, particularly on the grounds that it fails to take into consideration another important factor, namely, the number of scientists contributing to a specific field at any one time. Growth in the number of contributing scientists tends over time to reduce the decline in use and has an opposite effect to that of the growth of the literature. If the literature growth rate balances the growth of contributing scientists, the rate of obsolescence remains unchanged.

Oliver[66] offers some substantiation of this claim in a study of five years of the literature of semiconductor physics. For this literature and period, Oliver found a literature growth rate of 13.4%, a scientist growth rate of 15%, and a constant obsolescence rate of approximately 79%. Sandison,[75] however, expresses doubt as to whether these data actually do support Brookes' contention.

MacRae[56] suggests that the age distribution of citations in science is a result of two principal factors: growth of the literature and citation behavior, the latter favoring the more recent literature. He combines the rate of decay and the rate of growth into a single exponential function.

Sandison[75] has criticized the use of half-life as a measure of obsolescence in library applications, unless this measure is corrected to consider literature growth. Instead, he prefers a measure of obsolescence that directly reflects the number of library uses per item of a given age. Decline in use can be expressed in terms of (a) "50% consultation probability age" (the number of years required for the relative probabilities of consultation of individual items to decline by 50%) and (b) an item-consultation decay rate ("the rate of decrease in the observed relative probabilities that each available item will be consulted with each additional year since publication"). In the citation study context, these measures would translate into item-citation decay rate and 50% citation-probability age.

Elsewhere, Sandison[76] has pointed out that raw citation frequency and raw statistics on library use of periodicals are both potentially misleading when used to rank journals for purposes of selection, retirement, or optimum allocation of storage space. It is important to relate data on numbers of items used to data on numbers available for use (i.e., to determine density of citation or use), a point made by Raisig[72] in 1962, but still frequently overlooked. He proposes that one applicable measure would be density of use per meter of shelf. In other words, volume of use is related to the amount of space occupied by a particular journal. Sandison applied this density-of-use measure to raw data on the use of 138 physics journals at the Science Library of MIT. His analysis revealed no evidence of obsolescence in the 1955–1968 volumes. Indeed, he claims some statistically significant evidence of greater density of use with greater age. The ranking of physics journals by density of use also was found to be quite different from their rankings by absolute (raw) use data.

Brookes[13] has pointed out that it is inefficient to adopt a discard policy that is based entirely on a single rate of obsolescence calculated for a particular subject field. Periodical *utility* also must be taken into consideration. The utility volume of a periodical is defined as the number of uses it can be expected to attract in a particular library during the remainder of its existence. A periodical, A, that contributes 200 papers a year to a given subject will, according to Brookes, "always remain twice as useful as periodical B, contributing 100 papers per annum to that same subject." It is, therefore, "not rational to discard them at the same age."

If periodical sets may be regarded as having "heads" (more recent issues) and "tails" (the older materials), the optimum policy would be to discard tails of equal utility, leaving heads of different lengths on the shelves, the more productive periodicals having the longer heads. Brookes proposes the concept of "utility contours" for periodical sets and describes a technique whereby an optimum discard policy can be used for periodicals in special libraries.

Kraft and Hill[46] applied a dynamic programming model to the problem of selection and retention of journals. The model, which incorporates an obsolescence factor, was designed to identify the particular journal issues (considering both journal titles and the length of time these titles are retained) that will satisfy the maximum number of demands for a specified level of investment. For one calendar year at a time, the model reveals the amount of money remaining for the acquisition of new journals after deducting the costs for the storage and use of former acquisitions. Decisions can then be made on the purchase of new journals to maximize the satisfaction of present and anticipated future demand, within the constraints of the present and probable future budget.

Bibliometrics

The application of various statistical analyses to study patterns of authorship, publication, and literature use was once referred to as "statistical bibliography." More recently, Pritchard[69] coined the term "bibliometrics" to describe this area of study. Donohue[29] identified a number of distinct techniques in bibliometrics that might have practical application in libraries:

1. The use of citation analysis to determine the scatter of papers by journal and by author (as in the work of Bradford).
2. The use of citation analysis to identify the "research fronts" of a particular field. A research front, as described by Price,[68] is an area of research whose scope is well illustrated by a small number of key papers "knit together" through frequent citation in more recent literature. The technique of bibliographic coupling, as defined by Kessler,[42] can be used to identify subareas in the total research front of a field. Bibliographic coupling involves searching for groups of papers having common references. After identifying the most-cited papers in a field representing the research front, an analysis can be made of how these papers couple bibliographically. Bibliographic coupling may subdivide the research front into easily identifiable subareas of research.

3. The epidemic analysis of the literature of a particular subject. Goffman[34] and Goffman and Newill[36] have drawn an analogy between the epidemic spread of infection and the epidemic spread of ideas. An "infective" is a scientist who is actively writing in a particular subject area. He becomes a "removal" one year after his last publication on the subject. Later, however, he may become reinfective. By subtracting removals from infectives for a particular period of time, changes can be studied in the publication patterns in a designated subject field. It is also possible to identify whether the field is growing or declining and, in particular, to determine when it reaches an epidemic state.

Donohue refers to patterns of authorship, citation, and publication as *literature statics* and to the change in these patterns over time (determined through epidemic analysis for example) as *literature dynamics*. He applies the various bibliometric techniques to the literature of information science.

Some Further Trade-off Considerations

The cost of acquiring and storing a serial versus the cost of obtaining it through interlibrary loan when needed is a trade-off of obvious importance to libraries. It is clear that, except perhaps for the large national libraries, no library can own all the serials likely to contribute to the literature of a particular subject area. Studies based on the Bradford and Zipf distributions can assist the librarian in deciding which journals are likely to provide the greatest yield in a particular subject field. As shown by Cole[27] and Brookes,[18] these analyses also can consider the "law of obsolescence" when deciding how far back the journals should be retained to achieve an optimum allocation of storage space. This matter also has been addressed by Buckland et al.,[22] who point out that it is "clearly economical to retain any purchased title until the age at which its usefulness has dropped to the level at which the requests which still occur can be more cheaply satisfied by interlibrary loan than by continued storage." (The retention of a journal in the library, of course, has the added advantage of convenience of location and speed of delivery.) Addressing the subject of purchase, they point out that a journal would be worth purchasing only if the costs of satisfying anticipated demands by interlibrary loan were greater than the combined cost of purchase and storage while retained. Table 88 illustrates a "minimal cost policy" they proposed for a hypothetical petroleum library, including the storage-cost variable associated with expensive and inexpensive real estate. Note that

TABLE 88   Minimal Cost Policy for a Special Library Considering Variations in Cost of Real Estate[22]

	City library	Rural library
Assumptions		
Acquisitions cost	£5 per title	£5 per title
Storage cost	£0.125 per volume	£0.03 per volume
Interlibrary loan cost	£1 per loan	£1 per loan
Conclusions		
Titles taken	50	60
Retention range	11–24 years	16–30 years
Total volumes	744	1,230
Overall cost (Γ)	£1,160	£1,095
Satisfaction from stock	38%	63%

in the rural location, a library can afford to acquire more titles and hold them for longer periods, thereby satisfying a higher proportion of demands from its own collection and needing to borrow less frequently from outside sources.

Buckland et al.[22] also state that "there is in any given circumstances a solution which minimises the cost to the library budget of meeting a given demand, and this solution involves satisfying a particular proportion of demand from stock." The librarian may, however, deliberately choose a solution other than that of minimal cost to the library, to obtain a premium on accessibility and speed of delivery. The justification for this approach is the repeated finding that physical accessibility is a major factor influencing the use of library and information services in general. Even with an excellent interlibrary loan service, items not immediately available in the collection will seem less accessible to users and will not be used as much as they might have been if held by the library. The subject of optimum allocation of a library budget to acquisition and storage costs was discussed in Chapter 5, and is further discussed by Buckland and Woodburn.[23]

In the Project for Evaluating the Benefits from University Libraries (PEBUL) conducted by the University of Durham,[84] it was calculated that the average cost of purchasing a book in the arts or social sciences was approximately five times higher than the average cost of borrowing it (£4.47 as opposed to £0.89). If a typical book is expected to be used more than five times, purchasing apparently is cheaper than borrowing; but this calculation does not consider the cost of housing the book. Nor does it allow for the "costs" that may be associated with delays to the user.

Moreover, a book on the shelf of a particular library is likely to generate a higher level of demand than the demand for the same book if it were located elsewhere (e.g., in another library). In other words, a book has some browsing value.

Brookes[14] has described a graphical method, based on the law of scatter, to aid the librarian in deciding which periodicals to subscribe to and which not to subscribe to. For the latter group, it is more cost-effective to acquire individual photocopies from larger resource libraries when the need arises.

Williams and Pings[89] discuss optimum allocation of resources in a hospital library. Large samples of citations, drawn from a "core" of 89 biomedical journals, indicated that 50% of the citations were to the journals appearing in the core collection. Of these references, 45% were 5 years old or less, and 90% were between 5 and 15 years old. The authors suggest that, for a hospital library, the small core collection of 89 journals retained for 5 years would represent the most efficient use of library space; no hospital libraries should retain journals for more than 15 years. It is clear, then, that the hospital library must rely on interlibrary loan (ILL) to obtain needed articles from noncore journals, as well as older articles from core journals. Another consideration, however, is that a library must have bibliographic tools to permit the verification of citations before ILL requests can be made. Unfortunately, several such tools, dating back approximately 20 years, would be needed to permit verification of a substantial percentage of the articles cited in the library's core collection.

Perhaps the most complete study of the comparative cost-effectiveness of owning versus borrowing serial publications was conducted by Westat Research, Inc. for the National Science Foundation. The methodology used and the results achieved are presented by Williams et al.[88] The Westat study involved the construction of mathematical models based on data supplied by four research libraries, which can be used by a library to predict at what level of demand it would be cheaper to own a serial than to obtain photocopies of articles when they are needed. At the mid-range of costs for the four libraries studied, and assuming an annual subscription price of $20, it is shown that, below a demand of six uses per year, it is cheaper to obtain photocopies from another source than to purchase and maintain the serial. The authors suggest that a large proportion (perhaps half or more) of the serial titles held by many large research libraries are used less-frequently than six times a year. The savings to a library through borrowing rather than purchasing a serial title that is used an average of only once a year amounts to approximately $50 per title per year, or approximately $50,000 per year for 1,000 titles.

Note, however, that these figures do not consider user costs associated with delay in obtaining a copy from another library. The investigators point out, however, that "if delays in access increase user cost and the aim is to minimize this cost, then what must be minimized is the average access time to all publications the patron uses—those locally owned as well as those borrowed or photocopied." Because substantial delays may be associated with access to frequently used serials held by the library (which, when needed, may be in use by another patron, misshelved, at the binders, or even lost), it may be more cost-effective to buy duplicate sets of such serials rather than purchasing and maintaining additional serial titles that are called for infrequently.

Input costs for any activity generally can be traded off against output costs, and vice versa; that is, economies that are made in system input usually will result in increased output costs, while an expensive input operation that is conducted with care and completeness will produce certain economies at output. This trade-off is likely to exist in a library as well as in any other situation. For example, one way to reduce input costs is by economizing on cataloging. If insufficient attention is given to the cataloging operation, or fewer entry points are provided, this will likely result in more catalog searching failures, reduced efficiency in searching, and increased searching time. Delays between acquisition and appearance on the shelf, however, are likely to decrease because of the reduced time spent on cataloging. Similarly, if less care and time is spent on book selection (with concomitant reduced costs), a poorer overall match can be expected between the collection and user interests. As a result, the collection is likely to be less used, and the cost per item circulated will increase. A similar effect may result from input economies, such as reduced purchase of duplicate copies. In addition to reducing satisfaction level, this policy could increase the staff time consumed in assisting library users and could increase the number of reservations placed, thereby creating more work for the staff in recalling requested books; and the net result would be an increase in the unit cost per circulation. A number of such input/output trade-offs exist within the sphere of library operations. The library manager must recognize that any changes he makes to an input operation could have repercussions on one or more output functions. He must be careful to recognize what these repercussions might be, taking into consideration long-term as well as short-term effects.

Indeed, the librarian, like any other manager, must give careful consideration to the probable effects of any policy decision. For example, by retiring a certain percentage of the total collection to a remote storage area, immediate savings in storage costs will be realized. But this action is likely to result in reduced circulation of the stored portion of the collection, inconvenience to users, and new costs associated with retrieving the books from the storage area when needed. The librarian must carefully consider whether these disadvantages are adequately compensated for by the savings in storage costs.

Some Cost-Performance-Benefit Studies in Libraries

Perhaps the most complete series of studies relating to the effectiveness and cost-effectiveness of library operations is that conducted at the University of Lancaster in England, which has been mentioned on several occasions in this book.

Other studies on cost-effectiveness or cost-benefit considerations have been conducted by Newhouse and Alexander[65] at the Beverly Hills Public Library, by the University of Durham,[84] and by Raffel and Shishko[71] at MIT.

The Newhouse and Alexander study is interesting in that it represents an attempt by two economists to determine how a public library should allocate its book budget, using tools from economic theory relating to the measurement of benefits and costs. The authors claim that a library should select books that "the community values most highly" and that "book selection should maximize benefit to the community." In their analysis, however, "benefit" and "value" of various categories of books are judged largely in terms of the amount of use they are likely to receive.

Their work was based on an analysis of materials circulated by the Beverly Hills Public Library during a 46-week period, the object being to identify categories of books that circulate most frequently. From these circulation data, an "allocation model" was derived, which considers "the circulation rate of each book, its price, the proportion of the community that would buy if the library did not own it, and the processing costs associated with it." A "discount rate" (i.e., decline in demand over time) also is considered. An important assumption of this analysis is that the borrower of a book derives a fraction of the benefits of ownership. On the basis of these various considerations, a cost-benefit calculation was made for each book category. Those with the highest payoff, from the viewpoint of the cost-benefit relationship, are those that are expensive and which circulate frequently. The analysis indicated that, in relation to costs, benefits to the community would increase if more resources were allocated to the purchase of books in the following categories: mysteries, preschool and young adult fiction, psychology, and art techniques.

The studies of Raffel and Shishko[71] at MIT delve into various aspects of the evaluation of library operations. Several of these have been mentioned elsewhere in this book. Perhaps the most important element of their work, however, was a study of user preferences in the allocation of resources to various activities or functions (i.e., alternatives competing for funds). The method used to study user preferences was unusual in the library environment, although it has been used in other situations (e.g., in studying preferences for transportation systems). It involved, essentially, a type of management "game" in which the players, in this case users of the MIT libraries, were given hypothetical library budgets and asked to allocate them over a range of possible library services. The way in which the users allocated their budgets presumably would reflect their preferences for various services and facilities, which would then permit the manager of the library to rank the services to reflect user desires.

To be more precise, a participant was given a list of 20 service alternatives, together with an indication of the cost of implementation and a summary of "benefit considerations" for each. Benefit considerations were both plus and minus; that is, they indicated the losses that might be associated with a particular action, as well as possible gains. The list of alternatives, with accompanying instructions, is reproduced in Table 89. The library user was given three budgets:

1. A supplemental budget of $200,000 (i.e., an increase of $200,000 over the library budget in effect at the time of the study).
2. A supplemental budget of $100,000.
3. No new funds; that is, the user must work with the present budget and reallocate it as he wishes—a new service or an improvement to an existing one can be implemented only if the needed funds are saved by the curtailment of some other operation.

The survey, which was mailed to 700 students and faculty members, was returned by 283, a response of approximately 40%. The major ranking of alternatives (reflecting the preferences of the entire group of respondents) is shown in Table 90, and the percentage of respondents choosing particular alternatives at each budget level in Table 91. Note that the rankings differ comparatively little among the three budget levels. Considering the entire group of respondents, it is evident that much emphasis was placed on the importance of improving availability and reducing the cost of materials for use outside the library. The majority of respondents would reallocate resources to permit a lowering of the cost of making Xerox copies.

In addition to this "general orientation," however, a number of special orientations were evident when library users were categorized as to type. One was a "research orientation" that favored marginal increases in

TABLE 89   Service Alternatives and Associated Benefit Considerations[71]

Alternative	Benefit Considerations	Annual Additional Cost to Present Library Budget
1. 50% of the library's holdings of books which account for about 25% of total library circulations for the year, would be removed to an on-campus storage facility. There, these books would be stored as they are presently arranged (i.e., according to conventional Library of Congress classification) but access to the stacks would be restricted. Librarians would retrieve requested books on demand.	1. Browsing possible only under special circumstances, such as for theses, special projects, etc. Users would also encounter an average delay of 1/2 hour to retrieve stored books.	1. $ −10,000
2. Again, 50% of the library's holdings of books which account for about 25% of total library circulations for the year, would be removed to an on-campus storage facility. There, these books would be stored *compactly* (i.e., shelved chronologically and by size). Access to the stacks would be closed, and librarians would retrieve requested books on demand. (Note: 1 and 2 cannot *both* be selected.)	2. Browsing impossible since books are not stored by subject classification. Users would also encounter an average delay of 1/2 hour to retrieve stored books.	2. $ −25,000
3. *Expand* seating (all types) in libraries by *10%*. (Note: From systems 3 through 6, only one may be selected.)	3. Users would be able to find "choice" seating accommodations more easily.	3. $ +25,000
4. *Expand* seating (all types) in libraries by *20%*.	4. Users would be able to find "choice" seating accommodations more easily.	4. $ +50,000
5. *Cut* seating (all types) in libraries by *10%*.	5. Users would find it more difficult to obtain a seat in the library.	5. $ −25,000
6. *Cut* seating (all types) in libraries by *20%*.	6. Users would find it more difficult to obtain a seat in the library.	6. $ −50,000
7. The decentralized reserve collections would be replaced by two main reserve-study centers (one already in the Student Center, and another similar facility located near the Sloan-Hermann complex). Overnight circulation would be permitted from this latter facility. Areas now in the libraries devoted to study-reserve would be converted into stacks.	7. Replacing the decentralized reserve systems with two main study-reserve centers would lessen the current convenience of the more localized reserve collections, but would allow students to do all their work at one location.	7. $ −75,000
8. The library would lower the charge for Xeroxing to local commercial rates, provide an operator, and encourage users to reproduce library material.	8. Users could duplicate important material at low cost and would be able to use the material outside the library.	8. $ +10,000

9. Ten supplemental *departmental* libraries located near class-rooms would be built to house 10 years of the 20 most used journals and a collection of 3,000 books, including some required and recommended reading. These libraries would also have about 15 seats, but would provide no services beyond minimal cataloging. These might be contiguous to graduate lounges and study areas.

10. Instead of providing a reserve article per 10 students, the libraries would make enough complete Xerox copies of all articles 60 pages or less for *each* student in the relevant course and would distribute these articles.

11. *Increase* annual acquisitions by *10%*. (Note: From systems 11 through 14, only one may be selected.)

12. *Increase* annual acquisitions by *20%*.

13. *Decrease* annual acquisitions by *10%*.

14. *Decrease* annual acquisitions by *20%*.

15. The amount of time spent by professional catalogers on each book would be limited to a shorter period. The proof-reading and checking of catalog cards would also be curtailed.

16. The library would cut its reference staff by *10%*.

17. The library would add to its reference staff by *10%*.

18. The library would implement a direct telephone line to, say, Wellesley, staffed by additional professional librarians on station at Wellesley. In addition, interlibrary loan would be improved by increasing internal operating efficiency and direct messenger pickup.

19. The library would operate a long-range messenger service to the Library of Congress in Washington.

20. The library would purchase paperbacks of about 1/2 of books on reserve. This would treble the book:student ratio from 1:10 to 3:10. Circulation periods for these books would be lengthened to two days.

9. Such departmental libraries would provide more conveniently located working collections, and increase the availability of required and recommended reading.

10. Students could have a complete file of required articles for future use, and could read and study them at any time, in or out of the library.

11. Libraries could buy more new books as well as older books to "round out" the M.I.T. collection.

12. Libraries could buy more new books as well as older books to "round out" the M.I.T. collection.

13. Libraries could buy fewer books.

14. Libraries could buy fewer books.

15. The number of subject references for a given book would be limited. There would also be minor errors and other shortcomings in the catalog.

16. Bibliographic services and information aids would suffer.

17. Bibliographic services and information aids would be improved.

18. Users would be able to find out about books at another university library and would be able to obtain books within hours.

19. Users would be able to obtain books from the Library of Congress if they could not be obtained from a nearby collection.

20. Users would find required reading more readily available and would be able to take out these books for longer periods.

9. $+160,000

10. $+80,000

11. $+80,000

12. $+160,000

13. $−80,000

14. $−160,000

15. $−75,000

16. $−25,000

17. $+25,000

18. $+30,000

19. $+10,000

20. $+50,000

TABLE 90 Ranking of Service Alternatives by Budget Level[71]

	Budget Levels		
	$200,000	$100,000	$0
Positive Cost Systems			
Increase acquisitions	1*	2	2
Lower Xerox rates	2	1	1
LC messenger	3	3	3
Expand seating	4	4	4
Add reserve copies	5	5	4
Add reference	6	7	6
Increase access	7	6	7
Departmental libraries	8	9	9
All-Xerox reserve	9	8	8
Negative Cost Systems			
Centralize reserve	1*	1	1
Inexpensive storage	2	2	2
Cut reference	3	3	4
Cut seating	4	4	3
Decrease acquisitions	5	5	5

*Rank of system where rank of 1 means the system was chosen the most at that budget level.

acquisitions at the expense of other activities. It was noteworthy, however, that few (approximately 20%) favored radical increases in acquisitions at present budget levels and that virtually no one wanted to see acquisitions cut in favor of another alternative. Given increased funding, however, substantial increases in acquisitions were favored by many respondents. The idea of centralizing the reserve collections was generally popular, but the proposed inexpensive storage systems were less popular (although approximately one-third of the respondents were willing to adopt such a system at the present budget level). Undergraduates tended to reallocate funds from research activities to improve reserve collections; graduate students were more oriented toward outside use of library materials (especially lower Xerox rates) and wanted improved access to collections of other libraries. Faculty expressed preferences for departmental libraries and were less opposed to methods for inexpensive storage. Those respondents who claimed heavy use of the library generally were research-oriented; while those who indicated light use preferred to use materials outside the library.

A major conclusion of this study was that the library should "use current reproduction technology and paperback books to encourage people to use library materials outside the library."

Raffel and Shishko view the value of this type of survey in the following terms:

First, this survey gives an indication of the systems all members of the M.I.T. community would like to have. Second, the number of people supporting or vociferously opposing certain systems may be determined. The decrease in the popularity of a positive cost system as the budget level decreases may be a measure of the intensity of feeling, if any, for that system. Thus those items vigorously supported by a minority may be located. Few librarians feel comfortable basing their decisions only on the vocalized fears of a few concerned faculty members. Third, the inclusion of costs as a decision criterion eliminates the necessity of speculating (by the respondent or the decision maker) as to whether individuals would continue to support a given system if "they knew what it cost." Fourth, the survey can provide librarians with information to permit them to encourage the use of the library and to support library programs which they feel are educationally superior.

Another approach to the allocation of resources within a university

TABLE 91   Percentage of Respondents Choosing Alternative Services at Three Budget Levels[71]*

System	Budget Level		
	$200,000	$100,000	$0
[Increase acquisitions, 10% or 20%]	[78%]	[61%]	[41%]
Lower Xerox rates	74	65	54
LC messenger service	55	44	32
[Expand seating, 10% or 20%]	[48]	[32]	[16]
Add reserve copies	43	28	18
Increase acquisitions, 20%	43	8	4
Centralize reserve	41	48	62
Increase acquisitions, 10%	35	53	37
Add reference librarians	33	19	13
Expand seating, 10%	31	23	12
Increase access to other libraries	30	23	12
Departmental libraries	28	16	6
All-Xerox reserve	27	17	8
[Conventional or compact storage]	[24]	[24]	[34]
Expand seating, 20%	17	9	4
Conventional storage	16	16	21
[Cut seating, 10% or 20%]	[11]	[14]	[24]
Cut reference staff	10	16	20
Limit cataloging	8	12	17
Compact storage	8	8	13
Cut seating, 10%	8	10	12
Cut seating, 20%	3	4	12
Decrease acquisitions, 10%	0	0	3
Decrease acquisitions, 20%	0	0	0

*Related pairs of alternatives are combined within brackets.

library, this time an allocation of a book fund across the academic departments, has been described by McGrath et al.[62] The authors identified 22 variables that measure and quantify an academic department to reflect its needs for bibliographic support. Among the more important variables considered were the number of books published in subject areas of interest to the department, the present size of the holdings in these subjects, size of faculty, faculty teaching load, number of courses offered, student enrollment, volume of books circulated and interlibrary loans by departmental affiliation or subject areas of interest, and number of references occurring in graduate theses in the department. The technique of factor analysis was applied to the 22 × 22 correlation matrix, based on the 22 variables identified as being possibly significant. The factor analysis resulted in the identification of allocation factors. These factors were then incorporated into a formula which allowed the book fund to be allocated in an optimal fashion across the various departments.

The results of a study conducted by the University of Durham in England were published in 1969 in *Project for Evaluating the Benefits from University Libraries*.[84] The objective of the study was to devise procedures that might help the library manager to maximize benefits from existing library resources. An important assumption of the Durham project was that a library manager can optimize the allocation of his resources by adjusting the library's activities in such a way that a dollar's worth of resources allocated to a particular activity would not be of more value if it were spent on another activity. The Durham study incorporated several separate economic and operations research analyses of library activities. Many data on library use were collected by various methods, including an "instant diary" technique, in which users recorded details of a specific visit to the library on a brief questionnaire; a computer model was developed to simulate the decision processes of library users; a linear programming model for resource allocation purposes was derived and tested; and an experimental current-awareness service in the field of social science was initiated to gauge user reactions and demands and to investigate the effects of the service on the information-seeking behavior of users.

Although many data were collected during the Durham study and presented in the final report, it is not always clear how these various data are related, if indeed they are.

The 90 Percent Library

A concept important to efficient library operations is that of the 90 percent library. While the principle has been hinted at by several writers, it has been expressed most cogently by Bourne:[6]

The basic approach or point of view suggested here is first to envisage the library users as a composite or aggregate collection of people with a great variety of interests, approaches, needs, habits, and idiosyncracies, and then to ask the basic question, "What does the library have to do to satisfy 90 percent of this population's needs?" That is, what periodicals should be acquired so that 90 percent of the periodicals they use and make reference to are available? What literature searching speeds shall be provided in order to meet the response times required for 90 percent of the requests? By taking this point of view, our attention is focused on the actions or services necessary to satisfy a specified fraction of the user population. In this way, no attempt is made by the designer or operator to satisfy every possible request or need that might occur. Both the system designer and operator thus openly acknowledge that, in some instances, some users' needs will not be fully met. However, this approach keeps the library from being overdesigned or from going to extreme efforts in an attempt to make it all things to all people. Past experience by many types of organizations (e.g., transportation industry, retail sales) indicate that a disproportionate effort is usually required to raise the system performance from a capacity to satisfy some high fraction (e.g., 90 percent), to satisfying 100 percent of the user requirements. The libraries are no exception to this rule. The point of diminishing returns is such that it is probably more effective to run an information service at something less than a capability for 100 percent satisfaction of the users' requirements. The figure, 90 percent, is used in this paper as an example. Any other figure could of course be used, established by the people responsible for the design, operation, and support of the library. It would seem that many libraries in fact already subscribe to this principle even though it may not be stated so explicitly. For example, few, if any, local libraries try to duplicate the holdings of our national libraries in order to immediately fulfill any local request, but instead assume that they can satisfy "some reasonable fraction" of their requests from the local collection and handle the remainder in some other way.

Bourne points out that, while not all user requirements can be related to some specified level of satisfaction, many can. He uses the following statements as examples of requirements that could be stated in these terms:

Ninety percent of the information needs of a given user population are satisfied by:

1. Books that are less than ____ years old.
2. Periodicals that are less than ____ years old.
3. Retrospective search speeds of less than ____ days.
4. Document delivery speeds of less than ____ days.
5. A collection of less than ____ chosen journals and less than ____ chosen books.
6. A current-awareness service that periodically furnishes information at intervals of not more than ____ days.
7. A reference retrieval service that provides not more than ____ percent irrelevant material with the search results.

The specific numbers, of course, need to be supplied by the librarian on the basis of empirical data. While these numbers may vary somewhat from one library to the next, evidence indicates that these numbers may not differ too greatly among different user populations. Much of this book has been concerned with the identification of procedures that could be used or, in some cases, have been used to supply some of these missing numbers.

The empirical hyperbolic distributions previously mentioned, together with the "law of obsolescence," are extremely important in identifying a collection of materials capable of satisfying, say, 90% of all user requirements; that is, in any particular field of study, it should be possible to say that a specified fraction of all information needs can be satisfied from a specified number of sources (Bradford-Zipf distribution). It also should be possible to say that a specified fraction of information needs can be satisfied by sources that are no more than x years old (law of obsolescence).

Based upon an analysis of many different studies, Bourne was able to produce several useful plots to show the use of science literature as a function of age (including plots for particular scientific disciplines), drawing his data both from citation counts and from actual statistics of demand for materials in libraries. While these curves may differ somewhat in length (e.g., according to Figures 60 and 61, one would have to go back further in time to satisfy 95% of the demands in chemistry than to satisfy 95% of the demands in medicine), they all have the same basic shape. In fact, the distribution is essentially Zipfian. Figure 62 shows Bourne's composite curve for journal usage as a function of age in science and technology in general. Note that the "half-life" of both the medical literature and the chemistry literature appears to be quite similar. Bourne has pointed out, that, while there are differences in half-life from one scientific field to another, these differences are not dramatic.

The idea of a 90 percent library is important from the cost-effectiveness point of view. Unless a library has unlimited resources, it is unlikely that it will be able to satisfy 100% of all demands placed upon it. If it cannot satisfy all demands, it should identify a specified volume of demand that can be reasonably satisfied, both efficiently and economically. This level of demand may be 90%, 95%, or even a little higher. Library resources should then be allocated to permit the provision of this level of satisfaction as efficiently as possible. Studies of diminishing returns, involving the empirical distributions of Bradford and Zipf and the rate of obsolescence of bibliographic materials, should be of great value to the library manager in the optimum allocation of resources to achieve a specified performance level.

The 90 percent library concept may perhaps be best expressed in terms of a paraphrase: "You may satisfy some of the people all of the time and all of the people some of the time, but you can't satisfy all of the people all of the time."

This chapter has considered some factors affecting the cost-effectiveness of library services, has mentioned possible approaches to cost-effectiveness analysis, and has briefly outlined several studies that have been conducted. While some interesting and valuable work has been done in this area, particularly during the last 10 years, it is clear that systematic cost-effectiveness analysis, as applied to library operations, is still in its infancy. Library managers have not yet been given tools and techniques that they can apply routinely to assess the performance of their services and to relate performance levels to operating costs. Indeed, the widespread and routine use of such techniques is still a long way off.

REFERENCES

1. Arthur D. Little, Inc. *Program Evaluation of the State Technical Services.* Cambridge, Mass., 1969.
2. Basile, V. A. and Smith, R. W. "Evolving the 90% Pharmaceutical Library." *Special Libraries, 61*:81–86, 1970.
3. Bell, J. A. "The Academic Health Sciences Library and Serial Selection." *Bulletin of the Medical Library Association, 62*:281–285, 1974.
4. Bernal, J. D. "Preliminary Analysis of Pilot Questionnaire of the Use of Scientific Literature." *In: Report of the Royal Society Scientific Information Conference.* London, The Royal Society, 1948, pp. 589–637.
5. Boig, F. S. and Loftman, K. A. "Domestic and Foreign Periodicals in the Field of Petroleum Chemistry. A Statistical Analysis." *Oil and Gas Journal, 47*:199, 1949.
6. Bourne, C. P. "Some User Requirements Stated Quantitatively in Terms of the 90 Percent Library." *In: Electronic Information Handling.* Edited by A. Kent and O. E. Taulbee. Washington, D.C., Spartan Books, 1965, pp. 93–110.
7. Bradford, S. C. *Documentation.* London, Crosby Lockwood, 1948.
8. Bradford, S. C. "Sources of Information on Specific Subjects." *Engineering, 137*:85–86, 1934.
9. Brodman, E. "Choosing Physiology Journals." *Bulletin of the Medical Library Association, 32*:479–483, 1944.
10. Brookes, B. C. "Complete Bradford-Zipf Bibliograph." *Journal of Documentation, 25*:58–60, 1969.
11. Brookes, B. C. "The Derivation and Application of the Bradford-Zipf Distribution." *Journal of Documentation, 24*:247–265, 1968.
12. Brookes, B. C. "Statistical Distributions in Documentation and Library Planning." *In: Planning Library Services.* Session 3, Paper 1. Edited by A. G. Mackenzie and I. M. Stuart. Lancaster, Eng., University of Lancaster Library, 1969.
13. Brookes, B. C. "Obsolescence of Special Library Periodicals: Sampling Errors and Utility Contours." *Journal of the American Society for Information Science, 21*:320–329, 1970.
14. Brookes, B. C. "Photocopies v. Periodicals: Cost-Effectiveness in the Special Library." *Journal of Documentation, 26*:22–29, 1970.

15. Brookes, B. C. "The Growth, Utility and Obsolescence of Scientific Periodical Literature." *Journal of Documentation, 26*:283–294, 1970.
16. Brookes, B. C. "The Design of Cost-Effective Hierarchical Information Systems." *Information Storage and Retrieval, 6*:127–136, 1970.
17. Brookes, B. C. "The Viability of Branch Libraries." *Journal of Librarianship, 2*:14–21, 1970.
18. Brookes, B. C. "Optimum P% Library of Scientific Periodicals." *Nature, 232*:458–461, 1971.
19. Brookes, B. C. "Numerical Methods of Bibliographic Analysis." *Library Trends, 22*:18–43, 1973.
20. Buckland, M. K. "Are Obsolescence and Scattering Related?" *Journal of Documentation, 28*:242–245, 1972.
21. Buckland, M. K. "Toward an Economic Theory of the Library." *In: Economics of Information Dissemination*. Edited by R. S. Taylor. Syracuse, N. Y., School of Library Science, Syracuse University, 1973, pp. 68–83.
22. Buckland, M. K. et al. *Systems Analysis of a University Library*. Lancaster, Eng., University of Lancaster Library, 1970, pp. 11–15.
23. Buckland, M. K. and Woodburn, I. *Some Implications for Library Management of Scattering and Obsolescence*. Lancaster, Eng., University of Lancaster Library, 1968.
24. Burton, R. E. and Kebler, R. W. "The 'Half-life' of Some Scientific and Technical Literatures." *American Documentation, 11*:18–22, 1960.
25. Cezairliyan, A. O. et al. "A New Method for the Search of Scientific Literature Through Abstracting Journals." *Journal of Chemical Documentation, 2*:86–92, 1962.
26. Cole, P. F. "A New Look at Reference Scattering." *Journal of Documentation, 18*:58–64, 1962.
27. Cole, P. F. "Journal Usage Versus Age of Journal." *Journal of Documentation, 19*:1–11, 1963.
28. Cooper, M. "Current Information Dissemination: Ideas and Practices." *Journal of Chemical Documentation, 8*:207–218, 1968.
29. Donohue, J. C. *Understanding Scientific Literatures: A Bibliometric Approach*. Cambridge, Mass., MIT Press, 1973.
30. Earle, P. and Vickery, B. C. "Social Science Literature Use in the UK as Indicated by Citations." *Journal of Documentation, 25*:123–141, 1969.
31. Fairthorne, R. A. "Empirical Hyperbolic Distributions (Bradford-Zipf-Mandelbrot) for Bibliometric Description and Prediction." *Journal of Documentation, 25*:319–343, 1969.
32. Fussler, H. H. and Simon, J. L. *Patterns in the Use of Books in Large Research Libraries*. Chicago, University of Chicago Press, 1969.
33. Garfield, E. "Citation Analysis as a Tool in Journal Evaluation." *Science, 178*:471–479, 1972.
34. Goffman, W. "Mathematical Approach to the Spread of Scientific Ideas—The History of Mast Cell Research." *Nature, 212*:449–452, 1966.
35. Goffman, W. and Morris, T. G. "Bradford's Law and Library Acquisitions." *Nature, 226*:922–923, 1970.
36. Goffman, W. and Newill, V. A. "Communication and Epidemic Processes." *Proceedings of the Royal Society, 298A*:316–334, 1967.
37. Groos, O. V. "Bradford's Law and the Keenan-Atherton Data." *American Documentation, 18*:46, 1967.
38. Gross, P. L. K. and Gross, E. M. "College Libraries and Chemical Education." *Science, 66*:385–389, 1927.
39. Hitch, C. J. and McKean, R. *The Economics of Defense in the Nuclear Age*. Cambridge, Mass., Harvard University Press, 1960.

40. Hockings, E. F. "Selection of Scientific Periodicals in an Industrial Research Library." *Journal of the American Society for Information Science, 25*:131–132, 1974.
41. Kendall, M. G. "Natural Law in the Social Sciences." *Journal of the Royal Statistical Society, Series A, 124*:1–18, 1961.
42. Kessler, M. M. "Bibliographic Coupling Between Scientific Papers." *American Documentation, 14*:10–25, 1963.
43. Kilgour, F. G. "Recorded Use of Books in the Yale Medical Library." *American Documentation, 12*:266–269, 1961.
44. Kilgour, F. G. "Use of Medical and Biological Journals in the Yale Medical Library." *Bulletin of the Medical Library Association, 50*:429–449, 1962.
45. Kilgour, F. G. and Fleming, T. P. "Moderately and Heavily Used Biomedical Journals." *Bulletin of the Medical Library Association, 52*:234–241, 1964.
46. Kraft, D. H. and Hill, T. W., Jr. "The Journal Selection Problem in a University Library System." Unpublished Paper. College Park, Md., School of Library and Information Sciences, University of Maryland, 1970.
47. Krauze, T. and Hillinger, C. "Citations, References and the Growth of Scientific Literature: A Model of Dynamic Interaction." *Journal of the American Society for Information Science, 22*:333–336, 1971.
48. Lancaster, F. W. *Evaluation of the MEDLARS Demand Search Service.* Bethesda, Md., National Library of Medicine, 1968.
49. Lancaster, F. W. *Vocabulary Control for Information Retrieval.* Washington, D. C., Information Resources Press, 1972.
50. Leimkuhler, F. F. "The Bradford Distribution." *Journal of Documentation, 23*:197–207, 1967.
51. Leith, J. D. "Biomedical Literature: An Analysis of Journal Articles Collected by a Radiation-and-Cell-Biologist." *American Documentation, 20*:143–148, 1969.
52. Line, M. B. "The 'Half-Life' of Periodical Literature: Apparent and Real Obsolescence." *Journal of Documentation, 26*:46–54, 1970.
53. Line, M. B. et al. *Patterns of Citations to Articles Within Journals: A Preliminary Test of Scatter, Concentration and Obsolescence.* Bath, Eng., Bath University, 1972. ED 076 197.
54. Line, M. B. and Sandison, A. "'Obsolescence' and Changes in the Use of Literature With Time." *Journal of Documentation, 30*:283–350, 1974.
55. Lotka, A. J. "The Frequency Distribution of Scientific Productivity." *Journal of the Washington Academy of Sciences, 16*:317–323, 1926.
56. MacRae, D., Jr. "Growth and Decay Curves in Scientific Citations." *American Sociological Review, 34*:631–635, 1969.
57. Magson, M. S. "Techniques for the Measurement of Cost-Benefit in Information Centres." *ASLIB Proceedings, 25*:164–185, 1973.
58. Martyn, J. "Unintentional Duplication of Research." *New Scientist, 21*:338, 1964.
59. Martyn, J. and Gilchrist, A. *An Evaluation of British Scientific Journals.* London, ASLIB, 1968.
60. Mason, D. "PPBS: Application to an Industrial Information and Library Service." *Journal of Librarianship, 4*:91–105, 1972.
61. McDonough, A. M. *Information Economics and Management Systems.* New York, McGraw-Hill, 1963.
62. McGrath, W. E. et al. "An Allocation Formula Derived from a Factor Analysis of Academic Departments." *College and Research Libraries, 30*:51–62, 1969.
63. Mueller, M. W. *Time, Cost and Value Factors in Information Retrieval.* Paper presented at the IBM Information Systems Conference, Poughkeepsie, N.Y., September 21–23, 1959.

64. Murphy, L. J. "Lotka's Law in the Humanities?" *Journal of the American Society for Information Science, 24*:461–462, 1973.
65. Newhouse, J. P. and Alexander, A. J. *An Economic Analysis of Public Library Services.* Lexington, Mass., Lexington Books, 1972.
66. Oliver, M. R. "The Effect of Growth on the Obsolescence of Semiconductor Physics Literature." *Journal of Documentation, 27*:11–17, 1971.
67. Postell, W. "Further Comments on the Mathematical Analysis of Evaluating Scientific Journals." *Bulletin of the Medical Library Association, 34*:107–109, 1946.
68. Price, D. J. de Solla. "Networks of Scientific Papers." *Science, 149*:510–515, 1965.
69. Pritchard, A. "Statistical Bibliography or Bibliometrics?" *Journal of Documentation, 25*:348–349, 1969.
70. Quade, E. S. *Systems Analysis Techniques for Planning-Programming-Budgeting.* Santa Monica, Calif., Rand Corporation, 1966.
71. Raffel, J. A. and Shishko, R. *Systematic Analysis of University Libraries.* Cambridge, Mass., MIT Press, 1969.
72. Raisig, L. M. "Statistical Bibliography in the Health Sciences." *Bulletin of the Medical Library Association, 50*:450–461, 1962.
73. Raisig, L. M. "World Biomedical Journals, 1951–1960." *Bulletin of the Medical Library Association, 54*:108–125, 1966.
74. Rosenberg, K. C. "Evaluation of an Industrial Library: A Simple-Minded Technique." *Special Libraries, 60*:635–638, 1969.
75. Sandison, A. "The Use of Older Literature and its Obsolescence." *Journal of Documentation, 27*:184–199, 1971.
76. Sandison, A. "Densities of Use, and Absence of Obsolescence, in Physics Journals at MIT." *Journal of the American Society for Information Science, 25*:172–182, 1974.
77. Soper, M. E. "The Relationship Between Personal Collections and the Selection of Cited References." Doctoral Dissertation. Urbana, Ill., Graduate School of Library Science, University of Illinois, 1972.
78. Stevens, R. E. *The Characteristics of Subject Literatures.* ACRL Monographs, Nos. 5–7. Association of College and Research Libraries, 1953.
79. Strain, P. M. "A Study of the Usage and Retention of Technical Periodicals." *Library Resources and Technical Services, 10*:295–304, 1966.
80. Trueswell, R. W. "Two Characteristics of Circulation and Their Effect on the Implementation of Mechanized Circulation Control Systems." *College and Research Libraries, 25*:285–291, 1964.
81. Trueswell, R. W. "User Behavioral Patterns and Requirements and Their Effect on the Possible Applications of Data Processing and Computer Techniques in a University Library." Doctoral Dissertation. Evanston, Ill., Northwestern University, 1964.
82. Trueswell, R. W. "A Quantitative Measure of User Circulation and Its Possible Effect on Stack Thinning and Multiple Copy Determination." *American Documentation, 16*:20–25, 1965.
83. Trueswell, R. W. "Some Behavioral Patterns of Library Users: the 80/20 Rule." *Wilson Library Bulletin, 43*:458–461, 1969.
84. University of Durham. *Project for Evaluating the Benefits from University Libraries.* Durham, Eng., 1969.
85. Vickery, B. C. "Bradford's Law of Scattering." *Journal of Documentation, 4*:198–203, 1948.
86. Vickery, B. C. "Indicators of the Use of Periodicals." *Journal of Librarianship, 1*:170–182, 1969.
87. Wilkinson, E. A. "The Ambiguity of Bradford's Law." *Journal of Documentation, 28*:122–130, 1972.

88. Williams, G. E. et al. *Library Cost Models: Owning Versus Borrowing Serial Publications*. Chicago, The Center for Research Libraries, 1968.
89. Williams, J. F., II and Pings, V. M. "A Study of the Access to the Scholarly Record from a Hospital Health Science Core Collection." *Bulletin of the Medical Library Association, 61*:408–415, 1973.
90. Wood, D. N. and Bower, C. A. "The Use of Social Science Periodical Literature." *Journal of Documentation, 25*:108–122, 1969.
91. Zipf, G. K. *Psycho-Biology of Language*. Boston, Houghton Mifflin, 1935.
92. Zipf, G. K. *Human Behavior and the Principle of Least Effort*. Cambridge, Mass., Addison-Wesley Press, 1949.

14

Conclusion: Factors Affecting the Performance of Library Services

This book has reviewed various possible approaches to measuring and evaluating some of the major facets of library service. Orr[2] has referred to this as "measuring the goodness of library services." He recognizes two aspects of this measurement, which are reflected in the questions:

1. How good is the service?
2. How much good does it do?

Chapter 1 refers to the first of these aspects as measurement of *effectiveness* and to the second as measurement of *benefits*. The effectiveness of library services (as well as their *cost-effectiveness*) can be measured and evaluated; but, in many situations, the benefits of library service cannot be measured in any objective way. The emphasis of this book, therefore, has been on measurement of effectiveness and, to a lesser extent, the cost-effectiveness of library services.

The approach taken has been mainly fragmentary, in the sense that each of the several major facets of library operations or library service has been viewed independently. This is the only reasonable approach, because the evaluation of document delivery capabilities differs considerably from the evaluation of reference services, which differs from the evaluation of the catalog, and so on. Each of these facets can and should be evaluated separately; the evaluation of one is not dependent upon the evaluation of another. If a complete evaluation of a library were to be undertaken, each facet of service would, of course, be studied independently and then synthesized in some way to present a composite picture of library effectiveness.

If it were possible to derive an absolute numerical score for each facet of service (as it is possible to do for document delivery and reference services), it would be theoretically possible to derive some composite figure for library effectiveness as a whole. Such an index of effectiveness was proposed by Rzasa and Baker,[5] and this index has been used in two studies reported by Pritchard et al.[4] and Pritchard and Auckland.[3] As presented by Pritchard and Auckland, the overall index of library effectiveness is:

$$E = \frac{m}{N}\left(1 + \frac{n}{N}\right) + \frac{r_2}{N}\left(1 + \frac{r_1}{N}\right) + \frac{S}{N^?}$$

where

m = total number of items reshelved
N = total user population
n = total number who use the library
r_1 = total questions asked
r_2 = total questions answered satisfactorily
S = number of users studying with their own materials or who are there for social purposes.

It is obvious that such an equation is oversimplified. It does not represent all aspects of most library services and, more importantly, it combines qualitative with quantitative measures: In the case of reference service, it attempts to distinguish successes from failures; but in other uses of the library, it represents only the successes and does not attempt to represent the failures in any way (catalog searching failures and document delivery failures, for example).

It seems unlikely that it would be possible to derive a satisfactory "single figure of merit" for a library; and, indeed, such composite figures, because they deal with completely different types of service (which must be evaluated in completely different ways), seem of dubious value. The evaluation of any single aspect of library service, as, hopefully, has been demonstrated in this book, is quite complex. Factors affecting the success or failure of any of these aspects of service also are complex.

Although primarily concerned with evaluation procedures, a considerable amount of information also has been presented on factors that importantly affect the performance of library services. This chapter will summarize some of the important factors that affect library performance, judged in terms of user satisfaction.

The following situations will be considered:

1. A user comes to the library to look for a particular known item.
2. A user comes to the library to find books on a particular subject.
3. A user calls or visits the library to obtain an answer to a particular factual question.
4. A user asks the library to conduct a comprehensive literature search in a particular subject area.

For each of these situations, some of the important factors that determine whether or not the user'is satisfied by the library (i.e., whether or not his needs are met) will be explored.

The Known-Item Search

This situation involves the assumption that a user visits the library to find a particular book about which he has certain details. The probability of success in this situation is well-summarized in the following simple equation:*

USER + INFORMATION BROUGHT BY USER + COLLECTION +
BIBLIOGRAPHIC ACCESS + PHYSICAL ACCESS = USER + BOOK

The major factors affecting the probability of the success or failure of a known-item search are shown in Table 92. There is, of course, a danger of oversimplification in trying to tabulate a large number of factors in this way. The table may be incomplete, although the most important factors are represented. Moreover, all of the factors represented do not carry equal weight. It is quite clear that the single most important factor is whether or not the library owns the particular item sought. If it does not, the request cannot be satisfied immediately, although the item might be purchased or obtained through interlibrary loan. The "general" collection factors relate to the probability that the item will be held by the library. Most of the "specific" factors, on the other hand, relate to the probability that the item will be on the shelf when needed. Assuming that the item is owned by the library, the user still must obtain its call number and must locate it on the shelves. Whether he is able to do this depends largely on the completeness and accuracy of his bibliographic citation. Also impor-

*I am indebted to Judy Hattori, one of my students in 1974, for this simple and concise way of viewing the situation.

tant, however, are various personal factors relating to the user himself. The bibliographic access factors, together with the user factors, determine the probability that the user will be able to find an entry for the item in the catalog. The physical access factors, together with the user factors, relate to the probability that he will be able to find the item itself, assuming that he was able to determine its call number or otherwise identify it (e.g., verify the citation to request an interlibrary loan). The staff factors are shown to impinge on all others; that is, the user may need the assistance of the library staff to obtain bibliographic or physical access, or both. Librarians must be available to assist him if necessary. They must be approachable, knowledgeable, and helpful.

Search for Books on a Particular Subject

The assumption in this case is that a user comes to the library to seek books on a particular subject. He is not looking for any particular book, nor is he looking for the answer to a factual question. Instead, he wants to find one or more books that deal with a subject of current interest to him. He might, for example, be looking for books on economic conditions in Russia during the late nineteenth century. Once more, user factors, collection factors, bibliographic access factors, physical access factors, and staff factors can be identified, as shown in Table 93. Some of these factors duplicate those that affect the success or failure of the known-item search. Again, an inevitable danger of oversimplification exists in a table of this kind. One of the problems is that the user can employ a number of possible approaches. He may consult the catalog, identify relevant items, and then seek these items on the shelves. Alternatively, he may go directly to a particular section of the shelves and browse. In either case, he may or may not ask the library staff for assistance. Another complicating variable is the amount of literature the user needs, which could vary from a single book to a really comprehensive collection of materials.

The major factors affecting the success or failure of this situation are: the amount of materials published on the subject and whether or not the library collects such materials (and, if so, the comprehensiveness of its coverage). The collection bias, influenced by such things as extent of duplication and loan period, will determine whether or not the "best" or most up-to-date materials are on the shelf when needed. This factor will be particularly important in the case of the user who goes directly to the shelves to browse, rather than using the catalog. The items appearing under "collection factors" relate to the probability of the library holding materials in this subject area and to the probability of these materials

TABLE 92   Major Factors Influencing Success or Failure of a Known-Item Search

USER FACTORS	COLLECTION FACTORS		BIBLIOGRAPHIC ACCESS FACTORS	PHYSICAL ACCESS FACTORS
	General	*Related to Specific Item Sought*		
Motivation.	Size	Is specific item owned?	What is the extent of the backlog in technical processing?	Circulation policy: Does item circulate? What is loan period?
Perseverance.	Growth rate	Is it required reading for course?	What type of catalog? Dictionary Divided	How many sequences of shelving are there?
Accuracy.	Appropriateness (selection policy)	Is it in current popular demand?	What physical form of catalog? Card Printed On-line	Is call number explicit as to shelf location?
Intelligence.	Extent of duplication	How many copies are owned?	Size of catalog.	Is item on open shelves or in stacks?
Level of education.	Backlogs in acquisition	What is the likelihood of its being stolen?	How accessible is the catalog?	Is item in off-site storage area?
Ability to search systematically.			Are filing rules obvious?	Are shelves well guided?
Willingness to seek help if needed.			Is catalog complete and current?	Are there guides or maps to library arrangement?
Previous experience in the use of the library.			Is cataloging accurate and consistent?	Are shelves readily accessible?
Previous experience in the use of the catalog.			How many access points are provided per item?	Are there backlogs in reshelving?
				Is item at bindery?
				Is lighting adequate?
				Is item shelved correctly?

Has user received instruction in the use of library and/or catalog?

Information brought by user

(a) How complete and accurate is the citation?

(b) Is citation written or memorized?

Is it a circulating or a reference book?

Language in which the book is written?

Are title-added entries made?
Is guiding of the catalog adequate?
Are there instructions in use of the catalog?
Is the bibliographic description adequate for purposes of identification?
Is the reference structure complete?
Are other verification tools close at hand?

Security factors and rate of theft.
How much in-library use of collection?
Can book be recalled if on loan?
Can book be obtained on ILL if not in collection?

STAFF FACTORS: Are librarians available and willing to help when needed?

Are they approachable, knowledgeable, and helpful?

TABLE 93   Factors Influencing Success or Failure of a Search for Material on a Particular Subject

USER FACTORS	COLLECTION FACTORS	BIBLIOGRAPHIC ACCESS FACTORS	PHYSICAL ACCESS FACTORS
Does user know precisely what he is seeking?	Size.	How much backlog is there in technical processing (especially important if user is seeking very recent material)?	Circulation policies Do items in this area circulate? What is the loan period?
Can user describe his needs clearly to the library staff?	Growth rate.		What proportion of collection is on open shelves?
Motivation.	Appropriateness (selection policy).	What type of catalog? Dictionary Divided Classified	Does user have access to stacks? How many sequences of shelving are there?
Perseverance.	Extent of duplication in subject area.	What physical form? Card Printed On-Line	Are there guides or maps to library arrangement?
Accuracy.	Backlogs in acquisition.	Size of catalog.	Are shelves well guided?
Intelligence.	Is subject area within scope of library? Out of scope Marginal coverage Extensive coverage Comprehensive coverage	Accessibility of catalog. Is filing accurate and consistent? Are filing rules obvious? Is catalog complete and current?	Are shelves readily accessible? Are there backlogs in reshelving? Security factors and rate of theft. Is this subject in one place in the classification scheme or is it widely dispersed? Can materials be recalled if on loan?
Level of education.			
Ability to search systematically.			
Willingness to seek help if needed.			

Previous experience in the use of the library.

Previous experience in the use of the catalog.

Has user received instruction in use of library and/or catalog?

Is subject area covered by reference works, circulating items or both?

Age of material sought.

Language of material sought.

Is subject one that has been assigned for class study?

Is subject one in current popular demand?

How much has been written in this area?

Collection bias.

Is cataloging accurate and consistent?

How many subject access points are provided per item?

Are subject analytical entries made?

Does catalog have an adequate *see* and *see also* reference structure?

Are subject headings sufficiently specific?

Is guiding adequate?

Are there instructions in use of catalog?

Can user identify probably relevant items from bibliographic descriptions?

Can subject request be made to another library?

STAFF FACTORS: Are librarians available and willing to help when needed? Are they approachable, knowledgeable, and helpful?

Does staff member interview user to determine his real information need? How successful is this interaction?

being available when needed. The "bibliographic access factors" relate to the probability of the user being able to find citations to relevant materials through use of the catalog, especially the probability of his being able to conduct a comprehensive search, assuming this is needed. One possible approach to the problem is not directly accounted for in Table 93; that is, where the searcher makes use of various published bibliographies to identify materials relevant to the subject and then goes to the catalog to determine whether or not these are held by the library. In this case, the catalog search becomes a known-item search, and all the factors listed in Table 92 will apply. The "physical access factors" in Table 93 relate to the probability that a user will find materials on the shelves when he browses or when he visits the shelves to locate items previously identified in the catalog. Once more, several user factors and several staff factors can influence the entire operation.

Literature Search by a Library for a User

Assume that an industrial library is willing to conduct comprehensive literature searches for its users. The factors affecting a delegated search of this kind will be much the same whether it is conducted manually—for example, in printed indexes—or by means of a computer-based retrieval system. The major factors affecting the success or failure of such a literature search are depicted in Figure 65. Whether or not the user comes to a particular library or information center is presumably influenced by his awareness of its scope and coverage and of the services it provides. He comes with an information need that he is attempting to satisfy. The library, however, cannot act on a need as such—the need must be verbalized in the form of a stated request. Unfortunately, requests that individuals make to information centers are not always exact representations of actual information needs. How accurately the request reflects the true information need is dependent on several factors, including the user's interpretation of the system's capabilities (people have a tendency to ask for what they think the system can provide, which may not be what they really want), the ability of the user to express himself clearly, the clarity with which the user perceives his information need, the method by which the user communicates his need (by mail, telephone, personal visit), and the degree of assistance provided by the library. This assistance may vary: a detailed interview; a carefully structured request form; or some type of iterative search procedure, whereby a relatively crude search is conducted initially and the statement of need is modified on the basis of feedback from this "first approximation" search.

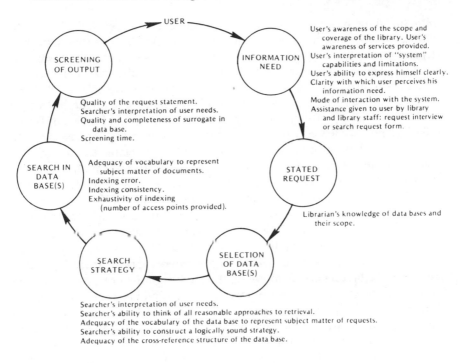

FIGURE 65 Factors affecting the success or failure of a delegated literature search.

Once the request is made, the librarian must decide which data base is the most appropriate to satisfy the requirements. The term "data base" is used somewhat loosely here. The data base selected may be a computer-based retrieval system (accessible in an on-line mode from the library itself or exploited from another information center) or it may simply be some type of printed index. It is clear that the success of the search will depend largely on which data base is chosen by the librarian, and this, in turn, will be governed by his knowledge of the scope of the data base. The librarian must choose the data base that is likely to be most productive for a particular request.

Once the librarian has decided which data base (bases) to consult, he must develop an appropriate searching strategy. In the case of a mechanized system operated in an off-line, batch-processing mode, he will prepare the strategy in advance, without direct interaction with the data base. In the case of a printed index or an on-line system, the strategy will not be developed "in advance." Instead, the librarian will interact with the data base in a heuristic fashion and will develop his search strategy as he goes along. How successful the search is at this point will depend on the searcher's interpretation of what the user really wants and his knowledge of all reasonable approaches to retrieval. This second factor is, in turn, dependent upon the assistance provided by the data base itself (e.g., by its cross-reference structure). In the case of a search strategy constructed for an off-line, batch-processing system, an important factor affecting performance is whether or not the search strategy is logically "correct." Another important performance factor relates to the vocabulary of the data base and its adequacy to represent the information needs of the requester. Specificity is especially important. For example, a search on "skin transplantation in monkeys" would be very difficult to conduct successfully in a data base that indexed only to the level of "transplantation," without further specifying what is transplanted and in what animal.

When the search is actually being conducted, in an off-line system, by a searcher at an on-line terminal, or in a printed index, further important performance factors come into play, the most significant being the quality and other properties of the indexing. It is obvious that, in terms of how much relevant literature can be retrieved (recall), a search is likely to be more successful if the indexing of the data base is reasonably exhaustive (i.e., if many access points are provided for each citation) and if the indexing has been carried out accurately and consistently. The vocabulary of the data base exerts as much influence at the indexing stage as it does at the time of searching; that is, the vocabulary (e.g., thesaurus, classification scheme, or list of subject headings) must be adequate to represent the subject matter discussed in the documents being entered into the system. In particular, it must be sufficiently specific to represent this subject matter with reasonable precision.

There also might be some "screening" of citations by the searcher. In the case of an on-line search, or a search in a printed index, the searcher will be conducting this screening continuously. This means that he will judge each citation he examines in terms of its probable relevance to the user for whom the search is being conducted. The searcher will retain or record only the citations that appear relevant to him. In the case of an off-line system, wherein search results are presented to the searcher in the form of a printout of citations, the screening operation will take place after the search is completed, if at all. In other words, the searcher will examine the search printout and will decide which citations appear to be relevant and which do not, sending only the seemingly relevant ones to the requester. How successful this screening operation is (i.e., how much agreement there is between the searcher's assessment of the relevance of citations and the assessment of relevance that the requester would make) again depends on a number of factors, including the quality of the original statement of information need, the searcher's interpretation of what the user really wants, the amount of time spent on screening, and the quality and completeness of the document representation appearing in the data base. Presumably, the searcher is likely to make more accurate relevance predictions on the basis of abstracts than from titles only.

Upon examining Figure 65, it becomes obvious that the conduct of a literature search by a library for one of its users is a complex undertaking and that many factors enter into determining whether a particular search will be successful. First and foremost, the success of the search will depend upon the interaction between the requester and the librarian. If, for one reason or another, the request statement inadequately represents the real information need of the user, the search is virtually doomed to at least partial failure, whatever the librarian may do. In fact, this user-system interaction is critical to the whole process. Unfortunately, as pointed out by Lancaster,[1] it is not always easy for a user to describe what he is looking for or for an information specialist to determine precisely the user's true information need. Even if this initial interaction is successful (i.e., if the request statement accurately reflects the information need) many other factors will influence the success or failure of a literature search, some completely beyond the control of the librarian. The librarian normally cannot control the characteristics of the data base he is using (e.g., the quality and accuracy of the indexing, indexing policy, and characteristics of the vocabulary of the system).

The Request for Factual Information

Table 94 presents some of the major factors that determine whether a request for factual information is handled completely, accurately, and rapidly. It is clear that the size and quality of the collection, especially the reference collection, will have a major influence on the outcome of a particular information search. More important perhaps are certain characteristics of the reference staff, because, for any particular request for information, the reference librarian is not "confined" to his own collection. He must, however, be familiar with outside sources of information and be willing to seek help from these sources if needed. The librarian's knowledge of current events, as indicated in Chapter 3, is particularly important.

In addition to collection factors and staff factors, the success of this

TABLE 94 Factors Affecting Success or Failure of Request for Factual Information

USER FACTORS	REQUEST FACTORS	COLLECTION FACTORS	STAFF FACTORS	OTHER FACTORS
Ability to express himself clearly.	Type of request: Complexity Subject area Highly current	Size of collection.	Size of reference staff.	Day and time at which request is made.
Accuracy.		Size of reference collection.	Approachability.	Number of staff available
Type of user.*	Mode of interaction with staff: Personal visit Telephone Does reference interview take place?	Growth rate.	Helpfulness.	Other demands occurring at the same time
		Scope of collection (range of subject areas covered and depth of the coverage).	Ability to determine precisely what the user is seeking.	Efficiency in allocation of duties among the staff.
	Response time requirement of user.	Currency of collection.	Knowledge of collection.	Subject specialization in handling inquiries
		Backlogs in acquisition (especially in acquisition of new editions of reference tools).	Knowledge of reference sources.	Clerical tasks reserved for clerical employees

Are supplementary tools
created by library staff?
Newspaper clippings
Vertical files
Special indexes

Subject knowledge.

Level and type of educa-
tion.

Knowledge of current
affairs.

Accessibility of reference
tools.

Willingness to seek help
from other staff
members.

Willingness to go beyond
the library for informa-
tion if necessary.

Service philosophy
(minimum, maximum).

Willingness of library to
allow staff members
time for keeping
current (e.g., reading
daily newspaper).

Continuing professional
education of staff
members.

*In certain types of libraries, certain categories of users may be given preferential treatment by the staff. For example, in an industrial library, special efforts may be made for a vice president, and in an academic library, a dean may receive the same type of preferential treatment.

type of demand will depend upon certain characteristics of the user, the request and how it is made to the system, and several other factors, including a number of administrative considerations.

The first chapter of this book emphasized the need for *microevaluation* of library service. Microevaluation is a diagnostic tool: as applied to library services, it implies the use of evaluative and analytical procedures to determine how well a particular library performs in a given situation and to identify major sources of weakness, failure, or inefficiency. It is obvious that such weakness or failure will vary significantly from library to library. An institution that performs one type of service well may perform another service poorly. Evaluation must occur at the level of the local institution, and it cannot be assumed that the limitations and failures encountered in one library also will apply to another, even one with the same general characteristics. Partly from the results of evaluations that have been conducted in libraries, however, and partly from common sense, it is possible to identify some major factors that are likely to influence the success or failure of the most important services that libraries offer. An attempt was made to present such factors in this book. Only by applying appropriate measurement and evaluation techniques can a library determine the circumstances under which it performs well or less well and identify the causes of its failures with sufficient precision to allow corrective actions to improve the overall level of performance and, presumably, to raise the level of user satisfaction with the services provided.

REFERENCES

1. Lancaster, F. W. "Interaction Between Requesters and a Large Mechanized Retrieval System." *Information Storage and Retrieval, 4*:239–252, 1968.
2. Orr, R. H. "Measuring the Goodness of Library Services: A General Framework for Considering Quantitative Measures." *Journal of Documentation, 29*:315–332, 1973.
3. Pritchard, A. and Auckland, M. *Library Effectiveness 1974.* London, City of London Polytechnic, 1974. ED 094 767.
4. Pritchard, A. et al. *Library Effectiveness Study.* London, City of London Polytechnic, 1971.
5. Rzasa, P. V. and Baker, N. R. "Measures of Effectiveness for a University Library." *Journal of the American Society for Information Science, 23*:248–253, 1972.

Index